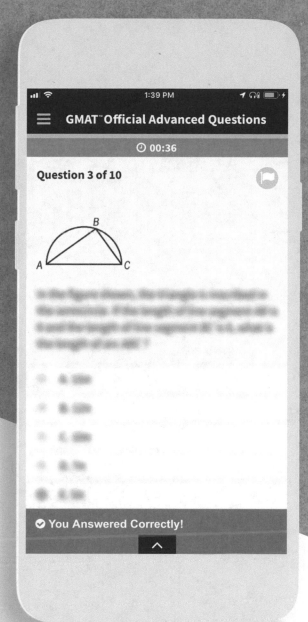

Access your Question Bank anywhere.

Practice with our mobile app!

Download once and practice online or offline anytime, anywhere.

⊙ **Download the App**
in the Apple App Store® or on Google Play. Search for "Wiley Efficient Learning."

⊙ **Login**
Enter the same email and passcode that you used to register on gmat.wiley.com.

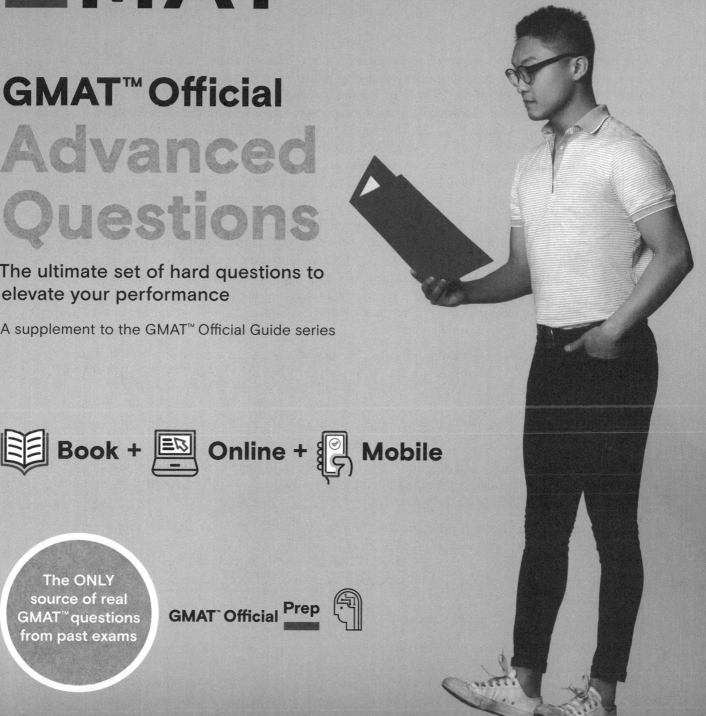

GMAT™

GMAT™ Official
Advanced
Questions

The ultimate set of hard questions to elevate your performance

A supplement to the GMAT™ Official Guide series

 Book + Online + Mobile

The ONLY source of real GMAT™ questions from past exams

GMAT™ Official **Prep**

This edition includes:

300 hard questions with answer explanations

Online access to track your performance

Mobile app to practice on-the-go

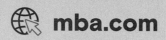 mba.com

GMAT™ Official Advanced Questions

For general information on our other products and services or for technical support, please contact our Customer Care Department within the United States at (800) 762–2974, outside the United States at (317) 572–3993 or fax (317) 572–4002.

Wiley publishes in a variety of print and electronic formats and by print-on-demand. Some material included with standard print versions of this book may not be included in e-books or in print-on-demand. If this book refers to media such as a CD or DVD that is not included in the version you purchased, you may download this material at http://booksupport.wiley.com. For more information about Wiley products, visit www.wiley.com.

ISBN 978-1-119-62095-2 (pbk); ISBN 978-1-119-62097-6 (ePUB)

Printed in the United States of America

V312607_081519

Table of Contents

Chapter 1 Introduction

Introduction

I. What is the GMAT™ Official Advanced Questions?

The GMAT™ Official Advanced Questions is a compilation of 300 hard Quantitative Reasoning and Verbal Reasoning questions, similar in difficulty level to hard questions found in the GMAT Official Guide series. Some of these questions have appeared in earlier editions of the GMAT Official Guide series; others have never been published before.

Like all GMAT questions, *hard* GMAT questions test higher-order reasoning skills identified as key factors of success in classrooms and job performances by educators and employers. They are unlike questions on other types of achievement-based exams, which focus more on mastery of mechanical cognitive skills and domain-specific knowledge. To solve GMAT questions, a test taker needs to demonstrate higher-order reasoning skills by understanding the underlying relationships between multiple concepts or arguments, identifying patterns, synthesizing information presented in various formats, and/or evaluating relevant information from different sources. What makes some GMAT questions harder than others is the level of complexity: hard GMAT questions typically involve multiple reasoning tasks or concepts and require more than one step to solve. They do not require mastery of skills and knowledge such as advanced-level mathematics, extensive calculations, or a large vocabulary in order to be solved.

II. Who should use the GMAT™ Official Advanced Questions?

The GMAT™ Official Advanced Questions is designed for test takers who have studied the questions in the GMAT Official Guide series and desire additional practice with hard questions.

For a simulation of the real exam experience, there are six GMAT Official Practice Exams—the first two are free to all mba.com registrants—which are available on mba.com and feature questions from past GMAT exams and use the same scoring algorithm as the actual exam.

III. How should I use the GMAT™ Official Advanced Questions?

Use the GMAT™ Official Advanced Questions for additional practice. The questions are organized by fundamental skills tested on the GMAT exam to better help you locate the specific skill type that you may want to improve. The fundamental skills are the same ones listed in the GMAT™ Enhanced Score Report, a non-official score report that provides more detailed information about your performance on the actual GMAT exam, which include:

Quantitative Reasoning

- *Geometry*—3-dimensional geometry; angles in the plane/lines and segments; circle/area; combo: circle/quadrangle/area/perimeter; coordinate geometry; polygon (5 or more sides); Pythagorean Theorem; quadrilateral area

- *Rates/Ratio/Percent*—conversion of fractions/decimals/percentages; graduated rate; percent (basic); ratio, proportion

- *Value/Order/Factors*—absolute value; computation-decimals; exponents; factors, multiples, divisibles; number linc and order; place value; positive and negative numbers; remainders

- *Equalities/Inequalities/Algebra*—algebraic manipulation; applying formula; linear equation; linear inequality; measurement conversion; newly defined functions; quadratic/other equalities/inequalities; systems of equations/inequalities; translation to algebraic expression

- *Counting/Sets/Series*—counting (combinatorics); estimation; series and sequences; sets

Verbal Reasoning

- *Critical Reasoning Analysis/Critique*—ability to analyze given information and make reasoned judgments by evaluating and breaking down an argument

- *Critical Reasoning Construction/Plan*—ability to construct a plan of action to find the best logical solution

- *Reading Comprehension Identify Inferred Idea*—ability to comprehend what a passage implies but does not explicitly mention

- *Reading Comprehension Identify Stated Idea*—ability to recognize and understand the ideas explicitly expressed in a passage

- *Sentence Correction Grammar*—ability to identify the answer that will create a sentence which is grammatically and structurally sound

- *Sentence Correction Communication*—ability to identify the answer that will create an effective sentence which expresses an idea or relationship clearly and concisely, as well as grammatically

For more information about the Enhanced Score Report and a description of each fundamental skill area, go to www.mba.com/esr-demo. *Note: The ratio of questions across different question types (e.g., data sufficiency, problem solving, etc.) and fundamental skills in GMAT™ Official Advanced Questions do not reflect the ratio of questions on the actual GMAT exam.*

Spend time reviewing the answer explanations and understanding the methods discussed. Like those in the GMAT Official Guide series, the answer explanations are written by GMAT subject matter experts with decades of experience writing and editing GMAT questions. Review these explanations carefully to understand the solution and identify techniques or approaches which may be applied to other GMAT questions.

Lastly, go online to gmat.wiley.com and access the Online Question Bank. The GMAT exam is administered on a computer, and it may be beneficial for you to practice answering on a computer. The Online Question Bank contains all of the questions that are in this book and allows you to create customized practice sets, use the timer, track your progress, and view performance metrics. You can also study on-the-go by accessing the Online Question Bank through the Wiley Efficient Learning mobile app, available in both the Apple App Store and the Google Play Store.

Chapter 2 Quantitative Reasoning

Practice Questions Quantitative Reasoning

[handwritten: abcdCf 24 / abcdfc 24 / abdCeC 24]

Problem Solving

[handwritten: aCbCef 24 / aCbeCf 24 / aCbefC 24]

Counting/Sets/Series

PS54110.01

1. The letters C, I, R, C, L, and E can be used to form 6-letter strings such as CIRCLE or CCIRLE. Using these letters, how many different 6-letter strings can be formed in which the two occurrences of the letter C are separated by at least one other letter?

   [handwritten: CaCbef 24 / 4 321 / CabCef 24 / CabeCf 24 / CabefC 24]

   (A)   96
   (B)   120
   (C)   144
   (D)   180
   (E)   240

PS24831.01

2.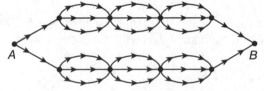

   The map above shows the trails through a wilderness area. If travel is in the direction of the arrows, how many routes along the marked trails are possible from point *A* to point *B*?

   [handwritten: 10 6 / 7 / 3·3·3 = 27 / 27·2]

   (A)   11
   (B)   18
   (C)   54
   (D)   108
   (E)   432

PS61551.01

3.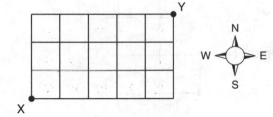

   In the figure above, X and Y represent locations in a district of a certain city where the streets form a rectangular grid. In traveling only north or east along the streets from X to Y, how many different paths are possible?

   [handwritten: 3N 5E / ₃C₈ = 5!·6·7·8 / 5!·1·2·3 = 56]

   (A)   720
   (B)   512
   (C)   336
   (D)   256
   (E)   56

PS92751.01

4.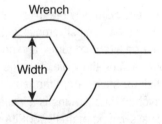

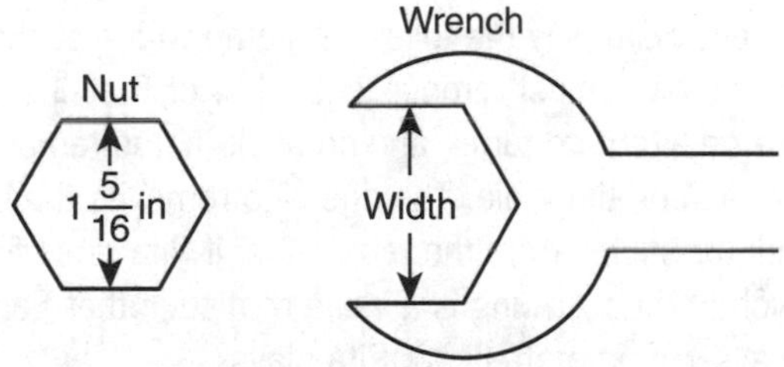

   The figures above show a hexagonal nut that has a width of $1\frac{5}{16}$ inches and a wrench that, in order to fit the nut, must have a width of at least $1\frac{5}{16}$ inches.

   Of all the wrenches that fit the nut and have widths that are whole numbers of millimeters, the wrench that fits the nut most closely has a width of how many millimeters?
   (*Note*: 1 inch ≈ 25.4 millimeters)

   (A)   30
   (B)   31
   (C)   32
   (D)   33
   (E)   34

[handwritten calculations at bottom left: 15.8 / 2 ; 254/16 ; 16 / 94 / 80 / 140]

[handwritten: (1 + 5/16)·(25.4) / 25.4 + 5/16·254/10 / 7.9 / 25.4 / 33.3]

PS45461.01

5.

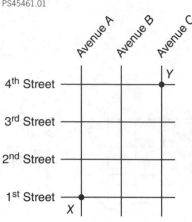

Pat will walk from intersection *X* to intersection *Y* along a route that is confined to the square grid of four streets and three avenues shown in the map above. How many routes from *X* to *Y* can Pat take that have the minimum possible length?

(A)   Six
(B)   Eight
(C)   Ten
(D)   Fourteen
(E)   Sixteen

PS95302.01

6.   Rita and Sam play the following game with *n* sticks on a table. Each must remove 1, 2, 3, 4 or 5 sticks at a time on alternate turns, and no stick that is removed is put back on the table. The one who removes the last stick (or sticks) from the table wins. If Rita goes first, which of the following is a value of *n* such that Sam can always win no matter how Rita plays?

(A)   7
(B)   10
(C)   11
(D)   12
(E)   16

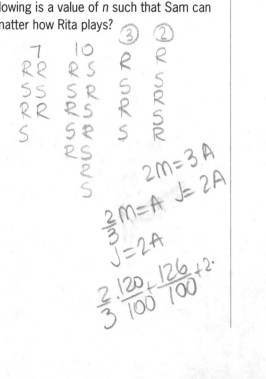

PS65402.01

7.   When $\frac{2}{9}$ of the votes on a certain resolution have been counted, $\frac{3}{4}$ of those counted are in favor of the resolution. What fraction of the remaining votes must be against the resolution so that the total count will result in a vote of 2 to 1 against the resolution?

(A) $\frac{11}{14}$

(B) $\frac{13}{18}$

(C) $\frac{4}{7}$

(D) $\frac{3}{7}$

(E) $\frac{3}{14}$

PS85402.01

8.   The sum of the first 100 positive integers is 5,050. What is the sum of the first 200 positive integers?

(A)   10,100
(B)   10,200
(C)   15,050
(D)   20,050
(E)   20,100

PS40502.01

9.

Month	Average Price per Dozen
April	$1.26
May	$1.20
June	$1.08

The table above shows the average (arithmetic mean) price per dozen eggs sold in a certain store during three successive months. If $\frac{2}{3}$ as many dozen were sold in April as in May, and twice as many were sold in June as in April, what was the average price per dozen of the eggs sold over the three-month period?

(A) $1.08
(B) $1.10
(C) $1.14
(D) $1.16
(E) $1.18

PS96602.01

10. Each of the integers from 0 to 9, inclusive, is written on a separate slip of blank paper and the ten slips are dropped into a hat. If the slips are then drawn one at a time without replacement, how many must be drawn to ensure that the numbers on two of the slips drawn will have a sum of 10?

0 1 2 3 4 5 6

(A) Three

(B) Four

(C) Five

(D) Six

(E) Seven

PS15402.01

11. King School has an enrollment of 900 students. The school day consists of 6 class periods during which each class is taught by one teacher. There are 30 students per class. Each teacher teaches a class during 5 of the 6 class periods and has one class period free. No students have a free class period. How many teachers does the school have?

(A) 25

(B) 30

(C) 36

(D) 60

(E) 150

PS07602.01

12. Ben and Ann are among 7 contestants from which 4 semifinalists are to be selected. Of the different possible selections, how many contain neither Ben nor Ann?

(A) 5

(B) 6

(C) 7

(D) 14

(E) 21

Equalities/Inequalities/Algebra

PS03551.01

13.

$n = 5$
$k = 3$

$n = 3$
$k = 1$

Let n and k be positive integers with $k \le n$. From an $n \times n$ array of dots, a $k \times k$ array of dots is selected. The figure above shows two examples where the selected $k \times k$ array is enclosed in a square. How many pairs (n, k) are possible so that exactly 48 of the dots in the $n \times n$ array are NOT in the selected $k \times k$ array?

$n^2 - k^2 = 48$
$(n-k)(n+k) = 48$
$1,2,3,4,5,6$ $8,12,16,24,48$

(A) 1

(B) 2

(C) 3

(D) 4

(E) 5

PS41471.01

14. If there is a least integer that satisfies the inequality $\frac{9}{x} \ge 2$, what is that least integer?

(A) 0

(B) 1

(C) 4

(D) 5

(E) There is not a least integer that satisfies the inequality.

PS18871.01

15.

x	C(x)
0	25,000
10	24,919
20	24,846
30	24,781
40	24,724
50	24,675

A certain manufacturer uses the function $C(x) = 0.04x^2 - 8.5x + 25{,}000$ to calculate the cost, in dollars, of producing x thousand units of its product. The table above gives values of this cost function for values of x between 0 and 50 in increments of 10. For which of the following intervals is the average rate of *decrease* in cost less than the average rate of *decrease* in cost for each of the other intervals?

(A) From $x = 0$ to $x = 10$

(B) From $x = 10$ to $x = 20$

(C) From $x = 20$ to $x = 30$

(D) From $x = 30$ to $x = 40$

(E) From $x = 40$ to $x = 50$

PS35302.01

16. On the day of the performance of a certain play, each ticket that regularly sells for less than $10.00 is sold for half price plus $0.50, and each ticket that regularly sells for $10.00 or more is sold for half price plus $1.00. On the day of the performance, a person purchases a total of y tickets, of which x regularly sell for $9.00 each and the rest regularly sell for $12.00 each. What is the amount paid, in dollars, for the y tickets?

(A) $7y - 2x$

(B) $12x - 7y$

(C) $\dfrac{9x + 12y}{2}$

(D) $7y + 4x$

(E) $7y + 5x$

PS47302.01

17. If $N = \dfrac{K}{T + \dfrac{x}{y}}$, where $T = \dfrac{K}{5}$ and $x = 5 - T$, which of the following expresses y in terms of N and T?

(A) $\dfrac{N(5 - T)}{T(5 - N)}$

(B) $\dfrac{N(T - 5)}{T(5 - N)}$

(C) $\dfrac{5 - T}{T(5 - N)}$

(D) $\dfrac{5N(5 - T)}{T(1 - 5N)}$

(E) $\dfrac{N(5 - T)}{5}$

PS78302.01

18. If $2x + 5y = 8$ and $3x = 2y$, what is the value of $2x + y$?

(A) 4

(B) $\dfrac{70}{19}$

(C) $\dfrac{64}{19}$

(D) $\dfrac{56}{19}$

(E) $\dfrac{40}{19}$

PS79302.01

19. If $_kS_n$ is defined to be the product of $(n + k)(n - k + 1)$ for all positive integers k and n, which of the following expressions represents $_{k+1}S_{n+1}$?

(A) $(n + k)(n - k + 2)$

(B) $(n + k)(n - k + 3)$

(C) $(n + k + 1)(n - k + 2)$

(D) $(n + k + 2)(n - k + 1)$

(E) $(n + k + 2)(n - k + 3)$

PS20502.01

20. There were 36,000 hardback copies of a certain novel sold before the paperback version was issued. From the time the first paperback copy was sold until the last copy of the novel was sold, 9 times as many paperback copies as hardback copies were sold. If a total of 441,000 copies of the novel were sold in all, how many paperback copies were sold?

(A) 45,000

(B) 360,000

(C) 364,500

(D) 392,000

(E) 396,900

PS30502.01

21. In the formula $w = \dfrac{P}{\sqrt[t]{v}}$, integers p and t are positive constants. If $w = 2$ when $v = 1$ and if $w = \dfrac{1}{2}$ when $v = 64$, then $t =$

(A) 1

(B) 2

(C) 3

(D) 4

(E) 16

PS03502.01

22.

The figure above represents a network of one-way streets. The arrows indicate the direction of traffic flow, and the numbers indicate the amount of traffic flow into or out of each of the four intersections during a certain hour. During that hour, what was the amount of traffic flow along the street from R to S if the total amount of traffic flow into P was 1,200? (Assume that none of the traffic originates or terminates in the network.)

(A) 200

(B) 250

(C) 300

(D) 350

(E) 400

PS23502.01

23. If C is the temperature in degrees Celsius and F is the temperature in degrees Fahrenheit, then the relationship between temperatures on the two scales is expressed by the equation $9C = 5(F - 32)$. On a day when the temperature extremes recorded at a certain weather station differed by 45 degrees on the Fahrenheit scale, by how many degrees did the temperature extremes differ on the Celsius scale?

(A) $\dfrac{65}{9}$

(B) 13

(C) 25

(D) 45

(E) 81

PS93502.01

24. If $d = \dfrac{a+b}{1+\dfrac{ab}{c^2}}$, $a = \dfrac{c}{2}$, and $b = \dfrac{3c}{4}$, what is the value of d in terms of c?

(A) $\dfrac{10c}{11}$

(B) $\dfrac{5c}{2}$

(C) $\dfrac{10c}{3}$

(D) $\dfrac{10}{11c}$

(E) $\dfrac{5}{2c}$

PS04502.01

25. A school supply store sells only one kind of desk and one kind of chair, at a uniform cost per desk or per chair. If the total cost of 3 desks and 1 chair is twice that of 1 desk and 3 chairs, then the total cost of 4 desks and 1 chair is how many times that of 1 desk and 4 chairs?

(A) 5

(B) 3

(C) $\dfrac{8}{3}$

(D) $\dfrac{5}{2}$

(E) $\dfrac{7}{3}$

PS35502.01

26. A certain truck traveling at 55 miles per hour gets 4.5 miles per gallon of diesel fuel consumed. Traveling at 60 miles per hour, the truck gets only 3.5 miles per gallon. On a 500-mile trip, if the truck used a total of 120 gallons of diesel fuel and traveled part of the trip at 55 miles per hour and the rest at 60 miles per hour, how many miles did it travel at 55 miles per hour?

(A) 140

(B) 200

(C) 250

(D) 300

(E) 360

PS45502.01

27. A merchant paid $300 for a shipment of x identical calculators. The merchant used two of the calculators as demonstrators and sold each of the others for $5 more than the average (arithmetic mean) cost of the x calculators. If the total revenue from the sale of the calculators was $120 more than the cost of the shipment, how many calculators were in the shipment?

(A) 24

(B) 25

(C) 26

(D) 28

(E) 30

PS06502.01

28. A car traveled 462 miles per tankful of gasoline on the highway and 336 miles per tankful of gasoline in the city. If the car traveled 6 fewer miles per gallon in the city than on the highway, how many miles per gallon did the car travel in the city?

(A) 14

(B) 16

(C) 21

(D) 22

(E) 27

PS56502.01

29. Machines X and Y run at different constant rates, and machine X can complete a certain job in 9 hours. Machine X worked on the job alone for the first 3 hours and the two machines, working together, then completed the job in 4 more hours. How many hours would it have taken machine Y, working alone, to complete the entire job?

(A) 18

(B) $13\dfrac{1}{2}$

(C) $7\dfrac{1}{5}$

(D) $4\dfrac{1}{2}$

(E) $3\dfrac{2}{3}$

PS77602.01

30. If $\dfrac{s}{t} = 2$, then the value of which of the following can be determined?

  I. $\dfrac{2t}{s}$

  II. $\dfrac{s-t}{t}$

  III. $\dfrac{t-1}{s-1}$

  (A) I only
  (B) III only
  (C) I and II only
  (D) II and III only
  (E) I, II, and III

PS58602.01

31. If $k \neq 0$ and $k - \dfrac{3 - 2k^2}{k} = \dfrac{x}{k}$, then $x =$

  (A) $-3 - k^2$
  (B) $k^2 - 3$
  (C) $3k^2 - 3$
  (D) $k - 3 - 2k^2$
  (E) $k - 3 + 2k^2$

PS68602.01

32. The sum of the ages of Doris and Fred is y years. If Doris is 12 years older than Fred, how many years old will Fred be y years from now, in terms of y?

  (A) $y - 6$
  (B) $2y - 6$
  (C) $\dfrac{y}{2} - 6$
  (D) $\dfrac{3y}{2} - 6$
  (E) $\dfrac{5y}{2} - 6$

Geometry

PS35461.01

33.

Note: Figure not drawn to scale.

The shaded region in the figure above represents a rectangular frame with length 18 inches and width 15 inches. The frame encloses a rectangular picture that has the same area as the frame itself. If the length and width of the picture have the same ratio as the length and width of the frame, what is the length of the picture, in inches?

  (A) $9\sqrt{2}$
  (B) $\dfrac{3}{2}$
  (C) $\dfrac{9}{\sqrt{2}}$
  (D) $15(1 - \dfrac{1}{\sqrt{2}})$
  (E) $\dfrac{9}{2}$

PS56271.01

34. The *surface distance* between 2 points on the surface of a cube is the length of the shortest path on the surface of the cube that joins the 2 points. If a cube has edges of length 4 centimeters, what is the surface distance, in centimeters, between the lower left vertex on its front face and the upper right vertex on its back face?

  (A) 8
  (B) $4\sqrt{5}$
  (C) $8\sqrt{2}$
  (D) $12\sqrt{2}$
  (E) $4\sqrt{2} + 4$

PS75571.01

35.

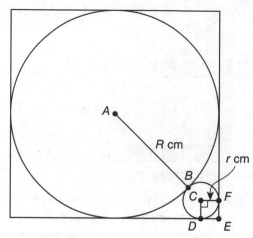

The figure above shows 2 circles. The larger circle has center A, radius R cm, and is inscribed in a square. The smaller circle has center C, radius r cm, and is tangent to the larger circle at point B and to the square at points D and F. If points A, B, C, and E are collinear, which of the following is equal to $\dfrac{R}{r}$?

(A) $\quad \dfrac{2}{\sqrt{2}+1}$

(B) $\quad \dfrac{2}{\sqrt{2}-1}$

(C) $\quad \dfrac{2}{2\sqrt{2}+1}$

(D) $\quad \dfrac{\sqrt{2}+1}{\sqrt{2}-1}$

(E) $\quad \dfrac{2\sqrt{2}+1}{2\sqrt{2}-1}$

PS15302.01

36.

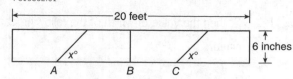

Note: Figure not drawn to scale.

The figure above shows the dimensions of a rectangular board that is to be cut into four identical pieces by making cuts at points A, B, and C, as indicated. If $x = 45$, what is the length AB ? (1 foot = 12 inches)

(A)   5 ft 6 in

(B)   5 ft $3\sqrt{2}$ in

(C)   5 ft 3 in

(D)   5 ft

(E)   4 ft 9 in

PS57302.01

37.

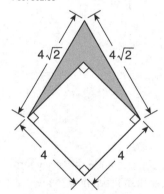

In the figure above, the area of the shaded region is

(A) $8\sqrt{2}$

(B) $4\sqrt{3}$

(C) $4\sqrt{2}$

(D) $8\left(\sqrt{3}-1\right)$

(E) $8\left(\sqrt{2}-1\right)$

PS18302.01

38.

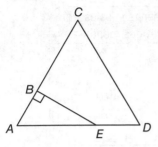

If each side of △ACD above has length 3 and if AB has length 1, what is the area of region BCDE ?

(A) $\dfrac{9}{4}$

(B) $\dfrac{7}{4}\sqrt{3}$

(C) $\dfrac{9}{4}\sqrt{3}$

(D) $\dfrac{7}{2}\sqrt{3}$

(E) $6 + \sqrt{3}$

PS76402.01

39.

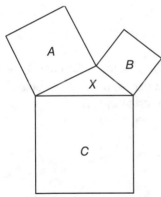

Note: Figure not drawn to scale.

In the figure above, three squares and a triangle have areas of A, B, C, and X as shown. If A = 144, B = 81, and C = 225, then X =

(A) 150

(B) 144

(C) 80

(D) 54

(E) 36

PS57402.01

40.

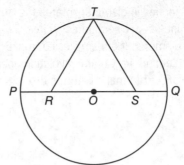

In the figure above, PQ is a diameter of circle O, PR = SQ, and △RST is equilateral. If the length of PQ is 2, what is the length of RT ?

(A) $\dfrac{1}{2}$

(B) $\dfrac{1}{\sqrt{3}}$

(C) $\dfrac{\sqrt{3}}{2}$

(D) $\dfrac{2}{\sqrt{3}}$

(E) $\sqrt{3}$

PS22502.01

41.

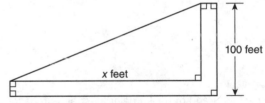

Note: Figure not drawn to scale.

The figure above shows some of the dimensions of a triangular plaza with an L-shaped walk along two of its edges. If the width of the walk is 4 feet and the total area of the plaza and walk together is 10,800 square feet, what is the value of x ?

(A) 200

(B) 204

(C) 212

(D) 216

(E) 225

PS88602.01

42. A circular rim 28 inches in diameter rotates the same number of inches per second as a circular rim 35 inches in diameter. If the smaller rim makes x revolutions per second, how many revolutions per minute does the larger rim make in terms of x?

(A) $\dfrac{48\pi}{x}$

(B) $75x$

(C) $48x$

(D) $24x$

(E) $\dfrac{x}{75}$

Rates/Ratios/Percent

PS17302.01

43. The annual stockholders' report for Corporation X stated that profits were up 10 percent over the previous year, although profits as a percent of sales were down 10 percent. Total sales for that year were approximately what percent of sales for the previous year?

(A) 78%

(B) 90%

(C) 110%

(D) 122%

(E) 190%

PS47402.01

44. A certain brand of house paint must be purchased either in quarts at $12 each or in gallons at $18 each. A painter needs a 3-gallon mixture of the paint consisting of 3 parts blue and 2 parts white. What is the least amount of money needed to purchase sufficient quantities of the two colors to make the mixture?
(4 quarts = 1 gallon)

(A) $54

(B) $60

(C) $66

(D) $90

(E) $144

PS43481.01

45.

Month	Change in sales from previous month
February	+10%
March	−15%
April	+20%
May	−10%
June	+5%

The table above shows the percent of change from the previous month in Company X's sales for February through June of last year. A positive percent indicates that Company X's sales for that month increased from the sales for the previous month, and a negative percent indicates that Company X's sales for that month decreased from the sales for the previous month. For which month were the sales closest to the sales in January?

(A) February

(B) March

(C) April

(D) May

(E) June

PS56302.01

46. A store bought 5 dozen lamps at $30 per dozen and sold them all at $15 per lamp. The profit on each lamp was what percent of its selling price?

(A) 20%

(B) 50%

(C) $83\dfrac{1}{3}$%

(D) 100%

(E) 500%

PS76302.01

47. Store N gives a 50 percent discount on the list price of all its items and Store W gives a 60 percent discount on the list price of all its items. If the list price of the same item is 20 percent higher in Store W, what percent (more or less) of the selling price in Store N is the selling price of the item in Store W ?

(A) 10% less

(B) 4% less

(C) 2% less

(D) 10% more

(E) 12% more

PS95402.01

48. A merchant purchased a jacket for $60 and then determined a selling price that equaled the purchase price of the jacket plus a markup that was 25 percent of the selling price. During a sale, the merchant discounted the selling price by 20 percent and sold the jacket. What was the merchant's gross profit on this sale?

(A) $0
(B) $3
(C) $4
(D) $12
(E) $15

PS12502.01

49. When a certain stretch of highway was rebuilt and straightened, the distance along the stretch was decreased by 20 percent and the speed limit was increased by 25 percent. By what percent was the driving time along this stretch reduced for a person who always drives at the speed limit?

(A) 16%
(B) 36%
(C) $37\frac{1}{2}$%
(D) 45%
(E) $56\frac{1}{4}$%

Value/Order/Factors

PS56441.01

50.

Components	Number of components:		
	Monday	Tuesday	Wednesday
A	3	6	3
B	6	3	4
C	4	7	4

A factory assembles Product X from three components, A, B, and C. One of each component is needed for each Product X and all three components must be available when assembly of each Product X starts. It takes two days to assemble one Product X. Assembly of each Product X starts at the beginning of one day and is finished at the end of the next day. The factory can work on at most five Product Xs at once. If components are available each day as shown in the table above, what is the largest number of Product Xs that can be assembled during the three days covered by the table?

(A) 3
(B) 5
(C) 6
(D) 9
(E) 10

PS04851.01

51. How many positive integers n have the property that both $3n$ and $\frac{n}{3}$ are 4-digit integers?

(A) 111
(B) 112
(C) 333
(D) 334
(E) 1,134

PS24851.01

52. If Whitney wrote the decimal representations for the first 300 positive integer multiples of 5 and did not write any other numbers, how many times would she have written the digit 5?

(A) 150
(B) 185
(C) 186
(D) 200
(E) 201

PS01661.01

53. The difference 942 − 249 is a positive multiple of 7. If a, b, and c are nonzero digits, how many 3-digit numbers abc are possible such that the difference abc − cba is a positive multiple of 7?

(A) 142
(B) 71
(C) 99
(D) 20
(E) 18

PS41661.01

54. Let S be the set of all positive integers having at most 4 digits and such that each of the digits is 0 or 1. What is the greatest prime factor of the sum of all the numbers in S?

(A) 11
(B) 19
(C) 37
(D) 59
(E) 101

PS43661.01

55.

Age	Tax only	Tax and fees	Fees only
18–39	20	30	30
≥40	10	60	100

The table above shows the number of residents in each of two age groups who support the use of each type of funding for a city initiative. What is the probability that a person randomly selected from among the 250 residents polled is younger than 40, or supports a type of funding that includes a tax, or both?

(A) $\frac{1}{5}$

(B) $\frac{8}{25}$

(C) $\frac{12}{25}$

(D) $\frac{3}{5}$

(E) $\frac{4}{5}$

PS55471.01

56. Which of the following describes the set of all possible values of the positive integer k such that, for each positive odd integer n, the value of $\frac{n}{k}$ is midway between consecutive integers?

(A) All positive integers greater than 2
(B) All prime numbers
(C) All positive even integers
(D) All even prime numbers
(E) All positive even multiples of 5

PS92981.01

57. A certain online form requires a 2-digit code for the day of the month to be entered into one of its fields, such as 04 for the 4th day of the month. The code is valid if it is 01, 02, 03, …, 31 and not valid otherwise. The transpose of a code xy is yx. For example, 40 is the transpose of 04. If N is the number of valid codes having a transpose that is not valid, what is the value of N?

(A) 12
(B) 13
(C) 18
(D) 19
(E) 20

PS25302.01

58. If x < y < z and y − x > 5, where x is an even integer and y and z are odd integers, what is the least possible value of z − x?

(A) 6
(B) 7
(C) 8
(D) 9
(E) 10

PS36302.01

59. An "Armstrong number" is an n-digit number that is equal to the sum of the nth powers of its individual digits. For example, 153 is an Armstrong number because it has 3 digits and $1^3 + 5^3 + 3^3 = 153$. What is the digit k in the Armstrong number 1,6k4?

(A) 2
(B) 3
(C) 4
(D) 5
(E) 6

PS30402.01

60. Five integers between 10 and 99, inclusive, are to be formed by using each of the ten digits exactly once in such a way that the sum of the five integers is as small as possible. What is the greatest possible integer that could be among these five numbers?

   (A) 98
   (B) 91
   (C) 59
   (D) 50
   (E) 37

PS66402.01

61. When the integer n is divided by 17, the quotient is x and the remainder is 5. When n is divided by 23, the quotient is y and the remainder is 14. Which of the following is true?

   (A) $23x + 17y = 19$
   (B) $17x - 23y = 9$
   (C) $17x + 23y = 19$
   (D) $14x + 5y = 6$
   (E) $5x - 14y = -6$

PS17402.01

62. Of the following, which is greatest?

   (A) $3\sqrt{2}$

   (B) $2\sqrt{3}$

   (C) $\dfrac{4\sqrt{3}}{5}$

   (D) $\dfrac{5\sqrt{2}}{4}$

   (E) $\dfrac{7}{\sqrt{3}}$

PS37402.01

63. If $n = p^2$ and p is a prime number greater than 5, what is the units digit of n^2?

   (A) 1
   (B) 3
   (C) 4
   (D) 7
   (E) 9

PS83502.01

64. A computer can perform 1,000,000 calculations per second. At this rate, how many *hours* will it take this computer to perform the 3.6×10^{11} calculations required to solve a certain problem?

   (A) 60
   (B) 100
   (C) 600
   (D) 1,000
   (E) 6,000

PS66602.01

65. In an auditorium, 360 chairs are to be set up in a rectangular arrangement with x rows of exactly y chairs each. If the only other restriction is that $10 < x < 25$, how many different rectangular arrangements are possible?

   (A) Four
   (B) Five
   (C) Six
   (D) Eight
   (E) Nine

PS28602.01

66. If the product of the integers w, x, y, and z is 770, and if $1 < w < x < y < z$, what is the value of $w + z$?

   (A) 10
   (B) 13
   (C) 16
   (D) 18
   (E) 21

PS78602.01

67.

1,234

1,243

1,324

....

....

+ 4,321

The addition problem above shows four of the 24 different integers that can be formed by using each of the digits 1, 2, 3, and 4 exactly once in each integer. What is the sum of these 24 integers?

(A) 24,000

(B) 26,664

(C) 40,440

(D) 60,000

(E) 66,660

Data Sufficiency

Counting/Sets/Series

DS19350.01

68. A country's per capita national debt is its national debt divided by its population. Is the per capita national debt of Country G within $5 of $500?

(1) Country G's national debt to the nearest $1,000,000,000 is $43,000,000,000.

(2) Country G's population to the nearest 1,000,000 is 86,000,000.

(A) Statement (1) ALONE is sufficient, but statement (2) alone is not sufficient.

(B) Statement (2) ALONE is sufficient, but statement (1) alone is not sufficient.

(C) BOTH statements TOGETHER are sufficient, but NEITHER statement ALONE is sufficient.

(D) EACH statement ALONE is sufficient.

(E) Statements (1) and (2) TOGETHER are NOT sufficient.

DS06351.01

69. The *cardinality* of a finite set is the number of elements in the set. What is the cardinality of set A?

(1) 2 is the cardinality of exactly 6 subsets of set A.

(2) Set A has a total of 16 subsets, including the empty set and set A itself.

(A) Statement (1) ALONE is sufficient, but statement (2) alone is not sufficient.

(B) Statement (2) ALONE is sufficient, but statement (1) alone is not sufficient.

(C) BOTH statements TOGETHER are sufficient, but NEITHER statement ALONE is sufficient.

(D) EACH statement ALONE is sufficient.

(E) Statements (1) and (2) TOGETHER are NOT sufficient.

DS59851.01

70. For each positive integer k, let $a_k = \left(1 + \dfrac{1}{k+1}\right)$. Is the product $a_1 a_2 \ldots a_n$ an integer?

(1) $n + 1$ is a multiple of 3.

(2) n is a multiple of 2.

(A) Statement (1) ALONE is sufficient, but statement (2) alone is not sufficient.

(B) Statement (2) ALONE is sufficient, but statement (1) alone is not sufficient.

(C) BOTH statements TOGETHER are sufficient, but NEITHER statement ALONE is sufficient.

(D) EACH statement ALONE is sufficient.

(E) Statements (1) and (2) TOGETHER are NOT sufficient.

DS95491.01

71. Let S be a set of outcomes and let A and B be events with outcomes in S. Let $\sim B$ denote the set of all outcomes in S that are not in B and let $P(A)$ denote the probability that event A occurs. What is the value of $P(A)$?

(1) $P(A \cup B) = 0.7$

(2) $P(A \cup \sim B) = 0.9$

(A) Statement (1) ALONE is sufficient, but statement (2) alone is not sufficient.

(B) Statement (2) ALONE is sufficient, but statement (1) alone is not sufficient.

(C) BOTH statements TOGETHER are sufficient, but NEITHER statement ALONE is sufficient.

(D) EACH statement ALONE is sufficient.

(E) Statements (1) and (2) TOGETHER are NOT sufficient.

DS41402.01

72. What is the number of integers that are common to both set *S* and set *T*?

    (1) The number of integers in *S* is 7, and the number of integers in *T* is 6.

    (2) *U* is the set of integers that are in *S* only or in *T* only or in both, and the number of integers in *U* is 10.

    (A) Statement (1) ALONE is sufficient, but statement (2) alone is not sufficient.

    (B) Statement (2) ALONE is sufficient, but statement (1) alone is not sufficient.

    (C) BOTH statements TOGETHER are sufficient, but NEITHER statement ALONE is sufficient.

    (D) EACH statement ALONE is sufficient.

    (E) Statements (1) and (2) TOGETHER are NOT sufficient.

DS51402.01

73. What is the sum of 3 consecutive integers?

    (1) The sum of the 3 integers is less than the greatest of the 3 integers.

    (2) Of the 3 integers, the ratio of the least to the greatest is 3.

    (A) Statement (1) ALONE is sufficient, but statement (2) alone is not sufficient.

    (B) Statement (2) ALONE is sufficient, but statement (1) alone is not sufficient.

    (C) BOTH statements TOGETHER are sufficient, but NEITHER statement ALONE is sufficient.

    (D) EACH statement ALONE is sufficient.

    (E) Statements (1) and (2) TOGETHER are NOT sufficient.

DS54402.01

74. How many people in Town *X* read neither the *World* newspaper nor the *Globe* newspaper?

    (1) Of the 2,500 people in Town *X*, 1,000 read no newspaper.

    (2) Of the people in Town *X*, 700 read the *Globe* only and 600 read the *World* only.

    (A) Statement (1) ALONE is sufficient, but statement (2) alone is not sufficient.

    (B) Statement (2) ALONE is sufficient, but statement (1) alone is not sufficient.

    (C) BOTH statements TOGETHER are sufficient, but NEITHER statement ALONE is sufficient.

    (D) EACH statement ALONE is sufficient.

    (E) Statements (1) and (2) TOGETHER are NOT sufficient.

DS16402.01

75. Bowls *X* and *Y* each contained exactly 2 jelly beans, each of which was either red or black. One of the jelly beans in bowl *X* was exchanged with one of the jelly beans in bowl *Y*. After the exchange, were both of the jelly beans in bowl *X* black?

    (1) Before the exchange, bowl *X* contained 2 black jelly beans.

    (2) After the exchange, bowl *Y* contained 1 jelly bean of each color.

    (A) Statement (1) ALONE is sufficient, but statement (2) alone is not sufficient.

    (B) Statement (2) ALONE is sufficient, but statement (1) alone is not sufficient.

    (C) BOTH statements TOGETHER are sufficient, but NEITHER statement ALONE is sufficient.

    (D) EACH statement ALONE is sufficient.

    (E) Statements (1) and (2) TOGETHER are NOT sufficient.

DS27602.01

76. All trainees in a certain aviator training program must take both a written test and a flight test. If 70 percent of the trainees passed the written test, and 80 percent of the trainees passed the flight test, what percent of the trainees passed both tests?

(1)   10 percent of the trainees did not pass either test.

(2)   20 percent of the trainees passed only the flight test.

(A)   Statement (1) ALONE is sufficient, but statement (2) alone is not sufficient.

(B)   Statement (2) ALONE is sufficient, but statement (1) alone is not sufficient.

(C)   BOTH statements TOGETHER are sufficient, but NEITHER statement ALONE is sufficient.

(D)   EACH statement ALONE is sufficient.

(E)   Statements (1) and (2) TOGETHER are NOT sufficient.

Equalities/Inequalities/Algebra

DS06110.01

77. Each of the five divisions of a certain company sent representatives to a conference. If the numbers of representatives sent by four of the divisions were 3, 4, 5, and 5, was the range of the numbers of representatives sent by the five divisions greater than 2?

(1)   The median of the numbers of representatives sent by the five divisions was greater than the average (arithmetic mean) of these numbers.

(2)   The median of the numbers of representatives sent by the five divisions was 4.

(A)   Statement (1) ALONE is sufficient, but statement (2) alone is not sufficient.

(B)   Statement (2) ALONE is sufficient, but statement (1) alone is not sufficient.

(C)   BOTH statements TOGETHER are sufficient, but NEITHER statement ALONE is sufficient.

(D)   EACH statement ALONE is sufficient.

(E)   Statements (1) and (2) TOGETHER are NOT sufficient.

DS24931.01

78. An investment has been growing at a fixed annual rate of 20% since it was first made; no portion of the investment has been withdrawn, and all interest has been reinvested. How much is the investment now worth?

(1)   The value of the investment has increased by 44% since it was first made.

(2)   If one year ago $600 had been withdrawn, today the investment would be worth 12% less than it is actually now worth.

(A)   Statement (1) ALONE is sufficient, but statement (2) alone is not sufficient.

(B)   Statement (2) ALONE is sufficient, but statement (1) alone is not sufficient.

(C)   BOTH statements TOGETHER are sufficient, but NEITHER statement ALONE is sufficient.

(D)   EACH statement ALONE is sufficient.

(E)   Statements (1) and (2) TOGETHER are NOT sufficient.

DS53841.01

79. X, 81, 73, 71, 98, 73, 64

What is the value of X in the above list of 7 numbers?

(1)   The average (arithmetic mean) of these 7 numbers is 80.

(2)   The range of these 7 numbers is 36.

(A)   Statement (1) ALONE is sufficient, but statement (2) alone is not sufficient.

(B)   Statement (2) ALONE is sufficient, but statement (1) alone is not sufficient.

(C)   BOTH statements TOGETHER are sufficient, but NEITHER statement ALONE is sufficient.

(D)   EACH statement ALONE is sufficient.

(E)   Statements (1) and (2) TOGETHER are NOT sufficient.

DS01451.01

80. In the first 2 hours after Meadow's self-service laundry opens, *m* large washing machines and *n* small washing machines are in continual use. Including the time for filling and emptying the washing machines, each load of laundry takes 30 minutes in a large washing machine and 20 minutes in a small washing machine. What is the total number of loads of laundry done at Meadow's self-service laundry during this 2-hour period?

(1) $n = 3m$

(2) $2m + 3n = 55$

(A) Statement (1) ALONE is sufficient, but statement (2) alone is not sufficient.

(B) Statement (2) ALONE is sufficient, but statement (1) alone is not sufficient.

(C) BOTH statements TOGETHER are sufficient, but NEITHER statement ALONE is sufficient.

(D) EACH statement ALONE is sufficient.

(E) Statements (1) and (2) TOGETHER are NOT sufficient.

DS76851.01

81. A box of light bulbs contains exactly 3 light bulbs that are defective. What is the probability that a sample of light bulbs picked at random from this box will contain at least 1 defective light bulb?

(1) The light bulbs in the sample will be picked 1 at a time without replacement.

(2) The sample will contain exactly 20 light bulbs.

(A) Statement (1) ALONE is sufficient, but statement (2) alone is not sufficient.

(B) Statement (2) ALONE is sufficient, but statement (1) alone is not sufficient.

(C) BOTH statements TOGETHER are sufficient, but NEITHER statement ALONE is sufficient.

(D) EACH statement ALONE is sufficient.

(E) Statements (1) and (2) TOGETHER are NOT sufficient.

DS01951.01

82. Khalil drove 120 kilometers in a certain amount of time. What was his average speed, in kilometers per hour, during this time?

(1) If Khalil had driven at an average speed that was 5 kilometers per hour faster, his driving time would have been reduced by 20 minutes.

(2) If Khalil had driven at an average speed that was 25% faster, his driving time would have been reduced by 20%.

(A) Statement (1) ALONE is sufficient, but statement (2) alone is not sufficient.

(B) Statement (2) ALONE is sufficient, but statement (1) alone is not sufficient.

(C) BOTH statements TOGETHER are sufficient, but NEITHER statement ALONE is sufficient.

(D) EACH statement ALONE is sufficient.

(E) Statements (1) and (2) TOGETHER are NOT sufficient.

DS70061.01

83. What is the median of the data set *S* that consists of the integers 17, 29, 10, 26, 15, and *x* ?

(1) The average (arithmetic mean) of *S* is 17.

(2) The range of *S* is 24.

(A) Statement (1) ALONE is sufficient, but statement (2) alone is not sufficient.

(B) Statement (2) ALONE is sufficient, but statement (1) alone is not sufficient.

(C) BOTH statements TOGETHER are sufficient, but NEITHER statement ALONE is sufficient.

(D) EACH statement ALONE is sufficient.

(E) Statements (1) and (2) TOGETHER are NOT sufficient.

DS47661.01

84. If $n > 4$, what is the value of the integer n?

    (1) $\dfrac{n!}{(n-3)!} = \dfrac{3!\,n!}{4!(n-4)!}$

    (2) $\dfrac{n!}{3!(n-3)!} + \dfrac{n!}{4!(n-4)!} = \dfrac{(n+1)!}{4!(n-3)!}$

    (A) Statement (1) ALONE is sufficient, but statement (2) alone is not sufficient.

    (B) Statement (2) ALONE is sufficient, but statement (1) alone is not sufficient.

    (C) BOTH statements TOGETHER are sufficient, but NEITHER statement ALONE is sufficient.

    (D) EACH statement ALONE is sufficient.

    (E) Statements (1) and (2) TOGETHER are NOT sufficient.

DS50571.01

85. Tami purchased several identically priced metal frames and several identically priced wooden frames for a total pretax price of $144. What was the total pretax price of the metal frames that Tami purchased?

    (1) The price of each metal frame was 60% greater than the price of each wooden frame.

    (2) Tami purchased twice as many wooden frames as metal frames.

    (A) Statement (1) ALONE is sufficient, but statement (2) alone is not sufficient.

    (B) Statement (2) ALONE is sufficient, but statement (1) alone is not sufficient.

    (C) BOTH statements TOGETHER are sufficient, but NEITHER statement ALONE is sufficient.

    (D) EACH statement ALONE is sufficient.

    (E) Statements (1) and (2) TOGETHER are NOT sufficient.

DS02871.01

86. A $10 bill (1,000 cents) was replaced with 50 coins having the same total value. The only coins used were 5-cent coins, 10-cent coins, 25-cent coins, and 50-cent coins. How many 5-cent coins were used?

    (1) Exactly 10 of the coins were 25-cent coins and exactly 10 of the coins were 50-cent coins.

    (2) The number of 10-cent coins was twice the number of 5-cent coins.

    (A) Statement (1) ALONE is sufficient, but statement (2) alone is not sufficient.

    (B) Statement (2) ALONE is sufficient, but statement (1) alone is not sufficient.

    (C) BOTH statements TOGETHER are sufficient, but NEITHER statement ALONE is sufficient.

    (D) EACH statement ALONE is sufficient.

    (E) Statements (1) and (2) TOGETHER are NOT sufficient.

DS56971.01

87. Merle's spare change jar has exactly 16 U.S. coins, each of which is a 1-cent coin, a 5-cent coin, a 10-cent coin, a 25-cent coin, or a 50-cent coin. If the total value of the coins in the jar is 288 U.S. cents, how many 1-cent coins are in the jar?

    (1) The exact numbers of 10-cent, 25-cent, and 50-cent coins among the 16 coins in the jar are, respectively, 6, 5, and 2.

    (2) Among the 16 coins in the jar there are twice as many 10-cent coins as 1-cent coins.

    (A) Statement (1) ALONE is sufficient, but statement (2) alone is not sufficient.

    (B) Statement (2) ALONE is sufficient, but statement (1) alone is not sufficient.

    (C) BOTH statements TOGETHER are sufficient, but NEITHER statement ALONE is sufficient.

    (D) EACH statement ALONE is sufficient.

    (E) Statements (1) and (2) TOGETHER are NOT sufficient.

DS48391.01

88. At a certain university recreation center, a member can receive a 30-minute massage, a 60-minute massage, or a 90-minute massage, and is charged $0.50 per minute for each massage. A member receiving a massage is charged the same fixed amount for each additional service, such as nutrition advice or a fitness evaluation. At this center, what is the total charge to a member for a 60-minute massage and 3 additional services?

    (1) At this recreation center, Jordan, a member, had a massage and 3 additional services for a total charge of $37.50.
    (2) At this recreation center, Ryan, a member, had a massage and 2 additional services for a total charge of $60.00.

    (A) Statement (1) ALONE is sufficient, but statement (2) alone is not sufficient.
    (B) Statement (2) ALONE is sufficient, but statement (1) alone is not sufficient.
    (C) BOTH statements TOGETHER are sufficient, but NEITHER statement ALONE is sufficient.
    (D) EACH statement ALONE is sufficient.
    (E) Statements (1) and (2) TOGETHER are NOT sufficient.

DS84302.01

89. If S is the sum of the first n positive integers, what is the value of n?

    (1) $S < 20$
    (2) $S^2 > 220$

    (A) Statement (1) ALONE is sufficient, but statement (2) alone is not sufficient.
    (B) Statement (2) ALONE is sufficient, but statement (1) alone is not sufficient.
    (C) BOTH statements TOGETHER are sufficient, but NEITHER statement ALONE is sufficient.
    (D) EACH statement ALONE is sufficient.
    (E) Statements (1) and (2) TOGETHER are NOT sufficient.

DS48302.01

90. Is $x^2 - y^2$ a positive number?

    (1) $x - y$ is a positive number.
    (2) $x + y$ is a positive number.

    (A) Statement (1) ALONE is sufficient, but statement (2) alone is not sufficient.
    (B) Statement (2) ALONE is sufficient, but statement (1) alone is not sufficient.
    (C) BOTH statements TOGETHER are sufficient, but NEITHER statement ALONE is sufficient.
    (D) EACH statement ALONE is sufficient.
    (E) Statements (1) and (2) TOGETHER are NOT sufficient.

DS89302.01

91. Alan and Sue have each been saving one dollar a day and will continue to do so for the next month. If Sue began saving several days before Alan, in how many days from today will Alan have saved one-half as much as Sue?

    (1) As of today, Alan has saved 7 dollars and Sue has saved 27 dollars.
    (2) Three days from today, Alan will have saved one-third as much as Sue.

    (A) Statement (1) ALONE is sufficient, but statement (2) alone is not sufficient.
    (B) Statement (2) ALONE is sufficient, but statement (1) alone is not sufficient.
    (C) BOTH statements TOGETHER are sufficient, but NEITHER statement ALONE is sufficient.
    (D) EACH statement ALONE is sufficient.
    (E) Statements (1) and (2) TOGETHER are NOT sufficient.

DS64402.01

92. What is the value of x ?

(1) $x^4 + x^2 + 1 = \dfrac{1}{x^4 + x^2 + 1}$

(2) $x^3 + x^2 = 0$

(A) Statement (1) ALONE is sufficient, but statement (2) alone is not sufficient.

(B) Statement (2) ALONE is sufficient, but statement (1) alone is not sufficient.

(C) BOTH statements TOGETHER are sufficient, but NEITHER statement ALONE is sufficient.

(D) EACH statement ALONE is sufficient.

(E) Statements (1) and (2) TOGETHER are NOT sufficient.

DS26402.01

93. Is x less than y ?

(1) $x - y + 1 < 0$

(2) $x - y - 1 < 0$

(A) Statement (1) ALONE is sufficient, but statement (2) alone is not sufficient.

(B) Statement (2) ALONE is sufficient, but statement (1) alone is not sufficient.

(C) BOTH statements TOGETHER are sufficient, but NEITHER statement ALONE is sufficient.

(D) EACH statement ALONE is sufficient.

(E) Statements (1) and (2) TOGETHER are NOT sufficient.

DS08402.01

94. State X has a sales tax rate of k percent on all purchases and State Y has a sales tax rate of n percent on all purchases. What is the value of $k - n$?

(1) The sales tax on a $15 purchase is 30 cents more in State X than in State Y.

(2) The sales tax rate in State X is 1.4 times the sales tax rate in State Y.

(A) Statement (1) ALONE is sufficient, but statement (2) alone is not sufficient.

(B) Statement (2) ALONE is sufficient, but statement (1) alone is not sufficient.

(C) BOTH statements TOGETHER are sufficient, but NEITHER statement ALONE is sufficient.

(D) EACH statement ALONE is sufficient.

(E) Statements (1) and (2) TOGETHER are NOT sufficient.

DS28402.01

95. Is $-3 \le x \le 3$?

(1) $x^2 + y^2 = 9$

(2) $x^2 + y \le 9$

(A) Statement (1) ALONE is sufficient, but statement (2) alone is not sufficient.

(B) Statement (2) ALONE is sufficient, but statement (1) alone is not sufficient.

(C) BOTH statements TOGETHER are sufficient, but NEITHER statement ALONE is sufficient.

(D) EACH statement ALONE is sufficient.

(E) Statements (1) and (2) TOGETHER are NOT sufficient.

DS69402.01

96. What is the value of x?

(1) $4^{x+1} + 4^x = 320$

(2) $x^2 = 9$

(A) Statement (1) ALONE is sufficient, but statement (2) alone is not sufficient.

(B) Statement (2) ALONE is sufficient, but statement (1) alone is not sufficient.

(C) BOTH statements TOGETHER are sufficient, but NEITHER statement ALONE is sufficient.

(D) EACH statement ALONE is sufficient.

(E) Statements (1) and (2) TOGETHER are NOT sufficient.

DS50502.01

97. Three dice, each with faces numbered 1 through 6, were tossed onto a game board. If one of the dice turned up 4, what was the sum of the numbers that turned up on all three dice?

(1) The sum of two of the numbers that turned up was 10.

(2) The sum of two of the numbers that turned up was 11.

(A) Statement (1) ALONE is sufficient, but statement (2) alone is not sufficient.

(B) Statement (2) ALONE is sufficient, but statement (1) alone is not sufficient.

(C) BOTH statements TOGETHER are sufficient, but NEITHER statement ALONE is sufficient.

(D) EACH statement ALONE is sufficient.

(E) Statements (1) and (2) TOGETHER are NOT sufficient.

DS81502.01

98. Of the numbers q, r, s, and t, which is greatest?

(1) The average (arithmetic mean) of q and r is s.

(2) The sum of q and r is t.

(A) Statement (1) ALONE is sufficient, but statement (2) alone is not sufficient.

(B) Statement (2) ALONE is sufficient, but statement (1) alone is not sufficient.

(C) BOTH statements TOGETHER are sufficient, but NEITHER statement ALONE is sufficient.

(D) EACH statement ALONE is sufficient.

(E) Statements (1) and (2) TOGETHER are NOT sufficient.

DS94502.01

99.

CAR RENTAL CHARGES AT THRIFTY AGENCY

Car Type	Charge per day	Charge per Week (7 days)
Economy	$28	$100
Compact	$30	$120
Midsize	$32	$140
Standard	$34	$160
Luxury	$39	$200

The table above shows the car rental charges at Thrifty Agency. The daily rate applies for each day or fraction of a day in excess of any multiple of a 7-day week, up to the charge per week. If Olga rented a car of one of the types indicated, which type was it?

(1) Olga's total rental charge, based only on the rates specified, was $184.

(2) Olga rented the car for 10 days.

(A) Statement (1) ALONE is sufficient, but statement (2) alone is not sufficient.

(B) Statement (2) ALONE is sufficient, but statement (1) alone is not sufficient.

(C) BOTH statements TOGETHER are sufficient, but NEITHER statement ALONE is sufficient.

(D) EACH statement ALONE is sufficient.

(E) Statements (1) and (2) TOGETHER are NOT sufficient.

DS76602.01

100. Is $xy < 6$?

(1) $x < 3$ and $y < 2$.

(2) $\frac{1}{2} < x < \frac{2}{3}$ and $y^2 < 64$.

(A) Statement (1) ALONE is sufficient, but statement (2) alone is not sufficient.

(B) Statement (2) ALONE is sufficient, but statement (1) alone is not sufficient.

(C) BOTH statements TOGETHER are sufficient, but NEITHER statement ALONE is sufficient.

(D) EACH statement ALONE is sufficient.

(E) Statements (1) and (2) TOGETHER are NOT sufficient.

DS86602.01

101. What is the value of $\dfrac{x}{yz}$?

(1) $x = \dfrac{y}{2}$ and $z = \dfrac{2x}{5}$.

(2) $\dfrac{x}{z} = \dfrac{5}{2}$ and $\dfrac{1}{y} = \dfrac{1}{10}$.

(A) Statement (1) ALONE is sufficient, but statement (2) alone is not sufficient.

(B) Statement (2) ALONE is sufficient, but statement (1) alone is not sufficient.

(C) BOTH statements TOGETHER are sufficient, but NEITHER statement ALONE is sufficient.

(D) EACH statement ALONE is sufficient.

(E) Statements (1) and (2) TOGETHER are NOT sufficient.

DS47602.01

102. In a certain group of people, the average (arithmetic mean) weight of the males is 180 pounds and of the females, 120 pounds. What is the average weight of the people in the group?

(1) The group contains twice as many females as males.

(2) The group contains 10 more females than males.

(A) Statement (1) ALONE is sufficient, but statement (2) alone is not sufficient.

(B) Statement (2) ALONE is sufficient, but statement (1) alone is not sufficient.

(C) BOTH statements TOGETHER are sufficient, but NEITHER statement ALONE is sufficient.

(D) EACH statement ALONE is sufficient.

(E) Statements (1) and (2) TOGETHER are NOT sufficient.

DS57602.01

103. If $y = 2^{x+1}$, what is the value of $y - x$?

(1) $2^{2x+2} = 64$

(2) $y = 2^{2x-1}$

(A) Statement (1) ALONE is sufficient, but statement (2) alone is not sufficient.

(B) Statement (2) ALONE is sufficient, but statement (1) alone is not sufficient.

(C) BOTH statements TOGETHER are sufficient, but NEITHER statement ALONE is sufficient.

(D) EACH statement ALONE is sufficient.

(E) Statements (1) and (2) TOGETHER are NOT sufficient.

DS67602.01

104. If $x \neq 1$, is y equal to $x + 1$?

(1) $\dfrac{y-2}{x-1} = 1$

(2) $y^2 = (x+1)^2$

(A) Statement (1) ALONE is sufficient, but statement (2) alone is not sufficient.

(B) Statement (2) ALONE is sufficient, but statement (1) alone is not sufficient.

(C) BOTH statements TOGETHER are sufficient, but NEITHER statement ALONE is sufficient.

(D) EACH statement ALONE is sufficient.

(E) Statements (1) and (2) TOGETHER are NOT sufficient.

DS18602.01

105. If $x + y + z > 0$, is $z > 1$?

(1) $z > x + y + 1$

(2) $x + y + 1 < 0$

(A) Statement (1) ALONE is sufficient, but statement (2) alone is not sufficient.

(B) Statement (2) ALONE is sufficient, but statement (1) alone is not sufficient.

(C) BOTH statements TOGETHER are sufficient, but NEITHER statement ALONE is sufficient.

(D) EACH statement ALONE is sufficient.

(E) Statements (1) and (2) TOGETHER are NOT sufficient.

Geometry

DS35210.01

106. In the rectangular coordinate system, line *k* passes through the point (n, –1). Is the slope of line *k* greater than zero?

    (1)   Line *k* passes through the origin.
    (2)   Line *k* passes through the point (1, $n + 2$).

    (A)   Statement (1) ALONE is sufficient, but statement (2) alone is not sufficient.
    (B)   Statement (2) ALONE is sufficient, but statement (1) alone is not sufficient.
    (C)   BOTH statements TOGETHER are sufficient, but NEITHER statement ALONE is sufficient.
    (D)   EACH statement ALONE is sufficient.
    (E)   Statements (1) and (2) TOGETHER are NOT sufficient.

DS88111.01

107. In quadrilateral *ABCD*, is angle *BCD* a right angle?

    (1)   Angle *ABC* is a right angle.
    (2)   Angle *ADC* is a right angle.

    (A)   Statement (1) ALONE is sufficient, but statement (2) alone is not sufficient.
    (B)   Statement (2) ALONE is sufficient, but statement (1) alone is not sufficient.
    (C)   BOTH statements TOGETHER are sufficient, but NEITHER statement ALONE is sufficient.
    (D)   EACH statement ALONE is sufficient.
    (E)   Statements (1) and (2) TOGETHER are NOT sufficient.

DS29831.01

108.

In the figure above, *B* is on $\overline{AC}$, *D* is on $\overline{AE}$, $\overline{AB}$ has the same length as $\overline{BC}$, and $\angle ABD$ has the same measure as $\angle ACE$. What is the length of $\overline{DB}$?

    (1)   The length of $\overline{EC}$ is 6.
    (2)   The length of $\overline{DE}$ is 5.

    (A)   Statement (1) ALONE is sufficient, but statement (2) alone is not sufficient.
    (B)   Statement (2) ALONE is sufficient, but statement (1) alone is not sufficient.
    (C)   BOTH statements TOGETHER are sufficient, but NEITHER statement ALONE is sufficient.
    (D)   EACH statement ALONE is sufficient.
    (E)   Statements (1) and (2) TOGETHER are NOT sufficient.

DS92931.01

109. Sprinklers are being installed to water a lawn. Each sprinkler waters in a circle. Can the lawn be watered completely by 4 installed sprinklers?

    (1)   The lawn is rectangular and its area is 32 square yards.
    (2)   Each sprinkler can completely water a circular area of lawn with a maximum radius of 2 yards.

    (A)   Statement (1) ALONE is sufficient, but statement (2) alone is not sufficient.
    (B)   Statement (2) ALONE is sufficient, but statement (1) alone is not sufficient.
    (C)   BOTH statements TOGETHER are sufficient, but NEITHER statement ALONE is sufficient.
    (D)   EACH statement ALONE is sufficient.
    (E)   Statements (1) and (2) TOGETHER are NOT sufficient.

DS18041.01

110. What is the length of the hypotenuse of $\triangle ABC$?

(1) The lengths of the three sides of $\triangle ABC$ are consecutive even integers.

(2) The hypotenuse of $\triangle ABC$ is 4 units longer than the shorter leg.

(A) Statement (1) ALONE is sufficient, but statement (2) alone is not sufficient.

(B) Statement (2) ALONE is sufficient, but statement (1) alone is not sufficient.

(C) BOTH statements TOGETHER are sufficient, but NEITHER statement ALONE is sufficient.

(D) EACH statement ALONE is sufficient.

(E) Statements (1) and (2) TOGETHER are NOT sufficient.

DS37571.01

111. Patricia purchased x meters of fencing. She originally intended to use all of the fencing to enclose a square region, but later decided to use all of the fencing to enclose a rectangular region with length y meters greater than its width. In square meters, what is the positive difference between the area of the square region and the area of the rectangular region?

(1) $xy = 256$

(2) $y = 4$

(A) Statement (1) ALONE is sufficient, but statement (2) alone is not sufficient.

(B) Statement (2) ALONE is sufficient, but statement (1) alone is not sufficient.

(C) BOTH statements TOGETHER are sufficient, but NEITHER statement ALONE is sufficient.

(D) EACH statement ALONE is sufficient.

(E) Statements (1) and (2) TOGETHER are NOT sufficient.

DS45771.01

112.

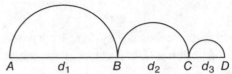

In the figure above, points A, B, C, and D are collinear and $\overgroup{AB}$, $\overgroup{BC}$, and $\overgroup{CD}$ are semicircles with diameters d_1 cm, d_2 cm, and d_3 cm, respectively. What is the sum of the lengths of $\overgroup{AB}$, $\overgroup{BC}$, and $\overgroup{CD}$, in centimeters?

(1) $d_1 : d_2 : d_3$ is 3:2:1.

(2) The length of $\overline{AD}$ is 48 cm.

(A) Statement (1) ALONE is sufficient, but statement (2) alone is not sufficient.

(B) Statement (2) ALONE is sufficient, but statement (1) alone is not sufficient.

(C) BOTH statements TOGETHER are sufficient, but NEITHER statement ALONE is sufficient.

(D) EACH statement ALONE is sufficient.

(E) Statements (1) and (2) TOGETHER are NOT sufficient.

DS16291.01

113. In the standard (x,y) coordinate plane, what is the slope of the line containing the distinct points P and Q?

(1) Both P and Q lie on the graph of $|x| + |y| = 1$.

(2) Both P and Q lie on the graph of $|x + y| = 1$.

(A) Statement (1) ALONE is sufficient, but statement (2) alone is not sufficient.

(B) Statement (2) ALONE is sufficient, but statement (1) alone is not sufficient.

(C) BOTH statements TOGETHER are sufficient, but NEITHER statement ALONE is sufficient.

(D) EACH statement ALONE is sufficient.

(E) Statements (1) and (2) TOGETHER are NOT sufficient.

DS61791.01

114. When opened and lying flat, a birthday card is in the shape of a regular hexagon. The card must be folded in half along 1 of its diagonals before being placed in an envelope for mailing. Assuming that the thickness of the folded card will not be an issue, will the birthday card fit inside a rectangular envelope that is 4 inches by 9 inches?

   (1) Each side of the regular hexagon is 4 inches long.

   (2) The area of the top surface (which is the same as the area of the bottom surface) of the folded birthday card is less than 36 square inches.

   (A) Statement (1) ALONE is sufficient, but statement (2) alone is not sufficient.

   (B) Statement (2) ALONE is sufficient, but statement (1) alone is not sufficient.

   (C) BOTH statements TOGETHER are sufficient, but NEITHER statement ALONE is sufficient.

   (D) EACH statement ALONE is sufficient.

   (E) Statements (1) and (2) TOGETHER are NOT sufficient.

DS77302.01

115.

In rectangular region *PQRS* above, *T* is a point on side *PS*. If *PS* = 4, what is the area of region *PQRS*?

   (1) $\triangle QTR$ is equilateral.

   (2) Segments *PT* and *TS* have equal length.

   (A) Statement (1) ALONE is sufficient, but statement (2) alone is not sufficient.

   (B) Statement (2) ALONE is sufficient, but statement (1) alone is not sufficient.

   (C) BOTH statements TOGETHER are sufficient, but NEITHER statement ALONE is sufficient.

   (D) EACH statement ALONE is sufficient.

   (E) Statements (1) and (2) TOGETHER are NOT sufficient.

DS58302.01

116. The top surface area of a square tabletop was changed so that one of the dimensions was reduced by 1 inch and the other dimension was increased by 2 inches. What was the surface area before these changes were made?

   (1) After the changes were made, the surface area was 70 square inches.

   (2) There was a 25 percent increase in one of the dimensions.

   (A) Statement (1) ALONE is sufficient, but statement (2) alone is not sufficient.

   (B) Statement (2) ALONE is sufficient, but statement (1) alone is not sufficient.

   (C) BOTH statements TOGETHER are sufficient, but NEITHER statement ALONE is sufficient.

   (D) EACH statement ALONE is sufficient.

   (E) Statements (1) and (2) TOGETHER are NOT sufficient.

DS49302.01

117. If the lengths of the legs of a right triangle are integers, what is the area of the triangular region?

   (1) The length of one leg is $\frac{3}{4}$ the length of the other.

   (2) The length of the hypotenuse is 5.

   (A) Statement (1) ALONE is sufficient, but statement (2) alone is not sufficient.

   (B) Statement (2) ALONE is sufficient, but statement (1) alone is not sufficient.

   (C) BOTH statements TOGETHER are sufficient, but NEITHER statement ALONE is sufficient.

   (D) EACH statement ALONE is sufficient.

   (E) Statements (1) and (2) TOGETHER are NOT sufficient.

DS12402.01

118. If cubical blocks in a display are stacked one on top of the other on a flat surface, what is the volume of the stack of blocks in cubic centimeters?

(1) The volume of the top block is 8 cubic centimeters.

(2) The height of the stack of blocks is 10 centimeters.

(A) Statement (1) ALONE is sufficient, but statement (2) alone is not sufficient.

(B) Statement (2) ALONE is sufficient, but statement (1) alone is not sufficient.

(C) BOTH statements TOGETHER are sufficient, but NEITHER statement ALONE is sufficient.

(D) EACH statement ALONE is sufficient.

(E) Statements (1) and (2) TOGETHER are NOT sufficient.

DS53402.01

119. Is the perimeter of a certain rectangular garden greater than 50 meters?

(1) The two shorter sides of the garden are each 15 meters long.

(2) The length of the garden is 5 meters greater than the width of the garden.

(A) Statement (1) ALONE is sufficient, but statement (2) alone is not sufficient.

(B) Statement (2) ALONE is sufficient, but statement (1) alone is not sufficient.

(C) BOTH statements TOGETHER are sufficient, but NEITHER statement ALONE is sufficient.

(D) EACH statement ALONE is sufficient.

(E) Statements (1) and (2) TOGETHER are NOT sufficient.

DS34402.01

120.

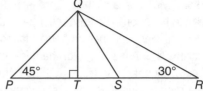

In the figure above, what is the perimeter of $\triangle PQR$?

(1) The length of segment PT is 2.

(2) The length of segment RS is $\sqrt{3}$.

(A) Statement (1) ALONE is sufficient, but statement (2) alone is not sufficient.

(B) Statement (2) ALONE is sufficient, but statement (1) alone is not sufficient.

(C) BOTH statements TOGETHER are sufficient, but NEITHER statement ALONE is sufficient.

(D) EACH statement ALONE is sufficient.

(E) Statements (1) and (2) TOGETHER are NOT sufficient.

DS07402.01

121.

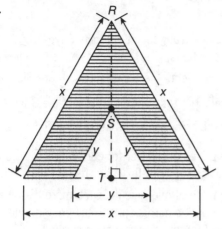

In the figure above, the shaded region represents the front of an upright wooden frame around the entrance to an amusement park ride. If $RS = \dfrac{5\sqrt{3}}{2}$ meters, what is the area of the front of the frame?

(1) $x = 9$ meters

(2) $ST = 2\sqrt{3}$ meters

(A)   Statement (1) ALONE is sufficient, but statement (2) alone is not sufficient.

(B)   Statement (2) ALONE is sufficient, but statement (1) alone is not sufficient.

(C)   BOTH statements TOGETHER are sufficient, but NEITHER statement ALONE is sufficient.

(D)   EACH statement ALONE is sufficient.

(E)   Statements (1) and (2) TOGETHER are NOT sufficient.

DS05502.01

122.

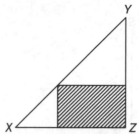

In the figure above, if the shaded region is rectangular, what is the length of XY ?

(1)   The perimeter of the shaded region is 24.

(2)   The measure of $\angle XYZ$ is 45°.

(A)   Statement (1) ALONE is sufficient, but statement (2) alone is not sufficient.

(B)   Statement (2) ALONE is sufficient, but statement (1) alone is not sufficient.

(C)   BOTH statements TOGETHER are sufficient, but NEITHER statement ALONE is sufficient.

(D)   EACH statement ALONE is sufficient.

(E)   Statements (1) and (2) TOGETHER are NOT sufficient.

DS87602.01

123.

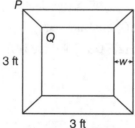

The figure above shows the dimensions of a square picture frame that was constructed using four identical pieces of frame as shown. If w is the width of each piece of the frame, what is the area of the front surface of each piece? (1 ft = 12 inches)

(1) $w = 3$ inches

(2) $PQ = \sqrt{18}$ inches

(A)   Statement (1) ALONE is sufficient, but statement (2) alone is not sufficient.

(B)   Statement (2) ALONE is sufficient, but statement (1) alone is not sufficient.

(C)   BOTH statements TOGETHER are sufficient, but NEITHER statement ALONE is sufficient.

(D)   EACH statement ALONE is sufficient.

(E)   Statements (1) and (2) TOGETHER are NOT sufficient.

DS48602.01

124.

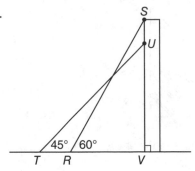

In the figure above, segments $\overline{RS}$ and $\overline{TU}$ represent two positions of the same ladder leaning against the side $\overline{SV}$ of a wall. The length of $\overline{TV}$ is how much greater than the length of $\overline{RV}$?

(1) The length of $\overline{TU}$ is 10 meters.

(2) The length of $\overline{RV}$ is 5 meters.

(A) Statement (1) ALONE is sufficient, but statement (2) alone is not sufficient.

(B) Statement (2) ALONE is sufficient, but statement (1) alone is not sufficient.

(C) BOTH statements TOGETHER are sufficient, but NEITHER statement ALONE is sufficient.

(D) EACH statement ALONE is sufficient.

(E) Statements (1) and (2) TOGETHER are NOT sufficient.

Rates/Ratios/Percent

DS67410.01

125. A large flower arrangement contains 3 types of flowers: carnations, lilies, and roses. Of all the flowers in the arrangement, $\frac{1}{2}$ are carnations, $\frac{1}{3}$ are lilies, and $\frac{1}{6}$ are roses. The total price of which of the 3 types of flowers in the arrangement is the greatest?

(1) The prices per flower for carnations, lilies, and roses are in the ratio 1:3:4, respectively.

(2) The price of one rose is $0.75 more than the price of one carnation, and the price of one rose is $0.25 more than the price of one lily.

(A) Statement (1) ALONE is sufficient, but statement (2) alone is not sufficient.

(B) Statement (2) ALONE is sufficient, but statement (1) alone is not sufficient.

(C) BOTH statements TOGETHER are sufficient, but NEITHER statement ALONE is sufficient.

(D) EACH statement ALONE is sufficient.

(E) Statements (1) and (2) TOGETHER are NOT sufficient.

DS34010.01

126. Town X has 50,000 residents, some of whom were born in Town X. What percent of the residents of Town X were born in Town X ?

(1) Of the male residents of Town X, 40 percent were not born in Town X.

(2) Of the female residents of Town X, 60 percent were born in Town X.

(A) Statement (1) ALONE is sufficient, but statement (2) alone is not sufficient.

(B) Statement (2) ALONE is sufficient, but statement (1) alone is not sufficient.

(C) BOTH statements TOGETHER are sufficient, but NEITHER statement ALONE is sufficient.

(D) EACH statement ALONE is sufficient.

(E) Statements (1) and (2) TOGETHER are NOT sufficient.

DS29931.01

127. A bank account earned 2% annual interest, compounded daily, for as long as the balance was under $1,000, starting when the account was opened. Once the balance reached $1,000, the account earned 2.5% annual interest, compounded daily until the account was closed. No deposits or withdrawals were made. Was the total amount of interest earned at the 2% rate greater than the total amount earned at the 2.5% rate?

(1) The account earned exactly $25 in interest at the 2.5% rate.

(2) The account was open for exactly three years.

(A) Statement (1) ALONE is sufficient, but statement (2) alone is not sufficient.

(B) Statement (2) ALONE is sufficient, but statement (1) alone is not sufficient.

(C) BOTH statements TOGETHER are sufficient, but NEITHER statement ALONE is sufficient.

(D) EACH statement ALONE is sufficient.

(E) Statements (1) and (2) TOGETHER are NOT sufficient.

DS53541.01

128. A novelist pays her agent 15% of the royalties she receives from her novels. She pays her publicist 5% of the royalties, plus a yearly fee. Did the novelist pay more to her agent last year than she paid to her publicist?

(1) The publicist's yearly fee is $2,000.

(2) The novelist earned an average of $3,500 in royalties last year on each of her novels.

(A) Statement (1) ALONE is sufficient, but statement (2) alone is not sufficient.

(B) Statement (2) ALONE is sufficient, but statement (1) alone is not sufficient.

(C) BOTH statements TOGETHER are sufficient, but NEITHER statement ALONE is sufficient.

(D) EACH statement ALONE is sufficient.

(E) Statements (1) and (2) TOGETHER are NOT sufficient.

Value/Order/Factors

DS85100.01

129. If x and z are integers, is $x + z^2$ odd?

(1) x is odd and z is even.

(2) $x - z$ is odd.

(A) Statement (1) ALONE is sufficient, but statement (2) alone is not sufficient.

(B) Statement (2) ALONE is sufficient, but statement (1) alone is not sufficient.

(C) BOTH statements TOGETHER are sufficient, but NEITHER statement ALONE is sufficient.

(D) EACH statement ALONE is sufficient.

(E) Statements (1) and (2) TOGETHER are NOT sufficient.

DS95850.01

130.

×	a	b	c
a	d	e	f
b	e	g	h
c	f	h	j

Each entry in the multiplication table above is an integer that is either positive, negative, or zero. What is the value of a ?

(1) $h \neq 0$

(2) $c = f$

(A) Statement (1) ALONE is sufficient, but statement (2) alone is not sufficient.

(B) Statement (2) ALONE is sufficient, but statement (1) alone is not sufficient.

(C) BOTH statements TOGETHER are sufficient, but NEITHER statement ALONE is sufficient.

(D) EACH statement ALONE is sufficient.

(E) Statements (1) and (2) TOGETHER are NOT sufficient.

DS36141.01

131. Given a positive number N, when N is rounded by a certain method (for convenience, call it Method Y), the result is 10^n if and only if n is an integer and $5 \times 10^{n-1} \le N < 5 \times 10^n$. In a certain gas sample, there are, when rounded by Method Y, 10^{21} molecules of H_2 and also 10^{21} molecules of O_2. When rounded by Method Y, what is the combined number of H_2 and O_2 molecules in the gas sample?

(1) The number of H_2 molecules and the number of O_2 molecules are each less than 3×10^{21}.

(2) The number of H_2 molecules is more than twice the number of O_2 molecules.

(A) Statement (1) ALONE is sufficient, but statement (2) alone is not sufficient.

(B) Statement (2) ALONE is sufficient, but statement (1) alone is not sufficient.

(C) BOTH statements TOGETHER are sufficient, but NEITHER statement ALONE is sufficient.

(D) EACH statement ALONE is sufficient.

(E) Statements (1) and (2) TOGETHER are NOT sufficient.

DS05541.01

132. If x is a positive integer, how many positive integers less than x are divisors of x ?

(1) x^2 is divisible by exactly 4 positive integers less than x^2.

(2) $2x$ is divisible by exactly 3 positive integers less than $2x$.

(A) Statement (1) ALONE is sufficient, but statement (2) alone is not sufficient.

(B) Statement (2) ALONE is sufficient, but statement (1) alone is not sufficient.

(C) BOTH statements TOGETHER are sufficient, but NEITHER statement ALONE is sufficient.

(D) EACH statement ALONE is sufficient.

(E) Statements (1) and (2) TOGETHER are NOT sufficient.

DS33551.01

133. If m and n are positive integers, is n even?

(1) $m(m + 2) + 1 = mn$

(2) $m(m + n)$ is odd.

(A) Statement (1) ALONE is sufficient, but statement (2) alone is not sufficient.

(B) Statement (2) ALONE is sufficient, but statement (1) alone is not sufficient.

(C) BOTH statements TOGETHER are sufficient, but NEITHER statement ALONE is sufficient.

(D) EACH statement ALONE is sufficient.

(E) Statements (1) and (2) TOGETHER are NOT sufficient.

DS65291.01

134. If m and n are positive integers, what is the value of $\dfrac{3}{m} + \dfrac{n}{4}$?

(1) $mn = 12$

(2) $\dfrac{3}{m}$ is in lowest terms and $\dfrac{n}{4}$ is in lowest terms.

(A) Statement (1) ALONE is sufficient, but statement (2) alone is not sufficient.

(B) Statement (2) ALONE is sufficient, but statement (1) alone is not sufficient.

(C) BOTH statements TOGETHER are sufficient, but NEITHER statement ALONE is sufficient.

(D) EACH statement ALONE is sufficient.

(E) Statements (1) and (2) TOGETHER are NOT sufficient.

DS21891.01

135. The first four digits of the six-digit initial password for a shopper's card at a certain grocery store is the customer's birthday in day-month digit form. For example, 15 August corresponds to 1508 and 5 March corresponds to 0503. The 5th digit of the initial password is the units digit of seven times the sum of the first and third digits, and the 6th digit of the initial password is the units digit of three times the sum of the second and fourth digits. What month, and what day of that month, was a customer born whose initial password ends in 16 ?

(1) The customer's initial password begins with 21, and its fourth digit is 1.

(2) The sum of the first and third digits of the customer's initial password is 3, and its second digit is 1.

(A) Statement (1) ALONE is sufficient, but statement (2) alone is not sufficient.

(B) Statement (2) ALONE is sufficient, but statement (1) alone is not sufficient.

(C) BOTH statements TOGETHER are sufficient, but NEITHER statement ALONE is sufficient.

(D) EACH statement ALONE is sufficient.

(E) Statements (1) and (2) TOGETHER are NOT sufficient.

DS38302.01

136. If K is a positive integer less than 10 and $N = 4,321 + K$, what is the value of K ?

(1) N is divisible by 3.

(2) N is divisible by 7.

(A) Statement (1) ALONE is sufficient, but statement (2) alone is not sufficient.

(B) Statement (2) ALONE is sufficient, but statement (1) alone is not sufficient.

(C) BOTH statements TOGETHER are sufficient, but NEITHER statement ALONE is sufficient.

(D) EACH statement ALONE is sufficient.

(E) Statements (1) and (2) TOGETHER are NOT sufficient.

DS99302.01

137. If s is an integer, is 24 a divisor of s ?

(1) Each of the numbers 3 and 8 is a divisor of s.

(2) Each of the numbers 4 and 6 is a divisor of s.

(A) Statement (1) ALONE is sufficient, but statement (2) alone is not sufficient.

(B) Statement (2) ALONE is sufficient, but statement (1) alone is not sufficient.

(C) BOTH statements TOGETHER are sufficient, but NEITHER statement ALONE is sufficient.

(D) EACH statement ALONE is sufficient.

(E) Statements (1) and (2) TOGETHER are NOT sufficient.

DS32402.01

138. $n = 2^4 \cdot 3^2 \cdot 5^2$ and positive integer d is a divisor of n. Is $d > \sqrt{n}$?

(1) d is divisible by 10.

(2) d is divisible by 36.

(A) Statement (1) ALONE is sufficient, but statement (2) alone is not sufficient.

(B) Statement (2) ALONE is sufficient, but statement (1) alone is not sufficient.

(C) BOTH statements TOGETHER are sufficient, but NEITHER statement ALONE is sufficient.

(D) EACH statement ALONE is sufficient.

(E) Statements (1) and (2) TOGETHER are NOT sufficient.

DS52402.01

139. Exactly 3 deposits have been made in a savings account and the amounts of the deposits are 3 consecutive integer multiples of $7. If the sum of the deposits is between $120 and $170, what is the amount of each of the deposits?

(1) The amount of one of the deposits is $49.

(2) The amount of one of the deposits is $63.

(A) Statement (1) ALONE is sufficient, but statement (2) alone is not sufficient.

(B) Statement (2) ALONE is sufficient, but statement (1) alone is not sufficient.

(C) BOTH statements TOGETHER are sufficient, but NEITHER statement ALONE is sufficient.

(D) EACH statement ALONE is sufficient.

(E) Statements (1) and (2) TOGETHER are NOT sufficient.

DS44402.01

140. If x, y, and d are integers and d is odd, are both x and y divisible by d?

(1) $x + y$ is divisible by d.

(2) $x - y$ is divisible by d.

(A) Statement (1) ALONE is sufficient, but statement (2) alone is not sufficient.

(B) Statement (2) ALONE is sufficient, but statement (1) alone is not sufficient.

(C) BOTH statements TOGETHER are sufficient, but NEITHER statement ALONE is sufficient.

(D) EACH statement ALONE is sufficient.

(E) Statements (1) and (2) TOGETHER are NOT sufficient.

DS06402.01

141. If x and y are integers, is $xy + 1$ divisible by 3 ?

(1) When x is divided by 3, the remainder is 1.

(2) When y is divided by 9, the remainder is 8.

(A) Statement (1) ALONE is sufficient, but statement (2) alone is not sufficient.

(B) Statement (2) ALONE is sufficient, but statement (1) alone is not sufficient.

(C) BOTH statements TOGETHER are sufficient, but NEITHER statement ALONE is sufficient.

(D) EACH statement ALONE is sufficient.

(E) Statements (1) and (2) TOGETHER are NOT sufficient.

DS00502.01

142. If x and y are integers between 10 and 99, inclusive, is $\dfrac{x - y}{9}$ an integer?

(1) x and y have the same two digits, but in reverse order.

(2) The tens' digit of x is 2 more than the units' digit, and the tens' digit of y is 2 less than the units' digit.

(A) Statement (1) ALONE is sufficient, but statement (2) alone is not sufficient.

(B) Statement (2) ALONE is sufficient, but statement (1) alone is not sufficient.

(C) BOTH statements TOGETHER are sufficient, but NEITHER statement ALONE is sufficient.

(D) EACH statement ALONE is sufficient.

(E) Statements (1) and (2) TOGETHER are NOT sufficient.

DS85502.01

143. If b is the product of three consecutive positive integers c, $c + 1$, and $c + 2$, is b a multiple of 24 ?

(1) b is a multiple of 8.

(2) c is odd.

(A) Statement (1) ALONE is sufficient, but statement (2) alone is not sufficient.

(B) Statement (2) ALONE is sufficient, but statement (1) alone is not sufficient.

(C) BOTH statements TOGETHER are sufficient, but NEITHER statement ALONE is sufficient.

(D) EACH statement ALONE is sufficient.

(E) Statements (1) and (2) TOGETHER are NOT sufficient.

DS17602.01

144. If ⊛ denotes a mathematical operation, does $x ⊛ y = y ⊛ x$ for all x and y ?

(1) For all x and y, $x ⊛ y = 2(x^2 + y^2)$.

(2) For all y, $0 ⊛ y = 2y^2$.

(A) Statement (1) ALONE is sufficient, but statement (2) alone is not sufficient.

(B) Statement (2) ALONE is sufficient, but statement (1) alone is not sufficient.

(C) BOTH statements TOGETHER are sufficient, but NEITHER statement ALONE is sufficient.

(D) EACH statement ALONE is sufficient.

(E) Statements (1) and (2) TOGETHER are NOT sufficient.

DS37602.01

145. If n is an integer, is $\dfrac{n}{15}$ an integer?

(1) $\dfrac{3n}{15}$ is an integer.

(2) $\dfrac{8n}{15}$ is an integer.

(A) Statement (1) ALONE is sufficient, but statement (2) alone is not sufficient.

(B) Statement (2) ALONE is sufficient, but statement (1) alone is not sufficient.

(C) BOTH statements TOGETHER are sufficient, but NEITHER statement ALONE is sufficient.

(D) EACH statement ALONE is sufficient.

(E) Statements (1) and (2) TOGETHER are NOT sufficient.

DS97602.01

146. If $1 < d < 2$, is the tenths digit of the decimal representation of d equal to 9 ?

(1) $d + 0.01 < 2$

(2) $d + 0.05 > 2$

(A) Statement (1) ALONE is sufficient, but statement (2) alone is not sufficient.

(B) Statement (2) ALONE is sufficient, but statement (1) alone is not sufficient.

(C) BOTH statements TOGETHER are sufficient, but NEITHER statement ALONE is sufficient.

(D) EACH statement ALONE is sufficient.

(E) Statements (1) and (2) TOGETHER are NOT sufficient.

DS08602.01

147. The 9 participants in a race were divided into 3 teams with 3 runners on each team. A team was awarded $6 - n$ points if one of its runners finished in nth place, where $1 \le n \le 5$. If all of the runners finished the race and if there were no ties, was each team awarded at least 1 point?

(1) No team was awarded more than a total of 6 points.

(2) No pair of teammates finished in consecutive places among the top five places.

(A) Statement (1) ALONE is sufficient, but statement (2) alone is not sufficient.

(B) Statement (2) ALONE is sufficient, but statement (1) alone is not sufficient.

(C) BOTH statements TOGETHER are sufficient, but NEITHER statement ALONE is sufficient.

(D) EACH statement ALONE is sufficient.

(E) Statements (1) and (2) TOGETHER are NOT sufficient.

DS38602.01
148. Can the positive integer n be written as the sum of two different positive prime numbers?

(1) n is greater than 3.

(2) n is odd.

(A) Statement (1) ALONE is sufficient, but statement (2) alone is not sufficient.

(B) Statement (2) ALONE is sufficient, but statement (1) alone is not sufficient.

(C) BOTH statements TOGETHER are sufficient, but NEITHER statement ALONE is sufficient.

(D) EACH statement ALONE is sufficient.

(E) Statements (1) and (2) TOGETHER are NOT sufficient.

DS73402.01
149. Is x an integer?

(1) x^2 is an integer.

(2) $\dfrac{x}{2}$ is not an integer.

(A) Statement (1) ALONE is sufficient, but statement (2) alone is not sufficient.

(B) Statement (2) ALONE is sufficient, but statement (1) alone is not sufficient.

(C) BOTH statements TOGETHER are sufficient, but NEITHER statement ALONE is sufficient.

(D) EACH statement ALONE is sufficient.

(E) Statements (1) and (2) TOGETHER are NOT sufficient.

DS46402.01
150. If b is an integer, is $\sqrt{a^2 + b^2}$ an integer?

(1) $a^2 + b^2$ is an integer.

(2) $a^2 - 3b^2 = 0$

(A) Statement (1) ALONE is sufficient, but statement (2) alone is not sufficient.

(B) Statement (2) ALONE is sufficient, but statement (1) alone is not sufficient.

(C) BOTH statements TOGETHER are sufficient, but NEITHER statement ALONE is sufficient.

(D) EACH statement ALONE is sufficient.

(E) Statements (1) and (2) TOGETHER are NOT sufficient.

Answer Key Quantitative Reasoning

Problem Solving

Counting/Sets/Series

1. E
2. C
3. E
4. E
5. C
6. D
7. A
8. E
9. D
10. E
11. C
12. A

Equalities/Inequalities/Algebra

13. C
14. B
15. E
16. A
17. A
18. D
19. D
20. C
21. C
22. B
23. C
24. A
25. E
26. E
27. E
28. B
29. A
30. C
31. C
32. D

Geometry

33. A
34. B
35. D
36. C
37. D
38. B
39. D
40. D
41. A
42. C

Rates/Ratios/Percent

43. D
44. C
45. D
46. C
47. B
48. C
49. B

Value/Order/Factors

50. B
51. B
52. E
53. E
54. E
55. D
56. D
57. D
58. D
59. B
60. C
61. B
62. A
63. A
64. B

65. B
66. B
67. E

Data Sufficiency

Counting/Sets/Series

68. E
69. D
70. B
71. C
72. C
73. B
74. E
75. E
76. D

Equalities/Inequalities/Algebra

77. C
78. B
79. A
80. B
81. E
82. A
83. A
84. A
85. C
86. A
87. D
88. C
89. C
90. C
91. A
92. A
93. A
94. A
95. A

96. A
97. B
98. E
99. A
100. B
101. B
102. A
103. D
104. A
105. B

Geometry

106. C
107. E
108. A
109. E
110. A
111. B
112. B
113. E
114. A
115. A
116. D
117. B
118. E
119. A
120. A
121. D
122. C
123. D
124. D

Rates/Ratios/Percent

125. A
126. C
127. C
128. E

Value/Order/Factors

129. D
130. C
131. C
132. A
133. D
134. C
135. A
136. B
137. A
138. C
139. B
140. C
141. C
142. A
143. A
144. A
145. B
146. B
147. A
148. E
149. E
150. B

Answer Explanations Quantitative Reasoning

Problem Solving

Counting/Sets/Series

PS54110.01

1. The letters C, I, R, C, L, and E can be used to form 6-letter strings such as CIRCLE or CCIRLE. Using these letters, how many different 6-letter strings can be formed in which the two occurrences of the letter C are separated by at least one other letter?

(A) 96
(B) 120
(C) 144
(D) 180
(E) 240

Arithmetic Elementary combinatorics

This can be solved by using the Multiplication Principle. The answer is $m \times n$, where m is the number of ways to choose the 2 suitable positions in which to place the C's and n is the number of ways in which to place the 4 remaining letters in the 4 remaining positions.

The value of m can be found by a direct count of the number of suitable ways to choose the 2 positions in which to place the C's. In what follows, each * denotes one of the 4 remaining positions.

There are 4 possibilities when a C is in the first position:

C*C***	C**C**	C***C*	C****C

There are 3 more possibilities when a C is in the second position:

*C*C**	*C**C*	*C***C

There are 2 more possibilities when a C is in the third position:

**C*C*	**C**C

There is 1 more possibility when a C is in the fourth position:

***C*C

Therefore, $m = 4 + 3 + 2 + 1 = 10$.

Alternatively, the value of m can be found by subtracting the number of non-suitable ways to place the C's (i.e., the number of consecutive positions in the string) from the number of all possible ways to place the C's (suitable or not). This gives $m = 15 - 5 = 10$, where $15 = \binom{6}{2}$ is the number of all possible ways to place the C's ("6 choose 2") and 5 is the number of non-suitable ways to place the C's (shown below).

CC****	*CC***	**CC**	***CC*	****CC

> **Tip**
>
> The alternative approach for finding m is useful when a direct count of the number of suitable ways is more difficult than a direct count of the number of non-suitable ways. An example is determining the number of 8-letter strings that can be formed from the letters in REPEATED in which there is at least one pair of E's having at least one other letter between them. For this example, $m = \binom{8}{3} - 6 = 56 - 6 = 50$.

The value of n is equal to the number of ways to place the 4 remaining letters into 4 positions, where order matters and the letters are selected without replacement. Thus, $n = 4! = 24$.

Therefore, the answer is $m \times n = 10 \times 24 = 240$.

The correct answer is E.

PS24831.01

2.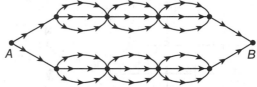

The map above shows the trails through a wilderness area. If travel is in the direction of the arrows, how many routes along the marked trails are possible from point A to point B ?

(A) 11
(B) 18
(C) 54
(D) 108
(E) 432

Arithmetic Elementary combinatorics

It is clear that the number of routes from point A to point B that begin by going up from point A ("up" relative to the orientation of the map) is the same as the number of routes from point A to point B that begin by going down from point A. Therefore, we only need to determine the number of routes from point A to point B that begin by going up and then double the result.

> **Tip**
>
> If these two numbers of routes were not the same, or at least if it was not clear whether they were the same, then we would simply determine each of the numbers separately and then add them.

To determine the number of routes that begin by going up from point A, we can apply the Multiplication Principle. There are 3 locations at which branches occur. Moreover, at each of these locations, there are 3 different trails that can be taken. Finally, the choices of which trail to take at each location can be made independently. Therefore, the Multiplication Principle applies and we get $(3)(3)(3) = 27$ for the number of routes that begin by going up from point A. Hence, the number of routes from point A to point B is $2(27) = 54$.

The correct answer is C.

PS61551.01

3.

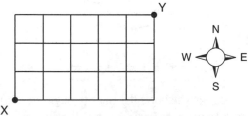

In the figure above, X and Y represent locations in a district of a certain city where the streets form a rectangular grid. In traveling only north or east along the streets from X to Y, how many different paths are possible?

(A) 720
(B) 512
(C) 336
(D) 256
(E) 56

Arithmetic Elementary combinatorics

Each possible path will consist of traveling a total of 3 grid segments north and 5 grid segments east. Thus, letting 'N' represent traveling north by one grid segment and 'E' represent traveling east by one grid segment, each path can be uniquely represented by an appropriate 8-character string of N's and E's. For example, as shown in the figure below, NEENEENE represents grid segments traveled in the order north, east, east, north, east, east, north, and east.

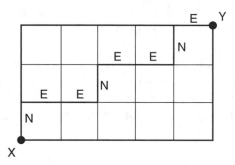

Therefore, the number of possible paths is equal to the number of appropriate 8-character strings of N's and E's, which is

$$\binom{8}{3} = \frac{8!}{3!(8-3)!} = \frac{(5!)(6)(7)(8)}{(2)(3)(5!)} = (7)(8) = 56,$$

since each appropriate string is determined when a specification is made for the 3 positions in the string at which the N's are to be placed. Alternatively, the number of possible paths is equal to the number of permutations of 8 objects in which 3 are identical (the N's) and the remaining 5 are identical (the E's), and thus equal to $\frac{8!}{(3!)(5!)}$.

The alternative approach has a well-known generalization that can be used to calculate the number of permutations of n objects when various subsets of those objects consist of objects to be treated as identical. We give four examples in which such a calculation can be used.

1. The number of 8-letter words that can be formed using the letters of PEPPERER is equal to
    $$\frac{8!}{(2!)(3!)(3!)} = 560.$$

    $P = 3$
    $E = 3$
    $R = 2$

2. Consider a 3-dimensional analog of the rectangular grid above, with dimensions 2 by 3 by 3. The number of paths from the front-left-down vertex to the back-right-up vertex such that each path consists of traveling only back, right, or up is equal to $\dfrac{8!}{(2!)(3!)(3!)} = 560.$

3. The number of ways to distribute 8 different books to David, Liam, and Sophia so that David is given 2 of the books, Liam is given 3 of the books, and Sophia is given 3 of the books is equal to $\dfrac{8!}{(2!)(3!)(3!)} = 560.$

4. The coefficient of $a^2b^3c^3$ in the expansion of $(a + b + c)^8$ after like terms are combined is equal to $\dfrac{8!}{(2!)(3!)(3!)} = 560.$

The correct answer is E.

PS92751.01

4.

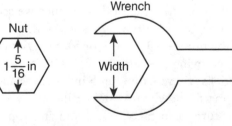

Nut

Wrench

Width

The figures above show a hexagonal nut that has a width of $1\frac{5}{16}$ inches and a wrench that, in order to fit the nut, must have a width of at least $1\frac{5}{16}$ inches.

Of all the wrenches that fit the nut and have widths that are whole numbers of millimeters, the wrench

that fits the nut most closely has a width of how many millimeters?
(*Note:* 1 inch ≈ 25.4 millimeters)

(A) 30
(B) 31
(C) 32
(D) 33
(E) 34

Arithmetic Measurement conversion

The width of the nut in millimeters is nearly equal to
$$\left(1+\frac{5}{16}\right)(25.4) = 25.4 + \left(\frac{5}{16}\right)\left(\frac{254}{10}\right) = 25.4 + \frac{127}{16}.$$

Since $25.4 + \dfrac{127}{16} = 25.4 + \dfrac{128}{16} - \dfrac{1}{16} = 33.4 - \dfrac{1}{16},$

it follows that the width of the nut is between 33 mm and 34 mm.

The correct answer is E.

PS45461.01

5.

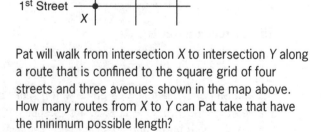

Pat will walk from intersection X to intersection Y along a route that is confined to the square grid of four streets and three avenues shown in the map above. How many routes from X to Y can Pat take that have the minimum possible length?

(A) Six
(B) Eight
(C) Ten
(D) Fourteen
(E) Sixteen

Arithmetic Elementary combinatorics

Each minimum-length route will consist of traveling a total of 3 grid segments up and 2 grid segments right. Thus, letting 'U' represent traveling up by one grid segment and 'R' represent traveling right by one grid segment, each minimum-length route can be uniquely represented by an appropriate 5-character string of U's and R's. For example, URUUR represents grid segments traveled in the order up, right, up, up, and right. Therefore, the number of possible minimum-length routes is equal to the number of appropriate 5-character strings of U's and R's, which is $\binom{5}{3} = \dfrac{5!}{3!(5-3)!} = 10$, since each appropriate string is determined when a specification is made for the 3 positions in the string at which the U's are to be placed.

> **Tip**
>
> The ideas involved in counting the number of 5-character strings of U's and R's can be extended to counting the number of n-character strings when various characters being used are the same. For example, MISSISSIPPI has one M, four I's, four S's, and two P's, and thus the number of 11-letter words that can be formed using the letters of MISSISSIPPI is equal to $\dfrac{11!}{(1!)(4!)(4!)(2!)} = \binom{11}{1} \cdot \binom{10}{4} \cdot \binom{6}{4} \cdot \binom{2}{2} = 34{,}650$.
> (Each of the two expressions we have given for 34,650 is intended to suggest a method for counting the number of 11-letter words.)

The correct answer is C.

PS95302.01

6. Rita and Sam play the following game with n sticks on a table. Each must remove 1, 2, 3, 4 or 5 sticks at a time on alternate turns, and no stick that is removed is put back on the table. The one who removes the last stick (or sticks) from the table wins. If Rita goes first, which of the following is a value of n such that Sam can always win no matter how Rita plays?

(A) 7

(B) 10

(C) 11

(D) 12

(E) 16

Arithmetic Elementary combinatorics

Let Player A be either Rita or Sam, and let Player B be the other player. If, after one of Player A's turns, there are exactly 6 sticks left, then Player A can win on his or her next turn. This is because if 6 sticks are left after Player A's turn, then regardless of whether Player B removes 1, 2, 3, 4, or 5 sticks, it follows that Player A can win on his or her next turn by removing, respectively, 5, 4, 3, 2, or 1 stick.

$\underline{n = 7}$: If Rita begins by removing 1 stick, then there will be 6 sticks left after Rita's turn. Therefore, by the remarks above, Rita can win. Hence, Sam cannot always win.

$\underline{n = 10}$: If Rita begins by removing 4 sticks, then there will be 6 sticks left after Rita's turn. Therefore, by the remarks above, Rita can win. Hence, Sam cannot always win.

$\underline{n = 11}$: If Rita begins by removing 5 sticks, then there will be 6 sticks left after Rita's turn. Therefore, by the remarks above, Rita can win. Hence, Sam cannot always win.

$\underline{n = 12}$: If Rita begins by removing 1 stick, then Sam can win by removing 5 sticks on his next turn, because 6 sticks will remain after Sam's turn. If Rita begins by removing 2 sticks, then Sam can win by removing 4 sticks on his next turn, because 6 sticks will remain after Sam's turn. By continuing in this manner, we see that if Rita begins by removing k sticks (where k is one of the numbers 1, 2, 3, 4, or 5), then Sam can win by removing $(6-k)$ sticks on his next turn because 6 sticks will remain after Sam's turn. Therefore, no matter how many sticks Rita removes on her first turn, Sam can win by removing appropriate numbers of sticks on his next two turns. Hence, Sam can always win.

$\underline{n = 16}$: If Rita removes 4 sticks on her first turn, then Sam will be in the same situation as Rita for $n = 12$ above, and therefore Rita can win no matter what Sam does. Hence, Sam cannot always win.

The correct answer is D.

PS65402.01

7. When $\frac{2}{9}$ of the votes on a certain resolution have been counted, $\frac{3}{4}$ of those counted are in favor of the resolution. What fraction of the remaining votes must be against the resolution so that the total count will result in a vote of 2 to 1 against the resolution?

(A) $\frac{11}{14}$

(B) $\frac{13}{18}$

(C) $\frac{4}{7}$

(D) $\frac{3}{7}$

(E) $\frac{3}{14}$

Arithmetic Operations on rational numbers

For this problem, by assigning carefully chosen numbers to quantities given in the problem, it can be made more concrete and some of the computations with fractions can be avoided.

Since $\frac{2}{9}$ of all the votes have been counted and $\frac{3}{4}$ of them are for the resolution, $36\ (= 9 \times 4)$ would be a good number to use as the total number of votes cast. Since the total count must result in a vote of 2 to 1 against the resolution, $\frac{2}{3}$ of all of the votes must be against the resolution. This information can be summarized in the following table.

	Total votes cast	Counted so far	Still to be counted
	36	$\frac{2}{9}(36) = 8$	$36 - 8 = 28$
For		$\frac{3}{4}(8) = 6$	
Against	$\frac{2}{3}(36) = 24$	$8 - 6 = 2$	$24 - 2 = 22$

From the table, it is clear that of the 28 votes still to be counted, 22 must be against the resolution.

Therefore, the fraction of the votes still to be counted that must be against the resolution is $\frac{22}{28} = \frac{11}{14}$.

In general, letting T represent the total number of votes cast, since the total count must result in a vote of 2 to 1 against the resolution, $\frac{2}{3}T$ votes must be against the resolution. The information is summarized in the following table.

	Total votes cast	Counted so far	Still to be counted
	T	$\frac{2}{9}T$	$T - \frac{2}{9}T = \frac{7}{9}T$
For		$\frac{3}{4}\left(\frac{2}{9}T\right) = \frac{1}{6}T$	
Against	$\frac{2}{3}T$	$\frac{1}{4}\left(\frac{2}{9}T\right) = \frac{1}{18}T$	$\frac{2}{3}T - \frac{1}{18}T = \frac{11}{18}T$

From the table, it is clear that of the $\frac{7}{9}T$ votes still to be counted $\frac{11}{18}T$ must be against the resolution. Therefore, the fraction of the votes still to be counted that must be against the resolution is $\dfrac{\frac{11}{18}T}{\frac{7}{9}T} = \frac{11}{14}$.

The correct answer is A.

Alternative explanation:
Assign actual numbers to the problem to make the math more concrete. Since we are dealing with $\frac{2}{9}$ of something and also $\frac{1}{4}$ of something, we will want our numbers to be convenient. Look for multiples of 36 (9 times 4) for which $\frac{2}{9}$ and $\frac{1}{4}$ will result in whole numbers. A number that will work well is 180.

Of the 180 votes, $\frac{2}{9}$ have been counted.

$\frac{2}{9}(180) = 40$ votes counted. This means 140 votes have not been counted.

Of those 40 counted votes, $\frac{3}{4}$ are in favor. $\frac{3}{4}$ (40) = 30 votes in favor (of the 40 counted).

This means 10 votes are not in favor (of the 40 counted).

Looking ahead to the desired end result, in order to achieve a 2:1 ratio against, $\frac{1}{3}$ of the votes will be for and $\frac{2}{3}$ will be against. Therefore we will need 120 votes against. So far we have 10 votes not in favor.

In order to reach a total of 120 uncounted votes, of the 140 uncounted votes, we will need 110 votes not in favor to combine with the 10 counted votes not in favor.

This is $\frac{110}{140}$ or $\frac{11}{14}$. The correct answer is A.

PS85402.01

8. The sum of the first 100 positive integers is 5,050. What is the sum of the first 200 positive integers?

(A) 10,100
(B) 10,200
(C) 15,050
(D) 20,050
(E) 20,100

Arithmetic Sequences

The sum of the first n positive integers is given by $\frac{n(n+1)}{2}$, so the sum of the first 200 positive integers is $\frac{200(201)}{2} = 20,100$.

Alternatively, letting $\sum_{i=1}^{100} i$ represent the sum of the first 100 positive integers, it is given that

$\sum_{i=1}^{100} i = 5,050$. Using this notation, $\sum_{i=1}^{200} i = \sum_{i=1}^{100} i +$

$\sum_{i=1}^{100}(100+i) = \sum_{i=1}^{100} i + \sum_{i=1}^{100} 100 + \sum_{i=1}^{100} i = 2\sum_{i=1}^{100} i +$

$100\sum_{i=1}^{100} 1 = 2(5,050) + 10,000$

$= 10,100 + 10,000 = 20,100$.

The correct answer is E.

PS40502.01

9.

Month	Average Price per Dozen
April	$1.26
May	$1.20
June	$1.08

The table above shows the average (arithmetic mean) price per dozen eggs sold in a certain store during three successive months. If $\frac{2}{3}$ as many dozen were sold in April as in May, and twice as many were sold in June as in April, what was the average price per dozen of the eggs sold over the three-month period?

(A) $1.08
(B) $1.10
(C) $1.14
(D) $1.16
(E) $1.18

Arithmetic Statistics

Given that the numbers of eggs sold in each of the three months are in the ratio 2:3:4, it follows that $\frac{2}{9}$ of the eggs sold in the three-month period were sold at an average of $1.26 per dozen, $\frac{3}{9} = \frac{1}{3}$ were sold at $1.20 per dozen, and $\frac{4}{9}$ were sold at $1.08 per dozen. Therefore, the average price per dozen of the eggs sold in the three-month period was $\frac{2}{9}(\$1.26) + \frac{1}{3}(\$1.20) + \frac{4}{9}(\$1.08) = \$1.16$.

The correct answer is D.

PS96602.01

10. Each of the integers from 0 to 9, inclusive, is written on a separate slip of blank paper and the ten slips are dropped into a hat. If the slips are then drawn one at a time without replacement, how many must be drawn to ensure that the numbers on two of the slips drawn will have a sum of 10?

(A) Three
(B) Four
(C) Five
(D) Six
(E) Seven

Arithmetic Elementary combinatorics

To simplify the discussion, we will refer to the drawing of the slip of paper with the integer n written on it as "drawing the integer n." The number of integers that must be drawn is at least seven, because if the six integers 0 through 5 were drawn, then no two of the integers drawn will have a sum of 10. In fact, it is easy to see that the sum of any two of these six integers is less than 10.

$$0, 1, 2, 3, 4, 5$$

Of the answer choices, only seven is not eliminated.

Although it is not necessary to show that seven is the least number of integers that must be drawn to ensure there exists a pair of the drawn integers that has a sum of 10, we provide a proof that seven is the least such number. Thus, we will show that if seven integers were drawn, then there exists a pair of the drawn integers that has a sum of 10. Since the integer 0 is such that none of the other integers can be paired with 0 to give a sum of 10, and similarly for the integer 5, it will suffice to show that if five integers were drawn from the eight integers 1, 2, 3, 4, 6, 7, 8, and 9, then there exists a pair of the drawn integers that has a sum of 10. Note that each of these eight integers differs from 5 by one of the numbers 1, 2, 3, or 4, as shown below.

$1 = 5 - 4$	$6 = 5 + 1$
$2 = 5 - 3$	$7 = 5 + 2$
$3 = 5 - 2$	$8 = 5 + 3$
$4 = 5 - 1$	$9 = 5 + 4$

With these preliminaries out of the way, assume that five integers have been drawn from these eight integers. Of the five integers that have been drawn, at least two must differ from 5 by the same number, say k, and since these two integers must be different, it follows that one of these two integers is $5 + k$ and the other is $5 - k$, and hence these two integers have a sum of 10.

The correct answer is E.

PS15402.01

11. King School has an enrollment of 900 students. The school day consists of 6 class periods during which each class is taught by one teacher. There are 30 students per class. Each teacher teaches a class during 5 of the 6 class periods and has one class period free. No students have a free class period. How many teachers does the school have?

(A) 25

(B) 30

(C) 36

(D) 60

(E) 150

Algebra Statistics

If each teacher has 5 class periods a day and each class has 30 students, then each teacher has (5)(30) students per day. Each of the 900 students has 6 classes per day, from which it follows that all the teachers combined have a total of (6)(900) students per day. Therefore, the school has

$$\frac{(6)(900)}{(5)(30)}$$ or 36 teachers.

The correct answer is C.

PS07602.01

12. Ben and Ann are among 7 contestants from which 4 semifinalists are to be selected. Of the different possible selections, how many contain neither Ben nor Ann?

(A) 5

(B) 6

(C) 7

(D) 14

(E) 21

Arithmetic Elementary combinatorics

The number of possible selections of 4 semifinalists that do not contain Ben or Ann is equal to the number of possible selections of 4 semifinalists from the remaining $7 - 2 = 5$ contestants, which is equal to $\binom{5}{4} = \frac{5!}{4!(5-4)!} = 5$. Alternatively, the number of possible selections of 4 semifinalists from the remaining 5 contestants is equal to the number of possible selections of exactly 1 non-semifinalist, which is equal to 5.

The correct answer is A.

Answer Explanations Quantitative Reasoning

Problem Solving

Equalities/Inequalities/Algebra

PS03551.01

13.

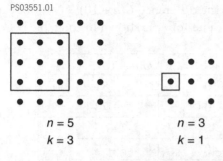

$n = 5$
$k = 3$

$n = 3$
$k = 1$

Let n and k be positive integers with $k \le n$. From an $n \times n$ array of dots, a $k \times k$ array of dots is selected. The figure above shows two examples where the selected $k \times k$ array is enclosed in a square. How many pairs (n, k) are possible so that exactly 48 of the dots in the $n \times n$ array are NOT in the selected $k \times k$ array?

(A) 1

(B) 2

(C) 3

(D) 4

(E) 5

Algebra Factoring; Simultaneous equations

The $n \times n$ array has n^2 dots and the $k \times k$ array has k^2 dots. The number of dots in the $n \times n$ array that are not in the $k \times k$ array is given by $n^2 - k^2 = (n - k)(n + k)$.

Therefore, $(n - k)(n + k) = 48$ is a necessary condition for there to be 48 dots not in the $k \times k$ array. This is also a sufficient condition, since it is clear that at least one $k \times k$ array of dots can be selected for removal from an $n \times n$ array of dots when $k \le n$.

The equation $(n - k)(n + k) = 48$ represents two positive integers, namely $n - k$ and $n + k$, whose product is 48. Thus, the smaller integer $n - k$ must be 1, 2, 3, 4, or 6, and the larger integer $n + k$ must be 48, 24, 16, 12, or 8. Rather than solving five pairs of simultaneous equations (for example, $n - k = 2$ and $n + k = 24$ is one such pair), it is more efficient to observe that the solution to the system $n - k = a$ and $n + k = b$ is $n = \frac{1}{2}(a + b)$ (add the equations, then divide by 2) and $k = \frac{1}{2}(b - a)$ (substitute $n = \frac{1}{2}(a + b)$ for n in either equation and solve for k; or subtract the equations, then

divide by 2). Therefore, the possible pairs (n, k) arise exactly when $48 = ab$ and both $a + b$ and $b - a$ are divisible by 2. This occurs exactly three times—$48 = (2)(24)$, $48 = (4)(12)$, and $48 = (6)(8)$.

The correct answer is C.

PS41471.01

14. If there is a least integer that satisfies the inequality $\frac{9}{x} \ge 2$, what is that least integer?

(A) 0

(B) 1

(C) 4

(D) 5

(E) There is not a least integer that satisfies the inequality.

Algebra Inequalities

It is clear that no negative integer satisfies the inequality (because $\dfrac{9}{\text{negative}} \ge 2$ is false) and zero does not satisfy the inequality (because $\frac{9}{0}$ is undefined). Thus, the integers, if any, that satisfy $\frac{9}{x} \ge 2$ must be among 1, 2, 3, 4, …. The least of these integers is 1, and it is easy to see that $x = 1$ satisfies the inequality $\frac{9}{x} \ge 2$. Therefore, the least integer that satisfies the inequality is 1.

Alternatively, the inequality can be solved algebraically. It will be convenient to consider three cases according to whether $x < 0$, $x = 0$, and $x > 0$.

Case 1: Assume $x < 0$. Then multiplying both sides of the inequality by x, which is negative, gives $9 \le 2x$, or $x \ge 4.5$. Because we are assuming $x < 0$, there are no solutions to $x \ge 4.5$. Therefore, no solutions exist in Case 1.

Case 2: Assume $x = 0$. Then $\frac{9}{x}$ is not defined, and thus $x = 0$ cannot be a solution.

Case 3: Assume $x > 0$. Then multiplying both sides of the inequality by x, which is positive, gives $9 \ge 2x$, or $x \le 4.5$. Because we are assuming $x > 0$, the solutions that exist in Case 2 are all real numbers x such that $0 < x \le 4.5$.

The set of all solutions to the inequality $\dfrac{9}{x} \geq 2$ will be all solutions found in Cases 1, 2, and 3.

Therefore, the solutions to the inequality consist of all real numbers x such that $0 < x \leq 4.5$. The least of these solutions that is an integer is 1.

The correct answer is B.

PS18871.01

15.

x	C(x)
0	25,000
10	24,919
20	24,846
30	24,781
40	24,724
50	24,675

A certain manufacturer uses the function $C(x) = 0.04x^2 - 8.5x + 25{,}000$ to calculate the cost, in dollars, of producing x thousand units of its product. The table above gives values of this cost function for values of x between 0 and 50 in increments of 10. For which of the following intervals is the average rate of *decrease* in cost less than the average rate of *decrease* in cost for each of the other intervals?

(A) From $x = 0$ to $x = 10$

(B) From $x = 10$ to $x = 20$

(C) From $x = 20$ to $x = 30$

(D) From $x = 30$ to $x = 40$

(E) From $x = 40$ to $x = 50$

Arithmetic Applied problems

Since the average rate of decrease of $C(x)$ in the interval from $x = a$ to $x = a + 10$ is

$$\dfrac{C(a+10)-C(a)}{(a+10)-a} = \dfrac{C(a+10)-C(a)}{10}, \text{ we are}$$

to determine for which value of a, chosen from the numbers 0, 10, 20, 30, and 40, the magnitude of $\dfrac{C(a+10)-C(a)}{10}$ is the least, or equivalently, for which of these values of a the magnitude of $C(a+10)-C(a)$ is the least. Probably the most straightforward method is to simply calculate or

estimate the difference $C(a+10)-C(a)$ for each of these values of a, as shown in the table below.

a to a + 10	C(a + 10) − C(a)
0 to 10	−81
10 to 20	−73
20 to 30	−65
30 to 40	−57
40 to 50	−49

Alternatively, since the graph of $C(x) = 0.04x^2 - 8.5x + 25{,}000$ is a parabola with vertex at $x = -\dfrac{b}{2a} = -\dfrac{-8.5}{2(0.04)} \approx \dfrac{8}{0.08} = 100$, it follows that the graph levels out as the value of x approaches a number that is approximately equal to 100. Therefore, among the intervals given, the least magnitude in the average rate of change of $C(x)$ occurs for the interval closest to the vertex, which is the interval from $x = 40$ to $x = 50$.

The correct answer is E.

PS35302.01

16. On the day of the performance of a certain play, each ticket that regularly sells for less than $10.00 is sold for half price plus $0.50, and each ticket that regularly sells for $10.00 or more is sold for half price plus $1.00. On the day of the performance, a person purchases a total of y tickets, of which x regularly sell for $9.00 each and the rest regularly sell for $12.00 each. What is the amount paid, in dollars, for the y tickets?

(A) $7y - 2x$

(B) $12x - 7y$

(C) $\dfrac{9x + 12y}{2}$

(D) $7y + 4x$

(E) $7y + 5x$

Algebra Applied problems

The amount paid for the y tickets is the sum of the amounts paid for two groups of tickets. The first group consists of x tickets, each of which regularly sells for $9.00. The second group consists of the remaining $(y - x)$ tickets, each of which regularly sells for $12.00. The amount paid for the first group was $x(\$4.50 + \$0.50) = \$5x$. The amount paid for the second group was $(y - x)(\$6.00 + \$1.00) = \$7(y - x)$, or $\$7y - \$7x$. Therefore, the amount paid for the y tickets was $\$5x + (\$7y - \$7x) = \$(7y - 2x)$.

The correct answer is A.

PS47302.01

17. If $N = \dfrac{K}{T + \dfrac{x}{y}}$, where $T = \dfrac{K}{5}$ and $x = 5 - T$, which of the following expresses y in terms of N and T?

(A) $\dfrac{N(5 - T)}{T(5 - N)}$

(B) $\dfrac{N(T - 5)}{T(5 - N)}$

(C) $\dfrac{5 - T}{T(5 - N)}$

(D) $\dfrac{5N(5 - T)}{T(1 - 5N)}$

(E) $\dfrac{N(5 - T)}{5}$

Algebra Simplifying algebraic expressions

To eliminate K and x in the first equation (the only equation in which y appears), use the second and third equations to replace K and x with expressions involving only N and T. Then solve for y in terms of N and T.

$$N = \dfrac{K}{T + \dfrac{x}{y}} \qquad \text{given equation}$$

$$N = \dfrac{5T}{T + \dfrac{5 - T}{y}} \qquad \begin{array}{l}\text{substitute using}\\ K = 5T \text{ and}\\ x = 5 - T\end{array}$$

$$N\left(T + \dfrac{5 - T}{y}\right) = 5T \qquad \begin{array}{l}\text{multiply both sides}\\ \text{by } T + \dfrac{5 - T}{y}\end{array}$$

$$NT + \dfrac{N(5 - T)}{y} = 5T \qquad \text{expand left side}$$

$$\dfrac{N(5 - T)}{y} = 5T - NT \qquad \begin{array}{l}\text{subtract } NT \text{ from}\\ \text{both sides}\end{array}$$

$$\dfrac{N(5 - T)}{y} = T(5 - N) \qquad \text{factor right side}$$

$$N(5 - T) = yT(5 - N) \qquad \begin{array}{l}\text{multiply both sides}\\ \text{by } y\end{array}$$

$$\dfrac{N(5 - T)}{T(5 - N)} = y \qquad \begin{array}{l}\text{divide both sides by}\\ T(5 - N)\end{array}$$

Alternatively, the algebraic manipulations involved in solving this type of problem as above can often be replaced with numerical computations by assigning values to the variables. The assigned values need to be consistent with all the constraints in the problem, and, for efficiency, the assigned values should be chosen to minimize the numerical computations. Letting $K = 10$, it follows from $T = \dfrac{K}{5}$ and $x = 5 - T$ that $T = 2$ and $x = 3$. Using these numerical values, the question can be rephrased as follows.

If $N = \dfrac{10}{2 + \dfrac{3}{y}}$, then which of the following expresses y in terms of N?

(A) $\dfrac{3N}{2(5 - N)}$

(B) $\dfrac{-3N}{2(5 - N)}$

(C) $\dfrac{3}{2(5 - N)}$

(D) $\dfrac{15N}{2(1 - 5N)}$

(E) $\dfrac{3N}{5}$

Letting $y = 1$, it follows that $N = \dfrac{10}{2 + 3} = 2$.

Plugging $N = 2$ into A, B, C, D, and E above gives, respectively, $1, -1, \dfrac{1}{2}, -\dfrac{5}{3}$, and $\dfrac{6}{5}$.

The correct answer is A.

PS78302.01

18. If $2x + 5y = 8$ and $3x = 2y$, what is the value of $2x + y$?

(A) 4

(B) $\dfrac{70}{19}$

(C) $\dfrac{64}{19}$

(D) $\dfrac{56}{19}$

(E) $\dfrac{40}{19}$

Algebra Simultaneous equations

From $3x = 2y$, it follows that $y = \dfrac{3}{2}x$, so $8 = 2x + 5$ $\left(\dfrac{3}{2}x\right) = \dfrac{19}{2}x$. Then $x = \dfrac{16}{19}$, $2x = \dfrac{32}{19}$, and $y = \dfrac{24}{19}$.

Thus $2x + y = \dfrac{56}{19}$.

The correct answer is D.

PS79302.01

19. If $_kS_n$ is defined to be the product of $(n + k)(n - k + 1)$ for all positive integers k and n, which of the following expressions represents $_{k+1}S_{n+1}$?

(A) $(n + k)(n - k + 2)$

(B) $(n + k)(n - k + 3)$

(C) $(n + k + 1)(n - k + 2)$

(D) $(n + k + 2)(n - k + 1)$

(E) $(n + k + 2)(n - k + 3)$

Algebra Substitution; Simplifying algebraic expressions

Substituting $n + 1$ for n and $k + 1$ for k in the definition gives $_{k+1}S_{n+1}$
$= (n + 1 + k + 1)(n + 1 - (k + 1) + 1)$
$= (n + k + 2)(n - k + 1)$.

The correct answer is D.

PS20502.01

20. There were 36,000 hardback copies of a certain novel sold before the paperback version was issued. From the time the first paperback copy was sold until the last copy of the novel was sold, 9 times as many paperback copies as hardback copies were sold. If a total of 441,000 copies of the novel were sold in all, how many paperback copies were sold?

(A) 45,000

(B) 360,000

(C) 364,500

(D) 392,000

(E) 396,900

Algebra First-degree equations

Let h be the number of hardback copies of the novel that were sold after the paperback version was issued. The following table summarizes the given information.

	Hardbacks sold	Paperbacks sold	Total
Before paperbacks	36,000	0	36,000
After paperbacks	h	$9h$	$10h$

Then, $441,000 = 36,000 + 10h$ or $h = 40,500$ and $9h = (9)(40,500) = 364,500$.

The correct answer is C.

Alternate Solution

Arithmetic Ratios

From the moment the paperback version was issued, $441,000 - 36,000 = 405,000$ copies of the novel were sold. Test the answer choices to see whether the ratio of paperbacks sold to hardbacks sold is 9:1. Start with the middle value, because the answer choices are usually listed in numerical order. This way, if you pick an answer that does not give the 9:1 ratio, you can learn whether it was too high or too low, thus allowing you to eliminate other answers that are too high or too low.

Testing answer choice C, if 364,500 paperbacks were sold, then $405,000 - 364,500 = 40,500$ hardbacks were sold after the initial 36,000 hardbacks were sold. Noting that 40,500 hardbacks is 10% of 405,000 and 364,500 paperbacks is 90% of 405,000, the ratio of paperbacks to hardbacks is 9:1.

The correct answer is C.

PS30502.01

21. In the formula $w = \dfrac{P}{\sqrt[t]{v}}$, integers p and t are positive constants. If $w = 2$ when $v = 1$ and if $w = \dfrac{1}{2}$ when $v = 64$, then $t =$

(A) 1
(B) 2
(C) 3
(D) 4
(E) 16

Algebra Exponents

It is given that $w = \dfrac{P}{\sqrt[t]{v}}$ and $w = 2$ when $v = 1$. Because 1 raised to any positive power is 1, it follows that $2 = P$. If $w = \dfrac{1}{2}$ when $v = 64$, then $\dfrac{1}{2} = \dfrac{2}{\sqrt[t]{64}}$ or $4 = \sqrt[t]{64}$. Then $\sqrt[t]{64} = 64^{\frac{1}{t}} = 4^{\frac{3}{t}}$ since $64 = 4^3$. So, $4 = 4^{\frac{3}{t}}$ and $t = 3$.

The correct answer is C.

PS03502.01

22.

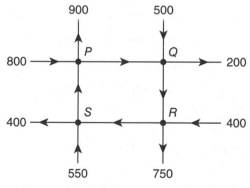

The figure above represents a network of one-way streets. The arrows indicate the direction of traffic flow, and the numbers indicate the amount of traffic flow into or out of each of the four intersections during a certain hour. During that hour, what was the amount of traffic flow along the street from R to S if the total amount of traffic flow into P was 1,200 ? (Assume that none of the traffic originates or terminates in the network.)

(A) 200
(B) 250

(C) 300
(D) 350
(E) 400

Arithmetic Computation with integers

In the following, the notation $A{\rightarrow}B$ will be used to represent the amount of traffic flow from A into B. Let x represent $R{\rightarrow}S$. From the figure, the amount of traffic flow into P was 800 plus $S{\rightarrow}P$. The total amount of traffic flow into P was 1,200, so $S{\rightarrow}P$ was 400. The amount of traffic flow into S was 550 plus $R{\rightarrow}S$, so $550 + x$. The amount of traffic flow out of S was 400 plus $S{\rightarrow}P$, or $400 + 400 = 800$. Since the amount of traffic flow into S must equal the amount of traffic flow out of S, $550 + x = 800$. Therefore, $x = 250$, so $R{\rightarrow}S$ was 250.

The correct answer is B.

PS23502.01

23. If C is the temperature in degrees Celsius and F is the temperature in degrees Fahrenheit, then the relationship between temperatures on the two scales is expressed by the equation $9C = 5(F - 32)$. On a day when the temperature extremes recorded at a certain weather station differed by 45 degrees on the Fahrenheit scale, by how many degrees did the temperature extremes differ on the Celsius scale?

(A) $\dfrac{65}{9}$
(B) 13
(C) 25
(D) 45
(E) 81

Algebra Formulas

Let F represent the larger extreme on the Fahrenheit scale. Then, $F - 45$ is the smaller extreme. It follows that the difference in the temperatures on the Celsius scale is $\dfrac{5}{9}(F - 32) - \dfrac{5}{9}\big[(F - 45) - 32\big] = 25$.

The correct answer is C.

PS93502.01

24. If $d = \dfrac{a+b}{1+\dfrac{ab}{c^2}}$, $a = \dfrac{c}{2}$, and $b = \dfrac{3c}{4}$, what is the value of d in terms of c ?

(A) $\dfrac{10c}{11}$

(B) $\dfrac{5c}{2}$

(C) $\dfrac{10c}{3}$

(D) $\dfrac{10}{11c}$

(E) $\dfrac{5}{2c}$

Algebra Simplifying algebraic expressions

First, $a + b = \dfrac{c}{2} + \dfrac{3c}{4} = \dfrac{5c}{4}$ and $1 + \dfrac{ab}{c^2} = 1 +$

$\dfrac{\left(\dfrac{c}{2}\right)\left(\dfrac{3c}{4}\right)}{c^2} = 1 + \dfrac{3}{8} = \dfrac{11}{8}$. Then, $d = \dfrac{a+b}{1+\dfrac{ab}{c^2}} = \dfrac{\dfrac{5c}{4}}{\dfrac{11}{8}} = \dfrac{10c}{11}$.

The correct answer is A.

PS04502.01

25. A school supply store sells only one kind of desk and one kind of chair, at a uniform cost per desk or per chair. If the total cost of 3 desks and 1 chair is twice that of 1 desk and 3 chairs, then the total cost of 4 desks and 1 chair is how many times that of 1 desk and 4 chairs?

(A) 5

(B) 3

(C) $\dfrac{8}{3}$

(D) $\dfrac{5}{2}$

(E) $\dfrac{7}{3}$

Algebra Simultaneous equations

Let d represent the cost of 1 desk and let c represent the cost of 1 chair. It is given that $3d + c = 2(d + 3c)$. It follows that $d = 5c$. Then $4d + c = 21c$ and $d + 4c = 9c$. Since $\dfrac{21c}{9c} = \dfrac{7}{3}$, the

total cost of 4 desks and 1 chair is $\dfrac{7}{3}$ times that of 1 desk and 4 chairs.

The correct answer is E.

PS35502.01

26. A certain truck traveling at 55 miles per hour gets 4.5 miles per gallon of diesel fuel consumed. Traveling at 60 miles per hour, the truck gets only 3.5 miles per gallon. On a 500-mile trip, if the truck used a total of 120 gallons of diesel fuel and traveled part of the trip at 55 miles per hour and the rest at 60 miles per hour, how many miles did it travel at 55 miles per hour?

(A) 140

(B) 200

(C) 250

(D) 300

(E) 360

Algebra Applied problems

Let m be the number of miles the truck traveled at 55 miles per hour. It follows that $500 - m$ is the number of miles the truck traveled at 60 miles per hour. Then, $\dfrac{m}{4.5}$ is the number of gallons the truck used while traveling at 55 miles per hour and $\dfrac{500 - m}{3.5}$ is the number of gallons the truck used while traveling at 60 miles per hour, so $\dfrac{m}{4.5} + \dfrac{500 - m}{3.5} = 120$. Solving this equation gives $m = 360$.

The correct answer is E.

PS45502.01

27. A merchant paid $300 for a shipment of x identical calculators. The merchant used two of the calculators as demonstrators and sold each of the others for $5 more than the average (arithmetic mean) cost of the x calculators. If the total revenue from the sale of the calculators was $120 more than the cost of the shipment, how many calculators were in the shipment?

(A) 24

(B) 25

(C) 26

(D) 28

(E) 30

Algebra Second-degree equations

The merchant paid \$300 for a shipment of x calculators, so the average cost, in dollars, per calculator was $\dfrac{300}{x}$. The merchant sold $(x-2)$ of them at the price of $5 + \dfrac{300}{x}$ dollars each, for a total revenue of $(x-2)\left(5 + \dfrac{300}{x}\right)$ dollars, which was $120 + 300 = 420$. Manipulating the equation $(x-2)\left(5 + \dfrac{300}{x}\right) = 420$ gives $x^2 - 26x - 120 = 0$ or $(x-30)(x+4) = 0$, which can be solved by factoring. It follows that there were 30 calculators in the shipment.

The correct answer is E.

We must determine machine Y's individual rate $\dfrac{1}{Y}$ for the whole job. First, add machine X's rate to machine Y's rate to get the combined rate.

Then,

$$\frac{1}{9} + \frac{1}{Y} = \frac{1}{6}$$

$$\frac{1}{Y} = \frac{1}{6} - \frac{1}{9}$$

$$\frac{1}{Y} = \frac{2}{36}$$

$$Y = 18$$

The correct answer is A.

PS77602.01

30. If $\dfrac{s}{t} = 2$, then the value of which of the following can be determined?

   I. $\dfrac{2t}{s}$

   II. $\dfrac{s-t}{t}$

   III. $\dfrac{t-1}{s-1}$

(A)   I only

(B)   III only

(C)   I and II only

(D)   II and III only

(E)   I, II, and III

Algebra Simplifying algebraic expressions

Substitute $2t$ for s in the expressions given in I, II, and III.

✔I. Value can be determined: $\dfrac{2t}{s} = \dfrac{2t}{2t} = 1$

✔II. Value can be determined:

$\dfrac{s-t}{t} = \dfrac{2t-t}{t} = \dfrac{t}{t} = 1$

✘III. Value cannot be determined: $\dfrac{t-1}{s-1} = \dfrac{t-1}{2t-1}$ equals 0 if $t = 1$, and equals $\dfrac{1}{3}$ if $t = 2$

The correct answer is C.

PS58602.01

31. If $k \neq 0$ and $k - \dfrac{3-2k^2}{k} = \dfrac{x}{k}$, then $x =$

(A) $-3 - k^2$

(B) $k^2 - 3$

(C) $3k^2 - 3$

(D) $k - 3 - 2k^2$

(E) $k - 3 + 2k^2$

Algebra Simplifying algebraic expressions

Multiplying both sides of the equation by k gives $k^2 - (3 - 2k^2) = x$ or $x = 3k^2 - 3$.

The correct answer is C.

PS68602.01

32. The sum of the ages of Doris and Fred is y years. If Doris is 12 years older than Fred, how many years old will Fred be y years from now, in terms of y?

(A) $y - 6$

(B) $2y - 6$

(C) $\dfrac{y}{2} - 6$

(D) $\dfrac{3y}{2} - 6$

(E) $\dfrac{5y}{2} - 6$

Algebra Applied problems

Let D and F represent Doris's and Fred's current ages, respectively. It is given that $D + F = y$ and $D = F + 12$. It follows that $(F + 12) + F = y$ and $F = \dfrac{y-12}{2} = \dfrac{y}{2} - 6$. Therefore, Fred's age y years from now will be $y + \left(\dfrac{y}{2} - 6 \right) = \dfrac{3y}{2} - 6$.

The correct answer is D.

Answer Explanations Quantitative Reasoning

Problem Solving

Geometry

33.

PS35461.01

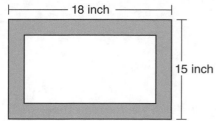

Note: Figure not drawn to scale.

The shaded region in the figure above represents a rectangular frame with length 18 inches and width 15 inches. The frame encloses a rectangular picture that has the same area as the frame itself. If the length and width of the picture have the same ratio as the length and width of the frame, what is the length of the picture, in inches?

(A) $9\sqrt{2}$

(B) $\dfrac{3}{2}$

(C) $\dfrac{9}{\sqrt{2}}$

(D) $15(1 - \dfrac{1}{\sqrt{2}})$

(E) $\dfrac{9}{2}$

Geometry Rectangles; Area

Let k be the proportionality constant for the fractional decrease from the dimensions of the frame to the dimensions of the picture. That is, let $18k$ be the length of the picture and let $15k$ be the width of the picture. We are given that $(18)(15) = 2(18k)(15k)$. Hence, $k^2 = \dfrac{1}{2}$ and $k = \dfrac{1}{\sqrt{2}}$.

Therefore, the length of the picture is

$$18k = \dfrac{18}{\sqrt{2}} = 9\sqrt{2}.$$

The correct answer is A.

PS56271.01

34.   The *surface distance* between 2 points on the surface of a cube is the length of the shortest path on the surface of the cube that joins the 2 points. If a cube

has edges of length 4 centimeters, what is the surface distance, in centimeters, between the lower left vertex on its front face and the upper right vertex on its back face?

(A)   8

(B) $4\sqrt{5}$

(C) $8\sqrt{2}$

(D) $12\sqrt{2}$

(E) $4\sqrt{2} + 4$

Geometry Rectangular solids

The left figure below shows a cube with edge length 4, where P is the lower left vertex on its front face and Q is the upper right vertex on its back face. It is clear that the shortest path on the surface between P and Q consists of a path on the front face joined to a path on the top face, or a path on the front face joined to a path on the right face. In fact, each of these two approaches can be used in essentially the same way to give a path from P to Q, whose length is the surface distance between P and Q. To simplify the exposition, we will consider the case where the surface distance is the length of a certain path P_F on the front face plus the length of a certain path P_T on the top face.

The middle figure below shows the top face of the cube lifted about 45 degrees, and the right figure below shows only the front and top faces of the cube after the top face has been lifted 90 degrees. Since rotations of the top face about this "hinge" do not change the length of any path on the front face or on the top face, this rotation by 90 degrees will not change the length of P_F or the length of P_T, and hence this rotation will not change the sum of the lengths of P_F and P_T.

In the right figure below, the shortest path from P to Q is the dashed segment shown in the figure. Moreover, the length of this dashed segment is the surface distance between P and Q because if P_F and P_T did not correspond to portions of this dashed segment on the front and top faces, respectively, then the sum of the lengths of P_F and

P_T would be greater than the length of the dashed segment, since the shortest distance between P and Q in the right figure below is the length of the line segment with endpoints P and Q.

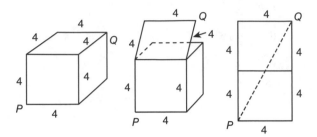

From the discussion above, it follows that the surface distance between P and Q is the length of the dashed segment in the right figure, which is easily found by using the Pythagorean theorem: $\sqrt{4^2 + 8^2} = \sqrt{4^2\left(1 + 2^2\right)} = 4\sqrt{5}$.

The correct answer is B.

PS75571.01

35.

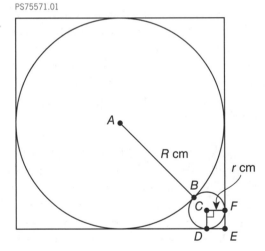

The figure above shows 2 circles. The larger circle has center A, radius R cm, and is inscribed in a square. The smaller circle has center C, radius r cm, and is tangent to the larger circle at point B and to the square at points D and F. If points A, B, C, and E are collinear, which of the following is equal to $\dfrac{R}{r}$?

(A) $\dfrac{2}{\sqrt{2} + 1}$

(B) $\dfrac{2}{\sqrt{2} - 1}$

(C) $\dfrac{2}{2\sqrt{2} + 1}$

(D) $\dfrac{\sqrt{2} + 1}{\sqrt{2} - 1}$

(E) $\dfrac{2\sqrt{2} + 1}{2\sqrt{2} - 1}$

Geometry Circles; Pythagorean theorem

Because $\overline{CE}$ is a diagonal of square $CDEF$, which has side length r, it follows from the Pythagorean theorem that $r^2 + r^2 = (CE)^2$, and hence $CE = r\sqrt{2}$.

> **Tip**
>
> A sometimes useful shortcut is the fact that, for a square we have $d = s\sqrt{2}$, where d is the diagonal length and s is the side length. This can be obtained by applying the Pythagorean theorem as above or by using properties of a 45–45–90 triangle.

Therefore, $BE = r + r\sqrt{2} = r(1 + \sqrt{2})$ and $AE = R + r(1 + \sqrt{2})$. Since $2(AE)$ is the diagonal length of the large square, which has side length $2R$, it follows from the above tip that $2(AE) = (2R)\sqrt{2}$, or $AE = R\sqrt{2}$. Alternatively, an appropriate application of the Pythagorean theorem gives $R^2 + R^2 = (AE)^2$, or $AE = R\sqrt{2}$. Now substitute for AE and solve for $\dfrac{R}{r}$.

$$AE = R\sqrt{2}$$

$$R + r(1 + \sqrt{2}) = R\sqrt{2} \qquad \text{substitute for } AE$$

$$r(\sqrt{2} + 1) = R(\sqrt{2} - 1) \quad \text{rearrange terms}$$

From the last equation we get $\dfrac{R}{r} = \dfrac{\sqrt{2} + 1}{\sqrt{2} - 1}$.

The correct answer is D.

PS15302.01

36.

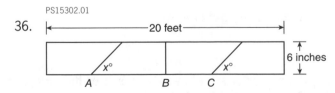

Note: Figure not drawn to scale.

The figure above shows the dimensions of a rectangular board that is to be cut into four identical

pieces by making cuts at points *A*, *B*, and *C*, as indicated. If *x* = 45, what is the length *AB* ?
(1 foot = 12 inches)

(A)   5 ft 6 in

(B)   5 ft 3$\sqrt{2}$ in

(C)   5 ft 3 in

(D)   5 ft

(E)   4 ft 9 in

Geometry Rectangles; Triangles

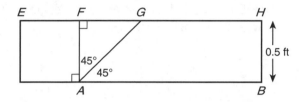

The figure above shows the left side of the rectangular board with points *E*, *F*, *G*, and *H* added and segment $\overline{FA}$ added. We are to determine the value of *AB*, which equals the value of *FH*. Since $\triangle AFG$ is an isosceles triangle, it follows that *FG* = *FA* = 0.5 ft. Moreover, *EF* = *GH* because the four pieces of the rectangular board have the same dimensions. Therefore, since *EH* is half the length of the 20 ft board, *EH* = 10 ft and we have *EF* + *FG* + *GH* = 10 ft, or 2(*GH*) + 0.5 ft = 10 ft, or *GH* = 4.75 ft. Hence, *AB* = *FH* = *FG* + *GH* = 0.5 ft + 4.75 ft = 5.25 ft, which equals 5 ft 3 in.

The correct answer is C.

PS57302.01

37.

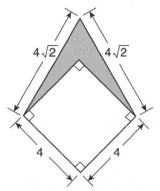

In the figure above, the area of the shaded region is

(A) $8\sqrt{2}$

(B) $4\sqrt{3}$

(C) $4\sqrt{2}$

(D) $8\left(\sqrt{3}-1\right)$

(E) $8\left(\sqrt{2}-1\right)$

Geometry Triangles; Area

First, the diagonal of the square with sides of length 4 is $4\sqrt{2}$. From this it follows that the area of the shaded region consists of the area of an equilateral triangle with sides $4\sqrt{2}$ minus $\dfrac{1}{2}$ the area of a square with sides of length 4. Thus, the area of the shaded region is

$$\frac{\sqrt{3}}{4}\left(4\sqrt{2}\right)^2 - \frac{1}{2}\left(4^2\right) = 8\left(\sqrt{3}-1\right).$$

The correct answer is D.

PS18302.01

38.

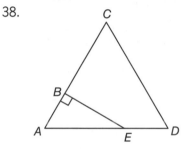

If each side of $\triangle ACD$ above has length 3 and if *AB* has length 1, what is the area of region *BCDE* ?

(A) $\dfrac{9}{4}$

(B) $\dfrac{7}{4}\sqrt{3}$

(C) $\dfrac{9}{4}\sqrt{3}$

(D) $\dfrac{7}{2}\sqrt{3}$

(E) $6 + \sqrt{3}$

Geometry Triangles; Area

The area of region *BCDE* is the area of $\triangle ACD$ minus the area of $\triangle ABE$. Since $\triangle ACD$ is equilateral, its area is $\dfrac{\sqrt{3}}{4}\left(3^2\right) = \dfrac{9\sqrt{3}}{4}$. $\triangle ABE$ is a 30–60–90 triangle with side lengths 1, $\sqrt{3}$, and 2 and area $\dfrac{\sqrt{3}}{2}$. Thus, the area of region $BCDE$ is

$$\dfrac{9\sqrt{3}}{4} - \dfrac{\sqrt{3}}{2} = \dfrac{7\sqrt{3}}{4}.$$

The correct answer is B.

PS76402.01

39.

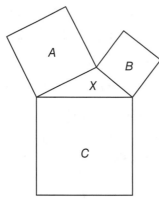

Note: Figure not drawn to scale.

In the figure above, three squares and a triangle have areas of A, B, C, and X as shown. If $A = 144$, $B = 81$, and $C = 225$, then $X =$

(A)   150

(B)   144

(C)   80

(D)   54

(E)   36

Geometry Triangles; Quadrilaterals; Area

The side lengths of the squares with areas 144, 81, and 225 are 12, 9, and 15, respectively, so the triangle with area X has sides 12, 9, and 15. Because $12^2 + 9^2 = 15^2$, the triangle with area X is a right triangle with legs of length 12 and 9. Thus, $X = \dfrac{1}{2}(12)(9) = 54$.

The correct answer is D.

PS57402.01

40.

In the figure above, PQ is a diameter of circle O, $PR = SQ$, and $\triangle RST$ is equilateral. If the length of PQ is 2, what is the length of RT?

(A) $\dfrac{1}{2}$

(B) $\dfrac{1}{\sqrt{3}}$

(C) $\dfrac{\sqrt{3}}{2}$

(D) $\dfrac{2}{\sqrt{3}}$

(E) $\sqrt{3}$

Geometry Triangles

Since $PR = SQ$, it follows that $RO = OS$, so O is the midpoint of $\overline{RS}$. Since $\triangle RST$ is equilateral and O is the midpoint of $\overline{RS}$, $\triangle ROT$ is a $30°$–$60°$–$90°$ triangle, and since $\overline{OT}$ is a radius of the circle with diameter 2, $OT = 1$. Using the ratios of the sides of a $30°$–$60°$–$90°$ triangle, it follows that $RT = \dfrac{2}{\sqrt{3}}$.

The correct answer is D.

PS22502.01

41.

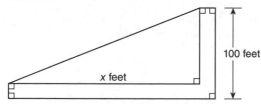

100 feet

x feet

Note: Figure not drawn to scale.

The figure above shows some of the dimensions of a triangular plaza with an L-shaped walk along two of its edges. If the width of the walk is 4 feet and the total area of the plaza and walk together is 10,800 square feet, what is the value of *x* ?

(A) 200

(B) 204

(C) 212

(D) 216

(E) 225

Geometry Polygons; Area

The area of the triangular plaza is given by $\frac{1}{2}x(100-4) = 48x$, and the area of the walkway is given by $(x+4)(4) + (96)(4)$. Since the total area of the plaza and walkway is 10,800, it follows that $52x + 400 = 10,800$ and $x = 200$.

The correct answer is A.

PS88602.01

42. A circular rim 28 inches in diameter rotates the same number of inches per second as a circular rim 35 inches in diameter. If the smaller rim makes *x* revolutions per second, how many revolutions per minute does the larger rim make in terms of *x*?

(A) $\dfrac{48\pi}{x}$

(B) $75x$

(C) $48x$

(D) $24x$

(E) $\dfrac{x}{75}$

Geometry Circles; Circumference

Since the smaller rim has diameter 28 inches and rotates x revolutions per second, it rotates $28\pi x$ inches per second. If y represents the number of revolutions the larger rim rotates per second, then the larger rim rotates $35\pi y$ inches per second. Since the rims rotate the same number of inches per second, it follows that $28\pi x = 35\pi y$.

Then $y = \dfrac{28x}{35} = \dfrac{4x}{5}$ inches per second or $\dfrac{4x}{5}(60) = 48x$ inches per minute.

The correct answer is C.

Answer Explanations Quantitative Reasoning

Problem Solving

Rates/Ratios/Percent

PS17302.01

43. The annual stockholders' report for Corporation *X* stated that profits were up 10 percent over the previous year, although profits as a percent of sales were down 10 percent. Total sales for that year were approximately what percent of sales for the previous year?

(A)   78%

(B)   90%

(C)   110%

(D)   122%

(E)   190%

Algebra Percents

Let P_1 and S_1 be the profit and sales for the previous year, and let P_2 and S_2 be the profit and sales for the following year. It is given that $P_2 = 1.1P_1$ and $\dfrac{P_2}{S_2} = 0.9\left(\dfrac{P_1}{S_1}\right)$. Substituting the first equation into the second equation gives

$$\frac{1.1\cancel{P}_1}{S_2} = 0.9\left(\frac{\cancel{P}_1}{S_1}\right), \text{ or } S_2 = \left(\frac{1.1}{0.9}\right)S_1 \approx (1.22)\,S_1.$$

Therefore, S_2 is approximately 122% of S_1.

The correct answer is D.

PS47402.01

44. A certain brand of house paint must be purchased either in quarts at $12 each or in gallons at $18 each. A painter needs a 3-gallon mixture of the paint consisting of 3 parts blue and 2 parts white. What is the least amount of money needed to purchase sufficient quantities of the two colors to make the mixture?

(4 quarts = 1 gallon)

(A) $54

(B) $60

(C) $66

(D) $90

(E) $144

Arithmetic Applied problems

To make 3 gallons of the mixture requires 12 quarts, and the least amount of money is achieved

by purchasing the greatest number of gallons and least number of quarts. Letting *B* be the number of quarts of blue paint needed and *W* be the number of quarts of white paint needed, it follows that $B + W = 12$, where $B = \dfrac{3}{2}W$ since the mixture has a blue to white ratio of 3 to 2. This gives $B = 7\dfrac{1}{5}$ and $W = 4\dfrac{4}{5}$. Since the paint can be purchased in whole quarts only, the painter must purchase 8 quarts or 2 gallons of blue, and 5 quarts or 1 gallon plus 1 quart of white for a total of $(2 + 1)(\$18) + \$12 = \$66$.

The correct answer is C.

PS43481.01

45.

Month	Change in sales from previous month
February	+10%
March	−15%
April	+20%
May	−10%
June	+5%

The table above shows the percent of change from the previous month in Company X's sales for February through June of last year. A positive percent indicates that Company X's sales for that month increased from the sales for the previous month, and a negative percent indicates that Company X's sales for that month decreased from the sales for the previous month. For which month were the sales closest to the sales in January?

(A)   February

(B)   March

(C)   April

(D)   May

(E)   June

Arithmetic Percents

Explicit calculation incorporating a few numerical shortcuts gives the following, where *J* is the January sales amount.

February sales: **$1.1J$**

March sales: $0.85(1.1J) = 0.85J + 0.85(0.1J) = 0.85J + 0.085J = \mathbf{0.935J}$

April sales: $1.2(0.935J) = 0.935J + 0.2(0.935J) = 0.935J + 0.187J = \mathbf{1.122J}$

May sales: $0.9(1.122J) = \mathbf{1.0098J}$

June sales: $\mathbf{1.05(1.0098J)}$ (May is clearly closer)

Alternatively, from

$$\left(1 + \frac{x}{100}\right)\left(1 + \frac{y}{100}\right) = 1 + \frac{x+y}{100} + \frac{x}{100}\left(\frac{y}{100}\right)$$

it follows that a percent change of $x\%$ followed by a percent change of $y\%$ is equal to a percent change of $(x + y)\%$ plus $x\%$ of y percentage points (equivalently, plus $y\%$ of x percentage points).

Percent change from January through February: The percent change is given as **+10%**.

Percent change from January through March: Using the rule above for $x = +10$ and $y = -15$ gives $(+10 - 15)\% + (+0.10)(-15\%)$, or $-5\% - 1.5\% = \mathbf{-6.5\%}$.

Percent change from January through April: This is equivalent to a -6.5% change (percent change from January through March) followed by a $+20\%$ change, and hence using the rule above for $x = -6.5$ and $y = +20$ gives $(-6.5 + 20)\% + (+0.20)(-6.5\%)$, or $+13.5\% - 1.3\% = \mathbf{+12.2\%}$.

Percent change from January through May: This is equivalent to a $+12.2\%$ change (percent change from January through April) followed by a -10% change, and hence using the rule above for $x = +12.2$ and $y = -10$ gives $(+12.2 - 10)\% + (-0.10)(+12.2\%)$, or $+2.2\% - 1.22\% = \mathbf{+0.98\%}$.

Percent change from January through June: This is clearly **greater than +0.98% + 5%**, and hence greater in magnitude than the result for May.

From the results above, the least change in the magnitude of the percent change from January occurred for May.

The correct answer is D.

PS56302.01

46. A store bought 5 dozen lamps at $30 per dozen and sold them all at $15 per lamp. The profit on each lamp was what percent of its selling price?

   (A)   20%
   (B)   50%
   (C) $83\frac{1}{3}\%$
   (D)   100%
   (E)   500%

Arithmetic Applied problems; Percents

For this problem it is especially important to keep your focus on what is asked and to ignore extraneous details.

The cost per lamp is $\dfrac{\$30}{\text{dozen}} = \dfrac{\$30}{12}$ and the selling price per lamp is $15, so the profit per lamp is $\$\left(15 - \dfrac{30}{12}\right)$. Therefore, for each lamp the profit as a percent of the selling price is

$$\frac{15 - \dfrac{30}{12}}{15} = 1 - \frac{\overset{2}{\cancel{30}}}{(12)(\cancel{15})} = 1 - \frac{1}{6} = 83\frac{1}{3}\%.$$

The correct answer is C.

PS76302.01

47. Store N gives a 50 percent discount on the list price of all its items and Store W gives a 60 percent discount on the list price of all its items. If the list price of the same item is 20 percent higher in Store W, what percent (more or less) of the selling price in Store N is the selling price of the item in Store W?

   (A)   10% less
   (B)   4% less
   (C)   2% less
   (D)   10% more
   (E)   12% more

Arithmetic Percents

Let $\$P$ be the list price of the item in Store N. The table shows the list and selling prices of the item in the two stores. For example, the selling price of the item in Store W is 60 percent less than the item's list price of $1.2P, or (0.4) ($1.2P) = $0.48P.

	List price ($)	Selling price ($)
Store N	P	0.5P
Store W	1.2P	0.48P

The amount, in dollars, by which the selling price of the item in Store W is less than the selling price of the item in Store N is $0.5P - 0.48P = 0.02P$, which is $\frac{0.02P}{0.5P} = 4\%$ less as a percent of the selling price in Store N.

Alternatively, we can assign a specific value to P and carry out the computations using this value. In percent problems, the computations are usually simpler when 100 is used, so let $P = 100$. (If, say, $33\frac{1}{3}\%$ of P had been involved, then $P = 300$ might be a better choice.) Therefore, the list price of the item in Store N is $100, the discount price of the item in Store N is (50%)($100) = $50, the list price of the item in Store W is (120%) ($100) = $120, and the discount price of the item in Store W is (40%)($120) = $48. Thus, the question becomes the following. What percent (more or less) of 50 is 48 ? A simple computation shows that 48 is $\left(\frac{50-48}{50} \times 100\right)\% = 4\%$ less than 50.

The correct answer is B.

PS95402.01
48. A merchant purchased a jacket for $60 and then determined a selling price that equaled the purchase price of the jacket plus a markup that was 25 percent of the selling price. During a sale, the merchant discounted the selling price by 20 percent and sold the jacket. What was the merchant's gross profit on this sale?

(A) $0
(B) $3
(C) $4
(D) $12
(E) $15

Algebra Percents

The purchase price, in dollars, of the jacket was 60. If S represents the selling price, in dollars, then $S = 60 + 0.25S$, from which $S = 80$. During the sale, the discounted selling price, in dollars, was $0.8(80) = 64$, so the merchant's gross profit, in dollars, was $64 - 60 = 4$.

The correct answer is C.

> **Tip**
>
> Read carefully. Usually, markup is a percent of the purchase price, but in this problem, it is a percent of the selling price.

PS12502.01
49. When a certain stretch of highway was rebuilt and straightened, the distance along the stretch was decreased by 20 percent and the speed limit was increased by 25 percent. By what percent was the driving time along this stretch reduced for a person who always drives at the speed limit?

(A) 16%
(B) 36%
(C) $37\frac{1}{2}\%$
(D) 45%
(E) $56\frac{1}{4}\%$

Arithmetic Applied problems; Percents

Let D and r be the distance and speed limit, respectively, along the stretch of highway before it was rebuilt. Then, the distance and speed limit along the stretch of highway after it was rebuilt are given by $0.8D$ and $1.25r$. It follows that the percent reduction in time is

$$\left[\left(\frac{\frac{D}{r} - \frac{0.8D}{1.25r}}{\frac{D}{r}}\right) \times 100\right]\% = \left[\left(1 - \frac{0.8}{1.25}\right) \times 100\right]\% = 36\%.$$

Alternatively, it helps to use actual numbers when calculating percent change, with 100 being the most mathematically convenient number to use. For this problem, set the speed limit at 100 miles per hour and the distance at 100 miles.

A 20 percent decrease in distance makes the new distance 80 miles. A 25 percent increase in speed limit makes the new speed limit 125 miles per hour, which, of course, is unrealistic, but very convenient to work with. Then, the new time

$\dfrac{\text{distance}}{\text{rate}}$ is $\dfrac{80}{125}$ hours. The percent change in time

is $\left[\left(1 - \dfrac{0.8}{1.25}\right) \times 100\right]\% = 36\%$.

The correct answer is B.

Answer Explanations Quantitative Reasoning

Problem Solving

Value/Order/Factors

PS56441.01

50.

Components	Number of components:		
	Monday	Tuesday	Wednesday
A	3	6	3
B	6	3	4
C	4	7	4

A factory assembles Product X from three components, A, B, and C. One of each component is needed for each Product X and all three components must be available when assembly of each Product X starts. It takes two days to assemble one Product X. Assembly of each Product X starts at the beginning of one day and is finished at the end of the next day. The factory can work on at most five Product Xs at once. If components are available each day as shown in the table above, what is the largest number of Product Xs that can be assembled during the three days covered by the table?

(A) 3
(B) 5
(C) 6
(D) 9
(E) 10

Arithmetic Applied problems

We will determine the largest number of Product Xs that can be assembled during all three days by considering separately the largest number that can be assembled if 0, 1, 2, or 3 Product Xs begin assembly on Monday.

0 Product Xs begin assembly on Monday: In this case, at most three Product Xs can begin assembly on Tuesday (because only three units of Component A are available on Wednesday), and hence at most $0 + 3 = $ **3 Product Xs** could be assembled during the three days.

1 Product X begins assembly on Monday: In this case, at most three Product Xs can begin assembly on Tuesday (because only three units of Component A are available on Wednesday), and hence at most $1 + 3 = $ **4 Product Xs** could be assembled during the three days.

2 Product Xs begin assembly on Monday: In this case, at most three Product Xs can begin

assembly on Tuesday (because only three units of Component A are available on Wednesday), and hence at most $2 + 3 = $ **5 Product Xs** could be assembled during the three days.

3 Product Xs begin assembly on Monday: In this case, at most two Product Xs can begin assembly on Tuesday (because the factory can work on at most five Product Xs at once), and hence at most $3 + 2 = $ **5 Product Xs** could be assembled during the three days.

Therefore, the largest number of Product Xs that can be assembled during the three days is 5.

The correct answer is B.

PS04851.01

51. How many positive integers n have the property that both $3n$ and $\frac{n}{3}$ are 4-digit integers?

(A) 111
(B) 112
(C) 333
(D) 334
(E) 1,134

Arithmetic Inequalities

If n is an integer, then $3n$ is always an integer. Also, $3n$ will be a 4-digit integer only when $1,000 \le 3n \le 9,999$. Therefore, n is an integer such that $333\frac{1}{3} \le n \le 3,333$. Equivalently, n is an integer such that $334 \le n \le 3,333$.

If n is an integer, then $\frac{n}{3}$ is an integer only when n is a multiple of 3. Also, $\frac{n}{3}$ will be a 4-digit integer only when $1,000 \le \frac{n}{3} \le 9,999$, or $3,000 \le n \le 29,997$. Therefore, n is a multiple of 3 such that $3,000 \le n \le 29,997$.

It follows that the values of n consist of all multiples of 3 between $3,000 = 3(1,000)$ and $3,333 = 3(1,111)$, inclusive. The number of such multiples of 3 is $(1,111 - 1,000) + 1 = 112$.

> **Tip**
>
> Be alert to possible easily overlooked constraints that may exist in a problem. For example, in applying the second requirement above, it is not sufficient to only consider integer values of n such that $1,000 \leq \dfrac{n}{3} \leq 9,999$. In addition, $\dfrac{n}{3}$ must also be an integer, and by applying this constraint it follows that the values of n must be multiples of 3.

The correct answer is B.

PS24851.01

52. If Whitney wrote the decimal representations for the first 300 positive integer multiples of 5 and did not write any other numbers, how many times would she have written the digit 5?

    (A)   150

    (B)   185

    (C)   186

    (D)   200

    (E)   201

Arithmetic Properties of integers

The number of times the digit 5 would be written is the number of times the digit 5 will appear in the units place plus the number of times the digit 5 will appear in the tens place plus the number of times the digit 5 will appear in the hundreds place.

Number of times the digit 5 will appear in the units place: This will be the number of terms in the sequence 5, 15, 25, 35, …, 1485, 1495. Adding 5 to each member of this sequence does not change the number of terms, and doing this gives the sequence 10, 20, 30, 40, …, 1490, 1500, which clearly has 150 terms (dividing the terms by 10 gives 1, 2, 3, 4, …, 149, 150). Thus, the digit 5 appears **150 times** in the units place.

Number of times the digit 5 will appear in the tens place: This will be the number of terms in the sequence 50, 55, 150, 155, 250, 255, …, 1450, 1455. The digit 5 appears in the tens place twice for each consecutive change in the hundreds digit. Thus, the digit 5 appears $2(15) = $ **30 times** in the tens place.

Number of times the digit 5 will appear in the hundreds place: This will be the number of terms in the sequence 500, 505, 510, 515, …, 590, 595, 1500. Thus, the digit 5 appears $20 + 1 = $ **21 times** in the hundreds place.

Therefore, the number of times the digit 5 would be written is $150 + 30 + 21 = 201$.

> **Tip**
>
> The method used above to count the number of terms in the sequence 5, 15, 25, 35, …, 1,485, 1,495 can be applied to any arithmetic sequence, and it avoids the necessity of remembering certain formulas. For example, to determine the number of terms in the sequence 13, 19, 25, 31, 37, 43, …, 301, we first observe that consecutive differences are equal to 6, so we subtract from each term a number chosen so that the first term becomes $(1)(6) = 6$. Thus, we subtract 7 from each term and obtain the sequence 6, 12, 18, 24, 30, 36, …, 294, which has the same number of terms as the original sequence. The number of terms in this new sequence is now easy to find—divide each term of this new sequence by 6, and it will be clear that the number of terms is 49.

Alternatively, in the 2-digit multiples of 5, namely the multiples of 5 in the interval 5–95, there are twelve occurrences of the digit 5. The same number of occurrences of the digit 5 appear in the multiples of 5 in each of the intervals 100–195, 200–295, 300–395, and 400–495. For the multiples of 5 in the interval 500–595, there are the same corresponding twelve occurrences of the digit 5 plus twenty more for the digit in hundreds place for each of the twenty multiples of 5 in 500–595, for a total of thirty-two occurrences of the digit 5. For the multiples of 5 in each of the intervals 600–695, 700–795, 800–895, 900–995, 1,000–1,095, 1,100–1,195, 1,200–1,295, 1,300–1,395, and 1,400–1,495, there are twelve occurrences of the digit 5. Finally, there is one occurrence of the digit 5 in 1,500. Therefore, the total number of occurrences of the digit 5 in the first 300 multiples of 5 is $14(12) + 32 + 1 = 201$.

The correct answer is E.

PS01661.01

53. The difference $942 - 249$ is a positive multiple of 7. If a, b, and c are nonzero digits, how many 3-digit

numbers *abc* are possible such that the difference *abc* − *cba* is a positive multiple of 7?

(A) 142

(B) 71

(C) 99

(D) 20

(E) 18

Arithmetic Place value

Since *abc* is numerically equal to $100a + 10b + c$ and *cba* is numerically equal to $100c + 10b + a$, it follows that *abc* − *cba* is numerically equal to $(100 − 1)a + (10 − 10)b + (1 − 100)c = 99(a − c)$. Because 7 and 99 are relatively prime, $99(a − c)$ will be divisible by 7 if and only if $a − c$ is divisible by 7. This leads to two choices for the nonzero digits *a* and *c*, namely $a = 9, c = 2$ and $a = 8, c = 1$. For each of these two choices for *a* and *c*, *b* can be any one of the nine nonzero digits. Therefore, there is a total of $2(9) = 18$ possible 3-digit numbers *abc*.

The correct answer is E.

PS41661.01

54. Let *S* be the set of all positive integers having at most 4 digits and such that each of the digits is 0 or 1. What is the greatest prime factor of the sum of all the numbers in *S*?

(A) 11

(B) 19

(C) 37

(D) 59

(E) 101

Arithmetic Properties of integers

By writing down all the positive integers in *S*, their sum can be found.

1	10	11	100	101
110	111	1,000	1,001	1,010
1,011	1,100	1,101	1,110	1,111

The sum of these integers is 8,888. Since this sum is $8 × 1,111 = 2^3 × 11 × 101$ (note that $1,111 = (11 × 100) + 11$), it follows that 101 is the largest prime factor of the sum.

Alternatively, we can simplify the description by letting the integers having fewer than four digits be represented by four-digit strings in which one or more of the initial digits is 0. For example, the two-digit number 10 can be written as $0010 = (0 × 10^3) + (0 × 10^2) + (1 × 10^1) + (0 × 10^0)$. Also, we can include $0 = 0000$, since the inclusion of 0 will not affect the sum. With these changes, it follows from the Multiplication Principle that there are $2^4 = 16$ integers to be added. Moreover, for each digit position (units place, tens place, etc.) exactly half of the integers will have a digit of 1 in that digit position. Therefore, the sum of the 16 integers will be $(8 × 10^3) + (8 × 10^2) + (8 × 10^1) + (8 × 10^0)$, or 8,888. Note that this alternative method of finding the sum is much quicker than the other method if "at most four digits" had been "at most seven digits." In the case of "at most seven digits," there will be $2^7 = 128$ integers altogether, and for each digit position, half of the integers will have a digit of 1 in that digit position and the other half will have a digit of 0 in that digit position. Thus, the sum will be $(64 × 10^6) + (64 × 10^5) + … + (64 × 10^0) = 71,111,104$. Incidentally, finding the greatest prime factor of 71,111,104 is not appropriate for a GMAT problem, but in this case a different question about the sum could have been asked.

The correct answer is E.

PS43661.01

55.

Age	Tax only	Tax and fees	Fees only
18–39	20	30	30
≥40	10	60	100

The table above shows the number of residents in each of two age groups who support the use of each type of funding for a city initiative. What is the probability that a person randomly selected from among the 250 residents polled is younger than 40, or supports a type of funding that includes a tax, or both?

(A) $\dfrac{1}{5}$

(B) $\dfrac{8}{25}$

(C) $\dfrac{12}{25}$

(D) $\dfrac{3}{5}$

(E) $\dfrac{4}{5}$

Arithmetic Probability

The requested probability is the number of residents described divided by the total number (250) of residents. The number of residents described is equal to the number of residents of age 18–39 (20 + 30 + 30 = 80) PLUS the number of residents of age ≥ 40 who support tax only (10) PLUS the number of residents of age ≥ 40 who support tax and fees (60). Therefore, the requested probability is $\dfrac{80 + 10 + 60}{250} = \dfrac{3}{5}$.

Alternatively, the requested probability is 1 minus the number of residents NOT described (100) divided by 250, or $1 - \dfrac{100}{250} = \dfrac{3}{5}$.

The correct answer is D.

PS55471.01

56. Which of the following describes the set of all possible values of the positive integer k such that, for each positive odd integer n, the value of $\dfrac{n}{k}$ is midway between consecutive integers?

(A) All positive integers greater than 2

(B) All prime numbers

(C) All positive even integers

(D) All even prime numbers

(E) All positive even multiples of 5

Arithmetic Properties of integers

The logical complexities involved in this question are lessened by testing individual values of k.

Does k *= 1 satisfy the condition?* NO. If $n = 1$, then $\dfrac{n}{k} = \dfrac{1}{1} = 1$ is not midway between consecutive integers.

Does k *= 2 satisfy the condition?* YES. For each positive odd integer n, the value of $\dfrac{n}{k} = \dfrac{n}{2}$ is an odd integer divided by 2, and hence is midway between consecutive integers.

Does k *= 3 satisfy the condition?* NO. If $n = 1$, then $\dfrac{n}{k} = \dfrac{1}{3}$ is not midway between consecutive integers.

It is easy to see that no other positive integer satisfies the condition, by considering the value of $\dfrac{n}{k}$ when $n = 1$. Therefore, 2 is the only positive integer value of k that satisfies the condition.

The correct answer is D.

PS92981.01

57. A certain online form requires a 2-digit code for the day of the month to be entered into one of its fields, such as 04 for the 4th day of the month. The code is *valid* if it is 01, 02, 03, …, 31 and *not valid* otherwise. The *transpose* of a code *xy* is *yx*. For example, 40 is the transpose of 04. If *N* is the number of valid codes having a transpose that is not valid, what is the value of *N*?

(A) 12

(B) 13

(C) 18

(D) 19

(E) 20

Arithmetic Operations with integers

It will be quicker to count the number of valid codes whose transposes are valid codes, and then subtract the result from 31 (the number of valid codes) to obtain the value of N.

Three such codes begin with 0: 01, 02, 03. The rest are such that their transposes are invalid codes.

Four such codes begin with 1: 10, 11, 12, 13. The rest are such that their transposes are invalid codes.

Three such codes begin with 2: 20, 21, 22. The rest are such that their transposes are invalid codes.

Two such codes begin with 3: 30, 31. The rest are invalid codes.

Therefore, the total number of valid codes whose transposes are valid codes is 3 + 4 + 3 + 2 = 12, and hence the total number of valid codes whose transposes are not valid is 31 − 12 = 19.

The correct answer is D.

PS25302.01

58. If $x < y < z$ and $y - x > 5$, where x is an even integer and y and z are odd integers, what is the least possible value of $z - x$?

(A)   6
(B)   7
(C)   8
(D)   9
(E)   10

Algebra Inequalities

Since $y - x > 5$, it follows that y must be one of the integers

$x + 6, x + 7, x + 8, x + 9, \ldots$

Also, because x is even and y is odd, y cannot be an even integer added to x, and thus y must be one of the integers

$x + 7, x + 9, x + 11, x + 13, \ldots$

Since $z > y$ and both y and z are odd integers, it follows that z must be one of the integers

$y + 2, y + 4, y + 6, y + 8, \ldots$

Therefore, the least possible value of $z - x$ occurs when y is 7 greater than x and z is 2 greater than y, which implies that z is $7 + 2 = 9$ greater than x.

The correct answer is D.

PS36302.01

59. An "Armstrong number" is an n-digit number that is equal to the sum of the nth powers of its individual digits. For example, 153 is an Armstrong number because it has 3 digits and $1^3 + 5^3 + 3^3 = 153$. What is the digit k in the Armstrong number $1,6k4$?

(A)   2
(B)   3
(C)   4
(D)   5
(E)   6

Arithmetic Operations with integers

If $k = 1$, then $1,6k4 = 1,614$ and $1^4 + 6^4 + 1^4 + 4^4$ is equal to $1 + 1,296 + 1 + 256 = 1,554 \neq 1,614$.

Therefore, $k = 1$ does not produce an Armstrong number.

If $k = 2$, then $1,6k4 = 1,624$ and $1^4 + 6^4 + 2^4 + 4^4$ is equal to $1 + 1,296 + 16 + 256 = 1,569 \neq 1,624$. Therefore, $k = 2$ does not produce an Armstrong number.

If $k = 3$, then $1,6k4 = 1,634$ and $1^4 + 6^4 + 3^4 + 4^4$ is equal to $1 + 1,296 + 81 + 256 = 1,634$. Therefore, $k = 3$ produces an Armstrong number.

Alternatively, the condition that $1,6k4$ is an Armstrong number can be expressed by the equation $1^4 + 6^4 + k^4 + 4^4 = 1,000 + 600 + 10k + 4$, or $1,553 + k^4 = 1,604 + 10k$. This can be rewritten as $k(k^3 - 10) = 51$. Therefore, k must be a factor of 51, and 3 is the only answer choice that is a factor of 51.

The correct answer is B.

PS30402.01

60. Five integers between 10 and 99, inclusive, are to be formed by using each of the ten digits exactly once in such a way that the sum of the five integers is as small as possible. What is the greatest possible integer that could be among these five numbers?

(A)   98
(B)   91
(C)   59
(D)   50
(E)   37

Arithmetic Place value

Note that 0 cannot be the tens digit of an integer between 10 and 99, inclusive. In order for the sum of the five integers to be as small as possible, their tens digits should be the five smallest remaining digits (that is, 1, 2, 3, 4, and 5), leaving the digits 0, 6, 7, 8, and 9 to be used as the ones digits. Let $a, b, c, d,$ and e represent distinct digits chosen from the digits 0, 6, 7, 8, and 9. The sum of the five integers formed in this way is as small as possible and equals $(10 + a) + (20 + b) + (30 + c) + (40 + d) + (50 + e) = 150 + (a + b + c + d + e) = 150 + 30 = 180$ regardless of how the digits 0, 6, 7, 8, and 9 are assigned to a, b, c, d, and e. By assigning 9 to e, it follows that one of the integers could be 59. Therefore, 59 is the greatest possible integer among the five integers whose sum is 180.

The correct answer is C.

PS66402.01

61. When the integer n is divided by 17, the quotient is x and the remainder is 5. When n is divided by 23, the quotient is y and the remainder is 14. Which of the following is true?

(A) $23x + 17y = 19$

(B) $17x - 23y = 9$

(C) $17x + 23y = 19$

(D) $14x + 5y = 6$

(E) $5x - 14y = -6$

Algebra Remainders; Simplifying algebraic expressions

It is given that $n = 17x + 5$ and $n = 23y + 14$. It follows that $17x + 5 = 23y + 14$, so $17x - 23y = 9$.

The correct answer is B.

PS17402.01

62. Of the following, which is greatest?

(A) $3\sqrt{2}$

(B) $2\sqrt{3}$

(C) $\dfrac{4\sqrt{3}}{5}$

(D) $\dfrac{5\sqrt{2}}{4}$

(E) $\dfrac{7}{\sqrt{3}}$

Arithmetic Operations with radical expressions

Probably the easiest way to determine which of the given radical expressions is greatest is to compare their squares, which are $18, 12, \dfrac{48}{25}$, $\dfrac{50}{16}$, and $\dfrac{49}{3}$. Clearly, 18 is the greatest of the squares, so $3\sqrt{2}$ is the greatest of the given radical expressions.

The correct answer is A.

PS37402.01

63. If $n = p^2$ and p is a prime number greater than 5, what is the units digit of n^2?

(A) 1

(B) 3

(C) 4

(D) 7

(E) 9

Arithmetic Properties of integers

First, all prime numbers greater than 5 are odd numbers with units digit 1, 3, 7, or 9. Note that no prime number greater than 5 has units digit 5. The following table summarizes the results for the possible cases.

Units digit of p	Units digit of $p^2 = n$	Units digit of $p^4 = n^2$
1	1	1
3	9	1
7	9	1
9	1	1

The correct answer is A.

PS83502.01

64. A computer can perform 1,000,000 calculations per second. At this rate, how many *hours* will it take this computer to perform the 3.6×10^{11} calculations required to solve a certain problem?

(A) 60

(B) 100

(C) 600

(D) 1,000

(E) 6,000

Arithmetic Measurement conversion

It will take this computer $\dfrac{3.6 \times 10^{11}}{10^6} = 3.6 \times 10^5$ seconds to perform the calculations. Since there are 3,600 seconds in 1 hour, this is equivalent to $\dfrac{3.6 \times 10^5}{3.6 \times 10^3} = 100$ hours.

The correct answer is B.

PS66602.01

65. In an auditorium, 360 chairs are to be set up in a rectangular arrangement with x rows of exactly y chairs each. If the only other restriction is that $10 < x < 25$, how many different rectangular arrangements are possible?

(A) Four
(B) Five
(C) Six
(D) Eight
(E) Nine

Arithmetic Properties of integers

Because a total of 360 chairs are distributed in x rows of exactly y chairs each, it follows that $xy = 360$. Also, $10 < x < 25$, and so x can only be an integer factor of $360 = 2^3 \times 3^2 \times 5$ that is between 10 and 25. Below is a list of all integers from 11 through 24. Since 2, 3, and 5 are the only prime factors of 360, any integer having a prime factor other than 2, 3, or 5 cannot be a factor of 360 and has been crossed out. For example, $21 = 3 \times 7$ has a prime factor of 7, and thus 21 has been crossed out.

~~11~~, 12, ~~13~~, ~~14~~, 15, 16, ~~17~~, 18, ~~19~~, 20, ~~21~~, ~~22~~, ~~23~~, 24

Of the six integers remaining, it is clear that each is a factor of $360 = 2^3 \times 3^2 \times 5$ except for $16 = 2^4$. Therefore, the number of possible rectangular arrangements is five.

The correct answer is B.

PS28602.01

66. If the product of the integers w, x, y, and z is 770, and if $1 < w < x < y < z$, what is the value of $w + z$?

(A) 10
(B) 13
(C) 16
(D) 18
(E) 21

Arithmetic Properties of integers

The prime factorization of 770 is $2 \times 5 \times 7 \times 11$, so $w = 2$, $z = 11$, and $w + z = 13$.

The correct answer is B.

PS78602.01

67.   1,234
         1,243
         1,324
          ....
          ....
       + 4,321

The addition problem above shows four of the 24 different integers that can be formed by using each of the digits 1, 2, 3, and 4 exactly once in each integer. What is the sum of these 24 integers?

(A) 24,000
(B) 26,664
(C) 40,440
(D) 60,000
(E) 66,660

Arithmetic Place value

Each digit 1, 2, 3, and 4 will appear six times in each of 1,000s place, 100s place, 10s place, and units place. Since $1 + 2 + 3 + 4 = 10$, it follows that the sum of the 24 integers is $(6)(10)(1,000) + (6)(10)(100) + (6)(10)(10) + (6)(10)(1) = 66,660$.

The correct answer is E.

Answer Explanations Quantitative Reasoning

Data Sufficiency

Counting/Sets/Series

DS19350.01

68. A country's per capita national debt is its national debt divided by its population. Is the per capita national debt of Country G within $5 of $500?

(1) Country G's national debt to the nearest $1,000,000,000 is $43,000,000,000.

(2) Country G's population to the nearest 1,000,000 is 86,000,000.

(A) Statement (1) ALONE is sufficient, but statement (2) alone is not sufficient.

(B) Statement (2) ALONE is sufficient, but statement (1) alone is not sufficient.

(C) BOTH statements TOGETHER are sufficient, but NEITHER statement ALONE is sufficient.

(D) EACH statement ALONE is sufficient.

(E) Statements (1) and (2) TOGETHER are NOT sufficient.

Arithmetic Estimation

Briefly, the question is whether

$$495 \le \frac{debt}{population} \le 505 \text{ is true.}$$

(1) We are given that 42.5 billion $\le$ debt < 43.5 billion. However, no information is given about the population; NOT sufficient.

(2) We are given that 85.5 million $\le$ population < 86.5 million. However, no information is given about the debt; NOT sufficient.

Given (1) and (2), then to determine whether $\frac{debt}{population}$ lies between 495 and 505, we will investigate the minimum possible value of $\frac{debt}{population}$ and the maximum possible value of $\frac{debt}{population}$. To simplify the discussion that follows, we will assume that the upper bounds given in (1) and (2) can be achieved. This will not affect our conclusions because with this assumption, the estimates we obtain will still justify our conclusions. The minimum possible value of $\frac{debt}{population}$ is

$$\frac{minimum\ debt}{maximum\ population} = \frac{42.5\ billion}{86.5\ million} = \frac{42.5}{86.5} \times 1,000.$$

Since $\frac{42.5}{86.5} = \frac{43.25}{86.5} - \frac{0.75}{86.5} = \frac{1}{2} - \frac{0.75}{86.5}$, which is less than $\frac{1}{2} - \frac{0.4325}{86.5} = \frac{1}{2} - \frac{1}{200}$, it follows that the minimum possible value of $\frac{debt}{population}$ is **less than** $\left(\frac{1}{2} - \frac{1}{200}\right) \times 1,000 = 500 - 5 = 495$.

The maximum possible value of $\frac{debt}{population}$ is

$$\frac{maximum\ debt}{minimum\ population} = \frac{43.5\ billion}{85.5\ million} = \frac{43.5}{85.5} \times 1,000.$$

Since $\frac{43.5}{85.5} = \frac{42.75}{85.5} + \frac{0.75}{85.5} = \frac{1}{2} + \frac{0.75}{86.5}$, which is greater than $\frac{1}{2} + \frac{0.4275}{85.5} = \frac{1}{2} + \frac{1}{200}$, it follows that the maximum possible value of $\frac{debt}{population}$ is **greater than** $\left(\frac{1}{2} + \frac{1}{200}\right) \times 1,000 = 500 + 5 = 505$.

Since the minimum possible value of $\frac{debt}{population}$ is less than 495 and the maximum possible value of $\frac{debt}{population}$ is greater than 505, it is not possible to determine whether or not $\frac{debt}{population}$ lies between 495 and 505.

The correct answer is E; both statements together are still not sufficient.

DS06351.01

69. The *cardinality* of a finite set is the number of elements in the set. What is the cardinality of set A?

(1) 2 is the cardinality of exactly 6 subsets of set A.

(2) Set A has a total of 16 subsets, including the empty set and set A itself.

(A) Statement (1) ALONE is sufficient, but statement (2) alone is not sufficient.

(B) Statement (2) ALONE is sufficient, but statement (1) alone is not sufficient.

(C) BOTH statements TOGETHER are sufficient, but NEITHER statement ALONE is sufficient.

(D) EACH statement ALONE is sufficient.

(E) Statements (1) and (2) TOGETHER are NOT sufficient.

Arithmetic Concepts of sets

Let n be the cardinality of the finite set A. What is the value of n?

(1) The number of 2-element subsets of A is equal to the number of unordered selections without replacement of 2 objects from a collection of n distinct objects, or "n choose 2." Therefore, we have $\binom{n}{2} = \dfrac{n(n-1)}{2} = 6$, or equivalently, $n^2 - n - 12 = 0$. Because this is a quadratic equation that may have two solutions, we need to investigate further to determine whether there is a unique value of n. Factoring leads to $(n-4)(n+3) = 0$, and thus $n = 4$ or $n = -3$. Since n must be a nonnegative integer, we discard the solution $n = -3$. Therefore, $n = 4$; SUFFICIENT.

(2) The number of subsets of set A is 2^n, because each subset of A corresponds to a unique sequence of answers to yes-no questions about membership in the subset (one question for each of the n elements). For example, let $A = \{1, 2, 3, 4, 5\}$, let Y represent "yes," and let N represent "no." Then the sequence NYNNN corresponds to the subset $\{2\}$, since the answers to "is 1 in the subset," "is 2 in the subset," "is 3 in the subset," etc. are "no," "yes," "no," etc. Also, the subset $\{1, 3, 4\}$ of A corresponds to the 5-letter sequence YNYYN. Since the number of 5-letter sequences such that each letter is either N or Y is 2^5, it follows that there are $2^5 = 32$ subsets of $\{1, 2, 3, 4, 5\}$. For Statement (2), we are given that $2^n = 16$, and hence $n = 4$; SUFFICIENT.

Alternatively, observe that $\{1\}$ has two subsets, $\{1, 2\}$ has four subsets, and each addition of a new element doubles the number of subsets, because the subsets after adding the new element will consist of all the previous subsets along with the new element included in each of the previous subsets. Thus, $\{1, 2, 3\}$ has $2(4) = 8$ subsets, $\{1, 2, 3, 4\}$ has $2(8) = 16$ subsets, $\{1, 2, 3, 4, 5\}$ has $2(16) = 32$ subsets, etc.

**The correct answer is D;
each statement alone is sufficient.**

DS59851.01

70. For each positive integer k, let $a_k = \left(1 + \dfrac{1}{k+1}\right)$. Is the product $a_1 a_2 \ldots a_n$ an integer?

(1) $n + 1$ is a multiple of 3.

(2) n is a multiple of 2.

(A) Statement (1) ALONE is sufficient, but statement (2) alone is not sufficient.

(B) Statement (2) ALONE is sufficient, but statement (1) alone is not sufficient.

(C) BOTH statements TOGETHER are sufficient, but NEITHER statement ALONE is sufficient.

(D) EACH statement ALONE is sufficient.

(E) Statements (1) and (2) TOGETHER are NOT sufficient.

Algebra Series and sequences

Since $1 + \dfrac{1}{k+1} = \dfrac{k+2}{k+1}$, it follows that the product can be written as

$$\left(\frac{\cancel{3}}{2}\right)\left(\frac{4}{\cancel{3}}\right)\left(\frac{\cancel{5}}{4}\right)\left(\frac{\cancel{6}}{\cancel{5}}\right)\cdots\left(\frac{\cancel{n}}{n-1}\right)\left(\frac{n+1}{\cancel{n}}\right)\left(\frac{n+2}{\cancel{n+1}}\right) =$$

$\dfrac{n+2}{2}$. Therefore, the product $a_1 a_2 \ldots a_n$ is an integer if and only if $\dfrac{n+2}{2}$ is an integer, or if and only if n is an even integer.

(1) If $n = 2$, then $n + 1 = 3$ is a multiple of 3 and the product is $\dfrac{n+2}{2} = \dfrac{2+2}{2}$, which is an integer. However, if $n = 5$, then

$n + 1 = 6$ is a multiple of 3 and the product is $\dfrac{n+2}{2} = \dfrac{5+2}{2}$, which is not an integer; NOT sufficient.

(2) If n is a multiple of 2, then by the remarks above it follows that the product is an integer; SUFFICIENT.

**The correct answer is B;
statement 2 alone is sufficient.**

DS95491.01

71. Let S be a set of outcomes and let A and B be events with outcomes in S. Let $\sim B$ denote the set of all outcomes in S that are not in B and let $P(A)$ denote the probability that event A occurs. What is the value of $P(A)$?

(1) $P(A \cup B) = 0.7$

(2) $P(A \cup \sim B) = 0.9$

(A)   Statement (1) ALONE is sufficient, but statement (2) alone is not sufficient.

(B)   Statement (2) ALONE is sufficient, but statement (1) alone is not sufficient.

(C)   BOTH statements TOGETHER are sufficient, but NEITHER statement ALONE is sufficient.

(D)   EACH statement ALONE is sufficient.

(E)   Statements (1) and (2) TOGETHER are NOT sufficient.

Arithmetic Probability; Sets

The general addition rule for sets applied to probability gives the basic probability equation

$$P(A \cup B) = P(A) + P(B) - P(A \cap B).$$

(1)   Given that $P(A \cup B) = 0.7$, it is not possible to determine the value of $P(A)$ because nothing is known about the relation of event A to event B. For example, if every outcome in event B is an outcome in event A, then $A \cup B = A$ and we have $P(A \cup B) = P(A) = 0.7$. However, if events A and B are mutually exclusive (i.e., $P(A \cap B) = 0$) and $P(B) = 0.2$, then the basic probability equation above becomes $0.7 = P(A) + 0.2 - 0$, and we have $P(A) = 0.5$; NOT sufficient.

(2)   Given that $P(A \cup \sim B) = 0.9$, it is not possible to determine the value of $P(A)$ because nothing is known about the relation of event A to event $\sim B$. For example, as indicated in the first figure below, if every outcome in event $\sim B$ is an outcome in event A, then $A \cup \sim B = A$ and we have $P(A \cup \sim B) = P(A) = 0.9$. However, as

indicated in the second figure below, if events A and $\sim B$ are mutually exclusive (i.e., $P(A \cap \sim B) = 0$) and $P(\sim B) = 0.2$, then the basic probability equation above, with $\sim B$ in place of B, becomes $0.9 = P(A) + 0.2 - 0$, and we have $P(A) = 0.7$; NOT sufficient.

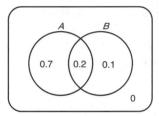 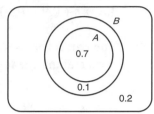

Given (1) and (2), if we can express event A as a union or intersection of events $A \cup B$ and $A \cup \sim B$, then the basic probability equation above can be used to determine the value of $P(A)$. The figure below shows Venn diagram representations of events $A \cup B$ and $A \cup \sim B$ by the shading of appropriate regions.

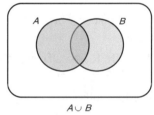 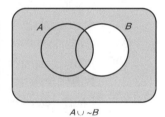

$A \cup B$ $A \cup \sim B$

Inspection of the figure shows that the only portion shaded in both Venn diagrams is the region representing event A. Thus, A is equal to the intersection of $A \cup B$ and $A \cup \sim B$, and hence we can apply the basic probability equation with event $A \cup B$ in place of event A and event $A \cup \sim B$ in place of event B. That is, we can apply the equation

$$P(C \cup D) = P(C) + P(D) - P(C \cap D)$$

with $C = A \cup B$ and $D = A \cup \sim B$. We first note that $P(C) = 0.7$ from (1), $P(D) = 0.9$ from (2), and $P(C \cap D) = P(A)$. As for $P(C \cup D)$, inspection of the figure above shows that $C \cup D$ encompasses all possible outcomes, and thus $P(C \cup D) = 1$. Therefore, the equation above involving events C and D becomes $1 = 0.7 + 0.9 - P(A)$, and hence $P(A) = 0.6$.

The correct answer is C;
both statements together are sufficient.

DS41402.01

72. What is the number of integers that are common to both set S and set T?

(1) The number of integers in S is 7, and the number of integers in T is 6.

(2) U is the set of integers that are in S only or in T only or in both, and the number of integers in U is 10.

(A) Statement (1) ALONE is sufficient, but statement (2) alone is not sufficient.

(B) Statement (2) ALONE is sufficient, but statement (1) alone is not sufficient.

(C) BOTH statements TOGETHER are sufficient, but NEITHER statement ALONE is sufficient.

(D) EACH statement ALONE is sufficient.

(E) Statements (1) and (2) TOGETHER are NOT sufficient.

Arithmetic Sets

In standard notation, $S \cap T$ and $S \cup T$ represent the intersection and union, respectively, of sets S and T, and $|S|$ represents the number of elements in a set S. Determine $|S \cap T|$.

(1) It is given that $|S| = 7$ and $|T| = 6$. If, for example, $S = \{1, 2, 3, 4, 5, 6, 7\}$ and $T = \{1, 2, 3, 4, 5, 6\}$, then $|S \cap T| = 6$. However, if $S = \{1, 2, 3, 4, 5, 6, 7,\}$ and $T = \{11, 12, 13, 14, 15, 16\}$, then $|S \cap T| = 0$; NOT sufficient.

(2) It is given that $|S \cup T| = 10$. If, for example, $S = \{1, 2, 3, 4, 5, 6, 7\}$ and $T = \{1, 2, 3, 8, 9, 10\}$, then $S \cup T = \{1, 2, 3, 4, 5, 6, 7, 8, 9, 10\}$, $|S \cup T| = 10$, and $|S \cap T| = 3$. However, if $S = \{1, 2, 3, 4, 5, 6, 7\}$ and

$T = \{11, 12, 13\}$, then $S \cup T = \{1, 2, 3, 4, 5, 6, 7, 11, 12, 13\}$, $|S \cup T| = 10$, and $|S \cap T| = 0$; NOT sufficient.

Taking (1) and (2) together along with the general addition rule for two sets A and B ($|A \cup B| = |A| + |B| - |A \cap B|$) applied to sets S and T gives $10 = 7 + 6 - |S \cap T|$, from which $|S \cap T|$ can be determined.

The correct answer is C;
both statements together are sufficient.

DS51402.01

73. What is the sum of 3 consecutive integers?

(1) The sum of the 3 integers is less than the greatest of the 3 integers.

(2) Of the 3 integers, the ratio of the least to the greatest is 3.

(A) Statement (1) ALONE is sufficient, but statement (2) alone is not sufficient.

(B) Statement (2) ALONE is sufficient, but statement (1) alone is not sufficient.

(C) BOTH statements TOGETHER are sufficient, but NEITHER statement ALONE is sufficient.

(D) EACH statement ALONE is sufficient.

(E) Statements (1) and (2) TOGETHER are NOT sufficient.

Algebra Sequences

Let k be the smallest of the three consecutive integers. It follows that $k + 1$ and $k + 2$ are the other two integers and $S = k + (k + 1) + (k + 2) = 3k + 3$, where S is the sum of the three consecutive integers. Determine S.

(1) It is given that $3k + 3 < k + 2$. It follows that $k < -\dfrac{1}{2}$. If $k = -1$, then $S = 0$. However, if $k = -2$, then $S = -3$; NOT sufficient.

(2) It is given that $\dfrac{k}{k + 2} = 3$. It follows that $k = -3$ and S can be determined;

SUFFICIENT.

The correct answer is B;
statement 2 alone is sufficient.

DS54402.01

74. How many people in Town *X* read neither the *World* newspaper nor the *Globe* newspaper?

(1) Of the 2,500 people in Town *X*, 1,000 read no newspaper.

(2) Of the people in Town *X*, 700 read the *Globe* only and 600 read the *World* only.

(A) Statement (1) ALONE is sufficient, but statement (2) alone is not sufficient.

(B) Statement (2) ALONE is sufficient, but statement (1) alone is not sufficient.

(C) BOTH statements TOGETHER are sufficient, but NEITHER statement ALONE is sufficient.

(D) EACH statement ALONE is sufficient.

(E) Statements (1) and (2) TOGETHER are NOT sufficient.

Arithmetic Sets

Determine the number of people in Town *X* who read neither the *World* newspaper nor the *Globe* newspaper.

(1) It is given that 1,000 of the 2,500 people in Town *X* read no newspaper, from which it follows that 1,500 people read at least one newspaper. It is possible that all of these 1,500 people read only the *Earth*, another newspaper that is read in Town *X*, so the number of people who read neither the *World* nor the *Globe* could be 2,500. It is also possible that all of the 1,500 people who read at least one newspaper read the *World*, so the number of people who read neither the *World* nor the *Globe* could be 1,000; NOT sufficient.

(2) It is given that 600 people read only the *World* and 700 people read only the *Globe*, but there is no information about the number of people in Town *X* and no information about other newspapers that might be read by the people in Town *X*; NOT sufficient.

Neither (1) nor (2) gives information as to whether other newspapers are read by people in Town *X*, and without this information, the number of people who read neither the *World* nor the *Globe* cannot be determined.

The correct answer is E;
both statements together are still not sufficient.

Tip

Just because the *World* and the *Globe* are the only newspapers mentioned, do not assume that they are the only newspapers read in Town *X*.

DS16402.01

75. Bowls *X* and *Y* each contained exactly 2 jelly beans, each of which was either red or black. One of the jelly beans in bowl *X* was exchanged with one of the jelly beans in bowl *Y*. After the exchange, were both of the jelly beans in bowl *X* black?

(1) Before the exchange, bowl *X* contained 2 black jelly beans.

(2) After the exchange, bowl *Y* contained 1 jelly bean of each color.

(A) Statement (1) ALONE is sufficient, but statement (2) alone is not sufficient.

(B) Statement (2) ALONE is sufficient, but statement (1) alone is not sufficient.

(C) BOTH statements TOGETHER are sufficient, but NEITHER statement ALONE is sufficient.

(D) EACH statement ALONE is sufficient.

(E) Statements (1) and (2) TOGETHER are NOT sufficient.

Arithmetic Sets

Determine after an exchange of one jelly bean if both jelly beans in bowl *X* are black.

(1) Bowl *X* has two black jelly beans, but bowl *Y* could have two red or two black or one of each color. If bowl *Y* has two red jelly beans, then bowl *X* will have one red and one black jelly bean after the exchange, not two black. However, if bowl *Y* has two black jelly beans, then bowl *X* will have two black after the exchange; NOT sufficient.

(2) After the exchange, bowl *Y* has one red and one black. If, before the exchange, bowl *X* had two black and bowl *Y* had two red, then after the exchange, each of bowl *Y* and bowl *X* will have one of each color. However, if bowl *Y* had two black jelly beans, bowl *X* had one of each color, and bowl *X* obtained a black in exchange for the red, then bowl *Y* will have one of each color and bowl *X* will have two black; NOT sufficient.

Taking (1) and (2) together, bowl X had two black jelly beans to start with and bowl Y ended up with one of each color after the exchange. bowl Y had to have had at least one red because bowl X had no red jelly beans to give to bowl Y. If bowl Y has two red and exchanges a red for one of bowl X's blacks, then, after the exchange, bowl Y will have one of each color, but bowl X will not have two black. On the other hand, if bowl Y has one of each color and exchanges its black for one of bowl X's blacks, then after the exchange, bowl Y will have one of each color and bowl X will have two blacks.

The correct answer is E; both statements together are still not sufficient.

DS27602.01

76. All trainees in a certain aviator training program must take both a written test and a flight test. If 70 percent of the trainees passed the written test, and 80 percent of the trainees passed the flight test, what percent of the trainees passed both tests?

(1) 10 percent of the trainees did not pass either test.

(2) 20 percent of the trainees passed only the flight test.

(A) Statement (1) ALONE is sufficient, but statement (2) alone is not sufficient.

(B) Statement (2) ALONE is sufficient, but statement (1) alone is not sufficient.

(C) BOTH statements TOGETHER are sufficient, but NEITHER statement ALONE is sufficient.

(D) EACH statement ALONE is sufficient.

(E) Statements (1) and (2) TOGETHER are NOT sufficient.

Algebra Sets

Let x be the percent of the trainees who passed both tests. The following Venn diagram represents the information that is given as well as information that can be derived from what is given. Note that $x - 50$ in the diagram can be found by using the requirement that the sum of the four values in the diagram is 100. What is the value of x?

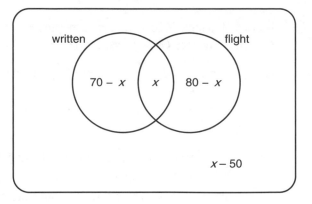

(1) Given that $x - 50 = 10$, it follows that $x = 60$; SUFFICIENT.

(2) Given that $80 - x = 20$, it follows that $x = 60$; SUFFICIENT.

Tip

A useful way to summarize the quantitative relations for a two-circle Venn diagram is

Total = $A + B$ − Both + Neither,

where A is the number of elements in Circle A, B is the number of elements in Circle B, "Both" is the number of elements in the intersection of the circles, and "Neither" is the number of elements that do not belong to either of the circles. If we think of A and B as the numbers of elements in the two 1-way intersections (i.e., Circle A alone and Circle B alone) and "Both" as the number of elements in the single 2-way intersection (i.e., Circle A intersects Circle B), then this equation can be written as

Total = (sum of 1-way) − (sum of 2-way) + None.

This second way of expressing the quantitative relations for a two-circle Venn diagram can be modified to give a similar way of expressing the quantitative relations for a three-circle Venn diagram:

Total = (sum of 1-way) − (sum of 2-way) + (sum of 3-way) + None.

Although Venn diagrams involving more than three circles will not likely be needed for the GMAT, we recommend researching the *inclusion-exclusion principle* if the reader is interested in further extensions of these ideas.

The correct answer is D; each statement alone is sufficient.

Answer Explanations Quantitative Reasoning

Data Sufficiency

Equalities/Inequalities/Algebra

DS06110.01

77. Each of the five divisions of a certain company sent representatives to a conference. If the numbers of representatives sent by four of the divisions were 3, 4, 5, and 5, was the range of the numbers of representatives sent by the five divisions greater than 2?

(1) The median of the numbers of representatives sent by the five divisions was greater than the average (arithmetic mean) of these numbers.

(2) The median of the numbers of representatives sent by the five divisions was 4.

(A) Statement (1) ALONE is sufficient, but statement (2) alone is not sufficient.

(B) Statement (2) ALONE is sufficient, but statement (1) alone is not sufficient.

(C) BOTH statements TOGETHER are sufficient, but NEITHER statement ALONE is sufficient.

(D) EACH statement ALONE is sufficient.

(E) Statements (1) and (2) TOGETHER are NOT sufficient.

Algebra Statistics

Let x be the unspecified number of representatives. By considering individual positive integer values of x, the median of the numbers is found to be 4 when $x = 1, 2, 3,$ or 4, and the median of the numbers is found to be 5 when $x \geq 5$. For example, the case in which $x = 2$ is shown below.

$$2, 3, \mathbf{4}, 5, 5$$

(1) In terms of x, the average of the numbers is $\dfrac{x + 3 + 4 + 5 + 5}{5} = \dfrac{x + 17}{5}$. If $x = 1$, then by the remarks above the median is 4, which is greater than $\dfrac{1 + 17}{5}$ (i.e., the median is greater than the average), and the range is $5 - 1 = 4$. If $x = 5$, then by the remarks above the median is 5, which is greater than $\dfrac{5 + 17}{5}$ (i.e., the median is greater than the average), and the range is $5 - 3 = 2$; NOT sufficient.

(2) Given the assumption that the median of the numbers is 4, it follows from the previous remarks that x can be any one of the numbers 1, 2, 3, and 4. If $x = 1$, then the range is $5 - 1 = 4$, which is greater than 2. If $x = 4$, then the range is $5 - 3 = 2$, which is not greater than 2; NOT sufficient.

Given (1) and (2), then from the previous remarks and (2) it follows that x must be among the numbers 1, 2, 3, and 4. From (2) it follows that $4 > \dfrac{x + 17}{5}$, or $x < 3$, and thus x is further restricted to be among the numbers 1 and 2. However, for each of these possibilities the range is greater than 2: If $x = 1$, then the range is $5 - 1 = 4 > 2$; and if $x = 2$, then the range is $5 - 2 = 3 > 2$.

The correct answer is C; both statements together are sufficient.

DS24931.01

78. An investment has been growing at a fixed annual rate of 20% since it was first made; no portion of the investment has been withdrawn, and all interest has been reinvested. How much is the investment now worth?

(1) The value of the investment has increased by 44% since it was first made.

(2) If one year ago $600 had been withdrawn, today the investment would be worth 12% less than it is actually now worth.

(A) Statement (1) ALONE is sufficient, but statement (2) alone is not sufficient.

(B) Statement (2) ALONE is sufficient, but statement (1) alone is not sufficient.

(C) BOTH statements TOGETHER are sufficient, but NEITHER statement ALONE is sufficient.

(D) EACH statement ALONE is sufficient.

(E) Statements (1) and (2) TOGETHER are NOT sufficient.

Algebra Applied problems

If the investment was initially worth P, then after one year the investment was worth $1.2P$, after two years the investment was worth $1.2(\$1.2P) = \$1.44P$, after three years the investment was worth $1.2(\$1.44P) = \$1.728P$, etc.

(1) Given that the investment was worth $\$(P + 0.44P) = \$1.44P$, it follows from the remarks above that the investment was first made two years ago. However, nothing is known about the value of P; NOT sufficient.

(2) Let $\$X$ be how much the investment was worth one year ago. Then the investment is now worth $\$1.2X$. However, if $600 had been withdrawn from the investment one year ago, then the investment would have been worth $\$(X - 600)$ one year ago and the investment would have been worth $\$1.2(X - 600) = \$(1.2X - 720)$ today. It is given that this amount, namely $\$(1.2X - 720)$, is 12 percent less than $\$1.2X$. Therefore, $1.2X - 720 = (0.88)(1.2X)$. This equation can be solved for X, and using this value of X, the value of $1.2X$ can be determined; SUFFICIENT.

The correct answer is B; statement 2 alone is sufficient.

DS53841.01

79. *X*, 81, 73, 71, 98, 73, 64

What is the value of *X* in the above list of 7 numbers?

(1) The average (arithmetic mean) of these 7 numbers is 80.

(2) The range of these 7 numbers is 36.

(A) Statement (1) ALONE is sufficient, but statement (2) alone is not sufficient.

(B) Statement (2) ALONE is sufficient, but statement (1) alone is not sufficient.

(C) BOTH statements TOGETHER are sufficient, but NEITHER statement ALONE is sufficient.

(D) EACH statement ALONE is sufficient.

(E) Statements (1) and (2) TOGETHER are NOT sufficient.

Arithmetic Statistics

(1) Since the average of the seven numbers is 80, it follows that the sum of the

seven numbers is $7(80) = 560$. Therefore, $X + 81 + 73 + 71 + 98 + 73 + 64 = 560$, which can be solved for a unique value of X; SUFFICIENT.

(2) The range of the numbers when X is not included is $98 - 64 = 34$. Therefore, if $X = 98 + 2 = 100$, then the range of the seven numbers is $100 - 64 = 36$, and if $X = 64 - 2 = 62$, then the range of the seven numbers is $98 - 62 = 36$. Therefore, more than one value of X satisfies the given information and statement 2; NOT sufficient.

The correct answer is A; statement 1 alone is sufficient.

DS01451.01

80. In the first 2 hours after Meadow's self-service laundry opens, *m* large washing machines and *n* small washing machines are in continual use. Including the time for filling and emptying the washing machines, each load of laundry takes 30 minutes in a large washing machine and 20 minutes in a small washing machine. What is the total number of loads of laundry done at Meadow's self-service laundry during this 2-hour period?

(1) $n = 3m$

(2) $2m + 3n = 55$

(A) Statement (1) ALONE is sufficient, but statement (2) alone is not sufficient.

(B) Statement (2) ALONE is sufficient, but statement (1) alone is not sufficient.

(C) BOTH statements TOGETHER are sufficient, but NEITHER statement ALONE is sufficient.

(D) EACH statement ALONE is sufficient.

(E) Statements (1) and (2) TOGETHER are NOT sufficient.

Algebra Simultaneous equations

During the two-hour period each large washer does four loads (the number of 30-minute periods in two hours is four) and each small washer does six loads (the number of 20-minute periods in two hours is six). Therefore, the total number of loads done during the two-hour period by *m* large washers and *n* small washers is $4m + 6n$.

(1) If $m = 1$ and $n - 3$, then $n = 3m$ and the total number of loads of laundry done in

the two-hour period is $4(1) + 6(3) = 22$. However, if $m = 2$ and $n = 6$, then $n = 3m$ and the total number of loads of laundry done in the two-hour period is $4(2) + 6(6) = 44$; NOT sufficient.

(2) Since $2m + 3n = 55$, it follows that $4m + 6n = 110$. Therefore, by the remarks above, the total number of loads done during the two-hour period is 110; SUFFICIENT.

The correct answer is B; statement 2 alone is sufficient.

DS76851.01
81. A box of light bulbs contains exactly 3 light bulbs that are defective. What is the probability that a sample of light bulbs picked at random from this box will contain at least 1 defective light bulb?

(1) The light bulbs in the sample will be picked 1 at a time without replacement.

(2) The sample will contain exactly 20 light bulbs.

(A) Statement (1) ALONE is sufficient, but statement (2) alone is not sufficient.

(B) Statement (2) ALONE is sufficient, but statement (1) alone is not sufficient.

(C) BOTH statements TOGETHER are sufficient, but NEITHER statement ALONE is sufficient.

(D) EACH statement ALONE is sufficient.

(E) Statements (1) and (2) TOGETHER are NOT sufficient.

Arithmetic Statistics

It is clear that neither (1) alone nor (2) alone is sufficient.

Given (1) and (2), if the box contains 22 light bulbs, then a sample of 20 light bulbs must contain at least one defective light bulb, and hence the desired probability is equal to 1. However, if the box contains 22,000 light bulbs, then it is clear that the probability that a sample of 20 light bulbs contains at least one defective light bulb is less than 1.

The correct answer is E; both statements together are still not sufficient.

DS01951.01
82. Khalil drove 120 kilometers in a certain amount of time. What was his average speed, in kilometers per hour, during this time?

(1) If Khalil had driven at an average speed that was 5 kilometers per hour faster, his driving time would have been reduced by 20 minutes.

(2) If Khalil had driven at an average speed that was 25% faster, his driving time would have been reduced by 20%.

(A) Statement (1) ALONE is sufficient, but statement (2) alone is not sufficient.

(B) Statement (2) ALONE is sufficient, but statement (1) alone is not sufficient.

(C) BOTH statements TOGETHER are sufficient, but NEITHER statement ALONE is sufficient.

(D) EACH statement ALONE is sufficient.

(E) Statements (1) and (2) TOGETHER are NOT sufficient.

Algebra Applied problems

Let r be Khalil's average speed in kilometers per hour and let t be Khalil's time in hours. Then $rt = 120$, or $t = \dfrac{120}{r}$. What is the value of r?

(1) If Khalil's speed had been $(r + 5)$ kilometers per hour, then his driving time would have been $\left(t - \dfrac{1}{3} \right)$ hours.

$$(r + 5)\left(t - \frac{1}{3} \right) = 120 \quad \text{Statement (1)}$$

$$(r + 5)\left(\frac{120}{r} - \frac{1}{3} \right) = 120 \quad \text{substitute } t = \frac{120}{r}$$

$$(r + 5)(360 - r) = 360r \quad \begin{array}{l}\text{multiply both}\\\text{sides by } 3r\end{array}$$

$$360r - r^2 + 1{,}800 - 5r = 360r \quad \text{expand left side}$$

$$-r^2 + 1{,}800 - 5r = 0 \quad \begin{array}{l}\text{subtract } 360r\\\text{from both sides}\end{array}$$

$$-(r + 45)(r - 40) = 0 \quad \text{factor the left side}$$

Although there are two possible values for r, namely $r = -45$ and $r = 40$, only the positive value of r is consistent with the context. Therefore, $r = 40$; SUFFICIENT.

(2) If Khalil's speed had been $1.25r$ kilometers per hour, then his driving time would have been $0.8t$ hours. It follows that $(1.25r)(0.8t) = 120$, or $rt = 120$, which provides no additional information to the given information; NOT sufficient.

The correct answer is A;
statement 1 alone is sufficient.

DS70061.01

83. What is the median of the data set S that consists of the integers 17, 29, 10, 26, 15, and x ?

(1) The average (arithmetic mean) of S is 17.

(2) The range of S is 24.

(A) Statement (1) ALONE is sufficient, but statement (2) alone is not sufficient.

(B) Statement (2) ALONE is sufficient, but statement (1) alone is not sufficient.

(C) BOTH statements TOGETHER are sufficient, but NEITHER statement ALONE is sufficient.

(D) EACH statement ALONE is sufficient.

(E) Statements (1) and (2) TOGETHER are NOT sufficient.

Arithmetic Statistics

(1) Since the average of the six numbers is 17, it follows that the sum of the six numbers is 6(17). Therefore, $17 + 29 + 10 + 26 + 15 + x = 6(17)$, which can be solved for a unique value of x, after which the median can be determined; SUFFICIENT.

(2) The range of the numbers when x is not included is $29 - 10 = 19$. Therefore, if $x = 29 + 5 = 34$, then the range of the seven numbers (10, 15, 17, 26, 29, 34) is

$34 - 10 = 24$ and the median of the seven numbers is $\dfrac{17 + 26}{2} = 21.5$.

However, if $x = 10 - 5 = 5$, then the range of the seven numbers (5, 10, 15, 17, 26, 29) is $29 - 5 = 24$ and the median of the seven numbers is $\dfrac{15 + 17}{2} = 16$; NOT sufficient.

The correct answer is A;
statement 1 alone is sufficient.

DS47661.01

84. If $n > 4$, what is the value of the integer n?

(1) $\dfrac{n!}{(n - 3)!} = \dfrac{3!n!}{4!(n - 4)!}$

(2) $\dfrac{n!}{3!(n - 3)!} + \dfrac{n!}{4!(n - 4)!} = \dfrac{(n + 1)!}{4!(n - 3)!}$

(A) Statement (1) ALONE is sufficient, but statement (2) alone is not sufficient.

(B) Statement (2) ALONE is sufficient, but statement (1) alone is not sufficient.

(C) BOTH statements TOGETHER are sufficient, but NEITHER statement ALONE is sufficient.

(D) EACH statement ALONE is sufficient.

(E) Statements (1) and (2) TOGETHER are NOT sufficient.

Algebra Simplifying algebraic expressions

(1) Because the numerators of the two fractions have several common factors, and similarly for the denominators, a reasonable strategy is to begin by appropriately canceling these common factors.

$\dfrac{n!}{(n - 3)!} = \dfrac{3!n!}{4!(n - 4)!}$	given
$\dfrac{1}{(n - 3)!} = \dfrac{3!}{4!(n - 4)!}$	divide both sides by $n!$
$\dfrac{1}{(n - 3)!} = \dfrac{1}{4(n - 4)!}$	$4! = 3! \times 4$
$4(n - 4)! = (n - 3)!$	cross-multiply
$4(n - 4)! = (n - 4)! \times (n - 3)$	
$4 = n - 3$	divide both sides by $(n - 4)!$
$n = 7$	

The manipulations above show that $n = 7$.

Alternatively, we could begin by reducing each of the fractions to lowest terms by using identities such as $n! = (n - 3)! \times (n - 2)(n - 1)(n)$, and then performing operations on the resulting equation; SUFFICIENT.

(2) For the same reason given in (1) above, we begin by canceling factors that are common on the left and right sides of the equality.

$$\frac{n!}{3!(n-3)!} + \frac{n!}{4!(n-4)!} = \frac{(n+1)!}{4!(n-3)!} \quad \text{given}$$

$$\frac{1}{3!(n-3)!} + \frac{1}{4!(n-4)!} = \frac{n+1}{4!(n-3)!} \quad \begin{array}{l}\text{divide both sides} \\ \text{by } n!\end{array}$$

$$\frac{4}{(n-3)!} + \frac{1}{(n-4)!} = \frac{n+1}{(n-3)!} \quad \begin{array}{l}\text{multiply both} \\ \text{sides by } 4! = \\ 3! \times 4\end{array}$$

$$4 + (n-3) = n+1 \quad \begin{array}{l}\text{multiply both} \\ \text{sides by } (n-3)! = \\ (n-4)! \times (n-3)\end{array}$$

The manipulations above show that the original equation is identically true for all integers greater than 4, and thus n can be any integer greater than 4.

Alternatively, we could begin by reducing each of the fractions to lowest terms by using identities such as $n! = (n-3)! \times (n-2)(n-1)(n)$, and then performing operations on the resulting equation; NOT sufficient.

**The correct answer is A;
statement 1 alone is sufficient.**

DS50571.01

85. Tami purchased several identically priced metal frames and several identically priced wooden frames for a total pretax price of $144. What was the total pretax price of the metal frames that Tami purchased?

(1) The price of each metal frame was 60% greater than the price of each wooden frame.

(2) Tami purchased twice as many wooden frames as metal frames.

(A) Statement (1) ALONE is sufficient, but statement (2) alone is not sufficient.

(B) Statement (2) ALONE is sufficient, but statement (1) alone is not sufficient.

(C) BOTH statements TOGETHER are sufficient, but NEITHER statement ALONE is sufficient.

(D) EACH statement ALONE is sufficient.

(E) Statements (1) and (2) TOGETHER are NOT sufficient.

Algebra Simultaneous equations

Let m and w, respectively, be the number of metal frames and wooden frames that Tami purchased, and let M and W, respectively, be their individual prices in dollars. We are given that $mM + wW = 144$. What is the value of mM?

(1) Given that $M = 1.6W = \frac{8}{5}W$, or $W = \frac{5}{8}M$,

we have $mM + w\left(\frac{5}{8}M\right) = 144$. Although it might seem there is not enough information to determine the value of mM, keep in mind that we are only seeking the value of the product mM, and not the individual values of m and M. Also, there are several implicit constraints involved, such as each of M and W must be a positive number less than 144 and each of m and w must be a positive integer. To see that more than one value of mM is possible, it will be convenient to specify a particular value for w, for example, $w = 16$. Then $mM + w\left(\frac{5}{8}M\right) = 144$

becomes $mM = 144 - 10M$, and non-sufficiency is now straightforward. If $w = 16$ and $M = 4$, then $mM = 104$. However, if $w = 16$ and $M = 8$, then $mM = 64$; NOT sufficient.

(2) Given that $w = 2m$, we have $mM + (2m)W = 144$, or $mM = 144 - 2mW$. If $m = 10$ and $W = 4$, then $mM = 64$. However, if $m = 10$ and $W = 5$, then $mM = 44$; NOT sufficient.

Given (1) and (2), we have $W = \frac{5}{8}M$ and $w = 2m$. Therefore, $mM + wW = 144$ becomes

$mM + (2m)\left(\frac{5}{8}M\right) = 144$, or $\left(1 + \frac{5}{4}\right)mM = 144$,

and hence the value of mM can be determined.

**The correct answer is C;
both statements together are sufficient.**

DS02871.01

86. A $10 bill (1,000 cents) was replaced with 50 coins having the same total value. The only coins used were 5-cent coins, 10-cent coins, 25-cent coins, and 50-cent coins. How many 5-cent coins were used?

(1) Exactly 10 of the coins were 25-cent coins and exactly 10 of the coins were 50-cent coins.

(2) The number of 10-cent coins was twice the number of 5-cent coins.

(A) Statement (1) ALONE is sufficient, but statement (2) alone is not sufficient.

(B) Statement (2) ALONE is sufficient, but statement (1) alone is not sufficient.

(C) BOTH statements TOGETHER are sufficient, but NEITHER statement ALONE is sufficient.

(D) EACH statement ALONE is sufficient.

(E) Statements (1) and (2) TOGETHER are NOT sufficient.

Algebra Simultaneous equations

Let a, b, c, and d be the number, respectively, of 5-cent, 10-cent, 25-cent, and 50-cent coins. We are given that $a + b + c + d = 50$ and $5a + 10b + 25c + 50d = 1,000$, or $a + 2b + 5c + 10d = 200$. Determine the value of a.

$$a + b + c + d = 50$$

$$a + 2b + 5c + 10d = 200$$

> **Tip**
>
> Note that each of a, b, c, and d must be a nonnegative integer, and so care must be taken in deducing non-sufficiency. For example, there are many real number pairs (x,y) that satisfy the equation $2x + y = 1$, but if each of x and y must be a nonnegative integer, then $x = 0$ and $y = 1$ is the only solution.

(1) We are given that $c = 10$ and $d = 10$. Substituting $c = 10$ and $d = 10$ into the two equations displayed above and combining terms gives $a + b = 30$ and $a + 2b = 50$. Subtracting these last two equations gives $b = 20$, and hence it follows that $a = 10$; SUFFICIENT.

(2) We are given that $b = 2a$. Substituting $b = 2a$ into the two equations displayed above and combining terms gives $a + 2a + c + d = 50$ and $a + 4a + 5c + 10d = 200$, which are equivalent to the following two equations.

$$3a + c + d = 50$$

$$a + c + 2d = 40$$

Subtracting these two equations gives $2a - d = 10$, or $2a = d + 10$. Since $2a$ is an even integer, d must be an even integer. At this point it is probably simplest to choose various nonnegative even integers for d to determine whether solutions for a, b, c, and d exist that have different values for a. Note that it is not enough to find different nonnegative integer solutions to $2a = d + 10$, since we must also ensure that c and d are nonnegative integers. If $d = 8$, then $2a = 8 + 10 = 18$, and we have $a = 9$, $b = 18$, $c = 15$, and $d = 8$. However, if $d = 10$, then $2a = 10 + 10 = 20$, and we have $a = 10$, $b = 20$, $c = 10$, and $d = 10$; NOT sufficient.

The correct answer is A; statement 1 alone is sufficient.

DS56971.01

87. Merle's spare change jar has exactly 16 U.S. coins, each of which is a 1-cent coin, a 5-cent coin, a 10-cent coin, a 25-cent coin, or a 50-cent coin. If the total value of the coins in the jar is 288 U.S. cents, how many 1-cent coins are in the jar?

(1) The exact numbers of 10-cent, 25-cent, and 50-cent coins among the 16 coins in the jar are, respectively, 6, 5, and 2.

(2) Among the 16 coins in the jar there are twice as many 10-cent coins as 1-cent coins.

(A) Statement (1) ALONE is sufficient, but statement (2) alone is not sufficient.

(B) Statement (2) ALONE is sufficient, but statement (1) alone is not sufficient.

(C) BOTH statements TOGETHER are sufficient, but NEITHER statement ALONE is sufficient.

(D) EACH statement ALONE is sufficient.

(E) Statements (1) and (2) TOGETHER are NOT sufficient.

Algebra Simultaneous equations

Let a, b, c, d, and e be the number, respectively, of 1-cent, 5-cent, 10-cent, 25-cent, and 50-cent coins. We are given the two equations shown below. Determine the value of a.

$$a + b + c + d + e = 16$$

$$a + 5b + 10c + 25d + 50e = 288$$

(1) We are given that $c = 6$, $d = 5$, and $e = 2$. Substituting these values into the two equations displayed above and combining terms gives $a + b = 3$ and $a + 5b = 3$. Subtracting these last two equations gives $4b = 0$, and therefore $b = 0$ and $a = 3$; SUFFICIENT.

(2) We are given that $c = 2a$. Substituting $c = 2a$ into the two equations displayed above and combining terms gives the following two equations.

$$3a + b + d + e = 16$$

$$21a + 5b + 25d + 50e = 288$$

From the first equation above we have $3a = 16 - b - d - e$. Therefore, $3a \leq 16$, and it follows that the value of a must be among 0, 1, 2, 3, 4, and 5. From the second equation above we have $5(b + 5d + 10e) = 288 - 21a$, and thus the value of $288 - 21a$ must be divisible by 5.

a	$288 - 21a$
0	288
1	267
2	246
3	**225**
4	204
5	183

The table above shows that $a = 3$ is the only nonnegative integer less than or equal to 5 such that $288 - 21a$ is divisible by 5; SUFFICIENT.

The correct answer is D; each statement alone is sufficient.

DS48391.01

88. At a certain university recreation center, a member can receive a 30-minute massage, a 60-minute massage, or a 90-minute massage, and is charged $0.50 per minute for each massage. A member receiving a massage is charged the same fixed amount for each additional service, such as nutrition advice or a fitness evaluation. At this center, what is the total charge to a member for a 60-minute massage and 3 additional services?

(1) At this recreation center, Jordan, a member, had a massage and 3 additional services for a total charge of $37.50.

(2) At this recreation center, Ryan, a member, had a massage and 2 additional services for a total charge of $60.00.

(A) Statement (1) ALONE is sufficient, but statement (2) alone is not sufficient.

(B) Statement (2) ALONE is sufficient, but statement (1) alone is not sufficient.

(C) BOTH statements TOGETHER are sufficient, but NEITHER statement ALONE is sufficient.

(D) EACH statement ALONE is sufficient.

(E) Statements (1) and (2) TOGETHER are NOT sufficient.

Algebra First-degree equations

Let x be the charge, in dollars, of each additional service. Determine the value of $(60)(0.5) + 3x$, or equivalently, determine the value of x.

(1) The table below shows the value of x for each of the three possible massages that Jordan had.

Massage	Total charge	x
30-minute	$15 + 3x = 37.50$	7.50
60-minute	$30 + 3x = 37.50$	2.50
90-minute	$45 + 3x = 37.50$	−2.50

From the table it follows that there are two possible values of x, namely $x = 7.5$ and $x = 2.5$; NOT sufficient.

(2) The table below shows the value of x for each of the three possible massages that Ryan had.

Massage	Total charge		x
30-minute	$15 + 2x = 60$		22.50
60-minute	$30 + 2x = 60$		15.00
90-minute	$45 + 2x = 60$		7.50

From the table it follows that there are three possible values of x, namely $x = 22.5$, $x = 15$, and $x = 7.5$; NOT sufficient.

Given (1) and (2), it follows that $x = 7.5$.

**The correct answer is C;
both statements together are sufficient.**

DS84302.01

89. If S is the sum of the first n positive integers, what is the value of n ?

(1) $S < 20$

(2) $S^2 > 220$

(A) Statement (1) ALONE is sufficient, but statement (2) alone is not sufficient.

(B) Statement (2) ALONE is sufficient, but statement (1) alone is not sufficient.

(C) BOTH statements TOGETHER are sufficient, but NEITHER statement ALONE is sufficient.

(D) EACH statement ALONE is sufficient.

(E) Statements (1) and (2) TOGETHER are NOT sufficient.

Arithmetic Sequences and series

(1) Given that $S < 20$, n could be 5 since
$\sum_{i=1}^{5} i = \frac{5(6)}{2} = 15 < 20$. However, n could also
be 4 since $\sum_{i=1}^{4} i = \frac{4(5)}{2} = 10 < 20$;
NOT sufficient.

(2) Given that $S^2 > 220$, n could be 5 since
$\sum_{i=1}^{5} i = \frac{5(6)}{2} = 15$ and $15^2 = 225 > 220$.
However, n could also be 6 since

$\sum_{i=1}^{6} i = \frac{6(7)}{2} = 21$ and $21^2 = 441 > 220$;
NOT sufficient.

Given (1) and (2) together, it is clear from the following table that $n = 5$.

n	S	S^2	allowed/not allowed
≤ 4	≤ 10	≤ 100	not allowed by (2)
5	15	225	allowed by (1) and (2)
≥ 6	≥ 21	≥ 441	not allowed by (1)

**The correct answer is C;
both statements together are sufficient.**

DS48302.01

90. Is $x^2 - y^2$ a positive number?

(1) $x - y$ is a positive number.

(2) $x + y$ is a positive number.

(A) Statement (1) ALONE is sufficient, but statement (2) alone is not sufficient.

(B) Statement (2) ALONE is sufficient, but statement (1) alone is not sufficient.

(C) BOTH statements TOGETHER are sufficient, but NEITHER statement ALONE is sufficient.

(D) EACH statement ALONE is sufficient.

(E) Statements (1) and (2) TOGETHER are NOT sufficient.

Algebra Factoring

Since $x^2 - y^2 = (x + y)(x - y)$, it follows that $x^2 - y^2$ will be a positive number if both $x + y$ and $x - y$ are positive numbers or if both are negative numbers.

(1) It is given that $x - y$ is a positive number. If, for example, $x = 2$ and $y = -3$, then $x - y$ is a positive number, but $x + y$ is not a positive number, so $x^2 - y^2$ is not a positive number. On the other hand, if $x = 3$ and $y = 1$, then $x - y$ is a positive number and $x + y$ is a positive number, so $x^2 - y^2$ is a positive number; NOT sufficient.

(2) It is given that $x + y$ is a positive number. If, for example, $x = -2$ and $y = 4$, then $x + y$ is

a positive number, but $x - y$ is not a positive number, so $x^2 - y^2$ is not a positive number. On the other hand, if $x = 3$ and $y = 1$, then $x + y$ is a positive number and $x - y$ is a positive number, so $x^2 - y^2$ is a positive number; NOT sufficient.

Taking (1) and (2) together, both $x + y$ and $x - y$ are positive numbers, so $x^2 - y^2$ is a positive number.

**The correct answer is C;
both statements together are sufficient.**

DS89302.01

91. Alan and Sue have each been saving one dollar a day and will continue to do so for the next month. If Sue began saving several days before Alan, in how many days from today will Alan have saved one-half as much as Sue?

(1) As of today, Alan has saved 7 dollars and Sue has saved 27 dollars.

(2) Three days from today, Alan will have saved one-third as much as Sue.

(A) Statement (1) ALONE is sufficient, but statement (2) alone is not sufficient.

(B) Statement (2) ALONE is sufficient, but statement (1) alone is not sufficient.

(C) BOTH statements TOGETHER are sufficient, but NEITHER statement ALONE is sufficient.

(D) EACH statement ALONE is sufficient.

(E) Statements (1) and (2) TOGETHER are NOT sufficient.

Algebra First-degree equations

Let A be the amount Alan has saved as of today. Let S be the amount Sue had already saved when Alan started saving. Then, as of today, Sue has saved $S + A$ dollars. Determine d, the number of days from today that Alan will have saved half as much as Sue. That is, determine d, where $A + d = \frac{1}{2}(S + A + d)$ or, after algebraic manipulation, determine d such that $d = S - A$.

(1) It is given that $A = 7$ and $S = 27$, so $d = 20$; SUFFICIENT.

(2) It is given that three days from today, Alan will have saved one-third as

much as Sue, from which it follows that $A + 3 = \frac{1}{3}(S + A + 3)$ or, after algebraic manipulation, $S = 2A + 6$. Then, $d = S - A = (2A + 6) - A = A + 6$. Since the value of A can vary, the value of d cannot be determined; NOT sufficient.

**The correct answer is A;
statement 1 alone is sufficient.**

DS64402.01

92. What is the value of x ?

(1) $x^4 + x^2 + 1 = \dfrac{1}{x^4 + x^2 + 1}$

(2) $x^3 + x^2 = 0$

(A) Statement (1) ALONE is sufficient, but statement (2) alone is not sufficient.

(B) Statement (2) ALONE is sufficient, but statement (1) alone is not sufficient.

(C) BOTH statements TOGETHER are sufficient, but NEITHER statement ALONE is sufficient.

(D) EACH statement ALONE is sufficient.

(E) Statements (1) and (2) TOGETHER are NOT sufficient.

Algebra Simplifying algebraic expressions

(1) If $x^4 + x^2 + 1 = \dfrac{1}{x^4 + x^2 + 1}$, then $x^4 + x^2 + 1$ is its own reciprocal. The only numbers that are their own reciprocals are -1 and 1. Since even powers of x are nonnegative, $x^4 + x^2 + 1 \neq -1$, so $x^4 + x^2 + 1 = 1$. It follows that $x^4 + x^2 = 0$ and $x = 0$; SUFFICIENT.

(2) If $x^3 + x^2 = 0$, then $x^2(x + 1) = 0$. It follows that $x = 0$ or $x = -1$; NOT sufficient.

**The correct answer is A;
statement 1 alone is sufficient.**

DS26402.01

93. Is x less than y ?

(1) $x - y + 1 < 0$

(2) $x - y - 1 < 0$

(A) Statement (1) ALONE is sufficient, but statement (2) alone is not sufficient.

(B)   Statement (2) ALONE is sufficient, but statement (1) alone is not sufficient.

(C)   BOTH statements TOGETHER are sufficient, but NEITHER statement ALONE is sufficient.

(D)   EACH statement ALONE is sufficient.

(E)   Statements (1) and (2) TOGETHER are NOT sufficient.

Algebra Inequalities

Determine if $x < y$ is true.

(1)   If $x - y + 1 < 0$, then $x < y - 1$. Since $y - 1 < y$, it follows that $x < y$; SUFFICIENT.

(2)   If $x = 1$ and $y = 2$, then $x - y - 1 = -2 < 1$ and $x < y$ is true. However, if $x = 1.5$ and $y = 1$, then $x - y - 1 = -0.5 < 1$ and $x < y$ is not true; NOT sufficient.

The correct answer is A;
statement 1 alone is sufficient.

> **Tip**
>
> In (1), manipulating the given inequality leads to $x < y - 1$, which leads directly to $x < y$ since $y - 1 < y$. This is not the case in (2), where manipulating the given inequality leads to $x < y + 1$ but not to $x < y$ since $y + 1 > y$. Examples can then be used to verify that $x < y$ can be, but doesn't have to be, true.

DS08402.01

94.   State X has a sales tax rate of k percent on all purchases and State Y has a sales tax rate of n percent on all purchases. What is the value of $k - n$?

(1)   The sales tax on a \$15 purchase is 30 cents more in State X than in State Y.

(2)   The sales tax rate in State X is 1.4 times the sales tax rate in State Y.

(A)   Statement (1) ALONE is sufficient, but statement (2) alone is not sufficient.

(B)   Statement (2) ALONE is sufficient, but statement (1) alone is not sufficient.

(C)   BOTH statements TOGETHER are sufficient, but NEITHER statement ALONE is sufficient.

(D)   EACH statement ALONE is sufficient.

(E)   Statements (1) and (2) TOGETHER are NOT sufficient.

Algebra Applied problems; Percents

(1)   It is given that $15\left(\dfrac{k}{100}\right) = 15\left(\dfrac{n}{100}\right) + 0.30$. It follows that $15(k - n) = 30$, from which the value of $k - n$ can be determined; SUFFICIENT.

(2)   It is given that $k = 1.4n$, from which $k - n$ cannot be determined. For example, if $n = 5$, then $k = 7$ and $k - n = 2$. However, if $n = 10$, then $k = 14$ and $k - n = 4$; NOT sufficient.

The correct answer is A;
statement 1 alone is sufficient.

DS28402.01

95.   Is $-3 \le x \le 3$?

(1) $x^2 + y^2 = 9$

(2) $x^2 + y \le 9$

(A)   Statement (1) ALONE is sufficient, but statement (2) alone is not sufficient.

(B)   Statement (2) ALONE is sufficient, but statement (1) alone is not sufficient.

(C)   BOTH statements TOGETHER are sufficient, but NEITHER statement ALONE is sufficient.

(D)   EACH statement ALONE is sufficient.

(E)   Statements (1) and (2) TOGETHER are NOT sufficient.

Algebra Properties of numbers; Inequalities

(1)   Given that $x^2 + y^2 = 9$, if $x < -3$ or if $x > 3$, then $x^2 > 9$ and $y^2 < 0$, which is not possible. Therefore, $-3 \le x \le 3$; SUFFICIENT.

(2)   Given that $x^2 + y \le 9$, if $x = 0$ and $y = 4$, then $x^2 + y \le 9$, and $-3 \le x \le 3$ is true. However, if $x = 4$ and $y = -7$, then $x^2 + y \le 9$, and $-3 \le x \le 3$ is not true; NOT sufficient.

The correct answer is A;
statement 1 alone is sufficient.

DS69402.01

96. What is the value of x?

(1) $4^{x+1} + 4^x = 320$

(2) $x^2 = 9$

(A) Statement (1) ALONE is sufficient, but statement (2) alone is not sufficient.
(B) Statement (2) ALONE is sufficient, but statement (1) alone is not sufficient.
(C) BOTH statements TOGETHER are sufficient, but NEITHER statement ALONE is sufficient.
(D) EACH statement ALONE is sufficient.
(E) Statements (1) and (2) TOGETHER are NOT sufficient.

Algebra Exponents

Determine the value of x.

(1) If $4^{x+1} + 4^x = 320$, then $4^x(4 + 1) = 320$, from which $4^x = 64$ and $x = 3$; SUFFICIENT.

(2) If $x^2 = 9$, then $x = -3$ or $x = 3$; NOT sufficient.

The correct answer is A; statement 1 alone is sufficient.

DS50502.01

97. Three dice, each with faces numbered 1 through 6, were tossed onto a game board. If one of the dice turned up 4, what was the sum of the numbers that turned up on all three dice?

(1) The sum of two of the numbers that turned up was 10.

(2) The sum of two of the numbers that turned up was 11.

(A) Statement (1) ALONE is sufficient, but statement (2) alone is not sufficient.
(B) Statement (2) ALONE is sufficient, but statement (1) alone is not sufficient.
(C) BOTH statements TOGETHER are sufficient, but NEITHER statement ALONE is sufficient.
(D) EACH statement ALONE is sufficient.
(E) Statements (1) and (2) TOGETHER are NOT sufficient.

Arithmetic Operations with integers

Determine the sum of the numbers that turned up when three dice were tossed, given that one of the dice turned up 4.

(1) Given that the sum of two of the numbers was 10, the numbers that turned up on the three dice could be 5, 4, and 5 ($5 + 5 = 10$) for a total sum of 14. On the other hand, they could be 2, 4, and 6 ($4 + 6 = 10$) for a total sum of 12; NOT sufficient.

(2) The number 4 could not have been one of the two numbers whose sum was 11 because $11 - 4 = 7$ and 7 is not a number that can turn up on the dice. Therefore, since 11 can be obtained only when the other two numbers are 5 and 6, the numbers that turned up on the three dice must be 4, 5, and 6 for a total sum of 15; SUFFICIENT.

The correct answer is B; statement 2 alone is sufficient.

DS81502.01

98. Of the numbers q, r, s, and t, which is greatest?

(1) The average (arithmetic mean) of q and r is s.

(2) The sum of q and r is t.

(A) Statement (1) ALONE is sufficient, but statement (2) alone is not sufficient.
(B) Statement (2) ALONE is sufficient, but statement (1) alone is not sufficient.
(C) BOTH statements TOGETHER are sufficient, but NEITHER statement ALONE is sufficient.
(D) EACH statement ALONE is sufficient.
(E) Statements (1) and (2) TOGETHER are NOT sufficient.

Algebra Statistics

Determine which of the numbers q, r, s, and t is the greatest.

(1) Given that $\frac{q+r}{2} = s$, then s is halfway between q and r and $q \leq s \leq r$ or $r \leq s \leq q$. So it is possible that q is the greatest,

it is possible that r is the greatest, and it is possible that t is the greatest since no information is given about t; NOT sufficient.

(2) Given that $t = q + r$, it is not possible to determine which of $q, r, s,$ and t is greatest. For example, if $q = 1, r = 5, s = 3,$ and $t = 6$, then t is the greatest, but if $q = 1, r = -5$, $s = -2,$ and $t = -4$, then q is the greatest; NOT sufficient.

Taking (1) and (2) together, it is still not possible to determine which of $q, r, s,$ and t is greatest because the examples used to show that (2) is not sufficient satisfy (1) also.

The correct answer is E; both statements together are still not sufficient.

DS94502.01

99.

CAR RENTAL CHARGES AT THRIFTY AGENCY

Car Type	Charge per day	Charge per Week (7 days)
Economy	$28	$100
Compact	$30	$120
Midsize	$32	$140
Standard	$34	$160
Luxury	$39	$200

The table above shows the car rental charges at Thrifty Agency. The daily rate applies for each day or fraction of a day in excess of any multiple of a 7-day week, up to the charge per week. If Olga rented a car of one of the types indicated, which type was it?

(1) Olga's total rental charge, based only on the rates specified, was $184.

(2) Olga rented the car for 10 days.

(A) Statement (1) ALONE is sufficient, but statement (2) alone is not sufficient.

(B) Statement (2) ALONE is sufficient, but statement (1) alone is not sufficient.

(C) BOTH statements TOGETHER are sufficient, but NEITHER statement ALONE is sufficient.

(D) EACH statement ALONE is sufficient.

(E) Statements (1) and (2) TOGETHER are NOT sufficient.

Arithmetic Interpretation of tables

Determine which type of car Olga rented.

(1) Since Olga's total rental charge was $184, determine for which type of car (economy, compact, midsize or standard) $\dfrac{184 - \text{charge per week}}{\text{charge per day}}$ is an integer. Note that Olga did not rent a luxury car because $184 < 200$ and 184 is not a multiple of 39.

Economy: $184 - 100 = 84 = 3(28)$
Compact: $184 - 120 = 64$, not a multiple of 30
Midsize: $184 - 140 = 44$, not a multiple of 32
Standard: $184 - 160 = 24$, not a multiple of 34

Olga rented an economy car; SUFFICIENT.

(2) Just knowing that Olga rented the car for 10 days is not enough information to determine which type of car she rented; NOT sufficient.

The correct answer is A; statement 1 alone is sufficient.

DS76602.01

100. Is $xy < 6$?

(1) $x < 3$ and $y < 2$.

(2) $\dfrac{1}{2} < x < \dfrac{2}{3}$ and $y^2 < 64$.

(A) Statement (1) ALONE is sufficient, but statement (2) alone is not sufficient.

(B) Statement (2) ALONE is sufficient, but statement (1) alone is not sufficient.

(C) BOTH statements TOGETHER are sufficient, but NEITHER statement ALONE is sufficient.

(D) EACH statement ALONE is sufficient.

(E) Statements (1) and (2) TOGETHER are NOT sufficient.

Algebra Inequalities

(1) Given that $x < 3$ and $y < 2$, it is not possible to determine whether or not $xy < 6$. For example, if $x = 1$ and $y = 1$, then $x < 3$, $y < 2$, and $xy = 1$. However, if $x = -3$ and

$y = -3$, then $x < 3$, $y < 2$, and $xy = 9$; NOT sufficient.

(2) Given that $y^2 < 64$, then it easily follows that $-8 < y < 8$. Thus, we have $\frac{1}{2} < x < \frac{2}{3}$ and $-8 < y < 8$. We consider two cases, according to the sign of y. *Case 1*: Suppose that $-8 < y \le 0$. Since $x > 0$ and $y \le 0$, it follows that $xy \le 0 < 6$. *Case 2*: Suppose that $0 < y < 8$. Then xy is the product of two positive quantities. Since the product of two positive quantities is greatest when each of the quantities is greatest, it follows that

$$xy < \left(\frac{2}{3}\right)(8) = \frac{16}{3} < 6.$$

Since $xy < 6$ in each case, and the two cases include all possible values of x and y, we have $xy < 6$; SUFFICIENT.

The correct answer is B; statement 2 alone is sufficient.

DS86602.01
101. What is the value of $\frac{x}{yz}$?

(1) $x = \frac{y}{2}$ and $z = \frac{2x}{5}$.

(2) $\frac{x}{z} = \frac{5}{2}$ and $\frac{1}{y} = \frac{1}{10}$.

(A) Statement (1) ALONE is sufficient, but statement (2) alone is not sufficient.

(B) Statement (2) ALONE is sufficient, but statement (1) alone is not sufficient.

(C) BOTH statements TOGETHER are sufficient, but NEITHER statement ALONE is sufficient.

(D) EACH statement ALONE is sufficient.

(E) Statements (1) and (2) TOGETHER are NOT sufficient.

Algebra Simplifying algebraic expressions

(1) Given that $x = \frac{y}{2}$ and $z = \frac{2x}{5}$, it follows that $\frac{x}{yz} = \frac{x}{(2x)\left(\frac{2x}{5}\right)} = \frac{5}{4x}$, which will have different values for different nonzero values of x; NOT sufficient.

(2) Given that $\frac{x}{z} = \frac{5}{2}$ and $\frac{1}{y} = \frac{1}{10}$, it follows that $\frac{x}{yz} = \frac{\frac{5z}{2}}{10z} = \frac{1}{4}$; SUFFICIENT.

The correct answer is B; statement 2 alone is sufficient.

DS47602.01
102. In a certain group of people, the average (arithmetic mean) weight of the males is 180 pounds and of the females, 120 pounds. What is the average weight of the people in the group?

(1) The group contains twice as many females as males.

(2) The group contains 10 more females than males.

(A) Statement (1) ALONE is sufficient, but statement (2) alone is not sufficient.

(B) Statement (2) ALONE is sufficient, but statement (1) alone is not sufficient.

(C) BOTH statements TOGETHER are sufficient, but NEITHER statement ALONE is sufficient.

(D) EACH statement ALONE is sufficient.

(E) Statements (1) and (2) TOGETHER are NOT sufficient.

Algebra Applied problems; Statistics

Let M and F, respectively, be the number of males and females in the group. Also, let $\sum M$ and $\sum F$, respectively, be the total weight, in pounds, of the males and females in the group. We are given that $\frac{\sum M}{M} = 180$ and $\frac{\sum F}{F} = 120$. What is the value of $\frac{\sum M + \sum F}{M + F}$?

(1) Given that $F = 2M$ (equivalently, $M = \frac{1}{2}F$), it follows that

$$\frac{\sum M + \sum F}{M + F} = \frac{\sum M}{M + F} + \frac{\sum F}{M + F} =$$

$$\frac{\sum M}{M + 2M} + \frac{\sum F}{\frac{1}{2}F + F} =$$

$$\frac{1}{3}\left(\frac{\sum M}{M}\right)+\frac{2}{3}\left(\frac{\sum F}{F}\right)=\frac{1}{3}(180)+\frac{2}{3}(120);$$

SUFFICIENT.

(2) We are given that $F = M + 10$. If $M = 2$ and $F = 12$, then there are six times as many females as males, and hence the average weight of the people in the group will be strongly skewed toward the average weight of the females. However, if $M = 100{,}000$ and $F = 100{,}010$, then the ratio of females to males is close to 1, and hence the average weight of the people in the group will be close to the average of 120 and 180.

> ### Tip
>
> In data sufficiency problems it is often helpful to consider contrasting extreme scenarios when they exist. If a variable can be any positive real number, then consider the scenario when the variable is very close to 0 and the scenario when the variable is very large. If a quadrilateral can be any rectangle, then consider the scenario when the rectangle is a square and the scenario when the rectangle is very long with a small width.

Alternatively,

$$\frac{\sum M+\sum F}{M+F}=\frac{180M+120(M+10)}{M+(M+10)}=\frac{150M+600}{M+5},$$

and by long division (takes one step), this can be written as $150 - \dfrac{150}{M+5}$, which can clearly vary when the value of M varies; NOT sufficient.

The correct answer is A; statement 1 alone is sufficient.

DS57602.01

103. If $y = 2^{x+1}$, what is the value of $y - x$?

(1) $2^{2x+2} = 64$

(2) $y = 2^{2x-1}$

(A) Statement (1) ALONE is sufficient, but statement (2) alone is not sufficient.

(B) Statement (2) ALONE is sufficient, but statement (1) alone is not sufficient.

(C) BOTH statements TOGETHER are sufficient, but NEITHER statement ALONE is sufficient.

(D) EACH statement ALONE is sufficient.

(E) Statements (1) and (2) TOGETHER are NOT sufficient.

Algebra Equations; Exponents

1. Given that $2^{2x+2} = 64 = 2^6$, it follows that $2x + 2 = 6$. Therefore, $x = 2$ and $y - x = 2^{2+1} - 2 = 6$; SUFFICIENT.

2. From the given information we have $y = 2^{x+1}$ and from (2) we have $y = 2^{2x-1}$. Therefore, $2^{x+1} = 2^{2x-1}$, and hence $x + 1 = 2x - 1$. Solving for x gives $x = 2$, and thus $y - x = 2^{2+1} - 2 = 6$; SUFFICIENT.

The correct answer is D; each statement alone is sufficient.

DS67602.01

104. If $x \neq 1$, is y equal to $x + 1$?

(1) $\dfrac{y-2}{x-1} = 1$

(2) $y^2 = (x + 1)^2$

(A) Statement (1) ALONE is sufficient, but statement (2) alone is not sufficient.

(B) Statement (2) ALONE is sufficient, but statement (1) alone is not sufficient.

(C) BOTH statements TOGETHER are sufficient, but NEITHER statement ALONE is sufficient.

(D) EACH statement ALONE is sufficient.

(E) Statements (1) and (2) TOGETHER are NOT sufficient.

Algebra Simplifying algebraic expressions

Determine if $y = x + 1$.

(1) Given $\dfrac{y-2}{x-1} = 1$, then $y - 2 = x - 1$ and $y = x + 1$; SUFFICIENT.

(2) Given $y^2 = (x + 1)^2$, then $y = x + 1$ or $y = -(x + 1)$; NOT sufficient.

The correct answer is A; statement 1 alone is sufficient.

DS18602.01

105. If $x + y + z > 0$, is $z > 1$?

(1) $z > x + y + 1$

(2) $x + y + 1 < 0$

(A)   Statement (1) ALONE is sufficient, but statement (2) alone is not sufficient.

(B)   Statement (2) ALONE is sufficient, but statement (1) alone is not sufficient.

(C)   BOTH statements TOGETHER are sufficient, but NEITHER statement ALONE is sufficient.

(D)   EACH statement ALONE is sufficient.

(E)   Statements (1) and (2) TOGETHER are NOT sufficient.

Algebra Inequalities

Determine if $z > 1$ is true.

(1)   Given that $z > x + y + 1$, by adding z to both sides, it follows that $2z > x + y + z + 1$. Also, $x + y + z + 1 > 1$ because $x + y + z > 0$. Thus, $2z > 1$ and $z > \dfrac{1}{2}$. It is possible that $z > 1$ is true and it is possible that $z > 1$ is not true. For example, if $z = 1.1$ and $x = y = 0$, then $x + y + z > 0$ and $z > x + y + 1$ are both true, and $z > 1$ is true. However, if $z = 1$, $x = -0.5$ and $y = -0.25$, $x + y + z > 0$ and $z > x + y + 1$ are both true, and $z > 1$ is not true; NOT sufficient.

(2)   Given that $x + y + 1 < 0$, it follows that $1 < -x - y$. It is also given that $x + y + z > 0$, so $z > -x - y$ or $-x - y < z$. Combining $1 < -x - y$ and $-x - y < z$ gives $1 < z$ or $z > 1$; SUFFICIENT.

**The correct answer is B;
statement 2 alone is sufficient.**

Answer Explanations Quantitative Reasoning

Data Sufficiency

Geometry

DS35210.01

106. In the rectangular coordinate system, line *k* passes through the point (*n*,–1). Is the slope of line *k* greater than zero?

(1)   Line *k* passes through the origin.

(2)   Line *k* passes through the point (1,*n* + 2).

(A)   Statement (1) ALONE is sufficient, but statement (2) alone is not sufficient.

(B)   Statement (2) ALONE is sufficient, but statement (1) alone is not sufficient.

(C)   BOTH statements TOGETHER are sufficient, but NEITHER statement ALONE is sufficient.

(D)   EACH statement ALONE is sufficient.

(E)   Statements (1) and (2) TOGETHER are NOT sufficient.

Geometry Simple coordinate geometry

(1)   The slope of a line through (*n*,–1) and (0,0) is $-\dfrac{1}{n}$, which is greater than zero if *n* < 0 and less than zero if *n* > 0; NOT sufficient.

(2)   Given that line *k* passes through the points (*n*,–1) and (1,*n* + 2), then the slope of line *k* (when it exists) is equal to $\dfrac{(n+2)-(-1)}{1-n} = \dfrac{n+3}{1-n}$. If *n* = 0, then the slope of line *k* is 3, which is positive. However, if *n* = 2, then the slope of line *k* is –5, which is negative; NOT sufficient.

Given (1) and (2), it follows that $-\dfrac{1}{n} = \dfrac{n+3}{1-n}$, which by cross-multiplying is equivalent to (–1)(1 − *n*) = *n*(*n* + 3) when *n* is not equal to 0 or 1. This is a quadratic equation that can be rewritten as $n^2 + 2n + 1 = 0$, or $(n+1)^2 = 0$. Therefore, *n* = –1 and the slope of line *k* is $-\dfrac{1}{n} = 1$, which is greater than zero.

The correct answer is C;
both statements together are sufficient.

DS88111.01

107. In quadrilateral *ABCD*, is angle *BCD* a right angle?

(1)   Angle *ABC* is a right angle.

(2)   Angle *ADC* is a right angle.

(A)   Statement (1) ALONE is sufficient, but statement (2) alone is not sufficient.

(B)   Statement (2) ALONE is sufficient, but statement (1) alone is not sufficient.

(C)   BOTH statements TOGETHER are sufficient, but NEITHER statement ALONE is sufficient.

(D)   EACH statement ALONE is sufficient.

(E)   Statements (1) and (2) TOGETHER are NOT sufficient.

Geometry Quadrilaterals

(1)   The figure below shows two possibilities for a quadrilateral *ABCD* such that angle *ABC* is a right angle. One quadrilateral is such that angle *BCD* is not a right angle (i.e., the answer to the question can be NO), and the other quadrilateral is a square (i.e., the answer to the question can be YES); NOT sufficient.

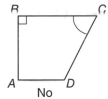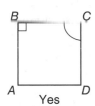

(2)   The figure below shows that relabeling the vertices of the examples used in (1) above will give an example such that angle *BCD* is not a right angle and an example such that angle *BCD* is a right angle; NOT sufficient.

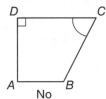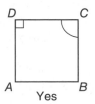

Given (1) and (2), the figure below indicates how an example satisfying both (1) and (2) can be constructed such that angle *BCD* is not a right angle. A right angle is constructed with vertex *B* and another right angle, appropriately rotated with respect to the first right angle, is constructed with vertex *D*. The rays of these two angles intersect at points *A* and *C* to form a quadrilateral *ABCD* that satisfies both (1) and (2) and is such that angle *BCD* is not a right angle (i.e., the answer to the question can be NO). For completeness, a square is also shown, which satisfies both (1) and (2) and is such that angle *BCD* is a right angle (i.e., the answer to the question can be YES).

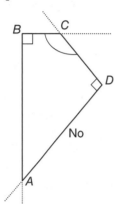

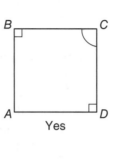

The correct answer is E;
both statements together are still not sufficient.

DS29831.01

108.

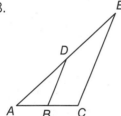

In the figure above, *B* is on $\overline{AC}$, *D* is on $\overline{AE}$, $\overline{AB}$ has the same length as $\overline{BC}$, and ∠*ABD* has the same measure as ∠*ACE*. What is the length of $\overline{DB}$?

(1)   The length of $\overline{EC}$ is 6.

(2)   The length of $\overline{DE}$ is 5.

(A)   Statement (1) ALONE is sufficient, but statement (2) alone is not sufficient.

(B)   Statement (2) ALONE is sufficient, but statement (1) alone is not sufficient.

(C)   BOTH statements TOGETHER are sufficient, but NEITHER statement ALONE is sufficient.

(D)   EACH statement ALONE is sufficient.

(E)   Statements (1) and (2) TOGETHER are NOT sufficient.

Geometry Triangles

The given information implies that △*ABD* is similar to △*ACE*, since ∠*ABD* and ∠*ACE* have the same measure and these two triangles share an angle at point *A*. Therefore, the lengths of corresponding sides of these two triangles are proportional. Using *AB* = *BC*, it follows that *AC* = 2(*AB*), and hence the lengths of the sides of △*ACE* are twice the lengths of the corresponding sides of △*ABD*.

(1)   Given that *EC* = 6, it follows from the remarks above that $DB = \frac{1}{2}(6) = 3$; SUFFICIENT.

(2)   The figure below shows two possibilities satisfying the given information and *DE* = 5 that have different values for *DB*; NOT sufficient.

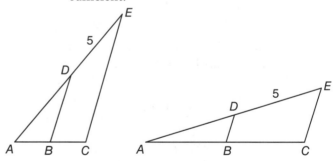

The correct answer is A;
statement 1 alone is sufficient.

DS92931.01

109. Sprinklers are being installed to water a lawn. Each sprinkler waters in a circle. Can the lawn be watered completely by 4 installed sprinklers?

(1)   The lawn is rectangular and its area is 32 square yards.

(2)   Each sprinkler can completely water a circular area of lawn with a maximum radius of 2 yards.

(A)   Statement (1) ALONE is sufficient, but statement (2) alone is not sufficient.

(B)   Statement (2) ALONE is sufficient, but statement (1) alone is not sufficient.

(C)   BOTH statements TOGETHER are sufficient, but NEITHER statement ALONE is sufficient.

(D)   EACH statement ALONE is sufficient.

(E)   Statements (1) and (2) TOGETHER are NOT sufficient.

Geometry Circles; Rectangles

(1)   No information is given about the area of the region that can be completely covered by four installed sprinklers; NOT sufficient.

(2)   No information is given about the area or the shape of the lawn; NOT sufficient.

Given (1) and (2), if the length of the rectangular lawn is sufficiently large, for example if the length is 32 yards and the width is 1 yard, then it is clear that the four sprinklers cannot completely water the lawn. However, if the lawn is in the shape of a square, then it is possible that four sprinklers can completely water the lawn. To see this, we first note that the side length of the square lawn is $\sqrt{32} = 4\sqrt{2}$ yards. To assist with the mathematical details, the figure below shows the square lawn positioned in the standard (x,y) coordinate plane so that the vertices of the lawn are located at $(0,0)$, $\left(0,4\sqrt{2}\right)$, $\left(4\sqrt{2},4\sqrt{2}\right)$, and $\left(4\sqrt{2},0\right)$. The two diagonals of the square, each of length 8, are shown as dashed segments, and the four sprinklers are at the four marked points located at the midpoints of the left and right halves of the diagonals. For example, one of the sprinklers is located at the point $\left(\sqrt{2},\sqrt{2}\right)$. Using the distance formula, it is straightforward to show that a circle centered at $\left(\sqrt{2},\sqrt{2}\right)$ with radius 2 passes through each of the points $(0,0)$, $\left(0,2\sqrt{2}\right)$, $\left(2\sqrt{2},2\sqrt{2}\right)$, and $\left(2\sqrt{2},0\right)$. Therefore, the interior of this circle covers the lower left square portion of the square lawn—that is, the square portion having vertices $(0,0)$, $\left(0,2\sqrt{2}\right)$, $\left(2\sqrt{2},2\sqrt{2}\right)$, and $\left(2\sqrt{2},0\right)$. Hence, the four sprinklers together, when located as described above, can completely water the square lawn. Therefore, it is possible that the lawn cannot be completely watered by the four sprinklers, and it is possible that the lawn can be completely watered by the four sprinklers.

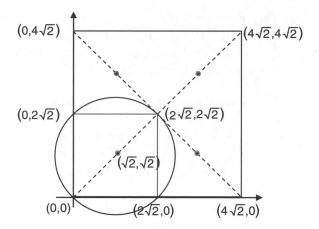

The correct answer is E; both statements together are still not sufficient.

DS18041.01

110.   What is the length of the hypotenuse of $\triangle ABC$?

(1)   The lengths of the three sides of $\triangle ABC$ are consecutive even integers.

(2)   The hypotenuse of $\triangle ABC$ is 4 units longer than the shorter leg.

(A)   Statement (1) ALONE is sufficient, but statement (2) alone is not sufficient.

(B)   Statement (2) ALONE is sufficient, but statement (1) alone is not sufficient.

(C)   BOTH statements TOGETHER are sufficient, but NEITHER statement ALONE is sufficient.

(D)   EACH statement ALONE is sufficient.

(E)   Statements (1) and (2) TOGETHER are NOT sufficient.

Geometry Pythagorean theorem

(1)   Let n, $n + 2$, and $n + 4$ be the consecutive even integers. Using the Pythagorean theorem, we have $n^2 + (n + 2)^2 = (n + 4)^2$. Because this is a quadratic equation that may have two solutions, we need to investigate further to determine whether there is a unique hypotenuse length.

$$n^2 + (n + 2)^2 = (n + 4)^2$$
$$n^2 + n^2 + 4n + 4 = n^2 + 8n + 16$$
$$n^2 - 4n - 12 = 0$$
$$(n - 6)(n + 2) = 0$$

Therefore, $n = 6$ or $n = -2$. Since $n = -2$ corresponds to side lengths of -2, 0, and 2, we discard $n = -2$. Therefore $n = 6$, the hypotenuse has length $n + 4 = 10$; SUFFICIENT.

(2) Let the side lengths be a, b, and $a + 4$. Using the Pythagorean theorem, we have $a^2 + b^2 = (a + 4)^2$. Expanding and solving for b in terms of a will facilitate our search for multiple hypotenuse length possibilities.

$$\begin{aligned} a^2 + b^2 &= (a + 4)^2 \\ a^2 + b^2 &= a^2 + 8a + 16 \\ b^2 &= 8a + 16 \\ b &= 2\sqrt{2a + 4} \end{aligned}$$

When $a = 1$, we obtain side lengths 1 and $2\sqrt{6}$, and hypotenuse length 5. When $a = 2$, we obtain side lengths 2 and $4\sqrt{2}$, and hypotenuse length 6; NOT sufficient.

**The correct answer is A;
statement 1 alone is sufficient.**

DS37571.01

111. Patricia purchased x meters of fencing. She originally intended to use all of the fencing to enclose a square region, but later decided to use all of the fencing to enclose a rectangular region with length y meters greater than its width. In square meters, what is the positive difference between the area of the square region and the area of the rectangular region?

(1) $xy = 256$

(2) $y = 4$

(A) Statement (1) ALONE is sufficient, but statement (2) alone is not sufficient.

(B) Statement (2) ALONE is sufficient, but statement (1) alone is not sufficient.

(C) BOTH statements TOGETHER are sufficient, but NEITHER statement ALONE is sufficient.

(D) EACH statement ALONE is sufficient.

(E) Statements (1) and (2) TOGETHER are NOT sufficient.

Geometry Rectangles; Perimeter

The square's perimeter is x meters, and thus the square has adjacent sides of length $\dfrac{x}{4}$ meters each. Since the rectangle's perimeter is also x meters, with adjacent side lengths that differ by y meters, it follows that the rectangle's length is $\left(\dfrac{x}{4} + \dfrac{y}{2}\right)$ meters (i.e., lengthen two opposite sides of the square by $\dfrac{y}{2}$ meters) and the rectangle's width is $\left(\dfrac{x}{4} - \dfrac{y}{2}\right)$ meters (i.e., shorten the two other opposite sides of the square by $\dfrac{y}{2}$ meters). Alternatively, letting L and W be the length and width, respectively and in meters, of the rectangle, then we can express each of L and W in terms of x and y by algebraically eliminating L and W from the equations $2L + 2W = x$ and $L = W + y$.

$$\begin{aligned} 2L + 2W &= x & \text{given} \\ 2(W + y) + 2W &= x & \text{substitute} \\ & & L = W + y \\ W &= \frac{x}{4} - \frac{y}{2} & \text{solve for } W \\ L &= \frac{x}{4} + \frac{y}{2} & \text{use } L = W + y \end{aligned}$$

Therefore, in square meters, the area of the square is $\left(\dfrac{x}{4}\right)^2$, the area of the rectangle is $\left(\dfrac{x}{4} + \dfrac{y}{2}\right)\left(\dfrac{x}{4} - \dfrac{y}{2}\right) = \left(\dfrac{x}{4}\right)^2 - \left(\dfrac{y}{2}\right)^2$, and the positive difference between these two areas is $\left(\dfrac{y}{2}\right)$. Determine the value of $\left(\dfrac{y}{2}\right)^2$.

(1) Given $xy = 256$, it is clearly not possible to determine the value of $\left(\dfrac{y}{2}\right)^2$; NOT sufficient.

(2) Given $y = 4$, the value of $\left(\dfrac{y}{2}\right)^2$ is equal to 4; SUFFICIENT.

**The correct answer is B;
statement 2 alone is sufficient.**

DS45771.01

112.

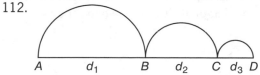

In the figure above, points A, B, C, and D are collinear and $\overparen{AB}$, $\overparen{BC}$, and $\overparen{CD}$ are semicircles with diameters d_1 cm, d_2 cm, and d_3 cm, respectively. What is the sum of the lengths of $\overparen{AB}$, $\overparen{BC}$, and $\overparen{CD}$, in centimeters?

(1) $d_1{:}d_2{:}d_3$ is 3:2:1.

(2)   The length of $\overline{AD}$ is 48 cm.

(A)   Statement (1) ALONE is sufficient, but statement (2) alone is not sufficient.

(B)   Statement (2) ALONE is sufficient, but statement (1) alone is not sufficient.

(C)   BOTH statements TOGETHER are sufficient, but NEITHER statement ALONE is sufficient.

(D)   EACH statement ALONE is sufficient.

(E)   Statements (1) and (2) TOGETHER are NOT sufficient.

Geometry Circles; Circumference

Since the circumference of a semicircle is $\pi\left(\dfrac{\text{diameter}}{2}\right)$, it follows that $\overparen{AB}$ has length $\pi\left(\dfrac{d_1}{2}\right)$ cm, $\overparen{BC}$ has length $\pi\left(\dfrac{d_2}{2}\right)$ cm, and $\overparen{CD}$ has length $\pi\left(\dfrac{d_3}{2}\right)$ cm. Therefore, the sum of the lengths, in centimeters, of $\overparen{AB}$, $\overparen{BC}$, and $\overparen{CD}$ is $\pi\left(\dfrac{d_1}{2}\right)+\pi\left(\dfrac{d_2}{2}\right)+\pi\left(\dfrac{d_3}{2}\right)=\dfrac{\pi}{2}\left(d_1+d_2+d_3\right)$.

Determine the value of $\dfrac{\pi}{2}\left(d_1+d_2+d_3\right)$.

(1)   Given that $d_1{:}d_2{:}d_3$ is 3:2:1, it is not possible to determine the value of $\dfrac{\pi}{2}\left(d_1+d_2+d_3\right)$ because d_1, d_2, and d_3 could be 3, 2, and 1 $(d_1+d_2+d_3=6)$ or d_1, d_2, and d_3 could be 6, 4, and 2 $(d_1+d_2+d_3=12)$; NOT sufficient.

(2)   Given that $AD=48$ and $AD=d_1+d_2+d_3$, it follows that $\dfrac{\pi}{2}\left(d_1+d_2+d_3\right)=\dfrac{\pi}{2}(48)$; SUFFICIENT.

The correct answer is B; statement 2 alone is sufficient.

DS16291.01

113.   In the standard (x,y) coordinate plane, what is the slope of the line containing the distinct points P and Q?

(1)   Both P and Q lie on the graph of $|x|+|y|=1$.

(2)   Both P and Q lie on the graph of $|x+y|=1$.

(A)   Statement (1) ALONE is sufficient, but statement (2) alone is not sufficient.

(B)   Statement (2) ALONE is sufficient, but statement (1) alone is not sufficient.

(C)   BOTH statements TOGETHER are sufficient, but NEITHER statement ALONE is sufficient.

(D)   EACH statement ALONE is sufficient.

(E)   Statements (1) and (2) TOGETHER are NOT sufficient.

Geometry Simple coordinate geometry

(1)   If $P=(1,0)$ and $Q=(0,1)$, then both P and Q lie on the graph of $|x|+|y|=1$ and the slope of the line containing P and Q is -1. However, if $P=(1,0)$ and $Q=(-1,0)$, then both P and Q lie on the graph of $|x|+|y|=1$ and the slope of the line containing P and Q is 0; NOT sufficient.

(2)   If $P=(1,0)$ and $Q=(0,1)$, then both P and Q lie on the graph of $|x+y|=1$ and the slope of the line containing P and Q is -1. However, if $P=(1,0)$ and $Q=(-1,0)$, then both P and Q lie on the graph of $|x+y|=1$ and the slope of the line containing P and Q is 0; NOT sufficient.

Taking (1) and (2) together is still not sufficient because the same examples used in (1) were also used in (2).

Although it is not necessary to visualize the graphs of $|x|+|y|=1$ and $|x+y|=1$ to solve this problem, some readers may be interested in their graphs. The graph of $|x|+|y|=1$ is a square with vertices at the four points $(\pm1,0)$ and $(0,\pm1)$. This can be seen by graphing $x+y=1$ in the first quadrant, which gives a line segment with endpoints $(1,0)$ and $(0,1)$, and then reflecting this line segment about one or both coordinate axes for the other quadrants (e.g., in the second quadrant, $x<0$ and $y>0$, and so $|x|+|y|=1$ becomes $-x+y=1$). The graph of $|x+y|=1$

is the union of two lines, one with equation $x + y = 1$ and the other with equation $x + y = -1$.

The correct answer is E;
both statements together are still not sufficient.

DS61791.01

114. When opened and lying flat, a birthday card is in the shape of a regular hexagon. The card must be folded in half along 1 of its diagonals before being placed in an envelope for mailing. Assuming that the thickness of the folded card will not be an issue, will the birthday card fit inside a rectangular envelope that is 4 inches by 9 inches?

(1) Each side of the regular hexagon is 4 inches long.

(2) The area of the top surface (which is the same as the area of the bottom surface) of the folded birthday card is less than 36 square inches.

(A) Statement (1) ALONE is sufficient, but statement (2) alone is not sufficient.

(B) Statement (2) ALONE is sufficient, but statement (1) alone is not sufficient.

(C) BOTH statements TOGETHER are sufficient, but NEITHER statement ALONE is sufficient.

(D) EACH statement ALONE is sufficient.

(E) Statements (1) and (2) TOGETHER are NOT sufficient.

Geometry Polygons

As shown in the figure above, a regular hexagon with sides of length s can be partitioned into six equilateral triangles. Using these triangles, it is possible to determine the length of each diagonal ($2s$), the height, shown as a dashed line, of each triangle $\left(\dfrac{s\sqrt{3}}{2}\right)$, the area of each triangular region $\left(\dfrac{s^2\sqrt{3}}{4}\right)$, and the area of the hexagonal region $\left(\dfrac{3s^2\sqrt{3}}{2}\right)$.

When the birthday card is folded in half along one of the diagonals it has the shape shown below.

(1) Given $s = 4$, the maximum width of the birthday card is $2s = 8$, which is less than the width of the envelope, and its height is $\left(\dfrac{4\sqrt{3}}{2}\right) = 2\sqrt{3}$, which is less than the height of the envelope because $2\sqrt{3} < 2\sqrt{4} = 4$. Thus, the birthday card will fit in the envelope; SUFFICIENT.

(2) Given that the surface area of the card when folded is less than 36 square inches, it follows that $\left(\dfrac{1}{2}\right)\left(\dfrac{3s^2\sqrt{3}}{2}\right) < 36$, which simplifies to $s < 4\sqrt[4]{3}$. If $s = 4$, then the birthday card will fit in the envelope, as shown in (1) above. However, if $s = 5$, then $s < 4\sqrt[4]{3}$ (note that $625 = 5^4 < (4\sqrt[4]{3})^4 = 768$), but the maximum width of the birthday card will be $2s = 10$, and the card will not fit in the envelope; NOT sufficient.

The correct answer is A;
statement 1 alone is sufficient.

DS77302.01

115.
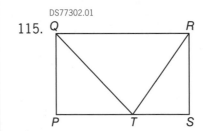

In rectangular region $PQRS$ above, T is a point on side PS. If $PS = 4$, what is the area of region $PQRS$?

(1) $\triangle QTR$ is equilateral.

(2) Segments PT and TS have equal length.

(A) Statement (1) ALONE is sufficient, but statement (2) alone is not sufficient.

(B) Statement (2) ALONE is sufficient, but statement (1) alone is not sufficient.

(C) BOTH statements TOGETHER are sufficient, but NEITHER statement ALONE is sufficient.

(D) EACH statement ALONE is sufficient.

(E) Statements (1) and (2) TOGETHER are NOT sufficient.

Geometry Triangles

It is given that *PQRS* is a rectangle and *PS* = 4. The area of *PQRS* can be determined if and only if *PQ* can be determined.

(1)

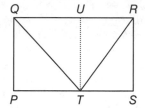

It is given that $\triangle QTR$ is equilateral. If $\overline{TU}$ is the height of $\triangle QTR$ as shown above, then $\triangle QUT$ is a 30–60–90° triangle with $UR = 2$. Using the ratios for 30–60–90 triangles, $TU = 2\sqrt{3}$. Since $PQ = TU$, the area of *PQRS* can be determined; SUFFICIENT.

(2) Given that $PT = TS$, PQ could be any positive number. Thus, it is not possible to determine *PQ* and therefore not possible to determine the area of *PQRS*; NOT sufficient.

The correct answer is A; statement 1 alone is sufficient.

DS58302.01

116. The top surface area of a square tabletop was changed so that one of the dimensions was reduced by 1 inch and the other dimension was increased by 2 inches. What was the surface area before these changes were made?

(1) After the changes were made, the surface area was 70 square inches.

(2) There was a 25 percent increase in one of the dimensions.

(A) Statement (1) ALONE is sufficient, but statement (2) alone is not sufficient.

(B) Statement (2) ALONE is sufficient, but statement (1) alone is not sufficient.

(C) BOTH statements TOGETHER are sufficient, but NEITHER statement ALONE is sufficient.

(D) EACH statement ALONE is sufficient.

(E) Statements (1) and (2) TOGETHER are NOT sufficient.

Geometry Quadrilaterals; First- and second-degree equations

Letting *S* be the side length of the square tabletop, the surface area before the change was S^2, and the area after the change is $(S-1)(S+2)$. Determine S^2.

(1) It is given that $(S-1)(S+2) = 70$. Solving this equation gives $S = -9$ and $S = 8$. Discarding $S = -9$, it follows that $S = 8$ and the surface area before the changes was 64 square inches; SUFFICIENT.

(2) Since only one dimension was increased and that increase was 2 inches, it follows from (2) that $S + 2 = 1.25S$. Solving this equation gives $S = 8$. Therefore, the surface area before the changes was 64 square inches; SUFFICIENT.

The correct answer is D; each statement alone is sufficient.

DS49302.01

117. If the lengths of the legs of a right triangle are integers, what is the area of the triangular region?

(1) The length of one leg is $\frac{3}{4}$ the length of the other.

(2) The length of the hypotenuse is 5.

(A) Statement (1) ALONE is sufficient, but statement (2) alone is not sufficient.

(B) Statement (2) ALONE is sufficient, but statement (1) alone is not sufficient.

(C) BOTH statements TOGETHER are sufficient, but NEITHER statement ALONE is sufficient.

(D) EACH statement ALONE is sufficient.

(E) Statements (1) and (2) TOGETHER are NOT sufficient.

Geometry Triangles

(1) Let *x* represent one leg of the triangle. Then the other leg is $\frac{3}{4}x$ and the area is $\frac{3}{8}x^2$. Since the value of *x* can be any positive multiple of 4, the area cannot be determined; NOT sufficient.

(2) Given that the lengths of the legs are the integers a and b and the length of the hypotenuse is 5, it follows that $a^2 + b^2 = 25$, where $1 \le a \le 4$ and $1 \le b \le 4$. The only pair of integers that meet these conditions are 3 and 4, so the area of the triangular region is 6; SUFFICIENT.

**The correct answer is B;
statement 2 alone is sufficient.**

DS12402.01

118. If cubical blocks in a display are stacked one on top of the other on a flat surface, what is the volume of the stack of blocks in cubic centimeters?

(1) The volume of the top block is 8 cubic centimeters.

(2) The height of the stack of blocks is 10 centimeters.

(A) Statement (1) ALONE is sufficient, but statement (2) alone is not sufficient.

(B) Statement (2) ALONE is sufficient, but statement (1) alone is not sufficient.

(C) BOTH statements TOGETHER are sufficient, but NEITHER statement ALONE is sufficient.

(D) EACH statement ALONE is sufficient.

(E) Statements (1) and (2) TOGETHER are NOT sufficient.

Geometry Volume

(1) It is given that the volume of the top cube in the stack is 8 cubic centimeters, from which it follows that the top block has edges of length 2 cm, but no information is given about the size of the other blocks in the stack or how many blocks the stack contains; NOT sufficient.

(2) It is given that the height of the stack of blocks is 10 cm, but no information is given about the size of any of the blocks in the stack or how many blocks are in the stack.

Taking (1) and (2) together gives no information about the size of the blocks below the top block or how many blocks are in the stack. For example, there could be two blocks with edges of lengths 2 cm and 8 cm. The volume of the top block would be 8 cubic centimeters, the height of the stack would be 10 cm, and the volume of the stack of

blocks would be 520 cubic centimeters. But there could also be three blocks with edges of lengths 2 cm, 3 cm, and 5 cm. The volume of the top block would be 8 cubic centimeters, the height of the stack would be 10 cm, and the volume of the stack of blocks would be 160 cubic centimeters.

**The correct answer is E;
both statements together are still not sufficient.**

Tip

Do not assume anything that is not explicitly stated in the problem. In this problem, it is tempting to assume that all of the blocks are identical, in which case there would be five blocks, each with height 2 cm to give the whole stack a height of 10 cm and a volume of 40 cubic centimeters. Under the assumption that all of the blocks are identical, the correct answer would be C.

DS53402.01

119. Is the perimeter of a certain rectangular garden greater than 50 meters?

(1) The two shorter sides of the garden are each 15 meters long.

(2) The length of the garden is 5 meters greater than the width of the garden.

(A) Statement (1) ALONE is sufficient, but statement (2) alone is not sufficient.

(B) Statement (2) ALONE is sufficient, but statement (1) alone is not sufficient.

(C) BOTH statements TOGETHER are sufficient, but NEITHER statement ALONE is sufficient.

(D) EACH statement ALONE is sufficient.

(E) Statements (1) and (2) TOGETHER are NOT sufficient.

Geometry Quadrilaterals; Perimeter

Let W represent the length of the shorter side (that is, the width) of the rectangular garden, and let L represent the length of the longer side (that is, the length). The perimeter is then $2(L + W)$. Determine if $2(L + W) > 50$ is true, or equivalently, if $L + W > 25$ is true.

(1) It is given that $W = 15$, from which it follows that $L > 15$. Then, $L + W > 15 + 15 > 25$; SUFFICIENT.

(2) It is given that $L = W + 5$, from which it follows that $L + W = 2W + 5$. If, for example, $W = 1$, then $2W + 5$ is not greater than 25, but if $W = 11$, then $2W + 5$ is greater than 25; NOT sufficient.

The correct answer is A; statement 1 alone is sufficient.

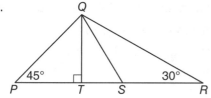

Tip

When determining whether a certain condition holds for an expression involving two variables, avoid assuming that the values of both variables must be known. In (1), knowing that L represents the length of the **longer** side and knowing the value of W, the length of the shorter side, is enough information to determine whether $L + W$ meets the given condition.

DS34402.01

120.

In the figure above, what is the perimeter of $\triangle PQR$?

(1) The length of segment PT is 2.
(2) The length of segment RS is $\sqrt{3}$.

(A) Statement (1) ALONE is sufficient, but statement (2) alone is not sufficient.

(B) Statement (2) ALONE is sufficient, but statement (1) alone is not sufficient.

(C) BOTH statements TOGETHER are sufficient, but NEITHER statement ALONE is sufficient.

(D) EACH statement ALONE is sufficient.

(E) Statements (1) and (2) TOGETHER are NOT sufficient.

Geometry Triangles; Perimeter

Determine the perimeter of $\triangle PQR$ by determining $PQ + QR + PR$.

(1) It is given that $PT = 2$. Since $\triangle PTQ$ is a 45°–45°–90° triangle, it follows that $QT = 2$ and $PQ = 2\sqrt{2}$. Since $\triangle QTR$ is a 30°–60°–90° triangle and $QT = 2$, it follows

that $QR = 4$ and $TR = 2\sqrt{3}$. $PT + TR = PR$, so PR, QR, and PQ are known and the perimeter of $\triangle PQR$ can be determined; SUFFICIENT.

(2) It is given that $RS = \sqrt{3}$, but no information is given to determine TS. If, for example, $TS = \sqrt{3}$, then $\triangle QTR$ is a 30°–60°–90° triangle with $TS + SR = TR = 2\sqrt{3}$. It follows that $QT = 2$ and $QR = 4$. Also, $\triangle PTQ$ is a 45°–45°–90° triangle with $QT = 2$. It follows that $PT = 2$ (hence $PR = 2 + 2\sqrt{3}$) and $PQ = 2\sqrt{2}$, so the perimeter of the triangle is $2\sqrt{2} + 4 + (2 + 2\sqrt{3})$. However, if $TS = 2\sqrt{3}$, then $\triangle QTR$ is a 30°–60°–90° triangle with $TS + SR = TR = 3\sqrt{3}$. It follows that $QT = 3$, and $QR = 6$. Also, $\triangle PTQ$ is a 45°–45°–90° triangle with $QT = 3$. It follows that $PT = 3$ (hence $PR = 3 + 3\sqrt{3}$) and $PQ = 3\sqrt{2}$, so the perimeter of the triangle is $3\sqrt{2} + 6 + (3 + 3\sqrt{3})$; NOT sufficient.

The correct answer is A; statement 1 alone is sufficient.

DS07402.01

121.

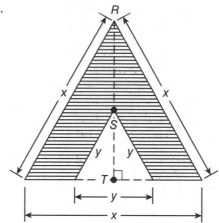

In the figure above, the shaded region represents the front of an upright wooden frame around the entrance to an amusement park ride. If $RS = \dfrac{5\sqrt{3}}{2}$ meters, what is the area of the front of the frame?

(1) $x = 9$ meters
(2) $ST = 2\sqrt{3}$ meters

(A) Statement (1) ALONE is sufficient, but statement (2) alone is not sufficient.

(B)   Statement (2) ALONE is sufficient, but statement (1) alone is not sufficient.

(C)   BOTH statements TOGETHER are sufficient, but NEITHER statement ALONE is sufficient.

(D)   EACH statement ALONE is sufficient.

(E)   Statements (1) and (2) TOGETHER are NOT sufficient.

Geometry Triangles

The front of the frame is in the shape of an equilateral triangle with sides of length x with an opening in the shape of an equilateral triangle with sides of length y, where $y < x$. The area of the front of the frame is the area of the larger triangle minus the area of the smaller triangle.

Note that the height of an equilateral triangle with sides of length s is given by $\dfrac{s\sqrt{3}}{2}$ and the area is given by $\dfrac{s^2\sqrt{3}}{4}$, both of which are easily derived using the ratios for the sides of a 30°–60°–90° triangle.

(1)   Given that $x = 9$, it follows that RT, the height of the large equilateral triangle, is $\dfrac{9\sqrt{3}}{2}$. Since $RS = \dfrac{5\sqrt{3}}{2}$ and $RT = RS + ST$, it follows that $ST = \dfrac{4\sqrt{3}}{2} = 2\sqrt{3}$, where ST is the height of the small equilateral triangle. Therefore, $y = 4$. With the side lengths of both triangles known, the area of the front of the frame can be determined; SUFFICIENT.

(2)   Given that $ST = 2\sqrt{3}$, it follows that $y = 4$. Also, since $RT = RS + ST$ and $RS = \dfrac{5\sqrt{3}}{2}$, it follows that $RT = \dfrac{9\sqrt{3}}{2}$ and $x = 9$. With the side lengths of both triangles known, the area of the front of the frame can be determined; SUFFICIENT.

The correct answer is D; each statement alone is sufficient.

DS05502.01

122.

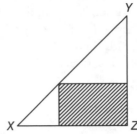

In the figure above, if the shaded region is rectangular, what is the length of XY?

(1)   The perimeter of the shaded region is 24.

(2)   The measure of $\angle XYZ$ is 45°.

(A)   Statement (1) ALONE is sufficient, but statement (2) alone is not sufficient.

(B)   Statement (2) ALONE is sufficient, but statement (1) alone is not sufficient.

(C)   BOTH statements TOGETHER are sufficient, but NEITHER statement ALONE is sufficient.

(D)   EACH statement ALONE is sufficient.

(E)   Statements (1) and (2) TOGETHER are NOT sufficient.

Geometry Triangles

Determine XY.

(1)   Letting L and W be the length and width of the shaded rectangular region, then from (1), $L + W = 12$. This does not give enough information about $\triangle XZY$ to determine XY; NOT sufficient.

(2)   From (2), $\triangle XZY$ is a 45°–45°–90° triangle, so $XZ = YZ$ and $XY = XZ\sqrt{2}$, but no information is given to determine XZ; NOT sufficient.

Taking (1) and (2) together and using the figure below, from (2), $\triangle XRP$ is a 45°–45°–90° triangle, so $XR = PR = QZ = W$. Likewise $\triangle PQY$ is a 45°–45°–90° triangle, so $PQ = YQ = RZ = L$. It follows that $XZ = XR + RZ = W + L$ and $W + L = 12$ from (1). Likewise, $YZ = YQ + QZ = L + W = 12$. Since the length of the legs of $\triangle XZY$ are known, XY can be determined.

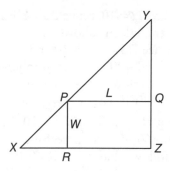

**The correct answer is C;
both statements together are sufficient.**

DS87602.01

123.

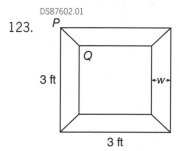

3 ft

3 ft

The figure above shows the dimensions of a square picture frame that was constructed using four identical pieces of frame as shown. If w is the width of each piece of the frame, what is the area of the front surface of each piece? (1 ft = 12 inches)

(1) $w = 3$ inches

(2) $PQ = \sqrt{18}$ inches

(A) Statement (1) ALONE is sufficient, but statement (2) alone is not sufficient.

(B) Statement (2) ALONE is sufficient, but statement (1) alone is not sufficient.

(C) BOTH statements TOGETHER are sufficient, but NEITHER statement ALONE is sufficient.

(D) EACH statement ALONE is sufficient.

(E) Statements (1) and (2) TOGETHER are NOT sufficient.

Geometry Quadrilaterals; Area

Determine the area of the surface of each of the four pieces of wood used to construct the square picture frame. In the following explanation, the larger square with one vertex labeled P will be referred to as Square P and the smaller square with one vertex labeled Q will be referred to as Square Q.

(1) It is given that the width of each piece of wood is 3 inches. Then, the area one piece of wood, in square inches, is

$$\frac{\text{area of Square } Q - \text{area of Square } P}{4} \text{ or}$$

$$\frac{36^2 - 30^2}{4}; \text{SUFFICIENT.}$$

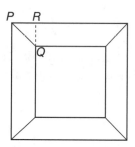

(2) It is given that $PQ = \sqrt{18} = 3\sqrt{2}$ inches. Since the pieces of the frame are identical, each of the angles at P is 45° and ΔPRQ in the figure above is a 45°–45°–90° triangle. It follows that $RQ = 3$. This is the same information given in (1), which was shown to be sufficient; SUFFICIENT.

**The correct answer is D;
each statement alone is sufficient.**

DS48602.01

124.

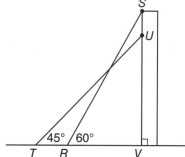

In the figure above, segments $\overline{RS}$ and $\overline{TU}$ represent two positions of the same ladder leaning against the side $\overline{SV}$ of a wall. The length of $\overline{TV}$ is how much greater than the length of $\overline{RV}$?

(1) The length of $\overline{TU}$ is 10 meters.

(2) The length of $\overline{RV}$ is 5 meters.

(A) Statement (1) ALONE is sufficient, but statement (2) alone is not sufficient.

(B)   Statement (2) ALONE is sufficient, but statement (1) alone is not sufficient.

(C)   BOTH statements TOGETHER are sufficient, but NEITHER statement ALONE is sufficient.

(D)   EACH statement ALONE is sufficient.

(E)   Statements (1) and (2) TOGETHER are NOT sufficient.

Geometry Triangles

Note that $TU = RS$ because they both represent the length of the same ladder. Determine $TV - RV$.

(1)   It is given that $TU = 10$. Since ΔTVU is a 45°–45°–90° triangle, it follows that $TV = 5\sqrt{2}$. Since $RS = TU = 10$ and ΔRVS is a 30°–60°–90° triangle, it follows that $RV = 5$. Therefore, $TV - RV$ can be determined; SUFFICIENT.

(2)   It is given that $RV = 5$. Then $RS = 10$ since ΔRVS is a 30°–60°–90° triangle. Since $RS = TU$, it follows that $TU = 10$. This is the same information as in (1); SUFFICIENT.

The correct answer is D; each statement alone is sufficient.

Answer Explanations Quantitative Reasoning

Data Sufficiency

Rates/Ratios/Percent

DS67410.01

125. A large flower arrangement contains 3 types of flowers: carnations, lilies, and roses. Of all the flowers in the arrangement, $\frac{1}{2}$ are carnations, $\frac{1}{3}$ are lilies, and $\frac{1}{6}$ are roses. The total price of which of the 3 types of flowers in the arrangement is the greatest?

(1) The prices per flower for carnations, lilies, and roses are in the ratio 1:3:4, respectively.

(2) The price of one rose is $0.75 more than the price of one carnation, and the price of one rose is $0.25 more than the price of one lily.

(A) Statement (1) ALONE is sufficient, but statement (2) alone is not sufficient.

(B) Statement (2) ALONE is sufficient, but statement (1) alone is not sufficient.

(C) BOTH statements TOGETHER are sufficient, but NEITHER statement ALONE is sufficient.

(D) EACH statement ALONE is sufficient.

(E) Statements (1) and (2) TOGETHER are NOT sufficient.

Algebra Applied problems; Ratios

Let T be the total number of flowers, and let $\$C$, $\$L$, and $\$R$ be the cost, respectively, of one carnation, one lily, and one rose.

(1) We are given that $L = 3C$ (because $C:L$ is 1:3) and $R = 4C$ (because $C:R$ is 1:4). The table below shows the total price for each type of flower.

Flower	Number of flowers	Price per flower	Total price
Carnation	$\frac{1}{2}T$	C	$\frac{1}{2}TC$
Lily	$\frac{1}{3}T$	$3C$	TC
Rosc	$\frac{1}{6}T$	$4C$	$\frac{2}{3}TC$

From the table it is clear that lilies have the greatest total cost; SUFFICIENT.

(2) We are given that $R = 0.75 + C$ and $R = 0.25 + L$. To simplify matters, we can use these equations to express each of the variables C, L, and R in terms of a single fixed variable, for example, $C = R - \frac{3}{4}$ and $L = R - \frac{1}{4}$. This will allow us to replace all appearances of C, L, and R with appearances of R only, thereby reducing by two the number of variables that have to be dealt with. The table below shows, for two values of T and R, the total price for each type of flower.

Flower	Number of flowers	Price per flower	Total price	Total price: $T = 24$, $R = 1$	Total price: $T = 24$, $R = 10$
Carnation	$\frac{1}{2}T$	$R - \frac{3}{4}$	$\frac{1}{2}TR - \frac{3}{8}T$	3	**111**
Lily	$\frac{1}{3}T$	$R - \frac{1}{4}$	$\frac{1}{3}TR - \frac{1}{12}T$	6	78
Rose	$\frac{1}{6}T$	R	$\frac{1}{6}TR$	4	40

From the table it is clear that the type of flower having the greatest total cost can vary; NOT sufficient.

Tip

Consider the expressions under "Total price" in the previous table. Note that, for a fixed value of T, as the value of R increases without bound, the total price for carnation will eventually exceed the total price for each of the other two types of flowers. Therefore, for non-sufficiency of (2), it is only necessary to determine whether there exist values for T and R such that carnations do not have the greatest total price. This suggests trying a small value for R, for example $R = 1$. Also, note that $T = 24$ was chosen to avoid fractions in the computations—24 is divisible by both 8 and 12.

The correct answer is A; statement 1 alone is sufficient.

DS34010.01

126. Town X has 50,000 residents, some of whom were born in Town X. What percent of the residents of Town X were born in Town X ?

(1) Of the male residents of Town X, 40 percent were not born in Town X.

(2) Of the female residents of Town X, 60 percent were born in Town X.

(A) Statement (1) ALONE is sufficient, but statement (2) alone is not sufficient.

(B) Statement (2) ALONE is sufficient, but statement (1) alone is not sufficient.

(C) BOTH statements TOGETHER are sufficient, but NEITHER statement ALONE is sufficient.

(D) EACH statement ALONE is sufficient.

(E) Statements (1) and (2) TOGETHER are NOT sufficient.

Algebra Applied problems

(1) We are given that 40 percent of the male residents were NOT born in Town X, or equivalently, that 60 percent of the male residents were born in Town X. However, no information is given about the number of female residents or about the percent of female residents born in Town X. By considering extreme cases, it is easy to see that the percent of residents born in Town X cannot be determined. For example, if only 10 of the 50,000 residents were male and 0 percent of the female residents were born in Town X, then only 6 residents (i.e., close to 0 percent of the residents) would have been born in Town X. However, if only 10 of the 50,000 residents were male and 100 percent of the female residents were born in Town X, then 49,996 residents (i.e., close to 100 percent of the residents) would have been born in Town X; NOT sufficient.

(2) We are given that 60 percent of the female residents were born in Town X. However, no information is given about the number of male residents or about the percent of male residents born in Town X. By considering extreme cases in the same manner that was done in (1), it is easy to see that the percent of residents born in Town X cannot be determined; NOT sufficient.

Given (1) and (2), it follows that 60 percent of the male residents and 60 percent of the female residents were born in Town X. Therefore, 60 percent of the residents were born in Town X.

The correct answer is C; both statements together are sufficient.

DS29931.01

127. A bank account earned 2% annual interest, compounded daily, for as long as the balance was under $1,000, starting when the account was opened. Once the balance reached $1,000, the account earned 2.5% annual interest, compounded daily until the account was closed. No deposits or withdrawals were made. Was the total amount of interest earned at the 2% rate greater than the total amount earned at the 2.5% rate?

  (1) The account earned exactly $25 in interest at the 2.5% rate.

  (2) The account was open for exactly three years.

  (A) Statement (1) ALONE is sufficient, but statement (2) alone is not sufficient.

  (B) Statement (2) ALONE is sufficient, but statement (1) alone is not sufficient.

  (C) BOTH statements TOGETHER are sufficient, but NEITHER statement ALONE is sufficient.

  (D) EACH statement ALONE is sufficient.

  (E) Statements (1) and (2) TOGETHER are NOT sufficient.

Algebra Applied problems

Let P_0, P_1, and P_2 be the initial balance, the balance after one year, and the balance after two years.

  (1) Since $25 is the exact amount of interest earned in one year by an initial amount of $1,000 earning 2.5 percent annual interest, compounded yearly, it follows that $25 is the total amount of interest earned in slightly less than one year by an initial amount of $1,000 earning 2.5 percent annual interest, compounded daily. However, the total amount of interest earned at the 2 percent rate could be less than $25 (for example, if $P_0 = \$990$, then the interest earned at the 2 percent rate is $10) and the total amount of interest earned at the 2 percent rate could be greater than $25 (for example, if $P_0 = \$900$, then the interest earned at the 2 percent rate is $100); NOT sufficient.

  (2) Given that the account was open for exactly three years, then the total amount of interest at the 2 percent rate could be less than the

total amount of interest at the 2.5 percent rate (for example, if the balance reached $1,000 a few days after the account was open). On the other hand, the total amount of interest at the 2 percent rate could also be greater than the total amount of interest at the 2.5 percent rate (for example, if the balance reached $1,000 a few days before the account was closed); NOT sufficient.

Given (1) and (2), it follows that the account earned interest at the 2.5 percent rate for slightly less than one year and the account earned interest at the 2 percent rate for slightly more than two years. Therefore, the balances of P_1 and P_2 were reached while the account was earning interest at the 2 percent rate. Since $P_0(1.02) < P_1$ and $P_1(1.02) < P_2$ (compounding daily for one year produces a greater amount than compounding annually for one year), the values of P_0, P_1, and P_2 satisfy the following inequalities.

$$P_0 < P_0(1.02) < P_1 < P_1(1.02) < P_2 < 1{,}000$$

Note that the difference $1{,}000 - P_0$ is the total amount of interest earned at the 2 percent rate. Thus, using (2), we wish to determine whether this difference is greater than 25. From $P_0(1.02) < P_1$ it follows that $P_0(1.02)^2 < P_1(1.02)$, and since $P_1(1.02) < 1{,}000$, we have $P_0(1.02)^2 < 1{,}000$. Therefore, $P_0 < \dfrac{1{,}000}{(1.02)^2}$, from which we can conclude the following inequality.

$$1{,}000 - P_0 > 1{,}000 - \frac{1{,}000}{(1.02)^2}$$

Since $1{,}000 - \dfrac{1{,}000}{(1.02)^2} > 25$ (see below), it follows that $1{,}000 - P_0 > 25$ and hence the total amount of interest earned at the 2 percent rate is greater than the total amount of interest earned at the 2.5 percent rate.

One way to verify that $1{,}000 - \dfrac{1{,}000}{(1.02)^2} > 25$ is to verify that $1 - \dfrac{1}{(1.02)^2} > \dfrac{1}{40}$, or equivalently, verify that $\dfrac{1}{(1.02)^2} < \dfrac{39}{40}$, or $40 < 39(1.02)^2$.

Now note that we can obtain this last inequality from $40 < 39(1.04)$ (because $39 + 39(0.04)$ is greater than $39 + 1$) and $1.04 < (1.02)^2$.

**The correct answer is C;
both statements together are sufficient.**

DS53541.01

128. A novelist pays her agent 15% of the royalties she receives from her novels. She pays her publicist 5% of the royalties, plus a yearly fee. Did the novelist pay more to her agent last year than she paid to her publicist?

(1) The publicist's yearly fee is $2,000.

(2) The novelist earned an average of $3,500 in royalties last year on each of her novels.

(A) Statement (1) ALONE is sufficient, but statement (2) alone is not sufficient.

(B) Statement (2) ALONE is sufficient, but statement (1) alone is not sufficient.

(C) BOTH statements TOGETHER are sufficient, but NEITHER statement ALONE is sufficient.

(D) EACH statement ALONE is sufficient.

(E) Statements (1) and (2) TOGETHER are NOT sufficient.

Arithmetic Applied problems

Let R be the novelist's royalties last year, and let Y be the yearly fee paid to the publicist. Determine whether $0.15R > 0.05R + Y$, or equivalently, whether $R > 10Y$.

(1) No information is given that allows us to determine whether R is greater than $10Y = 10(2,000) = 20,000$; NOT sufficient.

(2) No information is given that allows us to determine whether $3,500n$ is greater than $10Y$, where n is the number of novels; NOT sufficient.

Given (1) and (2) and letting n be the number of novels, we are to determine whether $3,500n > 20,000$. If $n = 1$, then the answer is NO. However, if $n = 10$, then the answer is YES.

**The correct answer is E;
both statements together are still not sufficient.**

Answer Explanations Quantitative Reasoning

Data Sufficiency

Value/Order/Factors

DS85100.01

129. If x and z are integers, is $x + z^2$ odd?

(1) x is odd and z is even.

(2) $x - z$ is odd.

(A) Statement (1) ALONE is sufficient, but statement (2) alone is not sufficient.

(B) Statement (2) ALONE is sufficient, but statement (1) alone is not sufficient.

(C) BOTH statements TOGETHER are sufficient, but NEITHER statement ALONE is sufficient.

(D) EACH statement ALONE is sufficient.

(E) Statements (1) and (2) TOGETHER are NOT sufficient.

Arithmetic Properties of integers

(1) We are given that x is odd and z is even. Therefore, z^2 is even and hence $x + z^2$ is odd, because an odd integer added to an even integer is an odd integer; SUFFICIENT.

(2) We are given that $x - z$ is odd. Since there is not a readily apparent useful algebraic relation between $x - z$ and $x + z^2$, we consider all possible cases.

x	z	z^2	$x - z$	$x + z^2$
even	even	even	even	even
even	odd	odd	odd	odd
odd	even	even	odd	odd
odd	odd	odd	even	even

From the table it is clear that if $x - z$ is odd, then $x + z^2$ is odd; SUFFICIENT.

The correct answer is D; each statement alone is sufficient.

DS95850.01

130.

×	a	b	c
a	d	e	f
b	e	g	h
c	f	h	j

Each entry in the multiplication table above is an integer that is either positive, negative, or zero. What is the value of a ?

(1) $h \neq 0$

(2) $c = f$

(A) Statement (1) ALONE is sufficient, but statement (2) alone is not sufficient.

(B) Statement (2) ALONE is sufficient, but statement (1) alone is not sufficient.

(C) BOTH statements TOGETHER are sufficient, but NEITHER statement ALONE is sufficient.

(D) EACH statement ALONE is sufficient.

(E) Statements (1) and (2) TOGETHER are NOT sufficient.

Arithmetic Properties of integers

(1) If a, b, c equal 1, 2, 3 in this order, then each entry will be an integer, $h \neq 0$, and $a = 1$. However, if a, b, c equal 2, 3, 4 in this order, then each entry will be an integer, $h \neq 0$, and $a = 2$. Hence, the value of a cannot be determined; NOT sufficient.

(2) The assumption $c = f$ is equivalent to $ac = c$, or $(a - 1)c = 0$. Hence, $c = f$ is equivalent to $a = 1$ or $c = 0$. If a, b, c equal 1, 2, 3 in this order, then each entry will be an integer, $c = f$, and $a = 1$. However, if a, b, c equal $-2, -1, 0$ in this order, then each entry will be an integer, $c = f$, and $a = -2$. Hence, the value of a cannot be determined; NOT sufficient.

Given (1) and (2), then from (1) we have $bc = h \neq 0$, and hence $b \neq 0$ and $c \neq 0$. From (2) we have $a = 1$ or $c = 0$, but since $c \neq 0$, it follows that $a = 1$. Hence, the value of a can be determined.

The correct answer is C; both statements together are sufficient.

DS36141.01

131. Given a positive number N, when N is rounded by a certain method (for convenience, call it Method Y), the result is 10^n if and only if n is an integer and $5 \times 10^{n-1} \le N < 5 \times 10^n$. In a certain gas sample, there are, when rounded by Method Y, 10^{21} molecules of H_2 and also 10^{21} molecules of O_2. When rounded by Method Y, what is the combined number of H_2 and O_2 molecules in the gas sample?

(1) The number of H_2 molecules and the number of O_2 molecules are each less than 3×10^{21}.

(2) The number of H_2 molecules is more than twice the number of O_2 molecules.

(A) Statement (1) ALONE is sufficient, but statement (2) alone is not sufficient.

(B) Statement (2) ALONE is sufficient, but statement (1) alone is not sufficient.

(C) BOTH statements TOGETHER are sufficient, but NEITHER statement ALONE is sufficient.

(D) EACH statement ALONE is sufficient.

(E) Statements (1) and (2) TOGETHER are NOT sufficient.

Arithmetic Rounding

Let H be the number of H_2 molecules and let O be the number of O_2 molecules. We are given that $0.5 \times 10^{21} \le H < 5 \times 10^{21}$ and $0.5 \times 10^{21} \le O < 5 \times 10^{21}$. When rounded by Method Y, what is the value of $H + O$?

(1) If $H = 2 \times 10^{21}$ and $O = 2 \times 10^{21}$, then each of H and O equals 10^{21} when rounded by Method Y, each of H and O is less than 3×10^{21}, and $H + O = 4 \times 10^{21}$, which equals 10^{21} when rounded by Method Y. However, if $H = 2.6 \times 10^{21}$ and $O = 2.6 \times 10^{21}$, then each of H and O equals 10^{21} when rounded by Method Y, each of H and O is less than 3×10^{21}, and $H + O = 5.2 \times 10^{21}$, which equals 10^{22} when rounded by Method Y; NOT sufficient.

(2) If $H = 2 \times 10^{21}$ and $O = 0.8 \times 10^{21}$, then each of H and O equals 10^{21} when rounded by Method Y, $H > 2 \times O$, and $H + O = 2.8 \times 10^{21}$, which equals 10^{21} when rounded by Method Y. However, if $H = 4.5 \times 10^{21}$ and $O = 2 \times 10^{21}$,

then each of H and O equals 10^{21} when rounded by Method Y, $H > 2 \times O$, and $H + O = 6.5 \times 10^{21}$, which equals 10^{22} when rounded by Method Y; NOT sufficient.

Given (1) and (2), since $O \ge 0.5 \times 10^{21}$ (given information), it follows from statement (2) that $H > 1 \times 10^{21}$. Also, since $H < 3 \times 10^{21}$ (statement (1)), it follows from statement (2) that $O < 1.5 \times 10^{21}$. Thus, $1 \times 10^{21} < H < 3 \times 10^{21}$ and $0.5 \times 10^{21} \le O < 1.5 \times 10^{21}$, and hence $1.5 \times 10^{21} < H + O < 4.5 \times 10^{21}$. Therefore, the value of $H + O$ equals 10^{21} when rounded by Method Y.

The correct answer is C; both statements together are sufficient.

DS05541.01

132. If x is a positive integer, how many positive integers less than x are divisors of x?

(1) x^2 is divisible by exactly 4 positive integers less than x^2.

(2) $2x$ is divisible by exactly 3 positive integers less than $2x$.

(A) Statement (1) ALONE is sufficient, but statement (2) alone is not sufficient.

(B) Statement (2) ALONE is sufficient, but statement (1) alone is not sufficient.

(C) BOTH statements TOGETHER are sufficient, but NEITHER statement ALONE is sufficient.

(D) EACH statement ALONE is sufficient.

(E) Statements (1) and (2) TOGETHER are NOT sufficient.

Arithmetic Properties of integers

Tip

For problems that involve how many divisors an unspecified integer has, it is sometimes useful to consider separate cases based on the number of repeated prime factors and the number of distinct prime factors the integer has. For example, let p, q, and r be distinct prime numbers. Then the factors of pq are 1, p, q, and pq; the factors of pqr are 1, p, q, r, pq, pr, qr, and pqr; the factors of p^3 are 1, p, p^2, and p^3; the factors of p^2q are 1, p, p^2, q, pq, and p^2q.

(1) If x has at least two prime factors, say p and q, then among the factors of x^2 are p, q, pq, p^2, q^2, p^2q, and pq^2, each of which is less than x^2 (because $x^2 \geq p^2q^2$). Thus, x cannot have at least two prime factors, otherwise, x^2 would have more than four divisors less than x^2. Therefore, x has the form $x = p^n$ for some prime number p and positive integer n. There are $2n$ divisors of $x^2 = (p^n)^2 = p^{2n}$ that are less than x^2, namely $1, p, p^2, p^3, \ldots, p^{2n-2}$, and p^{2n-1}. Statement (1) implies that $2n = 4$, and hence $n = 2$. It follows that $x = p^2$ for some prime number p, and so x has exactly two divisors less than x, namely 1 and p. Alternatively, the last part of this argument can be accomplished in a more concrete way by separately considering the number of prime factors of p, p^2, p^3, etc.; SUFFICIENT.

(2) Probably the simplest approach is to individually consider the divisors of $2x$ that are less than $2x$ for various values of x. If $x = 1$, then $2x = 2$ has one such divisor, namely 1. If $x = 2$, then $2x = 4$ has two such divisors, namely 1 and 2. If $x = 3$, then $2x = 6$ has three such divisors, namely 1, 2, and 3. If $x = 4$, then $2x = 8$ has three such divisors, namely 1, 2, and 4. At this point we have two integers satisfying statement (2), $x = 3$ and $x = 4$. Since $x = 3$ has one divisor less than $x = 3$ and $x = 4$ has two divisors less than $x = 4$; NOT sufficient.

The correct answer is A; statement 1 alone is sufficient.

DS33551.01

133. If m and n are positive integers, is n even?

(1) $m(m + 2) + 1 = mn$

(2) $m(m + n)$ is odd.

(A) Statement (1) ALONE is sufficient, but statement (2) alone is not sufficient.

(B) Statement (2) ALONE is sufficient, but statement (1) alone is not sufficient.

(C) BOTH statements TOGETHER are sufficient, but NEITHER statement ALONE is sufficient.

(D) EACH statement ALONE is sufficient.

(E) Statements (1) and (2) TOGETHER are NOT sufficient.

Arithmetic Properties of integers

(1) Given that $m(m + 2) + 1 = mn$, then m cannot be even, since if m were even, then we would have an odd integer, namely $m(m + 2) + 1$, equal to an even integer, namely mn. Therefore, m is odd. Hence, $m(m + 2)$ is odd, being the product of two odd integers, and thus $m(m + 2) + 1$ is even. Since $m(m + 2) + 1 = mn$, it follows that mn is even, and since m is odd, it follows that n is even; SUFFICIENT.

Alternatively, the table below shows that $m(m + 2) + 1 = mn$ is only possible when m is odd and n is even.

m	n	$m(m + 2) + 1$	mn
even	even	odd	even
even	odd	odd	even
odd	even	**even**	**even**
odd	odd	even	odd

(2) Since $m(m + n)$ is odd, it follows that m is odd and $m + n$ is odd. Therefore, $n = (m + n) - m$ is a difference of two odd integers and hence n is even; SUFFICIENT.

The correct answer is D; each statement alone is sufficient.

DS65291.01

134. If m and n are positive integers, what is the value of $\dfrac{3}{m} + \dfrac{n}{4}$?

(1) $mn = 12$

(2) $\dfrac{3}{m}$ is in lowest terms and $\dfrac{n}{4}$ is in lowest terms.

(A) Statement (1) ALONE is sufficient, but statement (2) alone is not sufficient.

(B) Statement (2) ALONE is sufficient, but statement (1) alone is not sufficient.

(C) BOTH statements TOGETHER are sufficient, but NEITHER statement ALONE is sufficient.

(D) EACH statement ALONE is sufficient.

(E) Statements (1) and (2) TOGETHER are NOT sufficient.

Arithmetic Fractions

(1) If $m = 1$ and $n = 12$, then m and n are positive integers, $mn = 12$, and $\dfrac{3}{m} + \dfrac{n}{4} = 6$. However, if $m = 3$ and $n = 4$, then m and n are positive integers, $mn = 12$, and $\dfrac{3}{m} + \dfrac{n}{4} = 2$; NOT sufficient.

(2) If $m = 2$ and $n = 1$, then m and n are positive integers, $\dfrac{3}{m}$ and $\dfrac{n}{4}$ are in lowest terms, and $\dfrac{3}{m} + \dfrac{n}{4} = \dfrac{3}{2} + \dfrac{1}{4}$. However, if $m = 2$ and $n = 3$, then m and n are positive integers, $\dfrac{3}{m}$ and $\dfrac{n}{4}$ are in lowest terms, and $\dfrac{3}{m} + \dfrac{n}{4} = \dfrac{3}{2} + \dfrac{3}{4}$; NOT sufficient.

Given (1) and (2), the table below shows that only one possibility exists for the values of m and n, and hence there is only one possible value of $\dfrac{3}{m} + \dfrac{n}{4}$.

(m,n)	$\dfrac{3}{m}$ lowest terms?	$\dfrac{n}{4}$ lowest terms?
(1,12)	$\dfrac{3}{1}$, YES	$\dfrac{12}{4}$, NO
(2,6)	$\dfrac{3}{2}$, YES	$\dfrac{6}{4}$, NO
(3,4)	$\dfrac{3}{3}$, NO	$\dfrac{4}{4}$, NO
(4,3)	$\dfrac{3}{4}$, **YES**	$\dfrac{3}{4}$, **YES**
(6,2)	$\dfrac{3}{6}$, NO	$\dfrac{2}{4}$, NO
(12,1)	$\dfrac{3}{12}$, NO	$\dfrac{1}{4}$, YES

**The correct answer is C;
both statements together are sufficient.**

DS21891.01

135. The first four digits of the six-digit initial password for a shopper's card at a certain grocery store is the customer's birthday in day-month digit form. For example, 15 August corresponds to 1508 and 5 March corresponds to 0503. The 5th digit of the initial password is the units digit of seven times the sum of the first and third digits, and the 6th digit of the initial password is the units digit of three times the sum of the second and fourth digits. What month, and what day of that month, was a customer born whose initial password ends in 16 ?

(1) The customer's initial password begins with 21, and its fourth digit is 1.

(2) The sum of the first and third digits of the customer's initial password is 3, and its second digit is 1.

(A) Statement (1) ALONE is sufficient, but statement (2) alone is not sufficient.

(B) Statement (2) ALONE is sufficient, but statement (1) alone is not sufficient.

(C) BOTH statements TOGETHER are sufficient, but NEITHER statement ALONE is sufficient.

(D) EACH statement ALONE is sufficient.

(E) Statements (1) and (2) TOGETHER are NOT sufficient.

Arithmetic Computation with integers

Let d_1, d_2, m_1, and m_2, respectively, represent the first four digits of the customer's initial password. Then, the entire password has the form $d_1 d_2 m_1 m_2 16$.

Because the maximum number of days per month is 31 and the number of months in a year is 12, d_1 can be only 0, 1, 2, or 3 and m_1 can be only 0 or 1. The following summarizes the possible values for d_1, d_2, m_1, and m_2.

d_1	d_2	m_1	m_2
0	1–9	0	1–9
1	0–9	1	0, 1, 2
2	0–9		
3	0, 1		

It is given that the fifth digit, which is 1, is the units digit of $7(d_1 + m_1)$. The only relevant multiple of 7 with units digit 1 is $(7)(3) = 21$, from which it follows that $d_1 + m_1 = 3$. Considering the restrictions on the values of the digits, then $d_1 = 2$ and $m_1 = 1$ or $d_1 = 3$ and $m_1 = 0$. Also, it is given that the sixth digit, which is 6, is the units digit of $3(d_2 + m_2)$. The only relevant multiples of 3 with units digit 6 are $(3)(2) = 6$ and $(3)(12) = 36$, from which it follows that $d_2 + m_2 = 2$ or $d_2 + m_2 = 12$.

Considering the restrictions on the values of the digits, if $d_2 + m_2 = 2$, then the only possibilities are $d_2 = 0$ and $m_2 = 2$ or $d_2 = 1$ and $m_2 = 1$ or $d_2 = 2$ and $m_2 = 0$. If $d_2 + m_2 = 12$, each of d_2 and m_2 is at least 3 because if either of the digits is less than 3, then the sum of the two digits cannot be 12. But if $d_1 = 2$ and $m_1 = 1$, which is one of the possibilities for d_1 and m_1 above, then m_2 can be only 0, 1, or 2; and if $d_1 = 3$ and $m_1 = 0$, which is the other possibility above for d_1 and m_1, then d_2 can be only 0 or 1. The table below summarizes the first four digits of the passwords that meet all conditions thus far.

First digit d_1	Second digit d_2	Third digit m_1	Fourth digit m_2
2	0	1	2
2	1	1	1
2	2	1	0
3	0	0	2
3	1	0	1
3	2	0	0

(1) It is given that the customer's password begins with 21 and the fourth digit is 1. In the table above, only one possible password meets these conditions, so the first four digits of the password are 2111 and the customer's birthday is the 21st day of November; SUFFICIENT.

(2) It is given that $d_1 + m_1 = 3$ and $d_2 = 1$. In the table above, the possibilities for the first four digits of the customer's password, where $d_2 = 1$, are 3101 and 2111, so the customer's birthday could be the 31st day of January or the 21st day of November; NOT sufficient.

The correct answer is A; statement 1 alone is sufficient.

DS38302.01

136. If K is a positive integer less than 10 and $N = 4{,}321 + K$, what is the value of K?

(1) N is divisible by 3.

(2) N is divisible by 7.

(A) Statement (1) ALONE is sufficient, but statement (2) alone is not sufficient.

(B) Statement (2) ALONE is sufficient, but statement (1) alone is not sufficient.

(C) BOTH statements TOGETHER are sufficient, but NEITHER statement ALONE is sufficient.

(D) EACH statement ALONE is sufficient.

(E) Statements (1) and (2) TOGETHER are NOT sufficient.

Arithmetic Computation with integers

(1) Dividing 4,321 by 3 gives a quotient of 1,440 and a remainder of 1, so $4{,}321 = 3(1{,}440) + 1$. It follows that $N = [3(1{,}440) + 1] + K = 3(1{,}440) + (1 + K)$. It is given that N is divisible by 3, from which it follows that $1 + K$ must be a multiple of 3. Therefore K can be 2, 5, or 8 since $K < 10$.

Alternatively, a number is divisible by 3 if and only if the sum of its digits is divisible by 3. If $K \neq 9$, the sum of the digits of $N = 4{,}321 + K$ is $4 + 3 + 2 + 1 + K = 10 + K = 1 + K$, which is divisible by 3 when $K = 2, 5,$ or 8; NOT sufficient.

(2) Dividing 4,321 by 7 gives a quotient of 617 and a remainder of 2, so $4{,}321 = 7(617) + 2$. It follows that $N = [7(617) + 2] + K = 7(617) + (2 + K)$. It is given that N is divisible by 7 from which it follows that $2 + K$ must be a multiple of 7. Thus, $K = 5$ since $K < 10$; SUFFICIENT.

The correct answer is B; statement 2 alone is sufficient.

DS99302.01

137. If s is an integer, is 24 a divisor of s?

(1) Each of the numbers 3 and 8 is a divisor of s.
(2) Each of the numbers 4 and 6 is a divisor of s.

(A) Statement (1) ALONE is sufficient, but statement (2) alone is not sufficient.
(B) Statement (2) ALONE is sufficient, but statement (1) alone is not sufficient.
(C) BOTH statements TOGETHER are sufficient, but NEITHER statement ALONE is sufficient.
(D) EACH statement ALONE is sufficient.
(E) Statements (1) and (2) TOGETHER are NOT sufficient.

Arithmetic Properties of integers

(1) If each of the numbers 3 and 8 is a divisor of s, then using the prime factorization of 8 gives $s = 2^3 \times 3 \times q = 24q$, for some positive integer q. Thus, 24 is a divisor of s; SUFFICIENT.

(2) If each of the numbers 4 and 6 is a divisor of s, then s could be 24 and it follows that 24 is a divisor of s. On the other hand, s could be 12 because 4 and 6 are both divisors of 12 and 24 is not a divisor of s; NOT sufficient.

The correct answer is A; statement 1 alone is sufficient.

Tip

If the integer n is divisible by each of the integers a and b and the greatest common factor of a and b is 1, then n is divisible by ab. However, if the greatest common divisor of a and b is greater than 1, then n may or may not be divisible by ab.

DS32402.01

138. $n = 2^4 \cdot 3^2 \cdot 5^2$ and positive integer d is a divisor of n. Is $d > \sqrt{n}$?

(1) d is divisible by 10.
(2) d is divisible by 36.

(A) Statement (1) ALONE is sufficient, but statement (2) alone is not sufficient.
(B) Statement (2) ALONE is sufficient, but statement (1) alone is not sufficient.
(C) BOTH statements TOGETHER are sufficient, but NEITHER statement ALONE is sufficient.
(D) EACH statement ALONE is sufficient.
(E) Statements (1) and (2) TOGETHER are NOT sufficient.

Arithmetic Properties of integers

Given $n = 2^4 \cdot 3^2 \cdot 5^2$, then $\sqrt{n} = (2^2)(3)(5) = 60$. If d is a divisor of n, determine whether $d > 60$ is true.

(1) It is given that d is divisible by 10. If $d = 10$, then d is divisible by 10 and d is a divisor of n since $n = (10)(2^3 \cdot 3^2 \cdot 5)$, but $d > 60$ is not true. However, if $d = 80$, then d is divisible by 10, d is a divisor of n since $n = (80)(3^2 \cdot 5)$, and $d > 60$ is true; NOT sufficient.

(2) It is given that d is divisible by 36. If $d = 36$, then d is divisible by 36 and d is a divisor of n since $n = (36)(2^2 \cdot 5^2)$, but $d > 60$ is not true. However, if $d = 72$, then d is divisible by 36, d is a divisor of n since $n = (72)(2 \cdot 5^2)$, and $d > 80$ is true; NOT sufficient.

Taking (1) and (2) together, it follows that d is divisible by $2^2 \cdot 3^2 \cdot 5 = 180$ and every multiple of 180 is greater than 60.

The correct answer is C; both statements together are sufficient.

DS52402.01

139. Exactly 3 deposits have been made in a savings account and the amounts of the deposits are 3 consecutive integer multiples of $7. If the sum of the deposits is between $120 and $170, what is the amount of each of the deposits?

(1) The amount of one of the deposits is $49.
(2) The amount of one of the deposits is $63.

(A) Statement (1) ALONE is sufficient, but statement (2) alone is not sufficient.
(B) Statement (2) ALONE is sufficient, but statement (1) alone is not sufficient.
(C) BOTH statements TOGETHER are sufficient, but NEITHER statement ALONE is sufficient.

(D)   EACH statement ALONE is sufficient.

(E)   Statements (1) and (2) TOGETHER are NOT sufficient.

Arithmetic Properties of integers

If k represents the least of the multiples of 7, then the three deposits, in dollars, are represented by $7k$, $7(k+1)$, and $7(k+2)$. The sum, in dollars, of the deposits is $21k + 21$, where $120 < 21k + 21 < 170$. It follows that the value of the integer k is 5, 6, or 7. If $k = 5$, then the deposits could be 35, 42, 49, with a sum of 126, which is between 120 and 170. If $k = 6$, then the deposits could be 42, 49, 56 with a sum of 147, which is between 120 and 170. If $k = 7$, then the deposits could be 49, 56, 63 with a sum of 168, which is between 120 and 170.

(1)   It is given that one of the deposits, in dollars, is 49. Since 49 is one of the amounts for each value of k in the remarks above, the amounts of the three deposits cannot be determined; NOT sufficient.

(2)   It is given that one of the deposits, in dollars, is 63. Since 63 occurs for exactly one value of k in the remarks above, the amounts, in dollars, of the deposits are 49, 56, and 63; SUFFICIENT.

The correct answer is B; statement 2 alone is sufficient.

DS44402.01

140. If x, y, and d are integers and d is odd, are both x and y divisible by d?

(1) $x + y$ is divisible by d.

(2) $x - y$ is divisible by d.

(A)   Statement (1) ALONE is sufficient, but statement (2) alone is not sufficient.

(B)   Statement (2) ALONE is sufficient, but statement (1) alone is not sufficient.

(C)   BOTH statements TOGETHER are sufficient, but NEITHER statement ALONE is sufficient.

(D)   EACH statement ALONE is sufficient.

(E)   Statements (1) and (2) TOGETHER are NOT sufficient.

Arithmetic Properties of integers

Determine whether both of the integers x and y are divisible by the odd integer d.

(1)   It is given that $x + y$ is divisible by d. It is possible that both x and y are divisible by d, and it is possible that they are not both divisible by d. For example, if $x = 4$, $y = 2$, and $d = 3$, then $4 + 2$ is divisible by 3, but neither 4 nor 2 is divisible by 3. On the other hand, if $x = 3$, $y = 6$, and $d = 3$, then $3 + 6$ is divisible by 3, and both 3 and 6 are divisible by 3; NOT sufficient.

(2)   It is given that $x - y$ is divisible by d. It is possible that both x and y are divisible by d, and it is possible that they are not both divisible by d. For example, if $x = 4$, $y = -2$, and $d = 3$, then $4 - (-2)$ is divisible by 3, but neither 4 nor -2 is divisible by 3. On the other hand, if $x = 3$, $y = -6$, and $d = 3$, then $3 - (-6)$ is divisible by 3, and both 3 and -6 are divisible by 3; NOT sufficient.

Taking (1) and (2) together, $x + y$ is divisible by d, so $\dfrac{x+y}{d}$ is an integer and $x - y$ is divisible by d, so $\dfrac{x-y}{d}$ is an integer. It follows that $\dfrac{x+y}{d} + \dfrac{x-y}{d} = \dfrac{2x}{d}$ is an integer and $\dfrac{x}{d}$ is an integer because d is odd. Similarly, $\dfrac{x+y}{d} - \dfrac{x-y}{d} = \dfrac{2y}{d}$ is an integer and $\dfrac{y}{d}$ is an integer because d is odd.

The correct answer is C; both statements together are sufficient.

DS06402.01

141. If x and y are integers, is $xy + 1$ divisible by 3?

(1)   When x is divided by 3, the remainder is 1.

(2)   When y is divided by 9, the remainder is 8.

(A)   Statement (1) ALONE is sufficient, but statement (2) alone is not sufficient.

(B)   Statement (2) ALONE is sufficient, but statement (1) alone is not sufficient.

(C)   BOTH statements TOGETHER are sufficient, but NEITHER statement ALONE is sufficient.

(D)   EACH statement ALONE is sufficient.

(E)   Statements (1) and (2) TOGETHER are NOT sufficient.

Arithmetic Properties of integers

Determine whether $xy + 1$ is divisible by 3, where x and y are integers.

(1)   It is given that the remainder is 1 when x is divided by 3. It follows that $x = 3q + 1$ for some integer q. So, $xy + 1 = (3q + 1)y + 1$. If $y = 2$, then $xy + 1 = 6q + 3$, which is divisible by 3. However, if $y = 1$, then $xy + 1 = 3q + 2$, which is not divisible by 3; NOT sufficient.

(2)   It is given that the remainder is 8 when y is divided by 9. It follows that $y = 9r + 8$ for some integer r. So, $xy + 1 = (9r + 8)x + 1$. If $x = 1$, then $xy + 1 = 9r + 9$, which is divisible by 3. However, if $x = 2$, then $xy + 1 = 18r + 17$, which is not divisible by 3; NOT sufficient.

Taking (1) and (2) together gives $x = 3q + 1$ and $y = 9r + 8$, from which it follows that $xy + 1 = (3q + 1)(9r + 8) + 1 = 27qr + 9r + 24q + 9 = 3(9qr + 3r + 8q + 3)$, which is divisible by 3.

The correct answer is C; both statements together are sufficient.

DS00502.01

142. If x and y are integers between 10 and 99, inclusive, is $\dfrac{x - y}{9}$ an integer?

(1) x and y have the same two digits, but in reverse order.

(2)   The tens' digit of x is 2 more than the units' digit, and the tens' digit of y is 2 less than the units' digit.

(A)   Statement (1) ALONE is sufficient, but statement (2) alone is not sufficient.

(B)   Statement (2) ALONE is sufficient, but statement (1) alone is not sufficient.

(C)   BOTH statements TOGETHER are sufficient, but NEITHER statement ALONE is sufficient.

(D)   EACH statement ALONE is sufficient.

(E)   Statements (1) and (2) TOGETHER are NOT sufficient.

Algebra Properties of integers

Determine whether $\dfrac{x - y}{9}$ is an integer, where x and y are 2-digit integers.

(1)   From (1), if $x = 10a + b$, then $y = 10b + a$. It follows that $x - y = 9(a - b)$, so $\dfrac{x - y}{9}$ is an integer; SUFFICIENT.

(2)   From (2), if $x = 10a + b$, then $a = b + 2$. If $y = 10c + d$, then $c = d - 2$. It is possible that $\dfrac{x - y}{9}$ is an integer (for example, if $x = 75$ and $y = 57$), and it is possible that $\dfrac{x - y}{9}$ is not an integer (for example, if $x = 75$ and $y = 46$); NOT sufficient.

The correct answer is A; statement 1 alone is sufficient.

DS85502.01

143. If b is the product of three consecutive positive integers c, $c + 1$, and $c + 2$, is b a multiple of 24 ?

(1) b is a multiple of 8.

(2) c is odd.

(A)   Statement (1) ALONE is sufficient, but statement (2) alone is not sufficient.

(B)   Statement (2) ALONE is sufficient, but statement (1) alone is not sufficient.

(C)   BOTH statements TOGETHER are sufficient, but NEITHER statement ALONE is sufficient.

(D)   EACH statement ALONE is sufficient.

(E)   Statements (1) and (2) TOGETHER are NOT sufficient.

Arithmetic Properties of integers

Since $24 = 2^3 \times 3$, and 1 is the only common factor of 2 and 3, any positive integer that is a multiple of 24 must be a multiple of both $2^3 = 8$ and 3. Furthermore, the product of any three consecutive positive integers is a multiple of 3. This can be shown as follows. In $b = c(c + 1)(c + 2)$, when the positive integer c is divided by 3, the remainder must be 0, 1, or 2. If the remainder is 0, then c itself is a multiple of 3.

If the remainder is 1, then $c = 3q + 1$ for some positive integer q and $c + 2 = 3q + 3 = 3(q + 1)$ is a multiple of 3. If the remainder is 2, then $c = 3r + 2$ for some positive integer r and $c + 1 = 3r + 3 = 3(r + 1)$ is a multiple of 3. In all cases, $b = c(c + 1)(c + 2)$ is a multiple of 3.

(1) It is given that b is a multiple of 8. It was shown above that b is a multiple of 3, so b is a multiple of 24; SUFFICIENT.

(2) It is given that c is odd. If $c = 3$, then $b = (3)(4)(5) = 60$, which is not a multiple of 24. If $c = 7$, then $b = (7)(8)(9) = (24)(7)(3)$, which is a multiple of 24; NOT sufficient.

The correct answer is A; statement 1 alone is sufficient.

DS17602.01
144. If ⊛ denotes a mathematical operation, does $x ⊛ y = y ⊛ x$ for all x and y ?

(1) For all x and y, $x ⊛ y = 2(x^2 + y^2)$.

(2) For all y, $0 ⊛ y = 2y^2$.

(A) Statement (1) ALONE is sufficient, but statement (2) alone is not sufficient.

(B) Statement (2) ALONE is sufficient, but statement (1) alone is not sufficient.

(C) BOTH statements TOGETHER are sufficient, but NEITHER statement ALONE is sufficient.

(D) EACH statement ALONE is sufficient.

(E) Statements (1) and (2) TOGETHER are NOT sufficient.

Algebra Functions

(1) For all x and y, $x ⊛ y = 2(x^2 + y^2)$ is equal to $y ⊛ x = 2(y^2 + x^2)$; SUFFICIENT.

(2) If $x ⊛ y = 2(x^2 + y^2)$ for all x and y, then $0 ⊛ y = 2y^2$ for all y and $x ⊛ y = y ⊛ x$ for all x and y. However, if $x ⊛ y = 2(x^3 + y^2)$ for all x and y, then $0 ⊛ y = 2y^2$ for all y, but $1 ⊛ 2 = 2(1^3) + 2(2^2) = 10$ and $2 ⊛ 1 = 2(2^3) + 2(1^2) = 18$; NOT sufficient.

The correct answer is A; statement 1 alone is sufficient.

DS37602.01
145. If n is an integer, is $\dfrac{n}{15}$ an integer?

(1) $\dfrac{3n}{15}$ is an integer.

(2) $\dfrac{8n}{15}$ is an integer.

(A) Statement (1) ALONE is sufficient, but statement (2) alone is not sufficient.

(B) Statement (2) ALONE is sufficient, but statement (1) alone is not sufficient.

(C) BOTH statements TOGETHER are sufficient, but NEITHER statement ALONE is sufficient.

(D) EACH statement ALONE is sufficient.

(E) Statements (1) and (2) TOGETHER are NOT sufficient.

Arithmetic Properties of integers

(1) We are given that $\dfrac{3n}{15} = \dfrac{n}{5}$ is an integer. If $n = 15$, then $\dfrac{n}{5}$ is an integer and $\dfrac{n}{15}$ is an integer. However, if $n = 5$, then $\dfrac{n}{5}$ is an integer and $\dfrac{n}{15}$ is not an integer; NOT sufficient.

(2) We are given that $\dfrac{8n}{15} = k$, where k is an integer. Since $8n = 15k$, it follows that both 3 and 5 are factors of $8n$. Therefore, the prime factorization of $8n = 2^3 \times n$ includes at least one factor of 3 and at least one factor of 5, and it is clear that each of these factors must be among the prime factors of n. Thus, both 3 and 5 are factors of n, and hence n is divisible by 15.

Alternatively, since 15 divides $8n$, and 8 and 15 are relatively prime, then it follows that 15 divides n; SUFFICIENT.

The correct answer is B; statement 2 alone is sufficient.

DS97602.01
146. If $1 < d < 2$, is the tenths digit of the decimal representation of d equal to 9 ?

(1) $d + 0.01 < 2$

(2) $d + 0.05 > 2$

(A) Statement (1) ALONE is sufficient, but statement (2) alone is not sufficient.

(B) Statement (2) ALONE is sufficient, but statement (1) alone is not sufficient.

(C) BOTH statements TOGETHER are sufficient, but NEITHER statement ALONE is sufficient.

(D) EACH statement ALONE is sufficient.

(E) Statements (1) and (2) TOGETHER are NOT sufficient.

Arithmetic Place value

Determine if the tenths digit of d, where $1 < d < 2$, is 9.

(1) Given $d + 0.01 < 2$, it follows that $d < 1.99$. It is possible that the tenths digit of d is 9 (for example, $1.98 < 1.99$, and the tenths digit of 1.98 is 9), and it is possible that the tenths digit of d is not 9 (for example, $1.88 < 1.99$, and the tenths digit of 1.98 is 8); NOT sufficient.

(2) Given $d + 0.05 > 2$, it follows that $d > 1.95$. Then $1.95 < d < 2$, since $d < 2$, so the tenths digit of d is 9; SUFFICIENT.

The correct answer is B; statement 2 alone is sufficient.

DS08602.01

147. The 9 participants in a race were divided into 3 teams with 3 runners on each team. A team was awarded $6 - n$ points if one of its runners finished in nth place, where $1 \leq n \leq 5$. If all of the runners finished the race and if there were no ties, was each team awarded at least 1 point?

(1) No team was awarded more than a total of 6 points.

(2) No pair of teammates finished in consecutive places among the top five places.

(A) Statement (1) ALONE is sufficient, but statement (2) alone is not sufficient.

(B) Statement (2) ALONE is sufficient, but statement (1) alone is not sufficient.

(C) BOTH statements TOGETHER are sufficient, but NEITHER statement ALONE is sufficient.

(D) EACH statement ALONE is sufficient.

(E) Statements (1) and (2) TOGETHER are NOT sufficient.

Arithmetic Operations with integers

Determine whether each team was awarded at least 1 point.

(1) It is given that no team was awarded more than 6 points. Since there were no ties, one of the nine runners had to have finished in first place. Say this runner was on Team A, and Team A was awarded 5 points. Since Team A was awarded at most 6 points, the best finish for one of the two other runners on Team A could be fifth place, leaving second place to a runner on one of the other teams. Say a runner on Team B finished in second place, and Team B was awarded 4 points. Since Team B was awarded at most 6 points, the best finish for one of the two other runners on Team B could be fourth place, leaving third place to a runner on the only team remaining, which would then be awarded 3 points. Thus, each team was awarded at least 1 point; SUFFICIENT.

(2) Given that no pair of teammates finished in consecutive places, it is possible that each team was awarded at least 1 point and it is also possible that at least one team was not awarded at least 1 point. For example, if the three runners on Team A placed first, third, and fifth and two runners on Team B placed second and fourth, then no pair of teammates finished in consecutive places, and Team C was awarded 0 points. On the other hand, if the three runners on Team A placed first, third, and fifth, a runner on Team B placed second, and a runner on Team C placed fourth, then no pair of teammates finished in consecutive places and each team was awarded at least 1 point; NOT sufficient.

The correct answer is A; statement 1 alone is sufficient.

DS38602.01

148. Can the positive integer n be written as the sum of two different positive prime numbers?

    (1) n is greater than 3.

    (2) n is odd.

    (A)   Statement (1) ALONE is sufficient, but statement (2) alone is not sufficient.

    (B)   Statement (2) ALONE is sufficient, but statement (1) alone is not sufficient.

    (C)   BOTH statements TOGETHER are sufficient, but NEITHER statement ALONE is sufficient.

    (D)   EACH statement ALONE is sufficient.

    (E)   Statements (1) and (2) TOGETHER are NOT sufficient.

Arithmetic Properties of integers

Determine if the positive integer n can be written as the sum of two different positive prime numbers.

    (1)   It is given that $n > 3$. If $n = 5$, then $n = 2 + 3$ and 2 and 3 are different positive prime numbers. However, $n = 11$, then n can be written as the following sums of two different positive numbers: $1 + 10, 2 + 9, 3 + 8, 4 + 7$, and $5 + 6$. In no case are the addends both prime; NOT sufficient.

    (2)   It is given that n is odd. The values of n in the examples used to show that (1) is not sufficient also satisfy (2); NOT sufficient.

Taken together, (1) and (2) are not sufficient because the same examples used to show that (1) is not sufficient also show that (2) is not sufficient.

The correct answer is E; both statements together are still not sufficient.

DS73402.01

149. Is x an integer?

    (1) x^2 is an integer.

    (2) $\dfrac{x}{2}$ is not an integer.

    (A)   Statement (1) ALONE is sufficient, but statement (2) alone is not sufficient.

    (B)   Statement (2) ALONE is sufficient, but statement (1) alone is not sufficient.

    (C)   BOTH statements TOGETHER are sufficient, but NEITHER statement ALONE is sufficient.

    (D)   EACH statement ALONE is sufficient.

    (E)   Statements (1) and (2) TOGETHER are NOT sufficient.

Algebra Properties of integers

Determine if x is an integer.

    (1)   It is given that x^2 is an integer. If, for example, $x^2 = 49$, then x is an integer. However, if $x^2 = 5$, then x is not an integer; NOT sufficient.

    (2)   It is given that $\dfrac{x}{2}$ is not an integer. If, for example, $x = 7$, then $\dfrac{x}{2}$ is not an integer, but x is an integer. However, if $x = \sqrt{5}$, then $\dfrac{x}{2}$ is not an integer and neither is x; NOT sufficient.

Taken together, (1) and (2) are not sufficient because the same examples used to show that (1) is not sufficient also show that (2) is not sufficient.

The correct answer is E; both statements together are still not sufficient.

DS46402.01

150. If b is an integer, is $\sqrt{a^2 + b^2}$ an integer?

    (1) $a^2 + b^2$ is an integer.

    (2) $a^2 - 3b^2 = 0$

    (A)   Statement (1) ALONE is sufficient, but statement (2) alone is not sufficient.

    (B)   Statement (2) ALONE is sufficient, but statement (1) alone is not sufficient.

    (C)   BOTH statements TOGETHER are sufficient, but NEITHER statement ALONE is sufficient.

    (D)   EACH statement ALONE is sufficient.

    (E)   Statements (1) and (2) TOGETHER are NOT sufficient.

Algebra Operations on radical expressions

Given that b is an integer, determine if $\sqrt{a^2 + b^2}$ is an integer.

(1) It is given that $a^2 + b^2$ is an integer. If $a = 3$ and $b = 4$, then $\sqrt{a^2 + b^2} = 5$, which is an integer. However, if $a = 1$ and $b = 2$, then $\sqrt{a^2 + b^2} = \sqrt{5}$, which is not an integer; NOT sufficient.

(2) It is given that $a^2 - 3b^2 = 0$, from which it follows that $a^2 = 3b^2$. Then, $\sqrt{a^2 + b^2} = \sqrt{3b^2 + b^2} = \sqrt{4b^2} = 2|b|$, which is an integer; SUFFICIENT.

The correct answer is B;
statement 2 alone is sufficient.

Chapter 3 Verbal Reasoning

Practice Questions Verbal Reasoning

Reading Comprehension

RC62100.01

Line   Anthropologists once thought that the ancestors
of modern humans began to walk upright because
it freed their hands to use stone tools, which they
had begun to make as the species evolved a brain of
(5)   increased size and mental capacity. But discoveries
of the three-million-year-old fossilized remains of
our hominid ancestor Australopithecus have yielded
substantial anatomical evidence that upright walking
appeared prior to the dramatic enlargement of the
(10)   brain and the development of stone tools.
        Walking on two legs in an upright posture (bipedal
locomotion) is a less efficient proposition than walking
on all fours (quadrupedal locomotion) because several
muscle groups that the quadruped uses for propulsion
(15)   must instead be adapted to provide the biped with
stability and control. The shape and configuration
of various bones must likewise be modified to allow
the muscles to perform these functions in upright
walking. Reconstruction of the pelvis (hipbones) and
(20)   femur (thighbone) of "Lucy," a three-million-year-old
skeleton that is the most complete fossilized skeleton
from the Australopithecine era, has shown that they
are much more like the corresponding bones of the
modern human than like those of the most closely
(25)   related living primate, the quadrupedal chimpanzee.
Lucy's wide, shallow pelvis is actually better suited to
bipedal walking than is the rounder, bowl-like pelvis of
the modern human, which evolved to form the larger
birth canal needed to accommodate the head of a
(30)   large-brained human infant. By contrast, the head of
Lucy's baby could have been no larger than that of a
baby chimpanzee.
        If the small-brained australopithecines were not
toolmakers, what evolutionary advantage did they
(35)   gain by walking upright? One theory is that bipedality
evolved in conjunction with the nuclear family:
monogamous parents cooperating to care for their
offspring. Walking upright permitted the father to
use his hands to gather food and carry it to his mate
(40)   from a distance, allowing the mother to devote more
time and energy to nurturing and protecting their
children. According to this view, the transition to
bipedal walking may have occurred as long as ten
million years ago, at the time of the earliest hominids,
(45)   making it a crucial initiating event in human evolution.

Questions 151–155 refer to the passage.

RC62100.01-10

151. The primary purpose of the passage is to

(A)   present an interpretation of the chronological
relationship between bipedal locomotion and
certain other key aspects of human evolution

(B)   compare the evolutionary advantages and
disadvantages of bipedal locomotion to those of
quadrupedal locomotion

(C)   argue that the transition to a nuclear family
structure was a more crucial step in human
evolution than was the development of stone tools

(D)   analyze anatomical evidence of bipedal
locomotion to show that the large brain of
modern humans developed at a later stage of
evolution than was previously believed

(E)   use examples of muscle and bone structure to
illustrate the evolutionary differences between
modern humans, australopithecines, and
chimpanzees

RC62100.01-20

152. The passage suggests that proponents of the theory
mentioned in lines 35–38 assume that which of the
following steps in human evolution occurred most
recently?

(A)   Development of a nuclear family structure

(B)   Transition from walking on all fours to walking
upright

(C)   Dramatic enlargement of the brain

(D)   Use of the hands to gather and carry food

(E)   Modification of propulsive muscles to provide
stability and control in locomotion

RC62100.01-30

153. According to the passage, the hominid australopithecine most closely resembled a modern human with respect to which of the following characteristics?

   (A)   Brain size

   (B)   Tool-making ability

   (C)   Shape of the pelvis

   (D)   Method of locomotion

   (E)   Preference for certain foods

RC62100.01-40

154. The passage suggests that, in comparison with the hominid australopithecines, modern humans are

   (A)   less well adapted to large-group cooperation

   (B)   less well adapted to walking upright

   (C)   more agile in running and climbing

   (D)   more well suited to a nuclear family structure

   (E)   more well suited to cooperative caring for their offspring

RC62100.01-50

155. The theory mentioned in lines 35–38 suggests that which of the following was true for the hominid ancestors of modern humans before they made the transition to walking upright?

   (A)   Their brains were smaller than the brains of present-day chimpanzees.

   (B)   They competed rather than cooperated in searching for food.

   (C)   Their mating patterns and family structure were closer to those of present-day chimpanzees than to those of modern humans.

   (D)   Males played a more significant role in child rearing than they played after the transition to walking upright.

   (E)   Females' ability to nurture and protect their offspring was limited by the need to find food for themselves.

RC04200.01

Line   Recent feminist scholarship concerning the United
States in the 1920s challenges earlier interpretations
that assessed the 1920s in terms of the unkept
"promises" of the women's suffrage movement. This
(5)   new scholarship disputes the long-held view that
because a women's voting bloc did not materialize
after women gained the right to vote in 1920,
suffrage failed to produce long-term political gains
for women. These feminist scholars also challenge
(10)   the old view that pronounced suffrage a failure for
not delivering on the promise that the women's vote
would bring about moral, corruption-free governance.
Asked whether women's suffrage was a failure, these
scholars cite the words of turn-of-the-century social
(15)   reformer Jane Addams, "Why don't you ask if suffrage
in general is failing?"
      In some ways, however, these scholars still present
the 1920s as a period of decline. After suffrage, they
argue, the feminist movement lost its cohesiveness,
(20)   and gender consciousness waned. After the mid-
1920s, few successes could be claimed by feminist
reformers: little could be seen in the way of legislative
victories.
      During this decade, however, there was intense
(25)   activism aimed at achieving increased autonomy for
women, broadening the spheres within which they
lived their daily lives. Women's organizations worked
to establish opportunities for women: they strove to
secure for women the full entitlements of citizenship,
(30)   including the right to hold office and the right to serve
on juries.

Questions 156–161 refer to the passage.

RC04200.01-10

156. The passage is primarily concerned with

(A)   providing evidence indicating that feminist
reformers of the 1920s failed to reach some of
their goals

(B)   presenting scholarship that contrasts suffragist
"promises" with the historical realities of the
1920s

(C)   discussing recent scholarship concerning the
achievements of women's suffrage during the
1920s and presenting an alternative view of
those achievements

(D)   outlining recent findings concerning events
leading to suffrage for women in the 1920s and
presenting a challenge to those findings

(E)   providing support for a traditional view of the
success of feminist attempts to increase gender
consciousness among women during the 1920s

RC04200.01-20

157. It can be inferred that the author of the passage
disagrees with the "new scholarship" mentioned in
line 5 regarding the

(A)   degree to which the "promises" of the suffrage
movement remained unkept

(B)   degree to which suffrage for women improved
the morality of governance

(C)   degree to which the 1920s represented a period
of decline for the feminist movement

(D)   degree of legislative success achieved by
feminist reformers during the 1920s

(E)   accuracy of the view that a women's voting bloc
did not materialize once suffrage was achieved

RC04200.01-30

158. The purpose of the second paragraph of the passage is to

   (A) suggest a reason why suffragist "promises" were not kept

   (B) contrast suffragist "promises" with the reality of the 1920s

   (C) deplore the lack of successful feminist reform in the 1920s

   (D) explain a view held by feminist scholars

   (E) answer the question asked by Jane Addams

RC04200.01-40

159. It can be inferred from the passage that recent scholars cite the words of Jane Addams primarily in order to

   (A) suggest that women's achievement of suffrage brought about changes in government that were not taken into account by early interpretations

   (B) point out contradictions inherent in the goals of the women's suffrage movement

   (C) show why a women's voting bloc was not formed when women won the right to vote

   (D) emphasize the place of social reform movements in the struggle for suffrage for women

   (E) suggest that the old view of women's suffrage was inappropriate

RC04200.01-50

160. It can be inferred that the analyses of the author of the passage and the scholars mentioned in lines 20–23 differ with regard to which of the following?

   (A) The criteria they use to evaluate the success of the feminist movement during the 1920s

   (B) Their interpretations of the "promises" of the suffragist movement

   (C) The suggestions they make for achieving feminist goals

   (D) Their definitions of what constitutes a legislative victory

   (E) Their estimations of the obstacles preventing women's having achieved a voting bloc in the 1920s

RC04200.01-60

161. The "new scholarship" mentioned in the first paragraph suggests which of the following concerning the "promises" mentioned in lines 4–5?

   (A) Failure to keep these promises is not a measure of the success of the suffrage movement.

   (B) Failure to keep these promises caused the feminist movement to lose cohesiveness during the 1920s.

   (C) Failure to keep these promises led recent feminist scholars to reevaluate the success of the suffrage movement.

   (D) These promises included securing for women the right to hold office and the right to serve on juries.

   (E) These promises were of little importance in winning suffrage for women.

RC60500.01

Line   *This passage is excerpted from material published in 1997.*

   Is there a massive black hole at the center of our galaxy, the Milky Way? The evidence is inconclusive.
(5) Just as the Sun's mass can be determined, given knowledge of other variables, by the velocity at which its planets orbit, the mass at the center of the Milky Way can be revealed by the velocities of stars and gas orbiting the galactic center. This dynamical
(10) evidence, based on recently confirmed assumptions about the stars' velocities, argues for an extremely compact object with a mass two to three million times the mass of our Sun. Although according to current theory this makes the mass at the center
(15) of the galaxy too dense to be anything but a black hole, the relative lack of energy radiating from the galactic center presents a serious problem. A black hole's gravity attracts surrounding matter, which swirls around the black hole, emitting some energy
(20) as it is engulfed. Scientists believe that the amount of energy that escapes the black hole should be about 10 percent of the matter's rest energy (the energy equivalent of its mass according to the equation $E=mc^2$). But when the energy coming from the
(25) galactic center is compared to widely held predictions based on how much matter should be falling into a theoretical central black hole, there is a discrepancy by a factor of a few thousand.

RC60500.01-10

162. The primary purpose of the passage is to

(A) present several theories that could account for a particular phenomenon

(B) argue that a certain question needs to be reframed in light of new evidence

(C) resolve an apparent inconsistency between two lines of evidence

(D) explain why a certain issue remains unresolved

(E) present evidence that calls into question certain assumptions of a current theory

RC60500.01-20

163. According to the passage, the dynamical evidence referred to in lines 9–10 supports which of the following?

(A) Recent assumptions about the velocities of stars

(B) Widely held predictions about the amount of matter a black hole will engulf

(C) The existence of an extremely dense object at the center of the Milky Way

(D) The contention that too much energy is coming from the mass at the Milky Way's galactic center for that mass to be a black hole

(E) The conclusion that a compact object of two to three million times the mass of our Sun is too dense to be anything but a black hole

RC60500.01-30

164. The "serious problem" referred to in line 17 could be solved if which of the following were true?

(A) Current assumptions about how much matter a black hole would engulf proved to be several thousand times too high.

(B) Current assumptions about how much matter a black hole would engulf proved to be a few thousand times too low.

(C) The object at the center of the Milky Way turned out to be far more dense than it is currently estimated to be.

(D) The object at the center of the Milky Way turned out to be far more massive than it is currently estimated to be.

(E) Matter being engulfed by a black hole radiated far more energy than is currently assumed.

RC60500.01-40

165. The "widely held predictions" mentioned in line 25 are predictions about the

    (A)   compactness of objects whose mass is millions of times the mass of our Sun

    (B)   velocities of stars orbiting the galactic center

    (C)   amount of matter swirling around the object at the center of the Milky Way

    (D)   amount of matter falling into a theoretical central black hole

    (E)   amount of energy that should be coming from a black hole at the center of the Milky Way

RC39461.01

Line   Despite their many differences of temperament and
of literary perspective, Emerson, Thoreau, Hawthorne,
Melville, and Whitman shared certain beliefs. Common
to all these writers is their humanistic perspective.
(5)   Its basic premises are that humans are the spiritual
center of the universe and that in them alone is the
clue to nature, history, and ultimately the cosmos.
Without denying outright the existence of a deity, this
perspective explains humans and the world in terms
(10)   of humanity.

    This common perspective is almost always
universalized. It emphasizes the human as universal,
freed from the accidents of time, space, birth, and
talent. Thus, for Emerson, the "American Scholar"
(15)   turns out to be simply "Man Thinking," while, for
Whitman, the "Song of Myself" merges imperceptibly
into a song of all the "children of Adam," where "every
atom belonging to me as good belongs to you."

    Also common to all five writers is the belief
(20)   that self-realization depends on the harmonious
reconciliation of two universal psychological
tendencies: first, the self-asserting impulse of
the individual to be responsible only to himself or
herself, and second, the self-transcending impulse
(25)   of the individual to know and become one with
that world. These conflicting impulses can be seen
in the democratic ethic. Democracy advocates
individualism, the preservation of the individual's
freedom and self-expression. But the democratic self
(30)   is torn between the duty to self, which is implied by
the concept of liberty, and the duty to society, which
is implied by the concepts of equality and fraternity.

    A third assumption common to the five writers is
that intuition and imagination offer a surer road to
(35)   truth than does abstract logic or scientific method. It
is illustrated by their emphasis upon introspection—
their belief that the clue to external nature is to be
found in the inner world of individual psychology—and
by their interpretation of experience as, in essence,
(40)   symbolic. Both these stresses presume an organic
relationship between the self and the cosmos of
which only intuition and imagination can properly take
account. These writers' faith in the imagination and
in themselves led them to conceive of the writer as a
(45)   seer.

Questions 166–172 refer to the passage.

RC39461.01-10

166. The author's discussion of Emerson, Thoreau,
Hawthorne, Melville, and Whitman is primarily
concerned with explaining

(A)   some of their beliefs about the difficulties
involved in self-realization

(B)   some of their beliefs concerning the world and
the place that humanity occupies in the universal
order

(C)   some of their beliefs concerning the relationship
between humanism and democracy

(D)   the way some of their beliefs are shaped by
differences in temperament and literary outlook

(E)   the effects of some of their beliefs on their
writings

RC39461.01-20

167. According to the passage, the five writers object to the
scientific method primarily because they think it

(A)   is not the best way to obtain an understanding
of the relationship between the individual and the
cosmos

(B)   is so specialized that it leads to an understanding
of separate parts of the universe but not of the
relationships among those parts

(C)   cannot provide an adequate explanation of
intuition and imagination

(D)   misleads people into believing they have an
understanding of truth, when they do not

(E)   prevents people from recognizing the symbolic
nature of experience

RC39461.01-30

168. The author quotes Whitman primarily in order to

   (A) show that the poet does not agree with Emerson

   (B) indicate the way the poet uses the humanist ideal to praise himself

   (C) suggest that the poet adapts the basic premises of humanism to his own individual outlook on the world

   (D) illustrate a way the poet expresses the relationship of the individual to the humanistic universe

   (E) demonstrate that the poet is concerned with the well-being of all humans

RC39461.01-40

169. It can be inferred that intuition is important to the five writers primarily because it provides them with

   (A) information useful for understanding abstract logic and scientific method

   (B) the discipline needed in the search for truth

   (C) inspiration for their best writing

   (D) clues to the interpretation of symbolic experience

   (E) the means of resolving conflicts between the self and the world

RC39461.01-50

170. The author discusses "the democratic ethic" (see lines 26–32) in order to

   (A) explain the relationship between external experience and inner imagination

   (B) support the notion that the self contains two conflicting and irreconcilable factions

   (C) illustrate the relationship between the self's desire to be individual and its desire to merge with all other selves

   (D) elaborate on the concept that the self constantly desires to realize its potential

   (E) give an example of the idea that, in order to be happy, the self must reconcile its desires with external reality

RC39461.01-60

171. It can be inferred that the idea of "an organic relationship between the self and the cosmos" (see lines 40–41) is necessary to the thinking of the five writers because such a relationship

   (A) enables them to assert the importance of the democratic ethic

   (B) justifies their concept of the freedom of the individual

   (C) sustains their faith in the existence of a deity

   (D) is the foundation of their humanistic view of existence

   (E) is the basis for their claim that the writer is a seer

RC39461.01-70

172. The passage is most relevant to which of the following areas of study?

   (A) Aesthetics and logic

   (B) History and literature

   (C) Theology and sociology

   (D) Anthropology and political science

   (E) Linguistics and art

RC49461.01

Line   The final quarter of the nineteenth century marked
a turning point in the history of biology—biologists
became less interested in applying an ideal of
historical explanation deductively to organic function
(5)   and more interested in discerning the causes of vital
processes through experimental manipulation. But it
is impossible to discuss the history of biology in the
nineteenth century without emphasizing that those
areas of biology most in the public eye had depended
(10)   on historical explanation. Wherever it was applied,
historical explanation was deemed causal explanation.
The biologist-as-historian and the general historian of
human events dealt with comparable phenomena and
assumed necessarily a common mode of explanation.
(15)   Nineteenth-century biologists found a historical
explanation of organic function attractive partly
because their observation of the formation of a
new cell from a preexisting cell seemed to confirm
a historical explanation of cell generation. The
(20)   same direct observation of continuous stages of
development was also possible when they examined
the complex sequence of events of embryogenesis.
In both cases, the observer received a concrete
impression that the daughter cell was brought into
(25)   being, or caused, by the prior cell. The argument
that these scientists employed confuses temporal
succession and causal explanation, of course,
but such confusion is the heart of most historical
explanation.
(30)   Not surprisingly, the evolutionary biologists of
the nineteenth century encountered a particularly
troublesome problem in their attempts to document
historical explanation convincingly: the factual record
of the history of life on earth (e.g., that provided by
(35)   fossils) was incomplete. The temporal continuity of
living forms was convincing, but was an assumption
that was difficult to uphold when one compared
species or organisms forming any two stages of the
evolutionary record. Nineteenth-century biologists
(40)   recognized this problem and attempted to resolve
it. Their solution today appears to be only verbal,
but was then regarded as eminently causal. The fact
of evolution demanded some connection between
all reproducing individuals and the species that they
(45)   compose, as well as between living species and
their extinct ancestors. Their solution, the concept
of heredity, seemed to fill in an admittedly deficient
historical record and seemed to complete the
argument for a historical explanation of evolutionary
(50)   events.

RC49461.01-10

173. The primary purpose of the passage is to

(A)   compare the information about organic function
made available by historical explanation with that
made available by the experimental investigation
of living organisms

(B)   assess the influence that theories of history had
on developments in the field of biology in the
nineteenth century

(C)   discuss the importance of historical explanation
in the thinking of nineteenth century biologists

(D)   contrast biologists' use of historical explanation
during the early nineteenth century with its use
during the final quarter of the nineteenth century

(E)   evaluate the way in which the concept of heredity
altered the use of historical explanation by
nineteenth-century biologists

RC49461.01-20

174. According to information presented in the passage,
which of the following is a true statement about
the methods of explanation used by biologists and
historians in the nineteenth century?

(A)   Neither biologists nor historians were able
to develop methods of explanation that were
accepted by the majority of their colleagues.

(B)   The methods used by biologists to explain
phenomena changed dramatically, whereas the
methods used by historians to explain events did
not change as noticeably.

(C)   Biologists believed that they had refined the
methods of explanation used by historians.

(D)   Biologists' and historians' methods of explaining
what they believed to be comparable phenomena
were similar.

(E)   Although biologists and historians adopted
similar methods of explanation, the biologists
were more apologetic about their use of these
methods.

RC49461.01-30

175. Which of the following best summarizes the "turning point" mentioned in line 2?

   (A) The beginning of the conflict between proponents of the ideal of historical explanation and the proponents of experimentation

   (B) The substitution of historical explanation for causal explanation

   (C) The shift from interest in historical explanation to interest in experimentation

   (D) The attention suddenly paid to problems of organic function

   (E) The growth of public awareness of the controversies among biologists

RC49461.01-40

176. The author implies that nineteenth-century biologists who studied embryogenesis believed that they

   (A) had discovered physical evidence that supported their use of historical explanation

   (B) were the first biologists to call for systematic experimentation on living organisms

   (C) were able to use historical explanation more systematically than were biologists who did not study embryogenesis

   (D) had inadvertently discovered an important part of the factual record of the history of living organisms on earth

   (E) had avoided the logical fallacies that characterize the reasoning of most nineteenth-century biologists

RC49461.01-50

177. The passage would be most likely to appear in which of the following?

   (A) An essay investigating the methodology used by historians of human events

   (B) A book outlining the history of biology in the nineteenth century

   (C) A seminar paper on the development of embryogenesis as a field of study in nineteenth-century biology

   (D) A review of a book whose topic is the discovery of fossils in the nineteenth century

   (E) A lecture whose subject is the limitations of experimental investigation in modern biology

RC59461.01

Line   Critics maintain that the fiction of Herman Melville
(1819–1891) has limitations, such as its lack
of inventive plots after *Moby-Dick* (1851) and its
occasionally inscrutable style. A more serious, yet
(5)   problematic, charge is that Melville is a deficient
writer because he is not a practitioner of the "art of
fiction," as critics have conceived of this art since the
late nineteenth-century essays and novels of Henry
James. Indeed, most twentieth-century commentators
(10)   regard Melville not as a novelist but as a writer of
romance, since they believe that Melville's fiction
lacks the continuity that James viewed as essential
to a novel: the continuity between what characters
feel or think and what they do, and the continuity
(15)   between characters' fates and their pasts or original
social classes. Critics argue that only *Pierre* (1852),
because of its subject and its characters, is close to
being a novel in the Jamesian sense.
      However, although Melville is not a Jamesian
(20)   novelist, he is not therefore a deficient writer. A more
reasonable position is that Melville is a different
kind of writer, who held, and should be judged
by, presuppositions about fiction that are quite
different from James's. It is true that Melville wrote
(25)   "romances"; however, these are not the escapist
fictions this word often implies, but fictions that
range freely among very unusual or intense human
experiences. Melville portrayed such experiences
because he believed these best enabled him to
(30)   explore moral questions, an exploration he assumed
was the ultimate purpose of fiction. He was content
to sacrifice continuity or even credibility as long
as he could establish a significant moral situation.
Thus Melville's romances do not give the reader
(35)   a full understanding of the complete feelings and
thoughts that motivate actions and events that shape
fate. Rather, the romances leave unexplained the
sequence of events and either simplify or obscure
motives. Again, such simplifications and obscurities
(40)   exist in order to give prominence to the depiction of
sharply delineated moral values, values derived from
a character's purely personal sense of honor, rather
than, as in a Jamesian novel, from the conventions of
society.

Questions 178–185 refer to the passage.

RC59461.01-10

178. The primary purpose of the passage is to

(A)   make a case for the importance of skillful
      psychological motivation in well-written novels
      and romances

(B)   contrast the romantic and novelistic traditions
      and assert the aesthetic superiority of the
      romantic tradition

(C)   survey some of the responses to Melville's fiction
      put forward by James and twentieth-century
      literary critics

(D)   argue that the charges made against Melville's
      fiction by literary critics are suspect and
      misleading

(E)   note several accusations made against Melville's
      fiction by literary critics and refute one of these
      accusations

RC59461.01-20

179. The author draws which of the following conclusions
about the fact that Melville's fiction often does not
possess the qualities of a Jamesian novel?

(A)   Literary critics should no longer use Jamesian
      standards to judge the value of novels.

(B)   Literary critics who have praised Melville's fiction
      at the expense of James's fiction should consider
      themselves justified.

(C)   Literary critics should no longer attempt to place
      writers, including Melville and James, in traditions
      or categories.

(D)   Melville and James should be viewed as different
      sorts of writers and one should not be regarded
      as inherently superior to the other.

(E)   Melville and James nevertheless share important
      similarities and these should not be overlooked
      or slighted when literary critics point out
      differences between the two writers.

RC59461.01-30
180. Which of the following would be the most appropriate title for the passage?

   (A) Melville's Unique Contribution to Romantic Fiction

   (B) Melville's Growing Reputation Among Twentieth-Century Literary Critics

   (C) Melville and the Jamesian Standards of Fiction: A Reexamination

   (D) Romantic and Novelistic: The Shared Assumptions of Two Traditions

   (E) The Art of Fiction: James's Influence on the Novelistic Tradition

RC59461.01-40
181. The author probably mentions Melville's *Pierre* to

   (A) refute those literary critics who have made generalizations about the quality of Melville's fiction

   (B) argue that the portrayal of characters is one of Melville's more accomplished literary skills

   (C) give an example of a novel that was thought by James to resemble his own fiction

   (D) suggest that literary critics find few exceptions to what they believe is a characteristic of Melville's fiction

   (E) reinforce the contention of literary critics

RC59461.01-50
182. Which of the following statements best describes the author's method of argumentation in lines 24–31?

   (A) The author describes an important standard of evaluation used by critics of Melville and then attacks that standard.

   (B) The author admits a contention put forward by critics of Melville but then makes a countercharge against those critics.

   (C) The author describes a charge advanced by critics of Melville and then points out a logical flaw in this charge.

   (D) The author provides evidence that seems to support a position held by critics of Melville but then demonstrates that the evidence actually supports a diametrically opposed position.

   (E) The author concedes an assertion made by critics of Melville but then mitigates the weight of the assertion by means of an explanation.

RC59461.01-60
183. Which of the following can logically be inferred from the passage about the author's application of the term "romance" to Melville's work?

   (A) The author uses the term in a broader way than did Melville himself.

   (B) The author uses the term in a different way than do many literary critics.

   (C) The author uses the term in a more systematic way than did James.

   (D) The author's use of the term is the same as the term's usual meaning for twentieth-century commentators.

   (E) The author's use of the term is less controversial than is the use of the term "novel" by many commentators.

RC59461.01-70

184. Which of the following can most logically be inferred about the author's estimation of the romantic and novelistic traditions of fiction?

(A) The romantic tradition should be considered at least as valuable as the novelistic tradition in the examination of human experience.

(B) The romantic tradition should be considered the more vital tradition primarily because Melville is part of that tradition.

(C) The romantic tradition should be considered the superior tradition because it is so widespread.

(D) The romantic tradition has had as much success in pleasing literary critics as has the novelistic tradition.

(E) The romantic and novelistic traditions have always made important contributions to literature, but their most important contributions have been in the twentieth century.

RC59461.01-80

185. The author of the passage would be most likely to agree that a writer's fiction should be evaluated by which of the following criteria?

(A) How consistently that fiction establishes credibility with the reader

(B) How skillfully that fiction supersedes the presuppositions or conventions of a tradition

(C) How completely that fiction satisfies the standards of judgment held by most literary critics

(D) How well that fiction fulfills the premises about fiction maintained by the writer of the fiction

(E) How well that fiction exhibits a continuity of subject and style over the course of the writer's career

RC69461.01

Line   Behind every book review there are two key figures: a book review editor and a reviewer. Editors decide whether a book is reviewed in their publication, when the review appears, how long it is, and who writes the

(5)   review.

        When many periodicals feature the same books, this does not prove that the editors of different periodicals have not made individual decisions. Before publication, editors receive news releases and

(10)   printer's proofs of certain books, signifying that the publishers will make special efforts to promote these books. They will be heavily advertised and probably be among the books that most bookstores order in quantity. Not having such books reviewed might give

(15)   the impression that the editor was caught napping, whereas too many reviews of books that readers will have trouble finding in stores would be inappropriate. Editors can risk having a few of the less popular titles reviewed, but they must consider what will be

(20)   newsworthy, advertised, and written about elsewhere.

        If these were the only factors influencing editors, few books that stand little chance of selling well would ever be reviewed. But editors feel some concern about what might endure, and therefore listen to

(25)   literary experts. A generation ago, a newspaper used a brilliant system of choosing which books to feature. The book review editor sent out a greater number of books than reviews he actually intended to publish. If a review was unenthusiastic, he reasoned that the

(30)   book was not important enough to be discussed immediately, and if good reviews of enough other books came in, the unenthusiastic review might never be printed. The unenthusiastic reviewers were paid promptly anyway, but they learned that if they wanted

(35)   their material to be printed, it was advisable to be kind.

        Most editors print favorable and unfavorable reviews; however, the content of the review may be influenced by the editor. Some editors would actually

(40)   feel that they had failed in their responsibility if they gave books by authors they admired to hostile critics or books by authors they disapproved of to critics who might favor them. Editors usually can predict who would review a book enthusiastically and who would

(45)   tear it to shreds.

RC69461.01-10

186. According to the passage, book review editors pay attention to all of the following in deciding which books should be reviewed in their publications EXCEPT

(A)   news releases from publishers

(B)   sales figures compiled by bookstores

(C)   the opinions of literary experts

(D)   the probability that the books will be extensively advertised

(E)   the likelihood that the books will be reviewed in other publications

RC69461.01-20

187. The main idea of the second paragraph is that

(A)   decisions made by book review editors are influenced by the business of selling books

(B)   book review editors must be familiar with all aspects of the book trade

(C)   advertising is the most important factor influencing book sales

(D)   book reviews usually have no influence on what books are ordered in quantity by stores

(E)   publishers deliberately try to influence the decisions of book review editors

RC69461.01-30

188. According to the passage, a major concern of the unenthusiastic book reviewers mentioned in line 33 was to

(A)   ensure prompt payment for their work

(B)   influence public opinion of books

(C)   confirm the opinions of other reviewers

(D)   promote new books by their favorite authors

(E)   have their reviews published in the newspaper

RC69461.01-40

189. The passage provides information to answer which of the following questions?

(A) Would most book review editors prefer to have books reviewed without regard to the probable commercial success of the books?

(B) Are publishers' efforts to persuade bookstores to order certain books generally effective?

(C) On what basis do literary experts decide that a book is or is not important?

(D) What criteria are used to determine the length of a particular book review?

(E) Have book review practices in general changed significantly since a generation ago?

RC69461.01-50

190. The passage suggests which of the following about book review readers?

(A) They pay careful attention to reviewers' biases as they read reviews.

(B) They disapprove of book review editors who try to influence what their reviewers write.

(C) They use book reviews in order to gauge whether a book is likely to endure.

(D) They expect to see timely reviews of widely publicized books in the periodicals they read.

(E) They are usually willing to search in several stores for a highly recommended book that is hard to find.

RC69461.01-60

191. Which of the following words, if substituted for "brilliant" in line 26, would LEAST change the meaning of the sentence?

(A) showy

(B) articulate

(C) literate

(D) stingy

(E) absurd

RC69461.01-70

192. Which of the following is an assumption made by the book review editor referred to in line 27?

(A) A book of great worth will receive only good reviews.

(B) An important book will endure despite possible bad reviews.

(C) Reviewers might hide their true opinions in order to have their reviews published.

(D) Book review editors should select reviewers whose opinions can be guessed in advance.

(E) Book review editors have an obligation to print extensive reviews of apparently important books.

RC69461.01-80

193. It can be inferred that, as a prospective book buyer, the author of the passage would generally respond to highly enthusiastic reviews of new books with

(A) resignation

(B) amusement

(C) condemnation

(D) skepticism

(E) disinterest

Line   There are two theories that have been used to explain ancient and modern tragedy. Neither quite explains the complexity of the tragic process or the tragic hero, but each explains important elements

(5) of tragedy, and, because their conclusions are contradictory, they represent extreme views. The first theory states that all tragedy exhibits the workings of external fate. Of course, the overwhelming majority of tragedies do leave us with a sense of the

(10) supremacy of impersonal power and of the limitation of human effort. But this theory of tragedy is an oversimplification, primarily because it confuses the tragic condition with the tragic process: the theory does not acknowledge that fate, in a tragedy,

(15) normally becomes external to the hero only after the tragic process has been set in motion. Fate, as conceived in ancient Greek tragedy, is the internal balancing condition of life. It appears as external only after it has been violated, just as justice is an

(20) internal quality of an honest person, but the external antagonist of the criminal. Secondarily, this theory of tragedy does not distinguish tragedy from irony. Irony does not need an exceptional central figure: as a rule, the more ignoble the hero the sharper the

(25) irony, when irony alone is the objective. It is heroism that creates the splendor and exhilaration that is unique to tragedy. The tragic hero normally has an extraordinary, often a nearly divine, destiny almost within grasp, and the glory of that original destiny

(30) never quite fades out of the tragedy.

    The second theory of tragedy states that the act that sets the tragic process in motion must be primarily a violation of moral law, whether human or divine; in short, that the tragic hero must have a

(35) flaw that has an essential connection with sin. Again it is true that the great majority of tragic heroes do possess hubris, or a proud and passionate mind that seems to make the hero's downfall morally explicable. But such hubris is only the precipitating

(40) agent of catastrophe, just as in comedy the cause of the happy ending is usually some act of humility, often performed by a noble character who is meanly disguised.

194. The primary purpose of the passage is to

  (A) compare and criticize two theories of tragedy

  (B) develop a new theory of tragedy

  (C) summarize the thematic content of tragedy

  (D) reject one theory of tragedy and offer another theory in its place

  (E) distinguish between tragedy and irony

195. The author states that the theories discussed in the passage "represent extreme views" (see line 6) because their conclusions are

  (A) unpopular

  (B) complex

  (C) paradoxical

  (D) contradictory

  (E) imaginative

196. The author objects to the theory that all tragedy exhibits the workings of external fate primarily because

  (A) fate in tragedies is not as important a cause of action as is the violation of a moral law

  (B) fate in tragedies does not appear to be something that is external to the tragic hero until after the tragic process has begun

  (C) the theory is based solely on an understanding of ancient Greek tragedy

  (D) the theory does not seem to be a plausible explanation of tragedy's ability to exhilarate an audience

  (E) the theory does not seem applicable to the large number of tragedies in which the hero overcomes fate

RC79461.01-40

197. Which of the following comparisons of the tragic with the ironic hero is best supported by information contained in the passage?

(A) A tragic hero's fate is an external condition, but an ironic hero's fate is an internal one.

(B) A tragic hero must be controlled by fate, but an ironic hero cannot be.

(C) A tragic hero's moral flaw surprises the audience, but an ironic hero's sin does not.

(D) A tragic hero and an ironic hero cannot both be virtuous figures in the same tragedy.

(E) A tragic hero is usually extraordinary, but an ironic hero may be cowardly or even villainous.

RC79461.01-50

198. The author contrasts an honest person and a criminal (see lines 19–21) primarily to

(A) prove that fate cannot be external to the tragic hero

(B) establish a criterion that allows a distinction to be made between irony and tragedy

(C) develop the distinction between the tragic condition and the tragic process

(D) introduce the concept of sin as the cause of tragic action

(E) argue that the theme of omnipotent external fate is shared by comedy and tragedy

RC79461.01-60

199. The author suggests that the tragic hero's "original destiny never quite fades out of the tragedy" (see lines 29–30) primarily to

(A) qualify the assertion that the theory of tragedy as a display of external fate is inconsistent

(B) introduce the discussion of the theory that tragedy is the consequence of individual sin

(C) refute the theory that the tragic process is more important than the tragic condition

(D) support the claim that heroism creates the splendor and exhilaration of tragedy

(E) distinguish between fate as conceived in ancient Greek tragedy and fate in more recent tragedy

RC79461.01-70

200. In the author's opinion, an act of humility in comedy is most analogous to

(A) a catastrophe in tragedy

(B) an ironic action in tragedy

(C) a tragic hero's pride and passion

(D) a tragic hero's aversion to sin

(E) a tragic hero's pursuit of an unusual destiny

Critical Reasoning

Analysis/Critique

CR31410.01

201. Most of Western music since the Renaissance has been based on a seven-note scale known as the diatonic scale, but when did the scale originate? A fragment of a bone flute excavated at a Neanderthal campsite has four holes, which are spaced in exactly the right way for playing the third through sixth notes of a diatonic scale. **The entire flute must surely have had more holes**, and the flute was made from a bone that was long enough for these additional holes to have allowed a complete diatonic scale to be played. Therefore, **the Neanderthals who made the flute probably used a diatonic musical scale**.

In the argument given, the two portions in **boldface** play which of the following roles?

(A) The first is presented as evidence that is confirmed by data presented elsewhere in the argument given; the second states a hypothesis that this evidence is used to undermine.

(B) The first is an opinion, for which no supporting evidence is presented in the argument given, that is used to support the main conclusion of the argument; the second is that main conclusion.

(C) The first describes a discovery as undermining the position against which the argument is directed; the second states the main conclusion of the argument.

(D) The first is a preliminary conclusion drawn on the basis of evidence presented elsewhere in the argument given; the second is the main conclusion that this preliminary conclusion supports.

(E) The first provides evidence to support the main conclusion of the argument; the second states a subsidiary conclusion that is drawn in order to support the main conclusion stated earlier in the argument.

CR53140.01

202. In a certain rural area, people normally dispose of household garbage by burning it. Burning household garbage releases toxic chemicals known as dioxins. New conservation regulations will require a major reduction in packaging—specifically, paper and cardboard packaging—for products sold in the area. Since such packaging materials contain dioxins, one result of the implementation of the new regulations will surely be a reduction in dioxin pollution in the area.

Which of the following, if true, most seriously weakens the argument?

(A) Garbage containing large quantities of paper and cardboard can easily burn hot enough for some portion of the dioxins that it contains to be destroyed.

(B) Packaging materials typically make up only a small proportion of the weight of household garbage, but a relatively large proportion of its volume.

(C) Per-capita sales of products sold in paper and cardboard packaging are lower in rural areas than in urban areas.

(D) The new conservation regulations were motivated by a need to cut down on the consumption of paper products in order to bring the harvesting of timber into a healthier balance with its regrowth.

(E) It is not known whether the dioxins released by the burning of household garbage have been the cause of any serious health problems.

CR45650.01

203. Suriland cannot both export wheat and keep bread plentiful and affordable in Suriland. Accordingly, Suriland's wheat farmers are required to sell their crop to the government, which pays them a dollar per bushel less than the price on the world market. Therefore, if the farmers could sell their wheat on the world market, they would make a dollar per bushel more, less any additional transportation and brokerage costs they would have to pay.

Which of the following, if true, most seriously weakens the argument?

(A) Suriland's wheat farmers have higher production costs than do farmers in many other wheat-producing countries.

(B) Sale of a substantial proportion of Suriland's wheat crop on the world market would probably depress the price of wheat.

(C) The transportation and brokerage costs that Suriland's farmers would face if they sold their wheat outside Suriland could amount to almost a dollar per bushel.

(D) Suriland is surrounded by countries that do not import any wheat.

(E) The price of a bushel of wheat on the world market occasionally drops below the average cost of producing a bushel of wheat in Suriland.

CR30370.01

204. Sasha: It must be healthy to follow a diet high in animal proteins and fats. Human beings undoubtedly evolved to thrive on such a diet, since our prehistoric ancestors ate large amounts of meat.

Jamal: But our ancestors also exerted themselves intensely in order to obtain this food, whereas most human beings today are much less physically active.

Jamal responds to Sasha by doing which of the following?

(A) Refuting her statement about our prehistoric ancestors

(B) Bringing forth a piece of information for the purpose of suggesting that she should qualify her main conclusion

(C) Citing additional evidence that indirectly supports her conclusion and suggests a way to broaden it

(D) Questioning whether her assumption about our prehistoric ancestors permits any conclusions about human evolution

(E) Expressing doubts about whether most human beings today are as healthy as our prehistoric ancestors were

CR70870.01

205. Some theorists and critics insist that no aesthetic evaluation of a work of art is sound if it is based even in part on data about the cultural background of the artist. This opinion is clearly false. The only sound aesthetic evaluations of artists' works are those that take into account factors such as the era and the place of the artists' births, their upbringing and education, and the values of their societies—in sum, those factors that are part of their cultural background.

The above argument is most vulnerable to which of the following objections?

(A) The argument presupposes the conclusion for which it purports to provide evidence.

(B) The argument cites evidence that undermines rather than supports the conclusion.

(C) The argument draws its conclusion by means of an equivocal interpretation of key terms.

(D) The argument assumes that the production of an effect is evidence of an intention to produce that effect.

(E) The argument assumes that evaluative disputes can be resolved by citing factual evidence.

CR53870.01

206. Banker: My country's laws require every bank to invest in its local community by lending money to local businesses, providing mortgages for local home purchases, and so forth. This is intended to revitalize impoverished local communities. But it is clear that the law will soon entirely cease to serve its intended purpose. An increasing number of banks incorporated in our country exist solely on the Internet and are not physically located in any specific community.

The banker's argument is most vulnerable to criticism on which of the following grounds?

(A) It overlooks the possibility that most banks that are physically located in specific communities in the banker's country are not located in impoverished communities.

(B) It takes for granted that a law that ceases to serve its originally intended purpose no longer serves any other beneficial purpose, either.

(C) It confuses a condition that would, if present, be likely to produce a given effect, with a condition that would probably be the cause if that effect were present.

(D) It overlooks the possibility that even if there is a strong correlation between two phenomena, neither of those phenomena are necessarily causally responsible for the other.

(E) It fails to adequately address the possibility that an increase in the number of banks of one kind in the banker's country will not lead to the complete elimination of banks of another kind.

CR15380.01

207. The contingency-fee system, which allows lawyers and their clients to agree that the lawyer will be paid only in the event of success, does not increase the number of medical malpractice lawsuits brought against doctors. As attorneys must cover the costs for their time and research, they want to be assured that any medical malpractice case they accept on a contingency-fee basis has substantial merit. Consequently, attorneys turn away many people who come to see them, for lack of a good case.

The argument above is most vulnerable to criticism on the grounds that it fails to

(A) specify the criteria attorneys use to judge the merits of a medical malpractice case

(B) consider whether, in the absence of a contingency-fee option, even people with meritorious cases are much less likely to initiate litigation if they believe they might incur large legal fees

(C) note whether, in successful medical malpractice lawsuits, the average monetary award after legal costs have been deducted is less under contingency-fee arrangements than otherwise

(D) consider the effect of the contingency-fee system on the number of lawsuits sought for reasons other than medical malpractice

(E) acknowledge the rising cost of medical malpractice insurance

CR66590.01

208. Shirla: In figure skating competitions that allow amateur and professional skaters to compete against each other, the professionals are bound to have an unfair advantage. After all, most of them became professional only after success on the amateur circuit.

Ron: But that means that it's been a long time since they've had to meet the more rigorous technical standards of the amateur circuit.

Which of the following is most likely a point at issue between Shirla and Ron?

(A) Whether there should be figure skating competitions that allow amateur and professional skaters to compete against each other

(B) Whether the scores of professional skaters competing against amateurs should be subject to adjustment to reflect the special advantages of professionals

(C) Whether figure skaters can successfully become professional before success on the amateur circuit

(D) Whether the technical standards for professional figure skating competition are higher than those for amateur figure skating competition

(E) Whether professional figure skaters have an unfair advantage over amateur figure skaters in competitions in which they compete against each other

CR03001.01

209. Recent observations suggest that small, earthlike worlds form a very low percentage of the planets orbiting stars in the galaxy other than the sun. Of over two hundred planets that astronomers have detected around other stars, almost all are hundreds of times larger and heavier than the earth and orbit stars much smaller than the sun.

Which of the following, if true, would most weaken the above justification of the claim that earthlike worlds form a low percentage of the total number of planets?

(A) There are millions of planets orbiting stars around which astronomers have not attempted to detect planets.

(B) The best current astronomical theories predict that almost all planets around other stars are probably hundreds of times larger than the earth.

(C) A planet orbiting a star similar to the sun would be more likely to be earthlike in size than would a planet orbiting a much smaller star.

(D) The smaller a planet is relative to the star it orbits, the more difficult it is for astronomers to detect.

(E) The observations would have detected any small, earthlike worlds orbiting the stars around which larger planets have been detected.

CR61021.01

210. Researchers in City X recently discovered low levels of several pharmaceutical drugs in public drinking water supplies. However, the researchers argued that the drugs in the water were not a significant public health hazard. They pointed out that the drug levels were so low that they could only be detected with the most recent technology, which suggested that the drugs may have already been present in the drinking water for decades, even though they have never had any discernible health effects.

Which of the following, if true, would most strengthen the researchers' reasoning?

(A) If a drug found in drinking water is not a significant public health hazard, then its presence in the water will not have any discernible health effects.

(B) There is no need to remove low levels of pharmaceutical drugs from public drinking water unless they present a significant public health hazard.

(C) Even if a substance in drinking water is a public health hazard, scientists may not have discerned which adverse health effects, if any, it has caused.

(D) Researchers using older, less sensitive technology detected the same drugs several decades ago in the public drinking water of a neighboring town but could find no discernible health effects.

(E) Samples of City X's drinking water taken decades ago were tested with today's most recent technology, and none of the pharmaceutical drugs were found.

CR20521.01

211. Errors in the performance of repetitive or "boring" tasks—often attributed to a momentary lapse in concentration—can be serious in such activities as flying a passenger aircraft. Is there any method that would provide warning of such lapses—for example by monitoring brain activity? Researchers scanned the brains of volunteers performing a repetitive task. When the tasks were being performed correctly, the volunteers' brains showed activity in cognitive-processing regions. However, these regions became less active several seconds before some errors were made, and another brain region, region X, became active. The researchers concluded that the monitoring of region X could provide warning of an impending error.

Which of the following, if true, most supports the researchers' conclusion?

(A) The cognitive effort required in performing a repetitive task diminishes significantly with increases in the number of repetitions of the task performance.

(B) Once a mistake was made and detected, brain activity in regions associated with cognitive effort sometimes increased.

(C) Other research found that whenever significant activity occurs in region X, it is generally with repetitive tasks, soon before an error occurs.

(D) The diminution of brain activity in cognitive processing regions and the increase of activity in region X began at least 5 seconds before the errors occurred.

(E) Reduced activity in brain regions associated with cognitive effort was accompanied by increased activity in regions that become active during sleep.

CR46521.01

212. City resident: These new digital electronic billboards should be banned for light pollution since they are much too bright.

Outdoor advertising spokesperson: No, that's not true. Testing with a sophisticated light meter shows that at night they throw off less light than traditional billboards that are reflectively lit. Your mistaken perception that they are brighter comes from looking directly at the light source—the screen itself.

The underlying strategy of the spokesperson's response to the resident is most analogous to the underlying strategy of which of the following?

(A) A doctor dismisses a patient's claim to have had a heart attack, citing a cardiac enzyme blood test.

(B) A politician rejects an accusation of perjury by denying the credibility of witness testimony.

(C) An insurance agent rejects a claim, on the grounds that there is insufficient evidence to support the claimant's testimony.

(D) An investigator casts doubt on the results of a lie detector, citing the subject's report of illness during the test.

(E) A psychologist treats a mental illness by encouraging a patient to abandon inconsistent beliefs.

CR02531.01

213. A fossil recently discovered in Marlandia, a chain of islands, proves that a present-day reptile indigenous to Marlandia is descended from an ancient reptile species that lived on the islands millions of years ago. The finding is surprising since the ancestral species was thought to have become extinct when Marlandia was submerged in a global sea-level rise twenty-five million years ago. Based on the new discovery, many scientists have concluded that the sea-level rise in question left at least part of Marlandia unsubmerged.

Which of the following would, if true, provide the most additional support for the scientists' conclusion?

(A) Reptiles in Marlandia have adapted to many environmental changes since the sea-level rise.

(B) Marlandia separated from a much larger landmass about eighty million years ago.

(C) No fossils that prove the relationship between the present-day species and the ancestral species have been found anywhere other than Marlandia.

(D) The present-day reptiles are able to thrive on very tiny Marlandia islands.

(E) The ancestral reptiles could not have survived long at sea.

CR21041.01

214. Advertisement: Our competitors' computer salespeople are paid according to the value of the products they sell, so they have a financial incentive to convince you to buy the most expensive units—whether you need them or not. But here at Comput-o-Mart, our salespeople are paid a salary that is not dependent on the value of their sales, so they won't try to tell you what to buy. That means when you buy a computer at Comput-o-Mart, you can be sure you're not paying for computing capabilities you don't need.

Which of the following would, if true, most weaken the advertisement's reasoning?

(A) Some less-expensive computers actually have greater computing power than more expensive ones.

(B) Salespeople who have a financial incentive to make sales generally provide more attentive service than do other salespeople.

(C) Extended warranties purchased for less-expensive computers can cost nearly as much as the purchase price of the computer.

(D) Comput-o-Mart is open only limited hours, which makes it more difficult for many shoppers to buy computers there than at other retail stores.

(E) Comput-o-Mart does not sell any computers that support only basic computing.

CR36441.01

215. Consumer advocate: In our nation, food packages must list the number of calories per food serving. But most of the serving sizes used are misleadingly small and should be updated. The serving sizes were set decades ago, when our nation's people typically ate smaller portions than they do today, and, as a result, people eating typical portions today consume more calories than the package labeling appears to indicate that they will. It is time package labeling reflected these changes.

Which of the following is the main point of the consumer advocate's argument?

(A) The number of calories per serving listed on most food packages in the consumer advocate's nation is misleadingly small.

(B) Most serving sizes used on food packages in the consumer advocate's nation should be increased to reflect today's typical portion sizes.

(C) People eating typical portions today often consume far more calories than the number of calories per serving listed on food packages in the consumer advocate's nation.

(D) The serving sizes used on food packages in the consumer advocate's nation were set when people ate smaller portions on average than they do today.

(E) The use of misleadingly small serving sizes on food packages in the consumer advocate's nation probably leads many people to consume more calories than they otherwise would.

CR05941.01

216. Columnist: Metro City has a lower percentage of residents with humanities degrees than any other city of comparable size in our nation. Nationwide, university graduates generally earn more than people who are not university graduates, but those with humanities degrees typically earn less than do graduates with degrees in other disciplines. So the main reason Metro City has higher income per capita than any other city of comparable size in our nation must be its low percentage of residents with humanities degrees.

Which of the following, if true, would most strengthen the columnist's argument?

(A) Metro City residents with humanities degrees have higher income per capita than do people with humanities degrees in any other city of comparable size in the nation.

(B) The percentage of residents with university degrees is lower in Metro City than in any other city of comparable size in the nation.

(C) Nationwide, university graduates without humanities degrees typically earn more than do individuals without university degrees.

(D) Metro City residents with degrees outside the humanities have per capita income no higher than the per capita income of such residents of other cities of comparable size in the nation.

(E) In Metro City, a lower proportion of university graduates have humanities degrees than in any other city of comparable size in the nation.

CR87051.01

217. Psychologist: In a survey, several hundred volunteers rated their own levels of self-control and their overall life satisfaction. The volunteers who rated themselves as having better self-control also reported greater satisfaction with their lives. This suggests that self-control is one factor that helps people avoid situations likely to produce dissatisfaction.

In order to assess the strength of the psychologist's argument, it would be most helpful to know whether

(A) people typically rate themselves as having significantly better self-control than expert psychological assessments would rate them as having

(B) people's perceptions of how satisfied they are with their lives could be affected by factors of which they are unaware

(C) there is a high level of self-control that tends to reduce overall life satisfaction

(D) people's ratings of their overall satisfaction with their lives tend to temporarily decrease in situations likely to produce dissatisfaction

(E) feelings of dissatisfaction significantly interfere with people's ability to exercise self-control

CR03161.01

218. Mansour: We should both plan to change some of our investments from coal companies to less polluting energy companies. And here's why. Consumers are increasingly demanding nonpolluting energy, and energy companies are increasingly supplying it.

Therese: I'm not sure we should do what you suggest. As demand for nonpolluting energy increases relative to supply, its price will increase, and then the more polluting energy will cost relatively less. Demand for the cheaper, dirtier energy forms will then increase, as will the stock values of the companies that produce them.

Therese responds to Mansour's proposal by doing which of the following?

(A) Advocating that consumers use less expensive forms of energy

(B) Implying that not all uses of coal for energy are necessarily polluting

(C) Disagreeing with Mansour's claim that consumers are increasingly demanding nonpolluting energy

(D) Suggesting that leaving their existing energy investments unchanged could be the better course

(E) Providing a reason to doubt Mansour's assumption that supply of nonpolluting energy will increase in line with demand

CR04161.01

219. Scientist: In an experiment, dogs had access to a handle they could pull to release food into a nearby enclosure that contained a familiar dog and nothing else, contained an unfamiliar dog and nothing else, or was empty. The dogs typically released more food to the familiar dog than to the unfamiliar dog. This suggests that dogs are more motivated to help other dogs they know than to help unfamiliar dogs.

The scientist's argument would be most strengthened if it were true that, in the experiment, the dogs with access to the handle tended to release more food when

(A) the behavior was being encouraged by a familiar person than when it was being encouraged by an unfamiliar person

(B) the enclosure was empty than when it contained an unfamiliar dog

(C) an unfamiliar dog in the enclosure was displaying hostility toward them than when an unfamiliar dog in the enclosure appeared friendly

(D) a dog in the enclosure appeared uninterested in food already released into the enclosure than when it appeared interested in that food

(E) a familiar dog was in the enclosure than when a familiar dog was visible but the enclosure was empty

CR09461.01

220. Most geologists believe oil results from chemical transformations of hydrocarbons derived from organisms buried under ancient seas. Suppose, instead, that oil actually results from bacterial action on other complex hydrocarbons that are trapped within the earth. As is well known, the volume of these hydrocarbons exceeds that of buried organisms. Therefore, our oil reserves would be greater than most geologists believe.

Which of the following, if true, gives the strongest support to the argument above about our oil reserves?

(A) Most geologists think optimistically about the earth's reserves of oil.

(B) Most geologists have performed accurate chemical analyses on previously discovered oil reserves.

(C) Ancient seas are buried within the earth at many places where fossils are abundant.

(D) The only bacteria yet found in oil reserves could have leaked down drill holes from surface contaminants.

(E) Chemical transformations reduce the volume of buried hydrocarbons derived from organisms by roughly the same proportion as bacterial action reduces the volume of other complex hydrocarbons.

CR66561.01

221. Meteorologists say that if only they could design an accurate mathematical model of the atmosphere with all its complexities, they could forecast the weather with real precision. But this is an idle boast, immune to any evaluation, for any inadequate weather forecast would obviously be blamed on imperfections in the model.

Which of the following, if true, could best be used as a basis for arguing against the author's position that the meteorologists' claim cannot be evaluated?

(A) Certain unusual configurations of data can serve as the basis for precise weather forecasts, even though the exact causal mechanisms are not understood.

(B) Most significant gains in the accuracy of the relevant mathematical models are accompanied by clear gains in the precision of weather forecasts.

(C) Mathematical models of the meteorological aftermath of such catastrophic events as volcanic eruptions are beginning to be constructed.

(D) Modern weather forecasts for as much as a full day ahead are broadly correct about 80 percent of the time.

(E) Meteorologists readily concede that the accurate mathematical model they are talking about is not now in their power to construct.

CR38561.01

222. The lobbyists argued that because there is no statistical evidence that breathing other people's tobacco smoke increases the incidence of heart disease or lung cancer in healthy nonsmokers, legislation banning smoking in workplaces cannot be justified on health grounds.

Of the following, which is the best criticism of the argument reported above?

(A) It ignores causes of lung cancer other than smoking.

(B) It neglects the damaging effects of smoke-filled air on nonsmokers who are not healthy.

(C) It fails to mention the roles played by diet, exercise, and heredity in the development of heart disease.

(D) It does not consider the possibility that nonsmokers who breathe smoke-filled air at work may become more concerned about their health.

(E) It does not acknowledge that nonsmokers, even those who breathe smoke-filled air at work, are in general healthier than smokers.

CR78561.01

223. Since 1978 when the copyright law was changed, books that are less than fifty years old must not be photocopied without the publisher's permission. Thus, any book that has been photocopied since 1978 without the publisher's permission must be at least fifty years old.

The reasoning above exhibits a flaw similar to one in which of the following?

(A) Any member of the solar system must be either a planet or a moon, so if an asteroid is neither a planet nor a moon, it must not be a member of the solar system.

(B) Anyone who rides a city bus must buy a bus pass, and since Demetrios has a bus pass, he must be riding on a city bus.

(C) A driver who turns right must signal, so any driver who did not signal must not have turned right.

(D) Anyone who legally crosses a national boundary must have a passport; thus anyone who does not have a passport cannot legally cross a national boundary.

(E) Any wage earner residing in the state must pay state taxes, so since Blodwen pays state taxes, she must be resident in the state.

CR10661.01

224. In the United States, injuries to passengers involved in automobile accidents are typically more severe than in Europe, where laws require a different kind of safety belt. It is clear from this that the United States needs to adopt more stringent standards for safety belt design to protect automobile passengers better.

Each of the following, if true, weakens the argument above EXCEPT:

(A) Europeans are more likely to wear safety belts than are people in the United States.

(B) Unlike United States drivers, European drivers receive training in how best to react in the event of an accident to minimize injuries to themselves and to their passengers.

(C) Cars built for the European market tend to have more sturdy construction than do cars built for the United States market.

(D) Automobile passengers in the United States have a greater statistical chance of being involved in an accident than do passengers in Europe.

(E) States that have recently begun requiring the European safety belt have experienced no reduction in the average severity of injuries suffered by passengers in automobile accidents.

CR60661.01

225. A country's Aeronautics Board (AB) employs inspectors who make routine annual inspections of all aircraft. On inspecting Azura Airlines' airplanes in December, they reported considerably more violations of AB rules this year, compared to a year ago. This fact explains why Azura had more accidents this year, compared to last year.

Which of the following, if true, would cast most doubt on the conclusion in the passage?

(A) Some aviation experts in other countries consider certain AB rules to be too lax and too easy to get around.

(B) Azura's routes are no more dangerous than are those of most other airlines.

(C) The AB increased the length and rigor of its inspections this year, compared to last year.

(D) Prior to last year Azura had an excellent safety record with very few accidents.

(E) In both years the AB report on Azura did not include violations on airplanes owned by Azura but leased by another airline.

CR13661.01

226. The more frequently employees take time to exercise during working hours each week, the fewer sick days they take. Even employees who exercise only once a week during working hours take less sick time than those who do not exercise. Therefore, if companies started fitness programs, the absentee rate in those companies would decrease significantly.

Which of the following, if true, most seriously weakens the argument above?

(A) Employees who exercise during working hours occasionally fall asleep for short periods of time after they exercise.

(B) Employees who are frequently absent are the least likely to cooperate with or to join a corporate fitness program.

(C) Employees who exercise only once a week in their company's fitness program usually also exercise after work.

(D) Employees who exercise in their company's fitness program use their working time no more productively than those who do not exercise.

(E) Employees who exercise during working hours take slightly longer lunch breaks than employees who do not exercise.

Construction/Plan

CR67370.01

227. Distressed by his own personal tragedies, the Roman philosopher Cicero once asked himself whether a wise person should try to achieve the Stoic ideal of complete emotionlessness. Cicero reasoned that, however desirable the goal may be, a wise person could never attain it, since emotions are not simply irrational urges. They are, rather, a product of one's estimate of the goodness and badness of the events, people, and actions one witnesses.

Which of the following is an assumption required by Cicero's reasoning?

(A) Wise people inevitably evaluate at least some of the things they observe.

(B) Irrationality makes evaluation of what one observes impossible.

(C) Wisdom precludes attempting to attain what one cannot.

(D) If evaluations are based only on reason, then they are inaccurate.

(E) A wise person will not evaluate what cannot be directly observed.

CR49770.01

228. First discovered several years ago in North American lakes and rivers, the northern snakehead is a nonnative fish with no local predators. To keep the northern snakehead's population from growing, for the past three years wildlife officials have been paying recreational fishers for each northern snakehead they catch. In this way, the officials hope to stop the northern snakeheads from eliminating rare native fish species.

To evaluate the likelihood that the wildlife officials' plan will succeed, it would be most useful to determine which of the following?

(A) Whether the northern snakehead's population in local lakes and rivers could be reduced by introducing predators from its native habitat

(B) How local population numbers of rare native fish species have been changing since the wildlife officials started paying recreational fishers to catch northern snakeheads

(C) Whether the fish species on which the northern snakehead preys in regions to which it is native and in which it is abundant have become significantly depleted in recent decades

(D) What total number of northern snakehead have been caught by recreational fishers since the wildlife officials began paying for them

(E) Whether rare native fish species in the region face any threats to their survival other than the proliferation of northern snakehead

CR51080.01

229. Scientist: A greenhouse gas, for example, carbon dioxide, forms a transparent layer that traps solar heat beneath it in the earth's atmosphere. Atmospheric levels of carbon dioxide are currently increasing, causing the climate to warm—an effect that is predicted by at least one computer model of the greenhouse effect. But the warming that has occurred is a great deal less than what would be expected based on the model. Therefore, _____.

Which of the following most logically completes the scientist's argument?

(A) better measurements of atmospheric levels of carbon dioxide are needed

(B) the definition of "greenhouse gas" should probably be reconsidered

(C) there are factors besides the increase in greenhouse-gas emissions contributing to the warming of the climate

(D) the computer model of the greenhouse effect must be incorrect in some respect

(E) the likely consequences of any warming of the climate are unlikely to be much less damaging than predicted

CR09090.01

230. Beets and carrots are higher in sugar than many other vegetables. They are also high on the glycemic index, a scale that measures the rate at which a food increases blood sugar levels. But while nutritionists usually advise people to avoid high-sugar and high-glycemic-index foods, despite any nutritional benefits they may confer, they are not very concerned about the consumption of beets and carrots.

Which of the following, if true, would best explain the nutritionists' lack of concern?

(A) Foods with added sugar are much higher in sugar, and have a larger effect on blood sugar levels, than do beets and carrots.

(B) Most consumption of beets and carrots occurs in combination with higher-protein foods, which reduce blood sugar fluctuations.

(C) Beets and carrots contain many nutrients, such as folate, beta-carotene, and vitamin C, of which many people fail to consume optimal quantities.

(D) The glycemic index measures the extent to which a food increases blood sugar levels as compared to white bread, a food that is much less healthy than beets and carrots.

(E) Nutritionists have only recently come to understand that a food's effect on blood sugar levels is an important determinant of that food's impact on a person's health.

CR36601.01

231. Ozone in the stratosphere blocks deadly ultraviolet rays from the sun, but chlorofluorocarbons (CFCs) in aerosols and other products have thinned this protective layer. Evidence of this is the ozone hole that forms over the South Pole every Antarctic spring as temperatures drop below −78°C, the temperature at which ozone depletion occurs. Measurements of the ozone hole taken at various times this spring show that, compared with the same times the previous year, its area diminished by four million square kilometers. Nevertheless, scientists have not concluded that the ozone layer is recovering.

Which of the following would, if true, provide the strongest reason for the scientists' reaction to the measurements?

(A) The ozone hole has steadily grown in size every year for the past decade except this year.

(B) The length of time that the ozone hole persists fluctuates from year to year.

(C) As a result of international treaties, CFCs have been completely banned for several years.

(D) Weather patterns allowed unusual amounts of warm air to mix into the polar regions this year.

(E) Human-made CFCs retain their ability to destroy ozone molecules for seventy-five to one hundred years.

CR29111.01

232. The recycling of municipal solid waste is widely seen as an environmentally preferable alternative to the prevailing practices of incineration and of dumping in landfills. Recycling is profitable, as the recycling programs already in operation demonstrate. A state legislator proposes that communities should therefore be required to adopt recycling and to reach the target of recycling 50 percent of all solid waste within 5 years.

Which of the following, if true, most seriously calls into question the advisability of implementing the proposal?

(A) Existing recycling programs have been voluntary, with citizen participation ranging from 30 percent in some communities to 80 percent in others.

(B) Existing recycling programs have been restricted to that 20 percent of solid waste that, when reprocessed, can match processed raw materials in quality and price.

(C) Existing recycling programs have had recurrent difficulties finding purchasers for their materials, usually because of quantities too small to permit cost-effective pickup and transportation.

(D) Some of the materials that can be recycled are the very materials that, when incinerated, produce the least pollution.

(E) Many of the materials that cannot be recycled are also difficult to incinerate.

CR30721.01

233. Biologist: Species with broad geographic ranges probably tend to endure longer than species with narrow ranges. The broader a species' range, the more likely that species is to survive the extinction of populations in a few areas. Therefore, it is likely that the proportion of species with broad ranges tends to gradually increase with time.

The biologist's conclusion follows logically from the above if which of the following is assumed?

(A) There are now more species with broad geographic ranges than with narrow geographic ranges.

(B) Most species can survive extinctions of populations in a few areas as long as the species' geographic range is not very narrow.

(C) If a population of a species in a particular area dies out, that species generally does not repopulate that area.

(D) If a characteristic tends to help species endure longer, then the proportion of species with that characteristic tends to gradually increase with time.

(E) Any characteristic that makes a species tend to endure longer will make it easier for that species to survive the extinction of populations in a few areas.

CR79731.01

234. Letter to the editor: If the water level in the Searle River Delta continues to drop, the rising sea level will make the water saltier and less suitable for drinking. Currently, 40 percent of the water from upstream tributaries is diverted to neighboring areas. To keep the delta's water level from dropping any further, we should end all current diversions from the upstream tributaries. Neighboring water utilities are likely to see higher costs and diminished water supplies, but these costs are necessary to preserve the delta.

Which of the following would, if true, indicate a serious potential weakness of the suggested plan of action?

(A) Desalination equipment would allow water from the delta to be used for drinking even it if became saltier.

(B) Water level is only one factor that affects salinity in the delta.

(C) The upstream tributaries' water levels are controlled by systems of dams and reservoirs.

(D) Neighboring areas have grown in population since the water was first diverted from upstream tributaries.

(E) Much of the recent drop in the delta's water level can be attributed to a prolonged drought that has recently ended.

CR47931.01

235. Researchers conditioned a group of flies to associate a particular odor with a weak electric shock. Twenty-four and forty-eight hours later the researchers conducted tests on the flies, both individually and in groups, to determine whether the flies retained the conditioning. When tested individually, the flies were significantly less likely to avoid areas marked with the odor. The researchers hypothesized that in the presence of the odor, a fly that retains the conditioned association gives off an alarm signal that arouses the attention of any surrounding flies, retriggering the association in them and thereby causing them to avoid the odor.

The researchers' hypothesis requires which of the following assumptions?

(A) The flies do not give off odors as alarm signals.

(B) Flies that did not avoid the odor when tested individually were not merely following other flies' movements when tested in a group.

(C) Flies that did not avoid the odor when tested individually were less likely than the other flies to avoid the odor when tested in a group.

(D) Prior to their conditioning, the flies would likely have found the odor used in the experiment to be pleasant.

(E) An electric shock was used during the flies' conditioning and during the later tests.

CR02741.01

236. Kayla: Many people are reluctant to shop in our neighborhood because street parking is scarce. The city plans to address this by adding parking meters with time limits that ensure that parking spaces are generally available. But this plan will surely backfire— shoppers dislike paying at parking meters, so most will probably drive to other neighborhoods to shop at malls with free parking.

Which of the following, if true, would be the most logically effective rebuttal a proponent of the city's plan could make to Kayla's objection?

(A) Most shoppers dislike hunting for scarce street parking spaces much more than they dislike paying for metered parking spaces.

(B) The city could post signs with street parking time limits to ensure that parking spaces become available without forcing shoppers to pay at meters.

(C) Currently, most shoppers in the neighborhood drive only occasionally to shop at malls in other neighborhoods.

(D) The neighborhood already contains a parking lot where shoppers must pay to park.

(E) The nearby malls with free parking have no parking time limits to help ensure that parking spaces in their lots become available.

CR78551.01

237. A new handheld device purports to determine the severity of concussions by reading the brain's electrical signals and comparing them to a database of 15,000 scans compiled at a brain research lab. The device is intended to help doctors decide whether an athlete who has received a blow to the head during a competition should be sent back into the game.

Which of the following would it be most useful to establish in order to evaluate the effectiveness of the device for its intended purpose?

(A) Whether the database of brain scans will regularly be updated with new scans

(B) Whether by use of this device doctors will be able to make a sound decision about whether to allow an athlete back into the competition before it ends

(C) Whether the device will be endorsed by a large number of medical professionals

(D) Whether the database includes scans of non-injured athletes in the same game as the injured athlete

(E) Whether team doctors have until now been mistaken in their assessments of whether an athlete can safely continue to play

CR30461.01

238. Mashika: We already know from polling data that some segments of the electorate provide significant support to Ms. Puerta. If those segments also provide significant support to Mr. Quintana, then no segment of the electorate that provides significant support to Mr. Quintana provides significant support to Mr. Ramirez.

Salim: But actually, as the latest polling data conclusively shows, at least one segment of the electorate does provide significant support to both Mr. Quintana and Mr. Ramirez.

Among the following statements, which is it most reasonable to infer from the assertions by Mashika and Salim?

(A) At least one segment of the electorate provides significant support neither to Mr. Quintana nor to Mr. Ramirez.

(B) At least one segment of the electorate provides significant support to Ms. Puerta but not to Mr. Quintana.

(C) Each segment of the electorate provides significant support to Ms. Puerta.

(D) Each segment of the electorate provides significant support to Mr. Quintana.

(E) Each segment of the electorate provides significant support to Mr. Ramirez.

CR98461.01

239. The proportion of manufacturing companies in Alameda that use microelectronics in their manufacturing processes increased from 6 percent in 1979 to 66 percent in 1990. Many labor leaders say that the introduction of microelectronics is the principal cause of the great increase in unemployment during that period in Alameda. In actual fact, however, most of the job losses were due to organizational changes. Moreover, according to new figures released by the labor department, there were many more people employed in Alameda in the manufacturing industry in 1990 than in 1979.

Which of the following, if true, best reconciles the discrepancy between the increase in unemployment and the increase in jobs in the manufacturing industry of Alameda?

(A) Many products that contain microelectronic components are now assembled completely by machine.

(B) Workers involved in the various aspects of the manufacturing processes that use microelectronic technology need extensive training.

(C) It is difficult to evaluate numerically what impact on job security the introduction of microelectronics in the workplace had before 1979.

(D) In 1990 over 90 percent of the jobs in Alameda's manufacturing companies were filled by workers who moved to Alameda because they had skills for which there was no demand in Alameda prior to the introduction of microelectronics there.

(E) Many workers who have retired from the manufacturing industry in Alameda since 1979 have not been replaced by younger workers.

CR00561.01

240. The retinas of premature babies are not fully developed at birth. Because their retinas are so delicate, premature babies sometimes lose their sight. Methods for preventing this syndrome, which is called retinopathy of prematurity, have improved, but the proportion of premature babies who lose their sight because of this syndrome has increased.

Which of the following, if true, best reconciles the apparent discrepancy described above?

(A) When premature babies are born, their retinas are developmentally unprepared to deal with light and air in the environment outside the womb.

(B) The oxygen that must be administered to premature babies at birth can sometimes have a damaging effect on the babies' retinas, but the oxygen is now administered in less damaging concentrations than it used to be.

(C) The effects of retinopathy of prematurity can be reduced by controlling the exposure of premature babies to light and oxygen, but this method cannot completely prevent the syndrome.

(D) The improvement of methods to prevent retinopathy of prematurity has been a gradual process, and there is still a need for further knowledge.

(E) Improved medical technology is saving the lives of premature babies who would previously have died, but these babies have even more delicate retinas than do other premature babies and are more apt to lose their sight.

CR60561.01

241. Although elementary school children have traditionally received considerable instruction in creating visual art, there has been no such instruction in music. Consequently, in contrast to the situation for visual art, most people as adults do not recognize the artistic intentions of composers. To remedy this situation, a few educators now recommend teaching elementary school students to compose music.

Which of the following, if true, is the strongest basis for arguing that implementation of the recommendation will not lead to the desired result?

(A) Few elementary school students are likely to create superior compositions.

(B) Traditional education facilitates the appreciation of visual art, but not the recognition of the artistic intentions of artists.

(C) More people report that they enjoy music than report that they enjoy visual art.

(D) Some composers have had little formal instruction in composition.

(E) The recommendation is based on the results of a controlled longitudinal study conducted in three schools within a single city.

CR47561.01

242. Pharmaceutical companies spend more than ever on research and development; yet the number of new drugs patented each year has dropped since 1963. At the same time, profits—at constant 1963 dollars—for the industry as a whole have been steadily increasing.

Which of the following, if true, is the single factor most likely to explain, at least in part, the three trends mentioned above for money spent, drugs patented, and profits made?

(A) Government regulations concerning testing requirements for novel drugs have become steadily more stringent.

(B) Research competition among pharmaceutical companies has steadily intensified as a result of a general narrowing of research targets to drugs for which there is a large market.

(C) Many pharmaceutical companies have entered into collaborative projects with leading universities, while others have hired faculty members away from universities by offering very generous salaries.

(D) The number of cases in which one company's researchers duplicated work done by another company's researchers has steadily grown.

(E) The advertising budgets of the major pharmaceutical companies have grown at a higher rate than their profits have.

CR97561.01

243. Under the agricultural policies of Country R, farmers can sell any grain not sold on the open market to a grain board at guaranteed prices. It seems inevitable that, in order to curb the resultant escalating overproduction, the grain board will in just a few years have to impose quotas on grain production, limiting farmers to a certain flat percentage of the grain acreage they cultivated previously.

Suppose an individual farmer in Country R wishes to minimize the impact on profits of the grain quota whose eventual imposition is being predicted. If the farmer could do any of the following and wants to select the most effective course of action, which should the farmer do now?

(A) Select in advance currently less profitable grain fields and retire them if the quota takes effect.

(B) Seek long-term contracts to sell grain at a fixed price.

(C) Replace obsolete tractors with more efficient new ones.

(D) Put marginal land under cultivation and grow grain on it.

(E) Agree with other farmers on voluntary cutbacks in grain production.

CR69561.01

244. Exports of United States wood pulp will rise considerably during this year. The reason for the rise is that the falling value of the dollar will make it cheaper for paper manufacturers in Japan and Western Europe to buy American wood pulp than to get it from any other source.

Which of the following is an assumption made in drawing the conclusion above?

(A) Factory output of paper products in Japan and Western Europe will increase sharply during this year.

(B) The quality of the wood pulp produced in the United States would be adequate for the purposes of Japanese and Western European paper manufacturers.

(C) Paper manufacturers in Japan and Western Europe would prefer to use wood pulp produced in the United States if cost were not a factor.

(D) Demand for paper products made in Japan and Western Europe will not increase sharply during this year.

(E) Production of wood pulp by United States companies will not increase sharply during this year.

CR79561.01

245. A company's personnel director surveyed employees about their satisfaction with the company's system for awarding employee performance ratings. The survey data indicated that employees who received high ratings were very satisfied with the system. The personnel director concluded from these data that the company's best-performing employees liked the system.

The personnel director's conclusion assumes which of the following?

(A) No other performance rating system is as good as the current system.

(B) The company's best-performing employees received high ratings.

(C) Employees who received low ratings were dissatisfied with the system.

(D) Employees who receive high ratings from a performance-rating system will like that system.

(E) The company's best-performing employees were motivated to perform well by the knowledge that they would receive performance ratings.

CR00661.01

246. There are fundamentally two possible changes in an economy that will each cause inflation unless other compensating changes also occur. These changes are either reductions in the supply of goods and services or increases in demand. In a pre-banking economy the quantity of money available, and hence the level of demand, is equivalent to the quantity of gold available.

If the statements above are true, then it is also true that in a pre-banking economy

(A) any inflation is the result of reductions in the supply of goods and services

(B) if other factors in the economy are unchanged, increasing the quantity of gold available will lead to inflation

(C) if there is a reduction in the quantity of gold available, then, other things being equal, inflation must result

(D) the quantity of goods and services purchasable by a given amount of gold is constant

(E) whatever changes in demand occur, there will be compensating changes in the supply of goods and services

CR20661.01

247. Clearbell Telephone provides slow-dialing (SD) service to customers for a low fee, and fast-dialing (FD) service to other customers who pay a somewhat higher fee. FD technology, however, is so efficient that it costs Clearbell substantially less per average call to provide than does SD. Nonetheless, accountants have calculated that Clearbell's profits would drop if it provided FD to all its customers at the current low-fee rate.

Assume that installation costs for FD are insignificant if the customer already has SD service. Which of the following, if true about Clearbell, best explains the results of the accountants' calculation?

(A) The extra revenue collected from customers who pay the high fee is higher than the extra cost of providing SD to customers who pay the low fee.

(B) The low fee was increased by 6 percent last year, whereas the higher fee was not increased last year.

(C) Although 96 percent of customers regard FD service as reliable and more convenient than SD, fewer than 10 percent of them choose to pay the higher fee for FD service.

(D) The company's competitors generally provide business customers with FD service at low-fee rates.

(E) Profits rose slightly each month for the first three months after FD was first offered to customers, then fell slightly each month for the succeeding three months.

CR23661.01

248. Manufacturers sometimes discount the price of a product to retailers for a promotion period when the product is advertised to consumers. Such promotions often result in a dramatic increase in amount of product sold by the manufacturers to retailers. Nevertheless, the manufacturers could often make more profit by not holding the promotions.

Which of the following, if true, most strongly supports the claim above about the manufacturers' profit?

(A) The amount of discount generally offered by manufacturers to retailers is carefully calculated to represent the minimum needed to draw consumers' attention to the product.

(B) For many consumer products the period of advertising discounted prices to consumers is about a week, not sufficiently long for consumers to become used to the sale price.

(C) For products that are not newly introduced, the purpose of such promotions is to keep the products in the minds of consumers and to attract consumers who are currently using competing products.

(D) During such a promotion retailers tend to accumulate in their warehouses inventory bought at discount; they then sell much of it later at their regular price.

(E) If a manufacturer fails to offer such promotions but its competitor offers them, that competitor will tend to attract consumers away from the manufacturer's product.

CR33661.01

249. Advertisement: Today's customers expect high quality. Every advance in the quality of manufactured products raises customer expectations. The company that is satisfied with the current quality of its products will soon find that its customers are not. At MegaCorp, meeting or exceeding customer expectations is our goal.

Which of the following must be true on the basis of the statements in the advertisement above?

(A) MegaCorp's competitors will succeed in attracting customers only if those competitors adopt MegaCorp's goal as their own.

(B) A company that does not correctly anticipate the expectations of its customers is certain to fail in advancing the quality of its products.

(C) MegaCorp's goal is possible to meet only if continuing advances in product quality are possible.

(D) If a company becomes satisfied with the quality of its products, then the quality of its products is sure to decline.

(E) MegaCorp's customers are currently satisfied with the quality of its products.

Sentence Correction

Communication

SC21011.01

250. The prime lending rate is a key rate in the economy: not only are the interest rates on most loans to small and medium-sized businesses tied to the prime, but also on a growing number of consumer loans, including home equity loans.

    (A) not only are the interest rates on most loans to small and medium-sized businesses tied to the prime, but also on

    (B) tied to the prime are the interest rates not only on most loans to small and medium-sized businesses, but also on

    (C) the interest rates not only on most loans to small and medium-sized businesses are tied to the prime, but also

    (D) not only the interest rates on most loans to small and medium-sized businesses are tied to the prime, but also on

    (E) the interest rates are tied to the prime, not only on most loans to small and medium-sized businesses, but also

SC83811.01

251. Lacking information about energy use, people tend to overestimate the amount of energy used by equipment, such as lights, that are visible and must be turned on and off and underestimate that used by unobtrusive equipment, such as water heaters.

    (A) equipment, such as lights, that are visible and must be turned on and off and underestimate that

    (B) equipment, such as lights, that are visible and must be turned on and off and underestimate it when

    (C) equipment, such as lights, that is visible and must be turned on and off and underestimate it when

    (D) visible equipment, such as lights, that must be turned on and off and underestimate that

    (E) visible equipment, such as lights, that must be turned on and off and underestimate it when

SC37561.01

252. Evidence of some shifts in the character of violence on television is emerging from a new study of 500 television programs by the Center for Media and Public Affairs, a nonprofit research center in Washington, D.C., a study that is underwritten by a number of educational institutions.

    (A) programs by the Center for Media and Public Affairs, a nonprofit research center in Washington, D.C., a study that is underwritten by a number of educational institutions

    (B) programs by the Center for Media and Public Affairs, a nonprofit research center in Washington, D.C., and it is underwritten by a number of educational institutions

    (C) programs underwritten by a number of educational institutions and conducted by the Center for Media and Public Affairs, a nonprofit research center based in Washington, D.C.

    (D) programs, a study underwritten by a number of educational institutions and conducted by the Center for Media and Public Affairs, a nonprofit research center in Washington, D.C.

    (E) programs, a study conducted by the Center for Media and Public Affairs, a nonprofit research center based in Washington, D.C., and it is underwritten by a number of educational institutions

SC48461.01

253. Judge Lois Forer's study asks why <u>do some litigants have a preferred status over others in the use of a public resource, the courts, which in theory are available to all but in fact are unequally distributed among</u> rich and poor.

- (A) do some litigants have a preferred status over others in the use of a public resource, the courts, which in theory are available to all but in fact are unequally distributed among

- (B) some litigants have a preferred status over others in the use of a public resource, the courts, which in theory are available to all but in fact are unequally distributed between

- (C) do some litigants have a preferred status over another in the use of a public resource, the courts, in theory available to all but in fact are unequally distributed among

- (D) some litigants have a preferred status to another in the use of a public resource, the courts, in theory available to all but in fact not equally distributed between

- (E) does one litigant have a preferred status over the other in the use of a public resource, the courts, in theory available to all but in fact they are not equally distributed among

SC30561.01

254. During an ice age, the buildup of ice at the poles and the drop in water levels near the equator speed up the earth's rotation, <u>like a spinning figure skater whose speed increases when her arms are drawn in</u>.

- (A) like a spinning figure skater whose speed increases when her arms are drawn in

- (B) like the increased speed of a figure skater when her arms are drawn in

- (C) like a figure skater who increases speed while spinning with her arms drawn in

- (D) just as a spinning figure skater who increases speed by drawing in her arms

- (E) just as a spinning figure skater increases speed by drawing in her arms

SC01561.01

255. <u>Added to the increase in hourly wages requested last July, the railroad employees are now seeking an expanded program of retirement benefits.</u>

- (A) Added to the increase in hourly wages requested last July, the railroad employees are now seeking an expanded program of retirement benefits.

- (B) Added to the increase in hourly wages which had been requested last July, the employees of the railroad are now seeking an expanded program of retirement benefits.

- (C) The railroad employees are now seeking an expanded program of retirement benefits added to the increase in hourly wages that were requested last July.

- (D) In addition to the increase in hourly wages that were requested last July, the railroad employees are now seeking an expanded program of retirement benefits.

- (E) In addition to the increase in hourly wages requested last July, the employees of the railroad are now seeking an expanded program of retirement benefits.

SC21561.01

256. The use of gravity waves, which do not interact with matter <u>in the way electromagnetic waves do, hopefully will enable</u> astronomers to study the actual formation of black holes and neutron stars.

- (A) in the way electromagnetic waves do, hopefully will enable

- (B) in the way electromagnetic waves do, will, it is hoped, enable

- (C) like electromagnetic waves, hopefully will enable

- (D) like electromagnetic waves, would enable, hopefully

- (E) such as electromagnetic waves do, will, it is hoped, enable

SC61561.01

257. <u>Many of them chiseled from solid rock centuries ago, the mountainous regions of northern Ethiopia are dotted with hundreds of monasteries.</u>

- (A) Many of them chiseled from solid rock ago, the mountainous regions of northern Ethiopia are dotted with hundreds of monasteries.
- (B) Chiseled from solid rock centuries ago, the mountainous regions of northern Ethiopia are dotted with many hundreds of monasteries.
- (C) Hundreds of monasteries, many of them chiseled from solid rock centuries ago, are dotting the mountainous regions of northern Ethiopia.
- (D) The mountainous regions of northern Ethiopia are dotted with hundreds of monasteries, many of which are chiseled from solid rock centuries ago.
- (E) The mountainous regions of northern Ethiopia are dotted with hundreds of monasteries, many of them chiseled from solid rock centuries ago.

SC81561.01

258. <u>Plausible though it sounds, the weakness of the hypothesis</u> is that it does not incorporate all relevant evidence.

- (A) Plausible though it sounds, the weakness of the hypothesis
- (B) Even though it sounds plausible, the weakness of the hypothesis
- (C) Though plausible, the hypothesis' weakness
- (D) Though the hypothesis sounds plausible, its weakness
- (E) The weakness of the hypothesis which sounds plausible

SC32561.01

259. <u>In despite of the steady population flow out from rural areas into urban clusters, nearly 5 million farm households are still in Japan</u> out of a total population of some 116 million people.

- (A) In despite of the steady population flow out from rural areas into urban clusters, nearly 5 million farm households are still in Japan
- (B) In spite of the steady population flow out from rural areas into urban clusters, nearly 5 million farm households are still in Japan
- (C) Despite the steady population flow from rural areas into urban clusters, Japan's farm households are still nearly 5 million
- (D) Despite the steady population flow from rural areas to urban clusters, there are still nearly 5 million farm households in Japan
- (E) In Japan, despite the steady population flow out from rural areas into urban clusters, still there are nearly 5 million farm households

SC52561.01

260. Financial uncertainties <u>from the accident at Three Mile Island may prove even more deterring to the nuclear industry than political opposition is.</u>

- (A) from the accident at Three Mile Island may prove even more deterring to the nuclear industry than political opposition is
- (B) from the accident at Three Mile Island may prove to be even more serious a deterrent to the nuclear industry than political opposition
- (C) from the accident at Three Mile Island may prove to be an even more serious deterrent to the nuclear industry than political opposition
- (D) resulting from the accident at Three Mile Island may prove to be an even more serious deterrent to the nuclear industry than is political opposition
- (E) resulting from the accident at Three Mile Island may prove even more deterring to the nuclear industry than political opposition

SC72561.01

261. <u>Remembered almost as an epic among America's 12,000 Bosnian Muslims is the digging of Chicago's subway tunnels in the early 1900s, one of the proudest of family legends.</u>

(A)   Remembered almost as an epic among America's 12,000 Bosnian Muslims is the digging of Chicago's subway tunnels in the early 1900s, one of the proudest of family legends.

(B)   Almost an epic among America's 12,000 Bosnian Muslims is the digging in the early 1900s of Chicago's subway tunnels, one of the proudest of family legends.

(C)   Digging Chicago's subway tunnels in the early 1900s, America's 12,000 Bosnian Muslims remember it almost as an epic and it is the one of the proudest of family legends.

(D)   America's 12,000 Bosnian Muslims remember almost as an epic the digging of Chicago's subway tunnels in the early 1900s, one of the proudest of family legends.

(E)   One of the proudest of family legends, remembered almost as an epic among America's 12,000 Bosnian Muslims, is the digging of Chicago's subway tunnels in the early 1900s.

SC92561.01

262. <u>Like the one reputed to live in Loch Ness, also an inland lake connected to the ocean by a river, inhabitants of the area around Lake Champlain claim sightings of a long and narrow "sea monster."</u>

(A)   Like the one reputed to live in Loch Ness, also an inland lake connected to the ocean by a river, inhabitants of the area around Lake Champlain claim sightings of a long and narrow "sea monster."

(B)   Inhabitants of the area around Lake Champlain claim sightings of a long and narrow "sea monster" similar to the one reputed to live in Loch Ness, which, like Lake Champlain is an inland lake connected to the ocean by a river.

(C)   Inhabitants of the area around Lake Champlain claim sightings of a long and narrow "sea monster" similar to Loch Ness's, which, like Lake Champlain, is an inland lake connected to the ocean by a river.

(D)   Like Loch Ness's reputed monster, inhabitants of the area around Lake Champlain, also an inland lake connected to the ocean by a river, claim sightings of a long and narrow "sea monster."

(E)   Similar to that reputed to live in Loch Ness, inhabitants of the area around Lake Champlain, also an inland lake connected to the ocean by a river, claim sightings of a long and narrow "sea monster."

SC43561.01

263. <u>A star will compress itself into a white dwarf, a neutron star, or a black hole after it passes through a red giant stage, depending on mass.</u>

(A) A star will compress itself into a white dwarf, a neutron star, or a black hole after it passes through a red giant stage, depending on mass.

(B) After passing through a red giant stage, depending on its mass, a star will compress itself into a white dwarf, a neutron star, or a black hole.

(C) After passing through a red giant stage, a star's mass will determine if it compresses itself into a white dwarf, a neutron star, or a black hole.

(D) Mass determines whether a star, after passing through the red giant stage, will compress itself into a white dwarf, a neutron star, or a black hole.

(E) The mass of a star, after passing through the red giant stage, will determine whether it compresses itself into a white dwarf, a neutron star, or a black hole.

SC53561.01

264. Although many art patrons can readily differentiate a good debenture from an undesirable one, they are <u>much less expert in distinguishing good paintings and poor ones, authentic art and</u> fakes.

(A) much less expert in distinguishing good paintings and poor ones, authentic art and

(B) far less expert in distinguishing good paintings from poor ones, authentic art from

(C) much less expert when it comes to distinguishing good paintings and poor ones, authentic art from

(D) far less expert in distinguishing good paintings and poor ones, authentic art and

(E) far less the expert when it comes to distinguishing between good painting, poor ones, authentic art, and

SC83561.01

265. <u>A site once used as an observatory by the Anasazi, ancient pueblo dwellers of New Mexico, has been recently discovered where patterns of light and shadow were employed to establish the precise limits of the positions of the Sun and Moon over a nineteen-year cycle.</u>

(A) A site once used as an observatory by the Anasazi, ancient pueblo dwellers of New Mexico, has been recently discovered where patterns of light and shadow were employed to establish the precise limits of the positions of the Sun and Moon over a nineteen-year cycle.

(B) A recently discovered site was once used as an observatory by the Anasazi, ancient pueblo dwellers of New Mexico, where patterns of light and shadow were employed to establish the precise limits of the positions of the Sun and Moon over a nineteen-year cycle.

(C) At a recently discovered site once used as an observatory by the Anasazi, ancient pueblo dwellers of New Mexico, patterns of light and shadow were employed to establish the precise limits of the positions of the Sun and Moon over a nineteen-year cycle.

(D) Patterns of light and shadow were employed to establish the precise limits of the positions of the Sun and Moon over a nineteen-year cycle at a site that was recently discovered and was once used by the Anasazi, ancient pueblo dwellers of New Mexico.

(E) Patterns of light and shadow were employed to establish the precise limits of the positions of the Sun and Moon over a nineteen-year cycle at a recently discovered place that the Anasazi, ancient pueblo dwellers of New Mexico, once used the site as an observatory.

SC93561.01

266. The cathedrals of the Middle Ages were <u>community centers just as much as they were purely religious edifices; and they were structures that represented a city's commitment to a public realm, the opposite of being a private one.</u>

(A) community centers just as much as they were purely religious edifices; and they were structures that represented a city's commitment to a public realm, the opposite of being a private one

(B) community centers as much as purely religious edifices; they were structures representing a city's commitment to a public realm, as opposed to private

(C) community centers as well as purely religious edifices; they were structures that represented a city's commitment to a public realm, not private ones

(D) as much community centers as purely religious edifices, structures that represented a city's commitment to a public realm, as opposed to a private one

(E) as much community centers as they were purely religious edifices, structures representing a city's commitment to a public realm, opposite of a private one

SC14561.01

267. The newspaper story accurately recounted the history of the colonial <u>mansion, that it contained thirteen rooms, and that it had a reputation for being a haunted house.</u>

(A) mansion, that it contained thirteen rooms, and that it had a reputation for being a haunted house

(B) mansion, that it contained thirteen rooms, and that it had a reputation of being haunted

(C) mansion, that the mansion contained thirteen rooms, and said that it had a reputation for being haunted

(D) mansion, said that it contained thirteen rooms and had a reputation for being a haunted house

(E) mansion and said that the mansion contained thirteen rooms and had the reputation of being haunted

SC24561.01

268. An archaeological excavation at <u>what might have been a workshop where statues were reproduced yielded 1,532 fragments of human figures, including</u> 7 intact statues.

(A) what might have been a workshop where statues were reproduced yielded 1,532 fragments of human figures, including

(B) what might have been a workshop where statues were reproduced yielded 1,532 fragments of human figures and

(C) the site of a possible workshop where statues were reproduced yielded 1,532 fragments of human figures and

(D) the site of a possible workshop where statues were reproduced yielded 1,532 fragments of human figures, including

(E) the site of a possible workshop where statues might have been reproduced yielded 1,532 fragments of human figures, including

SC34561.01

269. Sophisticated laser-guided land graders can now flatten uneven farmland almost perfectly <u>so as not to waste rainwater</u> in runoff down sloping fields.

(A) so as not to waste rainwater

(B) so that rainwater is not wasted

(C) so that there is no wasted rainwater

(D) and thereby not waste rainwater

(E) and there is no rainwater wasted

SC54561.01

270. Because there is not a linguistic census in France, as there is for Britain, there is difficulty in estimating the number of speakers of Breton, a Celtic language.

(A) Because there is not a linguistic census in France, as there is for Britain, there is difficulty in estimating

(B) Because there is no linguistic census in France, unlike Britain, it is difficult to estimate

(C) Unlike Britain, there is no linguistic census in France, and that fact makes for difficulty in estimating

(D) There is not a linguistic census in France, as there is for Britain, a fact making for difficulty in the estimation of

(E) There is no linguistic census in France, as there is in Britain, a fact that makes it difficult to estimate

SC65561.01

271. When adjusted for body weight, children of various age groups in the United States have a caffeine intake that ranges from 36 to 58 percent of the average amount consumed by adults.

(A) children of various age groups in the United States have a caffeine intake that ranges from 36 to 58 percent of the average amount consumed by adults

(B) the caffeine intake of children of various age groups in the United States ranges from 36 to 58 percent of the average amount consumed by adults

(C) various age groups of children in the United States range in caffeine intake from 36 to 58 percent of that consumed by the average adult

(D) in the United States, children of various age groups have a caffeine intake that ranges from 36 to 58 percent of the average adult's consumption

(E) in the United States, the caffeine intake of children in various age groups ranges from 36 to 58 percent of that consumed by the average adult

SC06561.01

272. When bitter managerial conflicts plague a small company, conflicts that in the past might have led to dissolution of the business, executives are likely to turn to outside professional counselors to help resolve disagreement.

(A) conflicts plague a small company, conflicts that in the past might have led to dissolution of the business, executives are likely to

(B) conflicts plague a small company, conflicts that might have in the past led to its dissolution, executives likely will

(C) conflicts plague a small company, which in the past it might have led to the business's dissolution, executives are liable to

(D) conflicts, which in the past might have led to dissolution of the business, plague a small company, executives are liable to

(E) conflicts, which in the past might have led to its dissolution, plague a small company, executives tend to

SC17561.01

273. A natural response of communities devastated by earthquake or flood is to rebuild on the same site, overlooking the possibility that the forces that caused it could be repeated.

(A) overlooking the possibility that the forces that caused it could be repeated

(B) overlooking the possibility that the forces causing it could be repeated

(C) overlooking that the forces that caused the disaster could also cause another one

(D) without considering that the forces causing the disaster could be repeated

(E) without considering that the forces that caused the disaster could also cause another such disaster

SC67561.01

274. <u>Avalanches at Rogers Pass in Glacier National Park killed more than 200 people between 1885 and 1910, but they</u> are now controlled if not prevented; cannons are fired at the slopes to make snow masses fall before they become dangerous.

   (A)   Avalanches at Rogers Pass in Glacier National Park killed more than 200 people between 1885 to 1910, but they

   (B)   More than 200 people have been killed by avalanches between 1885 and 1910 at Rogers Pass in Glacier National Park, but they

   (C)   Between 1885 and 1910, more than 200 people were killed by avalanches at Rogers Pass in Glacier National Park, but they

   (D)   More than 200 people have been killed by avalanches at Rogers Pass in Glacier National Park between 1885 and 1910, but such avalanches

   (E)   Avalanches at Rogers Pass in Glacier National Park killed more than 200 people between 1885 and 1910, but such avalanches

SC77561.01

275. Because 70 percent of the people of India use wood as their sole fuel, ten million acres of forest have been lost there since 1960, <u>resulting in wood now costing eight times as much to collect and distribute than</u> in 1960.

   (A)   resulting in wood now costing eight times as much to collect and distribute than

   (B)   resulting in wood now costing eight times as much to collect and distribute as

   (C)   resulting in wood now costing eight times as much to collect and distribute than it did

   (D)   and as a result wood now costs eight times as much to collect and distribute as it did

   (E)   and wood now costs eight times as much as a result to collect and distribute than

SC09561.01

276. In a crowded, acquisitive world, the disappearance of lifestyles such as those once followed by southern Africa's Bushmen and Australia's Aboriginal people, <u>requiring vast wild spaces and permitting little accumulation of goods, seem inevitably doomed</u>.

   (A)   requiring vast wild spaces and permitting little accumulation of goods, seem inevitably doomed

   (B)   requiring vast wild spaces and permitting little accumulation of goods, seems to be inevitably doomed

   (C)   which require vast wild spaces and permit little accumulation of goods, seem to be inevitably doomed

   (D)   lifestyles that require vast wild spaces and permit little accumulation of goods, seem inevitable

   (E)   lifestyles requiring vast wild spaces and permitting little accumulation of goods, seems inevitable

SC42561.01

277. Before Colette, the female writers of France had been aristocrats, from Mme de Lafayette to Anne de Noailles; there <u>were no Jane Austens or</u> Brontë sisters, perhaps because there were almost no clergymen's daughters.

   (A)   were no Jane Austens or

   (B)   were not Jane Austens or

   (C)   was not Jane Austen nor the

   (D)   was not a Jane Austen or the

   (E)   was no Jane Austen or no

SC73561.01

278. Chinese public buildings erected under a construction code of the Sung dynasty have withstood earthquakes well because the white cedar <u>used has four times the tensile strength of steel and the timber frame, incorporating</u> many joints and few nails, is flexible.

- (A) used has four times the tensile strength of steel and the timber frame, incorporating
- (B) used in them has four times the tensile strength of steel has and the timber frame, incorporating
- (C) that was used in them has four times the tensile strength steel has, and the timber frame, incorporating
- (D) that was used has four times as much tensile strength as steel, and the timber frame incorporates
- (E) that was used has four times the tensile strength steel does, and the timber frame incorporates

SC28561.01

279. Some historians of science have argued that science moves forward not so much <u>because of the insights of great thinkers but because of</u> more mundane developments, such as improved tools and technologies.

- (A) because of the insights of great thinkers but because of
- (B) because of the insights of great thinkers as the results of
- (C) because of the insights of great thinkers as because of
- (D) through the insights of great thinkers but through
- (E) through the insights of great thinkers but results from

Grammar

SC27561.01

280. Indoor air pollution can threaten the health of closely confined farm animals and the workers who tend them and <u>perhaps as well impairs the quality of such farm products like</u> eggs, poultry, and pork.

- (A) perhaps as well impairs the quality of such farm products like
- (B) perhaps as well impairs the quality of such farm products as
- (C) perhaps also impairs the quality of such farm products like
- (D) may also impair the quality of such farm products like
- (E) may also impair the quality of such farm products as

SC12811.01

281. Carbon-14 dating reveals that the megalithic monuments in Brittany are nearly 2,000 years <u>as old as any of their supposed</u> Mediterranean predecessors.

- (A) as old as any of their supposed
- (B) older than any of their supposed
- (C) as old as their supposed
- (D) older than any of their supposedly
- (E) as old as their supposedly

SC68461.01

282. Some biographers <u>have not only disputed the common notion that Edgar Allan Poe drank to excess but also questioned whether he drank</u> at all.

- (A) have not only disputed the common notion that Edgar Allan Poe drank to excess but also questioned whether he drank
- (B) not only have disputed the common notion that Edgar Allan Poe drank to excess but also over whether he drank
- (C) have disputed not only the common notion that Edgar Allan Poe drank to excess but also whether he may not have drunk
- (D) not only have disputed the common notion that Edgar Allan Poe drank to excess but also questioned whether or not he had drunk
- (E) have disputed the common notion not only that Edgar Allan Poe drank to excess but also questioned whether he may not have drunk

SC90561.01

283. The large populations and impressive cultural achievements of the Aztecs, the Mayas, and the Incas could not have come about without corn, <u>which was not only nutritious but also was able to be</u> dried, transported, and stored for long periods.

   (A)   which was not only nutritious but also was able to be

   (B)   which not only was nutritious but also could be

   (C)   which was not only nutritious but also it could be

   (D)   not only nutritious but it could also be

   (E)   not only nutritious but also able to be

SC91561.01

284. The Rorschach test is gaining new respect as a diagnostic tool because it takes only one hour to expose behavior and thought processes <u>that may be unlikely to emerge in other procedures or weeks of ordinary interviewing</u>.

   (A)   that may be unlikely to emerge in other procedures or weeks of ordinary interviewing

   (B)   whose emergence is unlikely in other procedures or weeks of ordinary interviews

   (C)   that might not emerge in other procedures or in weeks of ordinary interviews

   (D)   that may not emerge under other procedures or weeks of ordinary interviews

   (E)   likely not to emerge during weeks of ordinary interviewing or in other procedures

SC82561.01

285. The overall slackening of growth in productivity is influenced less by government regulation, although that is significant for specific industries like mining, than <u>the coming to an end of</u> a period of rapid growth in agricultural productivity.

   (A)   the coming to an end of

   (B)   the ending of

   (C)   by the coming to an end of

   (D)   by ending

   (E)   by the end of

SC13561.01

286. <u>It may someday be worthwhile to try to recover uranium from seawater</u>, but at present this process is prohibitively expensive.

   (A)   It may someday be worthwhile to try to recover uranium from seawater

   (B)   Someday, it may be worthwhile to try and recover uranium from seawater

   (C)   Trying to recover uranium out of seawater may someday be worthwhile

   (D)   To try for the recovery of uranium out of seawater may someday be worthwhile

   (E)   Recovering uranium from seawater may be worthwhile to try to do someday

SC23561.01

287. The spraying of pesticides can be carefully planned, but accidents, <u>weather conditions that could not be foreseen, and pilot errors often cause much larger deposits of spray than they had</u> anticipated.

   (A)   weather conditions that could not be foreseen, and pilot errors often cause much larger deposits of spray than they had

   (B)   weather conditions that cannot be foreseen, and pilot errors often cause much larger deposits of spray than

   (C)   unforeseeable weather conditions, and pilot errors are the cause of much larger deposits of spray than they had

   (D)   weather conditions that are not foreseeable, and pilot errors often cause much larger deposits of spray than

   (E)   unforeseeable weather conditions, and pilot errors often cause much larger deposits of spray than they had

SC33561.01

288. <u>To read of</u> Abigail Adams' lengthy separation from her family, her difficult travels, and her constant battles with illness is to feel intensely how harsh life was even for the so-called aristocracy of Revolutionary times.

   (A) To read of
   (B) Reading about
   (C) Having read about
   (D) Once one reads of
   (E) To have read of

SC74561.01

289. In the traditional Japanese household, most clothing could be packed <u>flatly, and so it was not necessary to have elaborate closet facilities</u>.

   (A) flatly, and so it was not necessary to have elaborate closet facilities
   (B) flat, and so elaborate closet facilities were unnecessary
   (C) flatly, and so there was no necessity for elaborate closet facilities
   (D) flat, there being no necessity for elaborate closet facilities
   (E) flatly, as no elaborate closet facilities were necessary

SC75561.01

290. Many states, in search of industries that are <u>clean, fast-growing, and pay</u> good wages to skilled workers, are trying to attract high-technology industries.

   (A) clean, fast-growing, and pay
   (B) clean, grow fast, and that pay
   (C) clean and fast-growing and that pay
   (D) clean and grow fast, paying
   (E) clean, fast-growing, and paying

SC95561.01

291. Much of the hope for continued improvement of the economy lies in the <u>projection of increasing consumer spending</u> this year.

   (A) projection of increasing consumer spending
   (B) projection of consumers increasing spending for
   (C) projected consumer spending increase
   (D) consumer spending that is projected to increase
   (E) increase in consumer spending that is projected for

SC46561.01

292. <u>Rejecting its argument that the Masters Dog Training Club's primary aim was to teach people to train dogs, the court ruled the club ineligible for tax exemption as an educational group.</u>

   (A) Rejecting its argument that the Masters Dog Training Club's primary aim was to teach people to train dogs, the court ruled the club ineligible for tax exemption as an educational group.
   (B) In rejecting the Masters Dog Training Club's argument that their primary aim was to teach people to train dogs, the court ruled the club ineligible to be exempted of taxes as an educational group.
   (C) Rejecting the argument that the primary aim of the Masters Dog Training Club was to teach people to train dogs, the court ruled that the club was ineligible for exemption from taxes as an educational group.
   (D) The club was not to be exempted of taxes as an educational group, ruled the court by rejecting its argument that the primary aim of the Masters Dog Training Club was teaching people to train dogs.
   (E) The court ruled the Masters Dog Training Club not eligible to be exempted from taxes as an educational group, rejecting the argument that the primary aim was to teach people to train dogs.

SC56561.01

293. Sartre, an inadvertent guru, had an opinion on everything, painfully considered, elaborately reasoned, <u>often changed</u>.

   (A) often changed
   (B) and it was usually changed
   (C) that was often changed
   (D) changing often
   (E) one he often changed

SC96561.01

294. One analyst of the liquor industry estimated that this year a few liquor stores have experienced <u>declining sales of up to fifty percent but predicted that the industry as a whole will maintain a volume of sales fairly close to last year</u>.

(A) declining sales of up to fifty percent but predicted that the industry as a whole will maintain a volume of sales fairly close to last year

(B) declines in sales of up to fifty percent but predicted that the industry as a whole would have maintained a volume of sales fairly close to last year

(C) up to fifty percent in declining sales but predicted that the industry as a whole would maintain a volume of sales fairly close to last year's

(D) sales declines of up to fifty percent but predicted that the industry as a whole would maintain a volume of sales fairly close to last year's

(E) declines up to fifty percent of sales but predicted that the industry as a whole will have maintained a volume of sales fairly close to last year's

SC08561.01

295. <u>Television programs developed in conjunction with the marketing of toys, which was once prohibited by federal regulations, are</u> thriving in the free market conditions permitted by the current Federal Communications Commission.

(A) Television programs developed in conjunction with the marketing of toys, which was once prohibited by federal regulations, are

(B) Television programs developed in conjunction with the marketing of toys, a practice that federal regulations once prohibited, is

(C) Developing television programs in conjunction with the marketing of toys, as once prohibited by federal regulations, is

(D) Federal regulations once prohibited developing television programs in conjunction with the marketing of toys, but they are

(E) Federal regulations once prohibited developing television programs in conjunction with the marketing of toys, but such programs are

SC98561.01

296. Statisticians studying the health effects of uranium mining on Navajo communities have found others besides miners and millworkers to be affected; birth defects, <u>children's cancer, and altered birth ratios of males and females are much higher</u> in mining than in non-mining communities.

(A) children's cancer, and altered birth ratios of males and females are much higher

(B) cancer among children, and altered male and female ratios at birth are much higher

(C) cancer among children, and altered birth ratios of males and females occur much more frequently

(D) altered birth ratios of males and females, and children's cancer are much higher

(E) altered male and female ratios at birth, and cancer among children occur much more

SC19561.01

297. <u>The effect of the earthquake that caused most of Port Royal to sink into the Caribbean was</u> like the eruption that buried ancient Pompeii: in each case a slice of civilization was instantly frozen in time.

(A) The effect of the earthquake that caused most of Port Royal to sink into the Caribbean was

(B) As the result of an earthquake, most of Port Royal sank into the Caribbean; the effect was

(C) In its effects, the sinking of most of Port Royal into the Caribbean was the result of an earthquake

(D) The earthquake that caused most of Port Royal to sink into the Caribbean was, in its effects,

(E) Most of Port Royal sank into the Caribbean because of an earthquake, the effect of which was

SC58461.01

298. Since the 1930s aircraft manufacturers have tried to build airplanes with frictionless <u>wings, shaped so smoothly and perfectly</u> that the air passing over them would not become turbulent.

   (A) wings, shaped so smoothly and perfectly

   (B) wings, wings so smooth and so perfectly shaped

   (C) wings that are shaped so smooth and perfect

   (D) wings, shaped in such a smooth and perfect manner

   (E) wings, wings having been shaped smoothly and perfectly so

SC29561.01

299. A study of children of divorced parents found that ten years after the parents' divorce, children who had been under six years of age at the time of the settlement were <u>not preoccupied, nor even very curious, about the reasons that led to their parents' divorces</u>.

   (A) not preoccupied, nor even very curious, about the reasons that led to their parents' divorces

   (B) not preoccupied with, or even very curious about, the reasons for their parents' divorce

   (C) neither preoccupied, nor even very curious, with the reasons that led to their parents divorce

   (D) neither preoccupied with the reasons that led to their parents' divorces or even very curious about them

   (E) neither preoccupied with the reasons that their parents divorced nor even very curious about it

SC49561.01

300. When Medicare was enacted in 1965, it was aimed <u>at the prevention of a catastrophic illness from financially destroying elderly patients.</u>

   (A) at the prevention of a catastrophic illness from financially destroying elderly patients

   (B) at being a preventive against catastrophic illness financially destroying elderly patients

   (C) at preventing a catastrophic illness from financially destroying the elderly patient

   (D) to prevent a catastrophic illness financially destroying an elderly patient

   (E) to prevent elderly patients being financially destroyed by a catastrophic illness

Answer Key Verbal Reasoning

Verbal Reasoning

Reading Comprehension

151. A
152. C
153. D
154. B
155. E
156. C
157. C
158. D
159. E
160. A
161. A
162. D
163. C
164. A
165. E
166. B
167. A
168. D
169. D
170. C
171. D
172. B
173. C
174. D
175. C
176. A
177. B
178. E
179. D
180. C
181. D
182. E
183. B
184. A

185. D
186. B
187. A
188. E
189. B
190. D
191. E
192. A
193. D
194. A
195. D
196. B
197. E
198. C
199. D
200. C

Critical Reasoning

Analysis/Critique

201. B
202. A
203. B
204. B
205. A
206. E
207. B
208. E
209. D
210. D
211. C
212. A
213. E
214. E
215. B
216. D

217. E
218. D
219. E
220. E
221. B
222. B
223. C
224. D
225. C
226. B

Construction/Plan

227. A
228. B
229. D
230. B
231. D
232. B
233. D
234. E
235. B
236. A
237. B
238. B
239. D
240. E
241. B
242. B
243. D
244. B
245. B
246. B
247. A
248. D
249. C

Sentence Correction

Communication

250. B
251. D
252. D
253. B
254. E
255. E
256. B
257. E
258. D
259. D
260. D
261. E
262. B
263. D
264. B
265. C
266. D
267. E
268. B
269. B
270. E
271. B
272. A
273. E
274. E
275. D
276. E
277. A
278. A
279. C

Grammar

280. E
281. B
282. A
283. B
284. C
285. C
286. A
287. B
288. A
289. B
290. C
291. E
292. C
293. A
294. D
295. E
296. C
297. D
298. B
299. B
300. C

Answer Explanations Verbal Reasoning

Reading Comprehension

Questions 151–155 refer to the passage on page 143.

RC62100.01-10

151. The primary purpose of the passage is to

(A) present an interpretation of the chronological relationship between bipedal locomotion and certain other key aspects of human evolution

(B) compare the evolutionary advantages and disadvantages of bipedal locomotion to those of quadrupedal locomotion

(C) argue that the transition to a nuclear family structure was a more crucial step in human evolution than was the development of stone tools

(D) analyze anatomical evidence of bipedal locomotion to show that the large brain of modern humans developed at a later stage of evolution than was previously believed

(E) use examples of muscle and bone structure to illustrate the evolutionary differences between modern humans, australopithecines, and chimpanzees

Main idea

To discern the primary purpose of a passage requires an understanding of the key messages within the passage. The passage states that a once-favored view was that modern human beings' ancestors began to walk upright around the same time that they began to use stone tools.

However, this argument has been weakened by archaeological discoveries indicating that these ancestors began to walk upright before the enlargement of the brain that led to the development of such tools.

Furthermore, the passage indicates that these ancestors had a shallow pelvis that would actually suit walking upright better than the bowl-shaped human pelvis, a development that allows for children to be born with larger brains and therefore heads.

Given that walking upright is less efficient than walking on all fours, the passage suggests that some sort of evolutionary advantage came from walking upright; the passage suggests that this advantage may have been that it allowed monogamous parents to cooperate in the care of offspring.

A **Correct.** As the review above indicates, the passage is primarily concerned with the chronological relationship between bipedal locomotion and certain other important developments in human evolution, such as fitness for cooperative parental roles.

B While the passage does mention the relative efficiency of bipedal and quadrupedal locomotion, it does so primarily to motivate the larger purpose of the passage. That is, it justifies the need to explain the development of bipedal locomotion. In other words, if bipedal locomotion were more efficient rather than less efficient, this efficiency boost would be sufficient to explain its evolution.

C The passage does not discuss whether the development of the nuclear family or the development of stone tools was the more crucial step in human evolution. Rather, it simply rules out the development of stone tools as an explanation for the development of bipedal locomotion and proposes the transition to a nuclear family as a possible explanation.

D The passage does present such evidence, but it does so merely as one step in pursuit of the primary purpose of presenting the chronological relationships among the evolution of bipedal locomotion and other key human developments.

E The passage does use such examples, but it does so merely as one step in pursuit of the overall, primary purpose of presenting the chronological relationships among the evolution of bipedal locomotion and other key human developments.

The correct answer is A.

RC62100.01-20

152. The passage suggests that proponents of the theory mentioned in lines 35–38 assume that which of the following steps in human evolution occurred most recently?

(A) Development of a nuclear family structure

(B) Transition from walking on all fours to walking upright

(C) Dramatic enlargement of the brain

(D) Use of the hands to gather and carry food

(E) Modification of propulsive muscles to provide stability and control in locomotion

Inference

The passage states that fossilized remains provide anatomical evidence that upright walking, which required a modification of propulsive muscles to provide stability and control in locomotion, occurred before the dramatic enlargement of the brain.

Proponents of the theory mentioned in lines 35–38 argue that walking upright may have evolved alongside the nuclear family structure because it allowed for cooperative caring for infants, which would have required the use of hands to gather and carry food. Thus, the dramatic enlargement of the brain was the most recent of the developments listed among the answer options.

A Proponents of the theory mentioned in lines 35–38 hold that the dramatic enlargement of the brain occurred more recently than the development of walking upright, which happened alongside the development of a nuclear family structure.

B Proponents of the theory mentioned in lines 35–38 hold that the dramatic enlargement of the brain occurred more recently than the transition from walking on all fours to walking upright.

C **Correct.** Proponents of the theory mentioned in lines 35–38 hold that the dramatic enlargement of the brain was the most recent of these developments to occur.

D Proponents of the theory mentioned in lines 35–38 hold that the dramatic enlargement of the brain occurred more recently than the use of hands to gather and carry food, which occurred alongside the development of walking upright.

E Proponents of the theory mentioned in lines 35–38 hold that the dramatic enlargement of the brain occurred more recently than the modification of propulsive muscles to provide stability and control in locomotion, which is a key factor in the development of walking upright.

The correct answer is C.

RC62100.01-30

153. According to the passage, the hominid australopithecine most closely resembled a modern human with respect to which of the following characteristics?

(A) Brain size

(B) Tool-making ability

(C) Shape of the pelvis

(D) Method of locomotion

(E) Preference for certain foods

Supporting idea

The passage directly states that australopithecines walked upright (used bipedal locomotion), as human beings do.

A The passage states that the dramatic enlargement of the brain among hominids occurred after the australopithecine era; it follows that the size of the australopithecine brain did not closely resemble that of the modern human brain.

B The passage states that stone-tool-making ability did not develop until some time after the australopithecine era. The passage suggests that study of Australopithecus indicates that there is substantial evidence that *upright walking appeared prior to . . . stone tools.*

C The passage specifies notable differences in shape between the australopithecine pelvis and the pelvis of modern human beings.

D **Correct.** As noted above, the passage indicates that australopithecines walked upright, or used bipedal locomotion, as modern human beings do.

(E)   The passage does not indicate the types of foods preferred by australopithecines.

The correct answer is D.

RC62100.01-40

154. The passage suggests that, in comparison with the hominid australopithecines, modern humans are

(A)   less well adapted to large-group cooperation

(B)   less well adapted to walking upright

(C)   more agile in running and climbing

(D)   more well suited to a nuclear family structure

(E)   more well suited to cooperative caring for their offspring

Inference

The information needed to answer this question is contained in the second paragraph. This is the only place in the passage where comparisons between australopithecines and modern human beings occur; the passage points out (1) that the pelvis and the femur of australopithecines are more similar to those of modern humans than they are to those of chimpanzees, the most closely related living primate, and (2) that the pelvis of australopithecines is better suited for bipedal locomotion than is the pelvis of modern humans.

A   The passage makes no mention of large-group cooperation.

B   Correct. As discussed above, the passage notes that the modern human pelvis is less suited for bipedal locomotion than was the australopithecine pelvis. This suggests that, in comparison with australopithecines, modern humans are *less well adapted* to walking upright.

C   The fact that australopithecines were better suited for walking upright than modern humans are would suggest if anything that australopithecines would also be better suited than humans to running and climbing (rather than vice versa). Regardless, the passage provides no clear evidence of whether modern humans or australopithecines were more agile.

D   In the third paragraph, the passage suggests that australopithecines may have been physically well suited to a nuclear family

structure. The passage gives no information as to whether australopithecines were more or less physically well suited to such a structure than are modern humans.

E   In the third paragraph, the passage suggests that australopithecines may have been physically well suited to cooperative caring for their offspring. The passage gives no information as to whether they were more or less physically well suited to such caring than modern humans.

The correct answer is B.

RC62100.01-50

155. The theory mentioned in lines 35–38 suggests that which of the following was true for the hominid ancestors of modern humans before they made the transition to walking upright?

(A)   Their brains were smaller than the brains of present-day chimpanzees.

(B)   They competed rather than cooperated in searching for food.

(C)   Their mating patterns and family structure were closer to those of present-day chimpanzees than to those of modern humans.

(D)   Males played a more significant role in child rearing than they played after the transition to walking upright.

(E)   Females' ability to nurture and protect their offspring was limited by the need to find food for themselves.

Inference

The theory mentioned in lines 35–38 holds that bipedality evolved among modern humans' hominid ancestors specifically because it granted monogamous couples the ability to cooperate in the care of their offspring.

According to this theory, because they could now walk upright, fathers were able to use their hands to gather food and carry it to their mates from a distance. This in turn allowed mothers to expend greater amounts of time and energy to the nurture and protection of their children.

This implies that prior to the development of walking upright, mothers had to spend more time acquiring their own food, and therefore less time nurturing and protecting their offspring.

A   According to the passage, the brains of baby australopithecine hominids *were no larger than* the brains of baby chimpanzees. This in no way implies that the brains of these ancestors were smaller than those of chimpanzees. Nothing in the passage indicates that the theory would disagree with this.

B   The theory states that walking upright allowed for cooperation for food within a monogamous couple; a simple lack of cooperation does not imply that these ancestors necessarily *competed* for food. For example, these groups could have engaged in cooperative hunting, just as many nonbipedal animals are now.

C   The theory does suggest that prior to the development of bipedality, these ancestors were not as capable of cooperative care. However, this still does not imply that their mating patterns and family structures were more similar to those of chimpanzees than to those of modern humans.

D   The theory actually suggests the opposite: that bipedality developed because it allowed for greater cooperative care among hominid parents.

E   **Correct.** As discussed above, the development of bipedality allowed fathers to assist mothers in acquiring food. This, thereby, freed up time and energy for mothers to nurture and protect their offspring.

The correct answer is E.

Questions 156–161 refer to the passage on page 145.

RC04200.01-10

156. The passage is primarily concerned with

(A) providing evidence indicating that feminist reformers of the 1920s failed to reach some of their goals

(B) presenting scholarship that contrasts suffragist "promises" with the historical realities of the 1920s

(C) discussing recent scholarship concerning the achievements of women's suffrage during the 1920s and presenting an alternative view of those achievements

(D) outlining recent findings concerning events leading to suffrage for women in the 1920s and presenting a challenge to those findings

(E) providing support for a traditional view of the success of feminist attempts to increase gender consciousness among women during the 1920s

Main idea

To understand the primary concern of the passage requires a clear understanding of the passage as a whole. This passage discusses recent scholarship concerning the 1920s that challenges an earlier interpretation in which the women's suffrage movement during the 1920s was considered a failure because it had not achieved long-term political goals. The scholars responsible for this earlier interpretation present the 1920s as a *period of decline,* and the passage presented here challenges this assessment.

A   The passage is primarily concerned with discussing how recent scholarship challenged an earlier assessment of the women's suffrage movement. The passage provides no specific evidence indicating that feminist reformers of the 1920s failed to reach their goals.

B   Although the passage refers to the *unkept "promises" of the women's suffrage movement,* the passage does not present scholarship that contrasts such a "promise" with the historical realities of the 1920s.

C   **Correct.** The passage discusses recent scholarship concerning the achievements of women's suffrage. In the final paragraph, the passage presents an alternative view of those achievements.

D   The passage does not outline findings regarding *what led to suffrage for women.* The passage's focus is on scholarship regarding *what followed women gaining suffrage.*

E   The passage does not provide support for a traditional view of 1920s feminists' success at increasing gender consciousness among women. In fact, the passage conflicts with the traditional view by suggesting that, during the 1920s, there existed intense activism aimed at increasing autonomy for women.

The correct answer is C.

RC04200.01-20

157. It can be inferred that the author of the passage disagrees with the "new scholarship" mentioned in line 5 regarding the

(A) degree to which the "promises" of the suffrage movement remained unkept

(B) degree to which suffrage for women improved the morality of governance

(C) degree to which the 1920s represented a period of decline for the feminist movement

(D) degree of legislative success achieved by feminist reformers during the 1920s

(E) accuracy of the view that a women's voting bloc did not materialize once suffrage was achieved

Inference

In the final paragraph of the passage, the author offers several points to counter the claim made by the *new scholarship* that the 1920s were still, in some ways, a period of decline.

A   Both the author and this *new scholarship* question the claims of the earlier interpretation that the "promises" of the women's suffrage movement were unkept.

B   There is no indication of agreement or disagreement between the author of the passage and this *new scholarship* about how much women improved the morality of governance in the 1920s.

C   **Correct.** In the final paragraph, the author gives a counterpoint to the claim of the *new scholarship* that the 1920s, in some ways, represented a period of decline for the feminist movement.

D   Nothing in the passage supports the claim that the author disagrees with the *new scholarship* regarding the degree of legislative success achieved by feminist reformers. Note that none of the achievements discussed

in the final paragraph are indicated to be legislative successes.

E   While the author of the passage mentions the *new scholarship*'s claim that a women's voting bloc failed to materialize once suffrage was achieved, the author does not explicitly disagree with this statement.

The correct answer is C.

RC04200.01-30

158. The purpose of the second paragraph of the passage is to

(A) suggest a reason why suffragist "promises" were not kept

(B) contrast suffragist "promises" with the reality of the 1920s

(C) deplore the lack of successful feminist reform in the 1920s

(D) explain a view held by feminist scholars

(E) answer the question asked by Jane Addams

Evaluation

The second paragraph of the passage describes certain views presented in the *recent feminist scholarship* discussed in the first paragraph. In the first paragraph, this *new scholarship* is described as challenging earlier interpretations that suggested that "promises" of the women's suffrage movement had not been kept.

Though this *new scholarship* argues that it is a mistake to view women's suffrage as a failure, the scholarship nonetheless does, in some ways, present the 1920s as a period of decline. The second paragraph of the passage explains precisely how the scholars present such a view.

A   Both the author and the *new scholarship* discussed in the passage reject the interpretation that suffragist "promises" remained unkept.

B   The second paragraph does not present a contrast between the reality of the 1920s and the suffragist "promises." This paragraph does present ways in which the new scholarship saw the 1920s as a period of decline. However, both the author and this *new scholarship* argue that it is improper to interpret the results of women's suffrage in the 1920s as *unkept "promises."*

C   As noted in the third paragraph, the author sees successful feminist reform in the 1920s. It is therefore incorrect to suggest that the author intends the second paragraph to deplore a lack of successful feminist reform during this period.

D   **Correct.** As discussed above, the second paragraph explains how this *new scholarship* presents the 1920s as a period of decline.

E   Jane Addams's question was rhetorical; there is no answer to this question in the passage.

The correct answer is D.

RC04200.01-40

159. It can be inferred from the passage that recent scholars cite the words of Jane Addams primarily in order to

(A)   suggest that women's achievement of suffrage brought about changes in government that were not taken into account by early interpretations

(B)   point out contradictions inherent in the goals of the women's suffrage movement

(C)   show why a women's voting bloc was not formed when women won the right to vote

(D)   emphasize the place of social reform movements in the struggle for suffrage for women

(E)   suggest that the old view of women's suffrage was inappropriate

Inference

The scholars cite the words of Jane Addams to suggest that it is no more appropriate to ask whether women's suffrage was a failure than to ask whether suffrage in general is a failure. The clear implication is that it is inappropriate to ask either question, presumably because suffrage has value in and of itself.

A   The scholars do not dispute the claim that women's suffrage failed to bring about significant changes in government. The point of Addams's statement is that it is inappropriate to call women's suffrage into question simply because it does not bring about all desired changes.

B   The scholars suggest no inherent contradictions in the goals of the women's suffrage movement. Even if such a claim had been made, there is little relation between that claim and Jane Addams's statement.

C   The scholars accept the earlier interpretation's assertion that a women's voting bloc was not formed; however, the scholars offer no explanation as to why such a bloc was not formed.

D   While it may be true that social reform movements played a significant role in the struggle for suffrage for women, this particular quotation does not convey that idea.

E   **Correct.** The old view suggested that in many ways the women's suffrage movement was a failure because it had failed to attain certain goals that had been associated with women's suffrage. The scholars quote Addams to suggest that this view is inappropriate: women's suffrage should no more be considered a failure for failing to reach all of its goals than suffrage in general should be considered a failure for failing to reach all of its goals.

The correct answer is E.

RC04200.01-50

160. It can be inferred that the analyses of the author of the passage and the scholars mentioned in lines 20–23 differ with regard to which of the following?

(A)   The criteria they use to evaluate the success of the feminist movement during the 1920s

(B)   Their interpretations of the "promises" of the suffragist movement

(C)   The suggestions they make for achieving feminist goals

(D)   Their definitions of what constitutes a legislative victory

(E)   Their estimations of the obstacles preventing women's having achieved a voting bloc in the 1920s

Inference

The author of the passage mentions ways in which the *new scholarship* mentioned in the first paragraph sees the 1920s as *a period of decline* for the feminist movement. For example, these scholars suggest that after the mid-1920s, *few successes could be claimed by feminist reformers: little could be seen in the way of legislative victories.*

The author points out actual gains for women, for example, the establishment by women's organizations of broader opportunities for women, striving *to secure for women the full entitlements of citizenship, including the right to hold office and the right to serve on juries.* The author thereby appears to counter these scholars' suggestion that the 1920s was a *period of decline* by suggesting other criteria that can be used to evaluate the attainments of the 1920s feminist movement.

A   **Correct.** As discussed above, the author applies different criteria from those attributed to the scholars mentioned in the second paragraph in evaluating the success of the feminist movement during the 1920s.

B   The author presents these scholars' discussion of these "promises" in the first paragraph; the author does not appear to disagree with the scholars' assessment.

C   The passage does not discuss any suggestions that these scholars have made about how to achieve feminist goals.

D   The passage mentions *legislative victories* but offers no definition of the term.

E   Nowhere does the passage discuss obstacles preventing the formation of a voting bloc in the 1920s.

The correct answer is A.

RC04200.01-60

161. The "new scholarship" mentioned in the first paragraph suggests which of the following concerning the "promises" mentioned in lines 4–5?

(A)   Failure to keep these promises is not a measure of the success of the suffrage movement.

(B)   Failure to keep these promises caused the feminist movement to lose cohesiveness during the 1920s.

(C)   Failure to keep these promises led recent feminist scholars to reevaluate the success of the suffrage movement.

(D)   These promises included securing for women the right to hold office and the right to serve on juries.

(E)   These promises were of little importance in winning suffrage for women.

Inference

The passage indicates that *new scholarship* disputed a long-held view that because certain promises of the women's suffrage movement— e.g., that a women's voting bloc would form; that the women's vote would bring about moral, corruption-free governance—went unkept, the movement was a failure. This scholarship rejected the view that *unkept "promises"* suggested a failure of the movement.

A   **Correct.** As indicated above, the *new scholarship* rejected the notion that the failure to keep these promises was a reasonable measure of the success or failure of the suffrage movement.

B   The second paragraph of the passage explains the *new scholarship's* view that the feminist movement lost its cohesiveness in the 1920s. However, there is no suggestion that a failure to keep the promises of the suffrage movement was actually a cause of this.

C   The *new scholarship* reevaluated the success of the suffrage movement. However, this scholarship did not suggest that it did so because the suffrage movement failed to keep its promises.

D   There is nothing in the passage to indicate that the *new scholarship* suggests that these promises include securing the right to hold office and the right to serve on juries for women.

E   There is nothing in the passage to suggest either that the promises were of little importance in winning suffrage for women or even that this *new scholarship* believed that they were.

The correct answer is A.

Questions 162–165 refer to the passage on page 147.

RC60500.01-10

162. The primary purpose of the passage is to

(A) present several theories that could account for a particular phenomenon

(B) argue that a certain question needs to be reframed in light of new evidence

(C) resolve an apparent inconsistency between two lines of evidence

(D) explain why a certain issue remains unresolved

(E) present evidence that calls into question certain assumptions of a current theory

Main idea

Our goal is to determine which of the five options best expresses the primary purpose of the passage. Note that this question regards the topic and how that topic is discussed: the issue that the passage primarily focuses on concerns the mass at the center of our galaxy. The passage primarily aims to explain why the specific nature of that mass had not—at least in 1997, when the passage was written—been adequately understood.

A While the passage draws upon certain theoretical findings, it does not present multiple theories.

B The passage suggests that the author is puzzled by the enormous mass at the center of the Milky Way, in light of evidence showing the relatively low level of energy radiating outward. Nevertheless, the passage never attempts to convince us that the question needs to be reframed.

C The passage describes an apparent inconsistency—or *discrepancy*—between two lines of evidence but does not seek to resolve that inconsistency.

D **Correct.** As indicated above, this choice expresses the primary purpose of the passage; that is, to explain why the nature of the mass at the center of our galaxy was not adequately understood.

E Although some of the evidence presented may cast doubt on one or more assumptions

of a theory that was current when the passage was written, the passage itself is not primarily focused on identifying any such assumptions.

The correct answer is D.

RC60500.01-20

163. According to the passage, the dynamical evidence referred to in lines 9–10 supports which of the following?

(A) Recent assumptions about the velocities of stars

(B) Widely held predictions about the amount of matter a black hole will engulf

(C) The existence of an extremely dense object at the center of the Milky Way

(D) The contention that too much energy is coming from the mass at the Milky Way's galactic center for that mass to be a black hole

(E) The conclusion that a compact object of two to three million times the mass of our Sun is too dense to be anything but a black hole

Supporting idea

What does the passage claim the dynamical evidence mentioned supports? The passage states that the dynamical evidence *argues for an extremely compact object with a mass two to three million times the mass of our Sun* at the center of the Milky Way. An extremely compact object with such a mass would, of course, be tremendously dense.

A The passage in no way suggests that the dynamical evidence mentioned supports assumptions about the velocities of stars. Rather, it states that the assumptions about the velocities of the stars have been "recently confirmed" and that the dynamical evidence is actually based on these assumptions. If the dynamical evidence is a product of these assumptions, then it cannot be used to support them.

B The passage suggests that the dynamical evidence is consistent with the existence in the Milky Way of an extremely dense object that is likely a black hole. However, the evidence in no way suggests that reliable predictions can be made about how much matter such a hypothetical black hole would engulf.

C   **Correct.** As indicated above, this refers to the extremely compact object of immense mass; this object would of course be "extremely dense."

D   This choice presents a suggestion opposite to the information in the passage. The passage suggests that the object at the center of the Milky Way is in fact radiating *too little* to be easily identifiable as a black hole.

E   The passage acknowledges that the density of the mass at the center of the Milky Way is consistent with the existence of a black hole there. However, the passage further suggests that an unexpectedly small quantity of energy radiating outward from the center of the Milky Way calls this into question.

The correct answer is C.

RC60500.01-30

164. The "serious problem" referred to in line 17 could be solved if which of the following were true?

(A)   Current assumptions about how much matter a black hole would engulf proved to be several thousand times too high.

(B)   Current assumptions about how much matter a black hole would engulf proved to be a few thousand times too low.

(C)   The object at the center of the Milky Way turned out to be far more dense than it is currently estimated to be.

(D)   The object at the center of the Milky Way turned out to be far more massive than it is currently estimated to be.

(E)   Matter being engulfed by a black hole radiated far more energy than is currently assumed.

Application

Which one of the five options would, if true, indicate a possible solution to the serious problem referred to? The serious problem is said to arise from the *relative lack of energy radiating from the galactic center* compared with the expected value if a matter-engulfing black hole were truly at the center of the Milky Way.

According to the passage, the radiated energy turned out to be a few thousand times less than had been expected, on theoretical grounds, to radiate from mass engulfed by the hypothetical black hole. However, if it were discovered that the matter engulfed were several thousand times less than previously estimated, the relatively low level of radiated energy observed would no longer seem at odds with the existence of the hypothesized black hole.

A   **Correct.** Reviewing the assumptions underlying *the widely held predictions* could lead to revised predictions that harmonize with the observational evidence regarding radiated energy from the galaxy's center.

B   The passage states that the assumed quantity of engulfed matter already seems to be radiating too little; this answer choice would actually make the "serious problem" in the passage worse. That is, assuming that there is actually more engulfed matter with such a small amount of radiation would simply worsen the problem.

C   The passage does not specify what impact a greater-than-estimated density would have on the quantity of energy that is radiated. That is, even if greater mass would change predictions, greater density may not do so.

D   If the object were more massive, then presumably the matter engulfed by this hypothetical *more massive* black hole would radiate a quantity of energy even greater than the observed quantity. This again would simply make the "serious problem" worse.

E   Given that not enough radiated energy is currently being observed, finding that the matter being engulfed radiates even more energy than expected would make the "serious problem" significantly worse. That is, the relatively low quantity of radiated energy observed would fall even farther short of the quantity expected.

The correct answer is A.

RC60500.01-40

165. The "widely held predictions" mentioned in line 25 are predictions about the

(A) compactness of objects whose mass is millions of times the mass of our Sun

(B) velocities of stars orbiting the galactic center

(C) amount of matter swirling around the object at the center of the Milky Way

(D) amount of matter falling into a theoretical central black hole

(E) amount of energy that should be coming from a black hole at the center of the Milky Way

Evaluation

What do the "widely held predictions" mentioned in the passage's final sentence refer to? Notice that the final sentence of the passage refers to a comparison between two things: *the energy coming from the galactic center* and the quantity of energy widely predicted to be radiated from matter being engulfed by a black hole. It follows that the best answer should present an option that refers to a predicted quantity of energy.

A   This choice fails to refer to any predicted quantity of energy.

B   This choice fails to refer to any predicted quantity of energy.

C   This choice fails to refer to any predicted quantity of energy.

D   This choice fails to refer to any predicted quantity of energy.

E   **Correct.** This choice presents the only option that refers to a predicted quantity of energy.

The correct answer is E.

Questions 166–172 refer to the passage on page 149.

RC39461.01-10

166. The author's discussion of Emerson, Thoreau, Hawthorne, Melville, and Whitman is primarily concerned with explaining

(A) some of their beliefs about the difficulties involved in self-realization

(B) some of their beliefs concerning the world and the place that humanity occupies in the universal order

(C) some of their beliefs concerning the relationship between humanism and democracy

(D) the way some of their beliefs are shaped by differences in temperament and literary outlook

(E) the effects of some of their beliefs on their writings

Main idea

Understanding the primary concern of the passage implies understanding the passage as a whole. The passage starts by stating that these five American writers have many differences, but that it will focus on those beliefs that they share. The passage suggests that all five of the writers hold that *humans are the spiritual center of the universe and that in them alone is the clue to nature, history, and ultimately the cosmos.*

The passage continues by providing more specific evidence for this assertion, outlining beliefs that the writers hold in common. Note that the first sentences of each paragraph from the second onward identify a particular perspective, belief, or assumption that the writers hold in common.

A   The scope of this choice is too narrow. The third paragraph of the passage discusses two apparently conflicting psychological tendencies that the writers suggest must be reconciled in order to achieve self-actualization. However, this point is not of great concern throughout the rest of the passage.

B   **Correct.** As discussed above, the passage is primarily concerned with beliefs the writers share concerning the fundamental role of humanity in the universal order.

C   The scope of this choice is too narrow. In the third paragraph, the passage considers the role of democracy in the five writers' thinking. However, it is only one of several such issues that the passage discusses.

D   This choice presents an idea contrary to the primary concern of the passage: the passage focuses not on the differences among these writers, but rather on the beliefs, concerns, and assumptions they share.

E   The passage primarily focuses on the common beliefs of these writers, not on any particular effects that these beliefs have on the writers' work.

The correct answer is B.

RC39461.01-20

167. According to the passage, the five writers object to the scientific method primarily because they think it

(A)   is not the best way to obtain an understanding of the relationship between the individual and the cosmos

(B)   is so specialized that it leads to an understanding of separate parts of the universe but not of the relationships among those parts

(C)   cannot provide an adequate explanation of intuition and imagination

(D)   misleads people into believing they have an understanding of truth, when they do not

(E)   prevents people from recognizing the symbolic nature of experience

Evaluation

The final paragraph of the passage indicates that the five writers suggest that the scientific method provides a less sure way to arrive at truth than do intuition and imagination. In particular, these authors propose that intuition and imagination allow us to recognize, in a way the scientific method cannot, the *organic relationship between the self and the cosmos.*

A   **Correct.** As indicated above, the passage indicates that these five writers believe that the scientific method is not a sure way to obtain an understanding of how the individual self relates to the cosmos.

B   The passage suggests that these five writers objected to use of the scientific method to obtain understanding of how the individual relates to the cosmos, not because it is too "specialized."

C   The passage suggests that these five writers believed that intuition and imagination were surer means of arriving at truth than the scientific method. This does not imply that the scientific method is incapable

of providing an adequate explanation of intuition and imagination themselves.

D   The passage does not indicate whether the writers believed that, as a result of the scientific method, people falsely believed that they understood the truth. The passage does suggest that the writers believed that the scientific method cannot lead to certain types of fundamental truths. However, this does not imply that these authors thought that any beliefs arrived at through the scientific method are inherently false.

E   The passage indicates that the writers did not believe that the scientific method could effectively lead to recognizing the symbolic nature of experience. Nevertheless, it does not indicate that they believe that the scientific method *prevents people* from recognizing the symbolic nature of experience.

The correct answer is A.

RC39461.01-30

168. The author quotes Whitman primarily in order to

(A)   show that the poet does not agree with Emerson

(B)   indicate the way the poet uses the humanist ideal to praise himself

(C)   suggest that the poet adapts the basic premises of humanism to his own individual outlook on the world

(D)   illustrate a way the poet expresses the relationship of the individual to the humanistic universe

(E)   demonstrate that the poet is concerned with the well-being of all humans

Evaluation

The second paragraph stresses that these five writers emphasize *the human as universal, freed from the accidents of time, space, birth, and talent*; they see this idea as falling within the general notion that humans are the spiritual center of the universe.

In this second paragraph the author presents two examples of writing, one from Emerson and one from Whitman, which demonstrate this emphasis. Answering the question requires recognizing that Whitman's statement illustrates the idea that each individual human has such a general relationship with the universe.

A   The quotations from Emerson and Whitman are intended to illustrate the same idea—namely, the human as universal—not to show how these two writers differ.

B   The author quotes Whitman to illustrate a general idea shared by the five writers rather than to indicate how Whitman uses the humanist ideal to praise himself. Furthermore, this choice is incorrect because the quotation itself indicates something true of *all the "children of Adam"*—all of humanity—rather than something true of Whitman specifically.

C   Once again, the author's quotation of Whitman is not meant to indicate anything distinctive about Whitman, but rather to illustrate a perspective he shared with the other four writers.

D   Correct. The author quotes Whitman to illustrate how Whitman expresses— as do each of the other writers under consideration—the relationship of each individual to a humanistic universe.

E   The quotation illustrates Whitman's view of the relationship of the individual to the universe. Even though Whitman may in fact be concerned with the well-being of all humans, the quotation itself in no way suggests this.

The correct answer is D.

RC39461.01-40

169. It can be inferred that intuition is important to the five writers primarily because it provides them with

(A)   information useful for understanding abstract logic and scientific method

(B)   the discipline needed in the search for truth

(C)   inspiration for their best writing

(D)   clues to the interpretation of symbolic experience

(E)   the means of resolving conflicts between the self and the world

Inference

The final paragraph states that the five writers all held that *intuition and imagination offer a surer road to truth than does abstract logic or scientific method.* Furthermore, the author states that this is illustrated, in part, by *their interpretation of experience as, in essence, symbolic.* This suggests that intuition's value is largely related to its ability to assist in interpreting symbolic experience.

A   The passage suggests that the writers believed intuition to be a surer road to truth than are abstract logic and the scientific method. Nevertheless, it does not indicate that these writers believed intuition to be useful for understanding abstract logic or the scientific method.

B   The passage suggests that the writers believed intuition to be helpful in arriving at the truth. However, it does not indicate that this is because it provides them with any sort of discipline needed in the search for the truth.

C   It may be true that intuition served as inspiration for the five writers' best writing. However, the passage provides no information that allows us to make such an inference.

D   Correct. The passage suggests that these writers believed intuition to be important because intuition (and imagination) assist in the interpretation of symbolic experience.

E   The passage nowhere indicates that intuition is involved in the resolution of conflicts between the self and the world.

The correct answer is D.

RC39461.01-50

170. The author discusses "the democratic ethic" (see lines 26–32) in order to

(A)   explain the relationship between external experience and inner imagination

(B)   support the notion that the self contains two conflicting and irreconcilable factions

(C)   illustrate the relationship between the self's desire to be individual and its desire to merge with all other selves

(D) elaborate on the concept that the self constantly desires to realize its potential

(E) give an example of the idea that, in order to be happy, the self must reconcile its desires with external reality

Evaluation

The passage discusses *the democratic ethic* as a specific instance of two conflicting impulses: the desire to be responsible to the self versus the desire to transcend the self and become one with the world. In particular, the democratic ethic relates to the conflict between one's duty to self and one's duty to society.

A   The passage's discussion of the democratic ethic relates to the conflict of the individual's self-asserting and self-transcending impulses. However, the democratic ethic is brought up to illustrate rather than explain this idea. Furthermore, the democratic ethic does not deal specifically with inner imagination and external experience, but rather with conflicting duties.

B   The passage nowhere indicates that the self has two irreconcilable factions. The discussion of the democratic ethic is part of a discussion regarding the importance of the harmonious reconciliation of two psychological tendencies.

C   **Correct.** As discussed above, the author's discussion of the democratic ethic is intended to illustrate the relationship between one's duty to oneself and one's duty to be a part of society; we can interpret the latter as one form of becoming one with the world.

D   The passage does not indicate that these five writers believed that the self constantly desires to realize its own potential.

E   The passage does not indicate that these five writers believed that happiness requires a reconciliation of the self's desires with external reality.

The correct answer is C.

RC39461.01-60

171. It can be inferred that the idea of "an organic relationship between the self and the cosmos" (see lines 40–41) is necessary to the thinking of the five writers because such a relationship

(A) enables them to assert the importance of the democratic ethic

(B) justifies their concept of the freedom of the individual

(C) sustains their faith in the existence of a deity

(D) is the foundation of their humanistic view of existence

(E) is the basis for their claim that the writer is a seer

Inference

The passage discusses the idea of *an organic relationship between the self and the cosmos* in the context of discussion of the five writers' shared beliefs *that the clue to external nature is to be found in the inner world of individual psychology* and that experience is, essentially, symbolic.

The passage indicates that these views presume the idea that there is an *organic relationship* between the self and the cosmos. This presumption of an organic relationship is, it seems, the basis of their humanistic view of existence.

A   It is possible to assert the importance of the democratic ethic without holding to these writers' view regarding an organic relationship between the self and the cosmos. In fact, this view may have played a part in their promotion of the democratic ethic. Nevertheless, the writers certainly could have asserted that this ethic was important without presuming such a view.

B   The passage indicates tension between the idea of individual freedom and the individual's duty to society, a view that these writers link to the organic relationship between the self and the cosmos. It is therefore unclear specifically how this idea justifies these five authors' conception of the freedom of the individual.

C   The passage indicates that these authors do not specifically deny the existence of a deity.

However, their belief in the humanistic view of existence stands in tension with a belief in a deity. Therefore, it is unlikely that the idea of an organic relationship between the self and the cosmos—a concept that underlies that humanistic view—would sustain whatever faith they might have in the existence of a deity distinct from the universe itself.

D   **Correct.** As indicated above, these five writers' humanistic view of existence presupposes an organic relationship between the self and the cosmos.

E   The passage indicates that the *writers' faith in the imagination and in themselves* underlies their claim that the writer is a seer, not their idea that there is an organic relationship between the self and the cosmos.

The correct answer is D.

RC39461.01-70

172. The passage is most relevant to which of the following areas of study?

(A)   Aesthetics and logic

(B)   History and literature

(C)   Theology and sociology

(D)   Anthropology and political science

(E)   Linguistics and art

Evaluation

The passage discusses five historically important literary figures; it follows that this passage is most relevant to *history and literature*.

A   Because the passage discusses only thematic characteristics of these five writers, it has little to do with aesthetics, that is, the study of beauty. Furthermore, it does not discuss any general features of reasoning and argumentation, so it has little to do with the study of logic.

B   **Correct.** Because the passage focuses on five historically important literary figures, it is most relevant to the study of history and literature.

C   The passage does not focus on the study of religion or on the structure and functioning of human society. Therefore, the passage

has little to do with to either theology or sociology.

D   The passage does not focus on either human society and culture or on political activity and behavior. Therefore, it has little to do with either anthropology or political science.

E   The passage does not engage in a study of language or the structure of language, so it has little to do with linguistics. Furthermore, it is relevant to only one particular type of art, literature, and so is of only limited relevance to the study of art in general.

The correct answer is B.

Questions 173–177 refer to the passage on page 151.

RC49461.01-10

173. The primary purpose of the passage is to

(A)   compare the information about organic function made available by historical explanation with that made available by the experimental investigation of living organisms

(B)   assess the influence that theories of history had on developments in the field of biology in the nineteenth century

(C)   discuss the importance of historical explanation in the thinking of nineteenth century biologists

(D)   contrast biologists' use of historical explanation during the early nineteenth century with its use during the final quarter of the nineteenth century

(E)   evaluate the way in which the concept of heredity altered the use of historical explanation by nineteenth-century biologists

Main idea

This question requires that we understand the fundamental purpose of the passage, which is a function of both its structure and content.

The first paragraph of the passage notes a turning point in the history of biology. In the late nineteenth century, biologists made a shift away from historical explanation of biology.

However, as the passage continues, it addresses the importance of historical explanation in biology throughout the nineteenth century.

A   The passage says little about the information about organic function that is made available by the experimental investigation of living organisms.

B   The passage focuses on historical explanation in biology. It does not discuss different theories of history. Therefore, it does not assess the influence of different theories of history on the influence on developments in biology.

C   **Correct.** The primary purpose of the passage is to discuss the importance of historical explanation in nineteenth-century biology.

D   The passage mentions the final quarter of the nineteenth century specifically to note the turning point when biologists began to use experimental manipulation as a way to discern the causes of vital processes. The passage does not contrast these biologists' use of historical explanation during the final quarter of the nineteenth century with their use of it earlier in the nineteenth century.

E   The final sentence of the passage suggests that the concept of heredity *seemed to complete the argument for a historical explanation of evolutionary events.* However, this is just one part of the passage's discussion of historical explanation in biology in the nineteenth century.

The correct answer is C.

RC49461.01-20

174. According to information presented in the passage, which of the following is a true statement about the methods of explanation used by biologists and historians in the nineteenth century?

(A)   Neither biologists nor historians were able to develop methods of explanation that were accepted by the majority of their colleagues.

(B)   The methods used by biologists to explain phenomena changed dramatically, whereas the methods used by historians to explain events did not change as noticeably.

(C)   Biologists believed that they had refined the methods of explanation used by historians.

(D)   Biologists' and historians' methods of explaining what they believed to be comparable phenomena were similar.

(E)   Although biologists and historians adopted similar methods of explanation, the biologists were more apologetic about their use of these methods.

Supporting idea

The passage states *The biologist-as-historian and the general historian of human events dealt with comparable phenomena and assumed necessarily a common mode of explanation.* This indicates, in other words, that biologists' and historians' methods were similar in explaining what they believed to be comparable phenomena.

A   The passage suggests that biologists through most of the nineteenth century tended to use historical explanation. Presumably, it is not true that biologists were unable to develop methods that were accepted by the majority of their colleagues.

B   The passage suggests that methods used by biologists changed significantly toward the end of the nineteenth century. However, nothing in the passage indicates to what extent, if at all, historians' methods changed.

C   The passage suggests that biologists believed that, in observing embryogenesis and cell formation, there existed a clear justification for the utility of historical explanation in biology. However, there is no indication that these biologists believed that they had refined the historical methods used by historians.

D   **Correct.** The final sentence of the first paragraph indicates that the methods of biologists and historians in the nineteenth century were similar.

E   The only evidence that biologists were apologetic about their methods in the nineteenth century is that a turning point in their methods existed toward the end of the century. This is of course only weak evidence that biologists were apologetic. And even if these biologists were apologetic, nothing in the passage indicates whether historians were more or less apologetic.

The correct answer is D.

175. Which of the following best summarizes the "turning point" mentioned in line 2?

(A) The beginning of the conflict between proponents of the ideal of historical explanation and the proponents of experimentation

(B) The substitution of historical explanation for causal explanation

(C) The shift from interest in historical explanation to interest in experimentation

(D) The attention suddenly paid to problems of organic function

(E) The growth of public awareness of the controversies among biologists

Evaluation

The *turning point* mentioned in the passage refers to a shift among biologists during the last quarter of the nineteenth century. Specifically, this shift was from favoring historical explanation to a greater interest in experimentation.

A The passage does not specify any sort of conflict between proponents of the ideal of historical explanation and the proponents of experimentation. The passage only notes that there was a shift in interest from historical explanation—applied deductively to organic function—to experimentation.

B The passage indicates, with some criticism, that historical explanation was seen as a type of causal explanation.

C **Correct.** As noted above, the *turning point* was a shift away from historical explanation—the dominant thread in biology throughout most of the nineteenth century—toward experimentation.

D The passage suggests that, throughout the nineteenth century, biology had been concerned with organic function: initially it explained organic function through historical processes and then it began to explain organic function through experimentation.

E The passage does not indicate whether public awareness of controversies among biologists grew.

The correct answer is C.

176. The author implies that nineteenth-century biologists who studied embryogenesis believed that they

(A) had discovered physical evidence that supported their use of historical explanation

(B) were the first biologists to call for systematic experimentation on living organisms

(C) were able to use historical explanation more systematically than were biologists who did not study embryogenesis

(D) had inadvertently discovered an important part of the factual record of the history of living organisms on earth

(E) had avoided the logical fallacies that characterize the reasoning of most nineteenth-century biologists

Implication

The author indicates that nineteenth-century biologists used a historical explanation of organic function. This use, they believed, was justified through observations of cell generation and stages in embryogenesis.

A **Correct.** The author suggests that nineteenth-century biologists who studied embryogenesis believed that they had discovered physical evidence supporting the use of historical explanation.

B The passage does not imply that biologists who studied embryogenesis were the first to call for systematic experimentation on living organisms.

C The passage does not imply that biologists who studied embryogenesis were any more successful in using historical explanation systematically than biologists who did not.

D The passage states that the fossil record was incomplete, so it is likely that this means many important things were missing. Any specific inadvertent discovery would have to be mentioned directly in the passage. The passage does not suggest any sort of discovery.

E The author, in the second paragraph, indicates that both those nineteenth-century biologists who studied cell generation and those who studied embryology confused temporal succession and causal explanation.

The correct answer is A.

RC49461.01-50

177. The passage would be most likely to appear in which of the following?

(A) An essay investigating the methodology used by historians of human events

(B) A book outlining the history of biology in the nineteenth century

(C) A seminar paper on the development of embryogenesis as a field of study in nineteenth-century biology

(D) A review of a book whose topic is the discovery of fossils in the nineteenth century

(E) A lecture whose subject is the limitations of experimental investigation in modern biology

Evaluation

The passage discusses a turning point in the late nineteenth century in the history of biology. It then focuses primarily on the use of historical explanation in the field of biology during the nineteenth century. Therefore, it seems that, among the five options here, the one this passage would be most likely to appear in would be a book discussing the history of biology in the nineteenth century.

A   The passage focuses on nineteenth-century biologists' use of historical explanation. It presents no specific investigation of how historians used that methodology. Therefore, it would not be of particular value in an essay investigating the methodology used by historians of human events.

B   **Correct.** The passage focuses mainly on nineteenth-century biologists' use of historical explanation. It also mentions a turning point in the history of biology. It references the history of human events primarily as an analogy to help clarify the biologists' use of this historical method. These facts about the passage suggest that, among the five options here, the one the passage would be most likely to appear in would be a book outlining the history of biology in the nineteenth century.

C   The passage spends only a portion of one paragraph saying anything about embryogenesis. Even that portion is primarily offered only to give some explanation of why nineteenth-century biologists were attracted to the use of historical explanation. It does not seem that it would appropriate to use the entire passage in a seminar paper on the topic of embryogenesis as a field of study in nineteenth-century biology.

D   There is no reference to a book whose topic is the discovery of fossils in the nineteenth century. The passage only briefly mentions fossils. It seems unlikely that the passage would be of any use to a review of such a book.

E   The passage says almost nothing about experimental investigation in modern biology, and says absolutely nothing about its limitations.

The correct answer is B.

Questions 178–185 refer to the passage on page 153.

RC59461.01-10

178. The primary purpose of the passage is to

(A) make a case for the importance of skillful psychological motivation in well-written novels and romances

(B) contrast the romantic and novelistic traditions and assert the aesthetic superiority of the romantic tradition

(C) survey some of the responses to Melville's fiction put forward by James and twentieth-century literary critics

(D) argue that the charges made against Melville's fiction by literary critics are suspect and misleading

(E) note several accusations made against Melville's fiction by literary critics and refute one of these accusations

Main idea

Our goal is to find the primary purpose of the passage, which requires a firm understanding of the structure of the passage and its objectives. The passage notes various criticisms of Melville's fiction, but its main argument is to support the idea that Melville's fiction is valid even though it does not follow Henry James's conception of the novel.

Furthermore, the passage defends Melville's fiction by arguing that Melville had an equally valid conception of the purpose of fiction: one that differed fundamentally from that of James. The passage indicates that Melville's strength does not derive from depictions of character motivation. Rather, it lies in Melville establishing a strong moral situation; occasionally this might be done at the expense of continuity or credibility.

A   The passage specifically refers to Melville's novels and does not suggest that *well-written novels or romances* all share any particular characteristic.

B   The passage is specifically concerned with Melville's novels, not the general romantic or novelistic traditions. Furthermore, the passage suggests that the romantic tradition in fiction has its own literary validity, as has the novelistic tradition, but does not indicate that one is superior to the other.

C   This passage does not simply give a survey of literary responses to Melville's fiction; the passage goes further in arguing for the literary worth of Melville's work.

D   Because the passage argues against certain criticisms of Melville's work, it might be argued that the author of the passage considers some criticisms of Melville "suspect." However, there is nothing in the passage to imply this applies to all criticisms of Melville's work. Furthermore, there is absolutely nothing in the passage to indicate that these critics' work is "misleading."

E   **Correct.** The primary purpose of the passage is to counter one of several negative evaluations of Melville's novels made by literary critics.

The correct answer is E.

RC59461.01-20

179. The author draws which of the following conclusions about the fact that Melville's fiction often does not possess the qualities of a Jamesian novel?

(A)   Literary critics should no longer use Jamesian standards to judge the value of novels.

(B)   Literary critics who have praised Melville's fiction at the expense of James's fiction should consider themselves justified.

(C)   Literary critics should no longer attempt to place writers, including Melville and James, in traditions or categories.

(D)   Melville and James should be viewed as different sorts of writers and one should not be regarded as inherently superior to the other.

(E)   Melville and James nevertheless share important similarities and these should not be overlooked or slighted when literary critics point out differences between the two writers.

Supporting idea

Which among the answer choices is a conclusion drawn by the author of the passage regarding the contrast between Melville's fiction and that of James? The second sentence of the final paragraph states this: *Melville is a different kind of writer, who held, and should be judged by, presuppositions about fiction that are quite different from James's.* In other words, Melville held different standards regarding fiction and one needs to evaluate Melville on these standards rather than on James's standards.

A   The passage suggests that Jamesian standards may be inappropriate for Melville's novels. However, it does not suggest that Jamesian standards are necessarily invalid for judging the value of other novels.

B   The passage mentions nothing about critics who have praised Melville's novels at the expense of James's novels. In fact, the passage never mentions James's novels.

C   The passage does not suggest that critics should avoid categorization of writers. In fact, the passage in lines 19–20 states that *Melville is not a Jamesian novelist*, which is in itself such a categorization.

D   **Correct.** This accurately expresses a conclusion drawn by the author, namely that Melville and James have valid, if different, approaches to fiction writing.

E   The author indicates no important similarities between Melville and James's writing. In fact, the author emphasizes certain key differences between the two authors' work.

The correct answer is D.

RC59461.01-30

180. Which of the following would be the most appropriate title for the passage?

(A) Melville's Unique Contribution to Romantic Fiction

(B) Melville's Growing Reputation Among Twentieth-Century Literary Critics

(C) Melville and the Jamesian Standards of Fiction: A Reexamination

(D) Romantic and Novelistic: The Shared Assumptions of Two Traditions

(E) The Art of Fiction: James's Influence on the Novelistic Tradition

Main idea

Given the content of the passage, which of these choices could most reasonably be used as a title? The passage's main purpose is to counter the criticisms of those critics who describe Melville's works of fiction as romances. These critics claim that Melville's works lack significant literary value because they fail to satisfy James's criteria for literary worth in novels, a standard that is widely accepted by literary critics. The passage argues that Melville's novels would be more appropriately evaluated using the criteria that Melville himself espoused; these criteria differ significantly from James's criteria.

A This choice is inappropriate because nothing in the passage suggests that Melville's approach was unique; that is, nothing in the passage indicates that Melville's contribution is the only one of its kind.

B This choice is inappropriate because the passage never states how Melville's literary reputation among twentieth-century critics evolved.

C **Correct.** This choice reflects the central idea of the passage that the literary worth of Melville's fiction is not appropriately judged using the Jamesian standard; rather, it is appropriately judged using Melville's own notion of *the ultimate purpose of fiction.*

D Although the passage suggests that issues of morality figured in the fiction of both James and Melville, the passage does not address any assumptions shared between James and Melville.

E Although the passage suggests that James had a significant influence on critical standards for the novel, the passage centers on Melville's works rather than James' influence.

The correct answer is C.

RC59461.01-40

181. The author probably mentions Melville's *Pierre* to

(A) refute those literary critics who have made generalizations about the quality of Melville's fiction

(B) argue that the portrayal of characters is one of Melville's more accomplished literary skills

(C) give an example of a novel that was thought by James to resemble his own fiction

(D) suggest that literary critics find few exceptions to what they believe is a characteristic of Melville's fiction

(E) reinforce the contention of literary critics

Evaluation

Why does the author of the passage mention Pierre*?* The final sentence of the first paragraph reads: *Critics argue that only* Pierre *(1852), because of its subject and characters, is close to being a novel in the Jamesian sense.*

This statement indicates that literary critics regard *Pierre* as the only possible exception to their negative characterization of Melville's fiction as *romance* because *Pierre* has at least some of the properties that James considered essential to novels of literary value.

A This is not a purpose of mentioning *Pierre.* The passage does not cite any critics who claim that most of Melville's novels satisfy Jamesian criteria.

B This is not a purpose of mentioning *Pierre.* The author of the passage does not endorse the view that character portrayal is a particular strength of Melville's novels.

In fact, the author suggests that Melville's novels tend to give questionable portrayals of what characters *feel or think*.

C   The passage lacks any information indicating James's personal view of *Pierre*. Given the information in the passage, it is entirely possible that James never even read *Pierre*.

D   Correct. The critics of Melville's novels generally characterize them as "romances" rather than "novels" given that they lack certain properties Henry James regarded as essential to novels. The mention of *Pierre* shows that the critics see it as the only one of Melville's novels that might fit the Jamesian criteria.

E   In the sentence in which *Pierre* is mentioned, the author of the passage does not endorse criticism suggesting that Melville's works are romances rather than novels. Furthermore, the sentence is not intended to endorse a contention of any other type of literary critic.

The correct answer is D.

RC59461.01-50

182. Which of the following statements best describes the author's method of argumentation in lines 24–31?

(A)   The author describes an important standard of evaluation used by critics of Melville and then attacks that standard.

(B)   The author admits a contention put forward by critics of Melville but then makes a countercharge against those critics.

(C)   The author describes a charge advanced by critics of Melville and then points out a logical flaw in this charge.

(D)   The author provides evidence that seems to support a position held by critics of Melville but then demonstrates that the evidence actually supports a diametrically opposed position.

(E)   The author concedes an assertion made by critics of Melville but then mitigates the weight of the assertion by means of an explanation.

Evaluation

Which answer choice best describes the reasoning in lines 24–32? The author suggests that Melville's novels can reasonably be called "romances," but also is careful to explain a sense of this designation that still regards Melville's novels as valid works of literature.

A   The text in lines 24–31 does not describe any standard of evaluation used by Melville's critics.

B   There is no countercharge against, or even mention of, Melville's critics in lines 24–31.

C   Again, there is no mention of criticisms of Melville's work in the lines 24–31; it follows that the author does not point out a "logical flaw" in such criticisms within lines 24–31.

D   In lines 24–31, the author accepts that Melville's novels can be called "romances." In lines 24–31, of course, the author presents no evidence to show that Melville's novels are not romances.

E   Correct. In lines 24–31, the author concedes that Melville's novels are romances. However, the author argues that this does not detract from the literary value of Melville's work.

The correct answer is E.

RC59461.01-60

183. Which of the following can logically be inferred from the passage about the author's application of the term "romance" to Melville's work?

(A)   The author uses the term in a broader way than did Melville himself.

(B)   The author uses the term in a different way than do many literary critics.

(C)   The author uses the term in a more systematic way than did James.

(D)   The author's use of the term is the same as the term's usual meaning for twentieth-century commentators.

(E)   The author's use of the term is less controversial than is the use of the term "novel" by many commentators.

Inference

Which of the following conclusions regarding the term "romance" as applied to Melville's work is most strongly supported by the information in the passage? The author of the passage uses the term without the negative connotation that the passage suggests the term carried for many twentieth-century critics of Melville.

A There is no information in the passage regarding how, or even whether, Melville used the term "romance."

B Correct. The author of the passage will call Melville's novels *romances* provided this term is used without the disparaging connotations of this term (particularly as used by many critics of Melville's work).

C Nothing in the passage specifies James's use of the term "romance."

D The author of the passage specifically applies the term "romance" in a way that avoids the disparaging connotations of escapism present in the use of the term by some critics of Melville's work.

E The passage provides no information by which we can gauge how controversial the author's use of "romance" as applied to Melville's works is, relative to other commentators' use of the term "novel."

The correct answer is B.

RC59461.01-70

184. Which of the following can most logically be inferred about the author's estimation of the romantic and novelistic traditions of fiction?

(A) The romantic tradition should be considered at least as valuable as the novelistic tradition in the examination of human experience.

(B) The romantic tradition should be considered the more vital tradition primarily because Melville is part of that tradition.

(C) The romantic tradition should be considered the superior tradition because it is so widespread.

(D) The romantic tradition has had as much success in pleasing literary critics as has the novelistic tradition.

(E) The romantic and novelistic traditions have always made important contributions to literature, but their most important contributions have been in the twentieth century.

Inference

We must determine which statement regarding the author's evaluation of the romantic and novelistic traditions of fiction is most strongly supported by the information in the passage. The passage states: *although Melville is not a Jamesian novelist, he is not therefore a deficient writer.* The author of the passage tells us that Melville sought to explore moral questions, an exploration that Melville assumed to be *the ultimate purpose of fiction.* These statements indicate that the author of the passage regards the romantic tradition's fictional examination of human experience as at least equal in value to the novelistic tradition's examination of it.

A Correct. The passage suggests that both traditions are concerned with the examination of human experience, yet their approaches to this examination differ. The passage argues that Melville's body of fiction is no less valuable as literature than James's.

B The passage provides nothing to indicate that Melville's position as a romantic writer therefore implies that romance is "more vital" than the novelistic tradition. Note that such a comparison would need to be clearly made for this to be a valid answer choice.

C The passage provides no information regarding how widespread the romantic tradition is.

D The passage provides no information to suggest that literary critics are more pleased by romantic works than they are by novelistic works. Note that such a comparison would need to be clearly made for this to be a valid answer choice.

E The passage provides no information to suggest that the most important contributions of the romantic and novelistic traditions have been during the twentieth century. In fact, given that Melville and James both worked in the nineteenth century, it seems doubtful that the passage would make such a claim.

The correct answer is A.

RC59461.01-80

185. The author of the passage would be most likely to agree that a writer's fiction should be evaluated by which of the following criteria?

(A) How consistently that fiction establishes credibility with the reader

(B) How skillfully that fiction supersedes the presuppositions or conventions of a tradition

(C) How completely that fiction satisfies the standards of judgment held by most literary critics

(D) How well that fiction fulfills the premises about fiction maintained by the writer of the fiction

(E) How well that fiction exhibits a continuity of subject and style over the course of the writer's career

Application

Which criteria would the author of the passage most likely agree to be useful for evaluating a writer's fiction? The passage argues that even though Melville's novels fail to satisfy Henry James's criteria for literary value in a novel, they still have a different kind of literary value. In particular, they match the criteria set out by Melville's own conception of fiction.

The author states that Melville sought in his fiction *to explore moral questions, an exploration he assumed was the ultimate purpose of fiction.* Therefore, the author would likely agree that the literary value of a writer's fiction is determined by the degree to which the writer's fiction fulfills the writer's own conception of what fiction should accomplish.

A The author of the passage would be unlikely to agree that fiction must establish credibility with the reader. In the passage, the author suggests that Melville was prepared to sacrifice some credibility in his fiction if doing so would help him to *establish a significant moral situation.*

B Nothing in the passage suggests that its author would agree with the idea that fiction must "supersede presuppositions or conventions of a tradition." While the author indicates that Melville's novels do not satisfy James's criteria for a good literary

novel, this does not indicate that Melville's work supersedes or replaces any tradition.

C The author of the passage clearly rejects this criterion and actually argues against the standards of many critics. Note the author's position that criticisms based on widespread acceptance by literary critics of James's standards for literary novels are not necessarily valid for all fiction.

D Correct. The author of the passage argues that Melville's fiction must be judged by reference to Melville's own criteria rather than by those of James or the critics who accepted James's criteria.

E Nowhere does the passage mention continuity of style over a career. Therefore, nothing in the passage suggests that the author would accept it.

The correct answer is D.

Questions 186–193 refer to the passage on page 156.

RC69461.01-10

186. According to the passage, book review editors pay attention to all of the following in deciding which books should be reviewed in their publications EXCEPT

(A) news releases from publishers

(B) sales figures compiled by bookstores

(C) the opinions of literary experts

(D) the probability that the books will be extensively advertised

(E) the likelihood that the books will be reviewed in other publications

Supporting idea

Which of the following is a factor that the passage does NOT indicate is considered by book review editors when deciding which book reviews to publish? The passage indicates that major decisions regarding which books will be reviewed in a given publication occur *before* the relevant books have been published; it follows that sales data for those books *would not exist* when initial decision making occurs.

This immediately suggests that answer choice B may be correct. But to verify that answer choice

B is correct, it will be important to quickly check two things: first, that the passage neither states nor implies review editors consider sales data and, second, that for each of the other factors listed, the passage either states or implies that review editors do consider that factor.

A   The passage indicates that book review editors do in fact consider news releases from publishers.

B   **Correct.** Nothing in the passage indicates that book review editors consider sales figures compiled by bookstores. Furthermore, the passage indicates that such data would NOT be available for certain books that the editors and book publishers consider most worth publishing. Even so, the passage does not exclude the possibility that book review editors may consider publishing reviews of books already in bookstores, based on a review of bookstore sales data. However, it is important to note that the passage neither states nor implies that this is so.

C   According to the passage, book review editors do in fact *listen to literary experts* regarding books that may sell well over time despite slow initial sales.

D   According to the passage, book review editors receive news releases and printers' proofs of certain books; this implies that the books will in fact be heavily advertised.

E   The passage states that book review editors *must consider what will be newsworthy, advertised, and written about elsewhere.* In other words, other publications' writing about the same books factor into the decisions of these editors.

The correct answer is B.

RC69461.01-20

187. The main idea of the second paragraph is that

(A)   decisions made by book review editors are influenced by the business of selling books

(B)   book review editors must be familiar with all aspects of the book trade

(C)   advertising is the most important factor influencing book sales

(D)   book reviews usually have no influence on what books are ordered in quantity by stores

(E)   publishers deliberately try to influence the decisions of book review editors

Evaluation

What idea is most central to the second paragraph? A good strategy here is to identify the two most plausible answer candidates by quickly eliminating the three least plausible.

Looking through the options, answer choices B, C, and D can be reasonably easily eliminated, leaving the remaining two options as the most plausible candidates. Note that the paragraph focuses on the idea that review editors' decisions are influenced by the business of selling books (answer choice A).

A   **Correct.** As indicated, this idea is the main theme of the paragraph.

B   The paragraph is focused on how editors' decisions are influenced by the business of selling books, not on how much knowledge book review editors must have.

C   Although the paragraph suggests that advertising may significantly influence book orders by bookstores, the paragraph does not indicate that advertising is the *most important factor.*

D   The paragraph does not indicate that book reviews usually have no influence on book orders by bookstores.

E   The paragraph does not indicate that publishers' pre-publication outreach to review editors is a deliberate effort to influence the editors' decisions.

The correct answer is A.

RC69461.01-30

188. According to the passage, a major concern of the unenthusiastic book reviewers mentioned in line 33 was to

(A)   ensure prompt payment for their work

(B)   influence public opinion of books

(C)   confirm the opinions of other reviewers

(D)   promote new books by their favorite authors

(E)   have their reviews published in the newspaper

Supporting idea

What does the passage suggest was a major concern of the unenthusiastic book reviewers mentioned? The necessary information is found in the final sentence of the third paragraph.

Given that the reviewers *were paid promptly anyway*, it follows that *prompt payment* would not be a *major concern* for them. This sentence goes on to suggest that having their material published in the newspaper was of concern, specifically implying that this concern may have induced some of them to provide more favorable reviews in order to ensure publication. While this is not directly stated, this line of reasoning is confirmed by the information that the review editor's *brilliant system* tended to publish only positive reviews.

A   The passage suggests that the practice was to promptly pay all reviewers—even those whose reviews were not published.

B   Nothing in the passage suggests that influencing public opinion was part of the agenda of *any* of the reviewers, even those occasionally writing unenthusiastic reviews.

C   Nothing in the passage suggests that writers of unenthusiastic book reviews were necessarily influenced by the opinions of other reviewers.

D   Nothing in the passage suggests that unenthusiastic book reviewers attempted to promote any book, let alone ones from their favorite authors.

E   **Correct.** The final sentence of the third paragraph indicates that this may have been a major concern of the unenthusiastic reviewers.

The correct answer is E.

RC69461.01-40

189. The passage provides information to answer which of the following questions?

(A)   Would most book review editors prefer to have

books reviewed without regard to the probable commercial success of the books?

(B)   Are publishers' efforts to persuade bookstores to order certain books generally effective?

(C)   On what basis do literary experts decide that a book is or is not important?

(D)   What criteria are used to determine the length of a particular book review?

(E)   Have book review practices in general changed significantly since a generation ago?

Inference

Which one of the five questions can be answered based on the information given in the passage? This implies that four of the answer choices will be questions that we cannot answer based on the passage. Certain among these choices are easily eliminated: the question regarding literary experts' evaluation and the question regarding criteria for length of reviews.

The question of whether book review practices in general have changed over the last generation is also fairly easily eliminated: the information about such practices a generation ago only concerns the system used by one review editor in one newspaper.

Thus we can narrow down our answer candidates to the following: the question about how expected commercial success relates to review editors' preferences, and the question about whether book publishers' outreach efforts for certain books succeed in persuading bookstores to order large quantities of those books. Which one of these two questions does the passage help answer?

A   The passage provides neither a definitive "yes" nor a definitive "no" answer to this question, at least as concerns "most" book editors. The second paragraph of the passage indicates that expectations regarding the books that bookstores will *order in quantity* does figure prominently in decision making regarding publication of reviews. However, this does not necessarily indicate what most editors *would prefer*. It is possible, if not likely, that book review editors differ widely in their preferences. This does not of course answer whether book review editors listen to their personal preferences when making decisions about publication of book reviews. Ultimately, we do not have the information to address either this question or its nuances.

B **Correct.** The passage tells us that the books that publishers heavily advertise will *probably be among the books that most bookstores order in quantity.* This provides a "yes" answer to the question.

C The passage provides no information regarding how *literary experts* decide whether a book is "important." Note that the passage specifically discusses book review editors. It is unclear whether this is the same thing as "literary expert," but we are given no reason to think so.

D The passage provides no information regarding how the length of a book review is determined.

E The passage indicates that a generation ago, a review editor for a newspaper had a *brilliant* system of publishing only the reviews that were enthusiastic about particular books. However, the passage does not indicate that this was common editorial practice at the time. Rather, the passage tells us that most editors currently publish both positive and negative reviews. Nothing in the passage indicates that this practice was different a generation ago.

The correct answer is B.

RC69461.01-50

190. The passage suggests which of the following about book review readers?

(A) They pay careful attention to reviewers' biases as they read reviews.

(B) They disapprove of book review editors who try to influence what their reviewers write.

(C) They use book reviews in order to gauge whether a book is likely to endure.

(D) They expect to see timely reviews of widely publicized books in the periodicals they read.

(E) They are usually willing to search in several stores for a highly recommended book that is hard to find.

Inference

What does the passage convey about readers of book reviews? Note that the question does not concern what is most likely true of *at least some* book review readers; rather, the passage most strongly suggests what is true of book review readers *in general*.

Nothing in the passage implies that any of the first three answer choices given is true of book review readers *in general*. This leaves the final two answer choices as possible candidates. Of the two, D more clearly describes something that the passage suggests is generally true of book review readers.

A No doubt some book review readers pay attention to reviewers' biases, but the passage does not imply that this is generally true of readers of book reviews.

B The passage does not tell us that readers of book reviews generally know whether review content is influenced by book review editors. Furthermore, it does not tell us whether these readers generally approve or disapprove of such editors.

C The passage nowhere suggests that readers of book reviews generally make judgments as to whether a book is likely to be a long-lasting cultural legacy.

D **Correct.** The passage indicates that book review editors in general feel responsible to meet their readers' expectations by providing reviews of books that are *newsworthy, advertised, and written about elsewhere.*

E The passage nowhere suggests that most book review readers will search in several stores for a highly recommended book. The passage refers to *books that readers will have trouble finding in stores;* however, this is more plausibly read as *readers of books* rather than *readers of book reviews.* Furthermore, it does not suggest that *most* readers—or most readers of book reviews—will go to several stores to search for a book.

The correct answer is D.

RC69461.01-60

191. Which of the following words, if substituted for "brilliant" in line 26, would LEAST change the meaning of the sentence?

(A) showy

(B) articulate

(C) literate

(D) stingy

(E) absurd

Evaluation

Which word, if substituted for "brilliant" in the sentence, would least alter the meaning of the sentence? In other words, we must pick the word we could substitute for *brilliant* in the sentence without significantly changing the meaning of the sentence.

Note that neither *articulate* nor *literate* would be an apt modifier of the word *system*. *Stingy* indicates a financial use of the *system*, which seems inappropriate.

Eliminating these options leaves only *showy* and *absurd* as candidates. Given these choices, it is fairly clear that brilliant is meant ironically. We are told that the unenthusiastic reviewers *quickly learned that if they wanted their material to be printed, it was advisable to be kind.*

A   Nothing in the passage conveys that the system, ironically designated *brilliant*, was showy, that is, eye-catching.

B   *Articulate* could describe fluent or coherent speech, description, or writing, but it does not appropriately modify the noun *system* in this context.

C   The adjective *literate* does not appropriately modify *system;* furthermore, it fails to convey a clear meaning that would match the ironic meaning of the modifier *brilliant.*

D   The system does not seem to have a monetary purpose, so *stingy* would not fit. Note that the final sentence of the paragraph suggests that the system self-selects for books that are likely to be successful, potentially at the expense of writers who write "unenthusiastic reviews." Nevertheless, the passage notes that the

unpublished writers would still be paid, so their risk lies in not having their work read rather than in not being paid for their work.

E   **Correct.** Among the answer choices, *absurd* best captures the ironic use of *brilliant* and preserves the meaning of the sentence as a whole.

The correct answer is E.

RC69461.01-70

192. Which of the following is an assumption made by the book review editor referred to in line 27?

(A) A book of great worth will receive only good reviews.

(B) An important book will endure despite possible bad reviews.

(C) Reviewers might hide their true opinions in order to have their reviews published.

(D) Book review editors should select reviewers whose opinions can be guessed in advance.

(E) Book review editors have an obligation to print extensive reviews of apparently important books.

Evaluation

Which one of the five options is an assumption the book review editor made in following the book review system described? The editor's policy was to publish the reviews that gave books a sufficiently positive evaluation while often refusing to publish unenthusiastic reviews; that is, reviews that did not rate books highly.

Given the information in the passage, it is likely that this editor followed other editors in *feeling some concern about what might endure.* That is, these editors would presumably not wish to risk ignoring *a book of great worth.* Therefore, this editor may have believed that his *brilliant system* of not publishing negative reviews would guard against such a risk. In other words, the editor assumed that unenthusiastic reviews accurately reflected the value of the books reviewed. By this logic, a book of great worth would, of course, receive only positive reviews.

A   **Correct.** The editor, in applying the *system* described, assumed that a book of *great worth* would receive only positive reviews.

B   If the editor assumed this, he would be justified in publishing bad reviews given that a good book would eventually be vindicated.

C   There is nothing to suggest that the editor thought the reviewers to be dishonest in representing their views of the books they review; that is, that the reviewers would lie in order to get their reviews published. While this may have been the case, the passage provides no evidence to suggest that the editor assumed this.

D   Nothing in the passage suggests that the editor's practice was governed by this sort of rule regarding how book review editors should select reviewers.

E   The passage suggests the book review editor wanted books of significant worth reviewed in his newspaper. However, it does not suggest that the editor assumed this rule should apply to all book review editors.

The correct answer is A.

RC69461.01-80

193. It can be inferred that, as a prospective book buyer, the author of the passage would generally respond to highly enthusiastic reviews of new books with

(A)   resignation

(B)   amusement

(C)   condemnation

(D)   skepticism

(E)   disinterest

Inference

What does the passage suggest about how its author might respond to highly enthusiastic *reviews of new books?* Nothing in the passage suggests the response would be resignation, amusement, or condemnation.

This narrows down the possibilities to skepticism or disinterest. The intended meaning of *disinterest* is "lack of interest." It is unlikely that the author of the passage would be generally uninterested in highly enthusiastic reviews of new books.

This of course leaves skepticism as the best candidate. The passage does suggest that this might be the passage author's attitude: the

passage discusses the impact of commercial considerations—the business of selling books— on review editors' choices regarding which books to review. It follows that *highly enthusiastic* reviews may, at least in some cases, be influenced by such considerations. With this in mind, the author of the passage is likely to approach such reviews with skepticism. In other words, the author holds a certain amount of doubt as to whether such reviews accurately reflect the true worth of the books reviewed.

A   Given the critical approach to reviewing practices conveyed in the passage, it is unlikely that the response of the author would be resignation.

B   The author of the passage might, for various reasons, be amused at some highly enthusiastic reviews. Nevertheless, the passage does not suggest that amusement would be the author's response to any highly enthusiastic review.

C   Nothing in the passage suggests that the author's general response to enthusiastic reviews would be condemnation.

D   **Correct.** As explained above, skepticism is most likely to be the author's most usual response.

E   Some book reviews, even highly enthusiastic ones, might not interest the author of the passage. However, nothing in the passage indicates that the author's general response would be to show no interest.

The correct answer is D.

Questions 194–200 refer to the passage on page 158.

RC79461.01-10

194. The primary purpose of the passage is to

(A)   compare and criticize two theories of tragedy

(B)   develop a new theory of tragedy

(C)   summarize the thematic content of tragedy

(D)   reject one theory of tragedy and offer another theory in its place

(E)   distinguish between tragedy and irony

Main idea

What is the primary purpose of the passage? The hypothesis that the primary purpose of the passage is to compare and criticize two theories of tragedy is attractive. After all, the substance of the passage consists mainly of a discussion of the two theories.

To confirm that answer choice A is the best choice, however, we need to quickly review the other options. Does the passage develop a new theory of tragedy? No. Does it summarize the thematic content of tragedy? This would be clear if so; it is not clear. Does it offer a theory of tragedy to replace a theory it rejects? Definitely not. Does it distinguish between tragedy and irony? This is discussed, but only in a manner incidental to the main idea of the passage. Given the unsuitability of the other answer choices, we are left with answer choice A: that the main purpose of the passage is to compare and criticize two theories of tragedy.

A   **Correct.** This best describes the main purpose of the passage, based on the analysis above.

B   The passage does not develop a new theory of tragedy.

C   While the passage summarizes the thematic content of tragedy in a very general way, it does so only as a means to providing a critical analysis of the two theories of tragedy discussed.

D   The passage does not advance a new theory of tragedy; it simply considers two existing theories.

E   The passage distinguishes between tragedy and irony; it does so only in service of the larger analysis that is the main focus of the passage.

The correct answer is A.

RC79461.01-20

195. The author states that the theories discussed in the passage "represent extreme views" (see line 6) because their conclusions are

(A)   unpopular

(B)   complex

(C)   paradoxical

(D)   contradictory

(E)   imaginative

Supporting idea

What reason does the author of the passage state for the claim that the two theories of tragedy discussed represent extreme views?

A careful reading of the first few sentences of the passage provides a quick answer to this question. In the second sentence of the passage, the author states that the two theories represent extreme views *because their conclusions are contradictory.*

It may be that the author has other reasons for this conclusion. However, no other such reasons are stated.

A   The author neither explicitly nor implicitly characterizes either of the theories as unpopular.

B   The author refers to *the complexity of the tragic process,* but this statement is not used to complain that the theories are extreme.

C   The author nowhere states that either of the theories—or their juxtaposition—is paradoxical.

D   **Correct.** The author presents this as reason for concluding that the theories are extreme.

E   The author nowhere refers to imaginativeness as a reason for the claim that the theories are extreme.

The correct answer is D.

RC79461.01-30

196. The author objects to the theory that all tragedy exhibits the workings of external fate primarily because

(A)   fate in tragedies is not as important a cause of action as is the violation of a moral law

(B)   fate in tragedies does not appear to be something that is external to the tragic hero until after the tragic process has begun

(C)   the theory is based solely on an understanding of ancient Greek tragedy

(D)   the theory does not seem to be a plausible explanation of tragedy's ability to exhilarate an audience

(E)   the theory does not seem applicable to the large number of tragedies in which the hero overcomes fate

Supporting idea

What is the author's main reason for objecting to the theory that all tragedy exhibits the workings of external fate?

This view is attributed, in the passage's third sentence, to the first of the two theories considered. The author characterizes this view as *an oversimplification, primarily because it confuses the tragic condition with the tragic process*. In other words, the tragic hero's relationship with fate changes as the *tragic process* continues: fate is used to balance the tragic hero's life, and becomes an external condition as the hero's life becomes unbalanced.

The author elaborates that in ancient Greek tragedy fate *normally becomes external to the hero only after the tragic process has begun*. Therefore, the correct answer will likely mention either the tragic "process" or the tragic "condition."

A   This option mentions neither the tragic condition nor the tragic process.

B   Correct. This option mentions the tragic process and accurately captures the reason presented by the author to support the objection raised.

C   The author invokes ancient Greek tragedy to illustrate and support the objection raised; it is not invoked to indicate a flaw in the theory objected to.

D   The author does not cite tragedy's ability to exhilarate an audience as a primary reason for the objection raised.

E   The author does not cite the large number of tragedies in which the hero overcomes fate as the primary reason for the objection raised.

The correct answer is B.

RC79461.01-40

197. Which of the following comparisons of the tragic with the ironic hero is best supported by information contained in the passage?

(A)   A tragic hero's fate is an external condition, but an ironic hero's fate is an internal one.

(B)   A tragic hero must be controlled by fate, but an ironic hero cannot be.

(C)   A tragic hero's moral flaw surprises the audience, but an ironic hero's sin does not.

(D)   A tragic hero and an ironic hero cannot both be virtuous figures in the same tragedy.

(E)   A tragic hero is usually extraordinary, but an ironic hero may be cowardly or even villainous.

Inference

Which one of the comparisons between the tragic hero and the ironic hero is most strongly supported by the information in the passage?

To eliminate some of the choices, note the following: first, the passage indicates that the tragic hero's fate is initially internal, but the passage does not apply this to the ironic hero's fate. Second, the passage does not suggest that an ironic hero cannot be controlled by fate. Third, the passage does not attribute a sin to the ironic hero, yet it does indicate that the character of the ironic hero tends to be *ignoble*.

In any case, the passage is silent as to whether a tragedy can feature two heroes, one tragic and the other ironic. Finally, the passage implies that tragedy, unlike irony, needs *an exceptional central figure*. Furthermore, the passage suggests the following about an ironic hero: *the more ignoble the hero the sharper the irony*.

A   The passage indicates that the tragic hero's fate is initially internal but becomes external as part of the *tragic process*. The passage does consider whether an ironic hero can be controlled by fate but also does not exclude that possibility. Therefore, the passage does not suggest that externalized fate is a factor that distinguishes the tragic hero from the ironic hero.

B   Nothing in the passage indicates that an ironic hero cannot be controlled by fate.

C   The passage indicates that the character of the ironic hero tends to be *ignoble*. However, it does not imply that a sin by the ironic hero is essential to the development of the irony.

D   The passage does not address whether a tragedy can feature two heroes, one of whom is tragic and one of whom is ironic.

E   **Correct.** Among the choices provided, this comparison is best supported: tragedy requires *an exceptional central* figure, while for irony, *the more ignoble the hero* the better.

The correct answer is E.

RC79461.01-50

198. The author contrasts an honest person and a criminal (see lines 19–21) primarily to

(A) prove that fate cannot be external to the tragic hero

(B) establish a criterion that allows a distinction to be made between irony and tragedy

(C) develop the distinction between the tragic condition and the tragic process

(D) introduce the concept of sin as the cause of tragic action

(E) argue that the theme of omnipotent external fate is shared by comedy and tragedy

Evaluation

For what reason does the author draw a contrast between an honest person and a criminal? The contrast is presented during the discussion of the first of the two theories of tragedy; in particular, it is introduced to question whether fate is necessarily external in the tragic hero. The author suggests that fate, as conceived in ancient Greek tragedy, is *initially the internal balancing condition of life.* However, fate becomes external once the tragic process is unleashed. The tragic process begins when the theory violates this internal balance, ultimately leading to the tragic condition.

From this perspective, fate is both internal and external during the tragic process. Attributing *sin* to the tragic hero pertains only to the discussion of the second theory of tragedy. Note that no reference to comedy occurs in the context of the contrast drawn between an honest person and a criminal.

A   The passage suggests that fate can be external as well as internal in ancient Greek tragedy.

B   The distinction between tragedy and irony is offered as a critique of the first theory of tragedy; it is not presented as derived from the preceding discussion about fate.

C   **Correct.** As explained above, the contrast between the internal and external forms of fate is presented to distinguish between the tragic process itself and the tragic condition that is the outcome of the tragic process.

D   The attribution of *sin* to the tragic hero figures only in the discussion of the second theory of tragedy; therefore it is not associated with the mentioned contrast.

E   While the passage briefly mentions comedy, it is not in association with the contrast mentioned.

The correct answer is C.

RC79461.01-60

199. The author suggests that the tragic hero's "original destiny never quite fades out of the tragedy" (see lines 29–30) primarily to

(A) qualify the assertion that the theory of tragedy as a display of external fate is inconsistent

(B) introduce the discussion of the theory that tragedy is the consequence of individual sin

(C) refute the theory that the tragic process is more important than the tragic condition

(D) support the claim that heroism creates the splendor and exhilaration of tragedy

(E) distinguish between fate as conceived in ancient Greek tragedy and fate in more recent tragedy

Evaluation

Which one of the five answer choices best describes the primary purpose of the author's claim that the glory of the tragic hero's "original destiny never quite fades out of the tragedy"? In the sentence immediately preceding this claim, we read: *It is heroism that creates the splendor and exhilaration that is unique to tragedy.* Tragedy persistently reminds us of the extraordinary destiny that could have been attained by the hero. This reminds the audience that this glorious destiny has been tragically lost. The final sentence of the first paragraph, therefore, serves to support the claim in the sentence that precedes it.

A   Nothing suggests that the author regards this claim as lessening the flaw that the

author sees in the theory of tragedy first
discussed.

B   This claim does not introduce the discussion
of the second theory in the sense of creating
a meaningful transition to it.

C   Nowhere does the passage address a theory
that the tragic process is more important
than the tragic condition; the author
suggests that both are inherent in tragedy.

D   **Correct.** The context indicates that the
author's suggestion is presented to support
the claim expressed in the sentence that
precedes it.

E   Nowhere does the passage mention a
distinction between ancient Greek tragedy
and more recent tragedy.

The correct answer is D.

RC79461.01-70

200. In the author's opinion, an act of humility in comedy is
most analogous to

(A)   a catastrophe in tragedy

(B)   an ironic action in tragedy

(C)   a tragic hero's pride and passion

(D)   a tragic hero's aversion to sin

(E)   a tragic hero's pursuit of an unusual destiny

Inference

*What would the author regard as most analogous to
an act of humility in comedy?* The author writes
that *a proud and passionate mind* is *the precipitating
agent of catastrophe, just as in comedy the cause of
the happy ending is usually some act of humility.* In
other words, in tragedy, the hero's hubris leads to
his or her downfall.

A   A catastrophe is an external event rather
than the quality of a character, whereas both
hubris and humility are qualities of human
characters.

B   Nowhere does the passage associate an ironic
action in tragedy with an act of humility.

C   **Correct.** The author compares how hubris
leads to catastrophe in tragedy with how an
act of humility leads to a happy ending in
comedy.

D   The author refers to how the second theory
associates the tragic hero with sin. However,
the author makes no reference to the tragic
hero's aversion to sin as analogous to an act
of humility in comedy.

E   The author does not propose any similarity
between the extraordinary aspiration of
the tragic hero—that is, the hero's *unusual
destiny*—and an act of humility in comedy.

The correct answer is C.

Answer Explanations Verbal Reasoning

Critical Reasoning

Analysis/Critique

CR31410.01

201. Most of Western music since the Renaissance has been based on a seven-note scale known as the diatonic scale, but when did the scale originate? A fragment of a bone flute excavated at a Neanderthal campsite has four holes, which are spaced in exactly the right way for playing the third through sixth notes of a diatonic scale. **The entire flute must surely have had more holes**, and the flute was made from a bone that was long enough for these additional holes to have allowed a complete diatonic scale to be played. Therefore, **the Neanderthals who made the flute probably used a diatonic musical scale**.

In the argument given, the two portions in **boldface** play which of the following roles?

(A)　The first is presented as evidence that is confirmed by data presented elsewhere in the argument given; the second states a hypothesis that this evidence is used to undermine.

(B)　The first is an opinion, for which no supporting evidence is presented in the argument given, that is used to support the main conclusion of the argument; the second is that main conclusion.

(C)　The first describes a discovery as undermining the position against which the argument is directed; the second states the main conclusion of the argument.

(D)　The first is a preliminary conclusion drawn on the basis of evidence presented elsewhere in the argument given; the second is the main conclusion that this preliminary conclusion supports.

(E)　The first provides evidence to support the main conclusion of the argument; the second states a subsidiary conclusion that is drawn in order to support the main conclusion stated earlier in the argument.

Argument Construction

To determine what roles the two portions in boldface play, it is useful to look first for certain "inference indicator" words: words that indicate that what follows is a premise (words like *because* and *since*) or a conclusion (words like *thus* and *therefore*).

Here, there is only one, *therefore*; it immediately precedes the second boldfaced portion. This

indicates that that portion is a conclusion. Because of this, we can effectively rule out answer choice A.

However, we must investigate the rest of the argument to determine whether this is the main conclusion. If it is, we can rule out answer choice E as well. Alternatively, it may be an intermediate conclusion, in which case E would be the correct answer.

To determine which sort of conclusion it is, ask whether this conclusion is used in support of another claim in the argument. This conclusion is not, which makes it the main conclusion. This rules out answer choice E.

To make a correct choice among options B, C, and D, we must determine the role of the first highlighted portion.

A　This choice is incorrect because the second boldfaced portion is a conclusion drawn in the argument. It is not, of course, a hypothesis that the first boldfaced portion is used to undermine. Furthermore, the argument presents no data to confirm the first boldfaced portion.

B　Correct. The first boldfaced portion is not a conclusion; it is merely an assertion that is not supported by any claims presented in the argument. This portion, along with the statement immediately following it, are offered in support of the second boldfaced portion. This second boldfaced portion is the argument's main conclusion.

C　The first boldfaced portion does not undermine a position that the argument is directed against. In fact, the argument is not explicitly directed against any position. Note that the argument is rhetorically positive, arguing for a specific position rather than against one.

D　The argument provides no evidence in support of the first boldfaced position.

E　As noted above, this cannot be the correct answer because the second boldfaced portion is in fact the main conclusion of the argument.

The correct answer is B.

CR53140.01

202. In a certain rural area, people normally dispose of household garbage by burning it. Burning household garbage releases toxic chemicals known as dioxins. New conservation regulations will require a major reduction in packaging—specifically, paper and cardboard packaging—for products sold in the area. Since such packaging materials contain dioxins, one result of the implementation of the new regulations will surely be a reduction in dioxin pollution in the area.

Which of the following, if true, most seriously weakens the argument?

(A) Garbage containing large quantities of paper and cardboard can easily burn hot enough for some portion of the dioxins that it contains to be destroyed.

(B) Packaging materials typically make up only a small proportion of the weight of household garbage, but a relatively large proportion of its volume.

(C) Per-capita sales of products sold in paper and cardboard packaging are lower in rural areas than in urban areas.

(D) The new conservation regulations were motivated by a need to cut down on the consumption of paper products in order to bring the harvesting of timber into a healthier balance with its regrowth.

(E) It is not known whether the dioxins released by the burning of household garbage have been the cause of any serious health problems.

Argument Evaluation

This question requires us to identify a claim that seriously weakens the argument that new conservation regulations that require a major reduction in paper and cardboard packaging will reduce dioxin pollution in a certain rural area.

Dioxins are released when household garbage is burned. It seems reasonable to think that reducing packaging material that contains dioxins would help reduce dioxin pollution. Nevertheless, suppose for some reason burning large amounts of paper and cardboard containing dioxins actually—however counterintuitively—leads to a

reduction in the amount of dioxins that pollute the environment. This would indicate a major weakness in the argument.

A **Correct.** This claim tells us that garbage containing large quantities of paper and cardboard burns at such a high temperature that a portion of the dioxins in the garbage is destroyed. If so, then reducing quantities of paper and cardboard in burned garbage might in fact increase dioxin pollution, not reduce it, despite the fact that paper and cardboard packaging contains dioxins.

B This choice does not weaken the argument: the amount of dioxin pollution could still be reduced by reducing the amount of dioxin-containing packaging.

C This choice is not relevant to the question. Even if per-capita sales of products sold in paper and cardboard packaging are relatively low in the area in question, it could still be the case that the amount of dioxin pollution in the area would be reduced if the amount of cardboard and paper packaging was reduced.

D This choice provides an additional reason for the regulations; it thus does nothing to weaken the argument.

E Health problems caused by burning dioxins are outside the scope of the argument. Remember, the argument is about whether the regulations will reduce dioxin pollution. Determining whether burning household garbage is harmful might be relevant to deciding whether the plan should be implemented. It is not relevant, though, to deciding whether the plan would work.

The correct answer is A.

CR45650.01

203. Suriland cannot both export wheat and keep bread plentiful and affordable in Suriland. Accordingly, Suriland's wheat farmers are required to sell their crop to the government, which pays them a dollar per bushel less than the price on the world market. Therefore, if the farmers could sell their wheat on the world market, they would make a dollar per bushel more, less any additional transportation and brokerage costs they would have to pay.

Which of the following, if true, most seriously weakens the argument?

(A) Suriland's wheat farmers have higher production costs than do farmers in many other wheat-producing countries.

(B) Sale of a substantial proportion of Suriland's wheat crop on the world market would probably depress the price of wheat.

(C) The transportation and brokerage costs that Suriland's farmers would face if they sold their wheat outside Suriland could amount to almost a dollar per bushel.

(D) Suriland is surrounded by countries that do not import any wheat.

(E) The price of a bushel of wheat on the world market occasionally drops below the average cost of producing a bushel of wheat in Suriland.

Argument Evaluation

To keep bread affordable in Suriland, the country's government requires that wheat farmers in the country sell their wheat to the government for one dollar per bushel less than the world market price.

This question requires us to identify a statement that seriously weakens the argument. The conclusion of the argument is that, if these wheat farmers could legally sell their wheat on the world market, they would make a dollar per bushel more, minus additional transportation and brokerage costs.

However, this argument assumes that the world market price for wheat is fixed and would not be affected by introducing Suriland's wheat supply. That is, it is possible that the world market price per bushel for wheat might decline as a result of an increase in the wheat supply available on that market. If this were the case, it would severely weaken the argument.

A   This choice is outside the scope of the argument: the argument is about Suriland's wheat farmers increasing how much money that can receive per bushel, not about how these farmers' costs compare to the costs of farmers in other countries. In any case, this claim does not indicate that Suriland's wheat farmers could make a dollar more, minus any additional transportation and brokerage costs, than they do now.

B   **Correct.** An increase in supply on the world market with no increased demand could easily depress the price of wheat on the market. It is still possible that Suriland's farmers would make more than they do now, even after subtracting additional transportation and brokerage costs. But the argument specifically says that the farmers would make a dollar more, minus those costs, and that does not follow if the claim made in this answer choice is true.

C   Note that the argument suggests that these farmers *would make a dollar per bushel more, less any additional transportation and brokerage costs they would have to pay.* That could still be true no matter what those costs are.

D   Whether Suriland's wheat is sold to near or distant countries is immaterial to the argument; note that the conclusion includes the qualification *less any additional transportation costs.*

E   This indicates that Suriland wheat farmers might sometimes lose money on their wheat if selling on the world market. This does not indicate, however, that they would not lose less on the world wheat market than they would selling to the government. Note that the government's price for wheat is pegged to the world market, so the price the world market offers and the price the government offers will always differ by the exact same amount: the government pays one dollar less.

The correct answer is B.

CR30370.01

204. Sasha: It must be healthy to follow a diet high in animal proteins and fats. Human beings undoubtedly evolved to thrive on such a diet, since our prehistoric ancestors ate large amounts of meat.

Jamal: But our ancestors also exerted themselves intensely in order to obtain this food, whereas most human beings today are much less physically active.

Jamal responds to Sasha by doing which of the following?

(A) Refuting her statement about our prehistoric ancestors

(B) Bringing forth a piece of information for the purpose of suggesting that she should qualify her main conclusion

(C) Citing additional evidence that indirectly supports her conclusion and suggests a way to broaden it

(D) Questioning whether her assumption about our prehistoric ancestors permits any conclusions about human evolution

(E) Expressing doubts about whether most human beings today are as healthy as our prehistoric ancestors were

Argument Construction

Sasha argues that, because our prehistoric ancestors consumed large amounts of meat, humans must have evolved to thrive on a diet of animal proteins and fats. She concludes from this that it must be good for us to consume such a diet.

Jamal responds by pointing out that our ancestors exerted themselves much more than we do, primarily to catch this food.

This question asks for the best characterization, among the answer choices, of Jamal's response.

A Jamal implicitly accepts Sasha's statement that our prehistoric ancestors consumed large amounts of meat. Therefore, Jamal does not refute this statement made by Sasha.

B **Correct.** Jamal's response indicates that our prehistoric ancestors were far more active than we are. This suggests not that Sasha is incorrect in her statement, but that her conclusion would benefit from this qualification: a diet high in animal protein and fat is healthy when one engages in intense physical activity at a level that is higher than what is normal for modern human beings.

C Jamal's response suggests that Sasha make her conclusion more restrictive rather than more broad.

D Jamal suggests a qualification of Sasha's argument based on the behavior of

prehistoric human beings versus modern human beings. This in no way suggests that her assumption about our prehistoric ancestors tells us anything about evolution.

E Jamal does not question whether most modern human beings are as healthy as our prehistoric ancestors. However, he does question whether a diet high in animal proteins and fats is healthy without adjusting one's level of intense physical activity.

The correct answer is B.

CR70870.01

205. Some theorists and critics insist that no aesthetic evaluation of a work of art is sound if it is based even in part on data about the cultural background of the artist. This opinion is clearly false. The only sound aesthetic evaluations of artists' works are those that take into account factors such as the era and the place of the artists' births, their upbringing and education, and the values of their societies—in sum, those factors that are part of their cultural background.

The above argument is most vulnerable to which of the following objections?

(A) The argument presupposes the conclusion for which it purports to provide evidence.

(B) The argument cites evidence that undermines rather than supports the conclusion.

(C) The argument draws its conclusion by means of an equivocal interpretation of key terms.

(D) The argument assumes that the production of an effect is evidence of an intention to produce that effect.

(E) The argument assumes that evaluative disputes can be resolved by citing factual evidence.

Argument Evaluation

This question asks us to identify which of the objections listed among the answer choices the argument is most vulnerable to.

The argument's conclusion is that the opinion, expressed by some theorists and critics, that *no aesthetic evaluation of a work of art is sound if it is based even in part on data about the cultural background of the artist*, is false.

The only reason given for this conclusion is essentially a reiteration of the conclusion: that the cultural background is in fact vital to aesthetic evaluation of the artist. Given that the only reason given against the theorists' and critics' opinion is an opposite opinion, the argument is circular.

Therefore, the answer to this question must identify this: that is, that the argument presupposes the truth of the conclusion for which it claims to provide evidence.

A **Correct.** As indicated above, the argument is vulnerable to this criticism.

B The argument does not cite evidence that undermines rather than supports the conclusion. In fact, the argument's "evidence" for its conclusion is simply a reiteration of the conclusion itself.

C The argument does not equivocate on any key terms.

D The argument does not assume that the production of an effect means that one intended to produce that effect.

E The argument does not assume that facts will resolve evaluative disputes.

The correct answer is A.

CR53870.01

206. Banker: My country's laws require every bank to invest in its local community by lending money to local businesses, providing mortgages for local home purchases, and so forth. This is intended to revitalize impoverished local communities. But it is clear that the law will soon entirely cease to serve its intended purpose. An increasing number of banks incorporated in our country exist solely on the Internet and are not physically located in any specific community.

The banker's argument is most vulnerable to criticism on which of the following grounds?

(A) It overlooks the possibility that most banks that are physically located in specific communities in the banker's country are not located in impoverished communities.

(B) It takes for granted that a law that ceases to serve its originally intended purpose no longer serves any other beneficial purpose, either.

(C) It confuses a condition that would, if present, be likely to produce a given effect, with a condition that would probably be the cause if that effect were present.

(D) It overlooks the possibility that even if there is a strong correlation between two phenomena, neither of those phenomena are necessarily causally responsible for the other.

(E) It fails to adequately address the possibility that an increase in the number of banks of one kind in the banker's country will not lead to the complete elimination of banks of another kind.

Argument Evaluation

This item requires us to identify a criticism to which this argument is vulnerable.

The argument is as follows: an increasing number of banks in a particular country exist in no specific community, but only on the Internet. The banker believes the country's law requiring banks to invest in their specific communities will soon cease to serve its purpose, namely, to help revitalize impoverished communities.

Note that the banker's conclusion is quite strong: *The law will soon entirely cease to serve its intended purpose.* The only reasons to believe that the law would *entirely cease to serve its…purpose* would be: (1) if circumstances led to the complete disappearance of banks that do exist in specific communities; (2) if somehow circumstances caused investment in impoverished local communities to fail to revitalize those communities.

A To propose that most banks that are physically located in specific communities are not located in impoverished communities would, if anything, help support the banker's argument. That is, these banks would not have local communities in need of help, so the law would have little real effect on the impoverished communities it is intended to serve.

B First, it is not clear that the argument does take for granted that the law will serve no other beneficial purpose even if it fails to serve its intended purpose. Even if the argument did take this statement as given, it does nothing to call into question the banker's argument.

C   The argument does not confuse cause and effect.

D   The argument does not confuse correlation with causation.

E   **Correct.** The argument's only reason given for its conclusion is that the number of Internet-only banks is growing. This does not mean, however, that banks within local communities will no longer exist, or that those banks' investments will fail to help revitalize impoverished communities. Even if the number of local banks declines, as long as some local banks remain, the law will not necessarily *cease to serve its intended purpose*.

The correct answer is E.

CR15380.01

207. The contingency-fee system, which allows lawyers and their clients to agree that the lawyer will be paid only in the event of success, does not increase the number of medical malpractice lawsuits brought against doctors. As attorneys must cover the costs for their time and research, they want to be assured that any medical malpractice case they accept on a contingency-fee basis has substantial merit. Consequently, attorneys turn away many people who come to see them, for lack of a good case.

The argument above is most vulnerable to criticism on the grounds that it fails to

(A)   specify the criteria attorneys use to judge the merits of a medical malpractice case

(B)   consider whether, in the absence of a contingency-fee option, even people with meritorious cases are much less likely to initiate litigation if they believe they might incur large legal fees

(C)   note whether, in successful medical malpractice lawsuits, the average monetary award after legal costs have been deducted is less under contingency-fee arrangements than otherwise

(D)   consider the effect of the contingency-fee system on the number of lawsuits sought for reasons other than medical malpractice

(E)   acknowledge the rising cost of medical malpractice insurance

Argument Evaluation

This question asks us to identify the best criticism of this argument among the given answer choices.

Based on the premise that attorneys will turn away many potential clients who are not likely to win their cases, the argument concludes that a contingency-fee system does not increase the number of medical malpractice lawsuits brought against doctors.

In order to understand the argument more fully, we would need to consider whether the alternative to a contingency-fee system—a system wherein a client pays the attorney's fees regardless of outcome—makes it less likely that a potential client would bring a medical malpractice lawsuit against a doctor.

A   While it is true that the argument fails to specify the criteria that attorneys use to judge the merits of a malpractice case, this in no way suggests that such criteria do not exist.

B   **Correct.** This claim suggests that in the absence of a contingency-fee option, potential clients might hesitate to bring to court even lawsuits with merit. This suggests that there might actually be fewer meritorious malpractice lawsuits against doctors without the contingency-fee option. This would result in an overall reduction in the number of malpractice lawsuits against doctors, which substantially weakens the conclusion.

C   This implies that the contingency-fee option would reduce costs. Therefore, there would be more incentive to bring cases under the contingency-fee option. This strengthens the argument.

D   This is outside the scope of the argument. Note that the conclusion is about medical malpractice lawsuits, so this criticism is immaterial to the argument.

E   Note that medical malpractice insurance is a cost paid by doctors themselves. Therefore, the rising cost of medical malpractice insurance has no effect on the likelihood that a medical malpractice case will be brought to court.

The correct answer is B.

CR66590.01

208. Shirla: In figure skating competitions that allow amateur and professional skaters to compete against each other, the professionals are bound to have an unfair advantage. After all, most of them became professional only after success on the amateur circuit.

Ron: But that means that it's been a long time since they've had to meet the more rigorous technical standards of the amateur circuit.

Which of the following is most likely a point at issue between Shirla and Ron?

(A) Whether there should be figure skating competitions that allow amateur and professional skaters to compete against each other

(B) Whether the scores of professional skaters competing against amateurs should be subject to adjustment to reflect the special advantages of professionals

(C) Whether figure skaters can successfully become professional before success on the amateur circuit

(D) Whether the technical standards for professional figure skating competition are higher than those for amateur figure skating competition

(E) Whether professional figure skaters have an unfair advantage over amateur figure skaters in competitions in which they compete against each other

Argument Construction

To answer this question, we must identify a point on which Shirla and Ron disagree.

Shirla argues that because professional figure skaters who compete against amateur skaters will already have had success on the amateur circuit, the professionals will have an unfair advantage over the amateurs.

Ron, on the other hand, points out that this means that it has been a long time since the professionals have had to meet the more rigorous technical standards of the amateur circuit.

What that indicates is that Ron is countering Shirla's reason for thinking that professional figure skaters would have an unfair advantage. However, it is not clear whether Ron is suggesting that amateurs now have an advantage or whether professionals and amateurs would be on a relatively equal plane. It is only clear that Ron disagrees with Shirla's claim about professionals having an unfair advantage.

A   Shirla believes that professionals would have an unfair advantage. It therefore seems reasonable to conclude that she would oppose figure skating competitions that allow amateur and professional skaters to compete against one another. Nevertheless, she does not specify this and so we cannot be certain. That said, it is even less clear what Ron would say about such competitions. Note that it is unclear where Ron stands with regard to which group actually holds an advantage, if either.

B   It is unclear whether Shirla would say that the scores of professional skaters competing against amateur skaters must be adjusted to reflect the professionals' advantage. It is possible, after all, that Shirla would instead argue that there should be no such competition at all. Ron, on the other hand, simply disagrees with the claim that professionals have an unfair advantage.

C   Shirla believes that professional figure skaters will have initially competed on the amateur circuit before becoming professional. There is no indication that Ron disagrees with this.

D   Ron believes that the technical standards for professional figure skating competitions are lower, not higher, than those for amateur figure skating. There is no indication that Shirla disagrees with this.

E   **Correct.** Shirla believes that professional figure skaters would have an unfair advantage in competitions with amateur figure skaters; Ron disagrees with this belief.

The correct answer is E.

CR03001.01

209. Recent observations suggest that small, earthlike worlds form a very low percentage of the planets orbiting stars in the galaxy other than the sun. Of over two hundred planets that astronomers have detected around other stars, almost all are hundreds of times larger and heavier than the earth and orbit stars much smaller than the sun.

Which of the following, if true, would most weaken the above justification of the claim that earthlike worlds form a low percentage of the total number of planets?

(A) There are millions of planets orbiting stars around which astronomers have not attempted to detect planets.

(B) The best current astronomical theories predict that almost all planets around other stars are probably hundreds of times larger than the earth.

(C) A planet orbiting a star similar to the sun would be more likely to be earthlike in size than would a planet orbiting a much smaller star.

(D) The smaller a planet is relative to the star it orbits, the more difficult it is for astronomers to detect.

(E) The observations would have detected any small, earthlike worlds orbiting the stars around which larger planets have been detected.

Argument Evaluation

This question asks you to identify a claim that would, if true, weaken the justification for the conclusion that only a small percentage of the total number of planets in our galaxy are formed by earthlike worlds.

The only justification given for this conclusion is that, of the *over 200 planets that astronomers have detected around other stars, almost all are hundreds of times larger and heavier than the earth and orbit stars much smaller than the sun.*

Any evidence suggesting that the planets the astronomers have detected may be unrepresentative of planets in general would weaken the justification this claim gives to the conclusion.

A   This may look like it weakens the justification. After all, if the total number

of planets were significantly smaller than millions, then the sample size of *over 200 planets* would allow us to make the inference with more confidence. Nevertheless, particularly when accounting for the vagueness of the conclusion, the size of the sample is large enough to give us a reasonable degree of certainty. More importantly, though, note that the conclusion is restricted to planets orbiting stars in our galaxy. There is nothing in this answer choice to suggest that the planets it refers to are actually in our galaxy.

B   This choice strengthens the justification for the conclusion.

C   This choice does not weaken the justification for the conclusion. The only way it might do so is if it provided information showing that astronomers have mainly looked at planets orbiting an unrepresentative sample of stars, that is, a sample that is more heavily populated with planets orbiting stars that are smaller than most stars in the total star population. We are given no reason to believe this is the case.

D   Correct. This gives us a reason to think that the sample may be unrepresentative. Planets more earthlike in size may be less likely to be detected than the much larger stars that astronomers have detected.

E   This claim strengthens, rather than weakens, the argument. It implies that the astronomers' detection methods would not have inadvertently underrepresented the number of earthlike worlds.

The correct answer is D.

CR61021.01

210. Researchers in City X recently discovered low levels of several pharmaceutical drugs in public drinking water supplies. However, the researchers argued that the drugs in the water were not a significant public health hazard. They pointed out that the drug levels were so low that they could only be detected with the most recent technology, which suggested that the drugs may have already been present in the drinking water for decades, even though they have never had any discernible health effects.

Which of the following, if true, would most strengthen the researchers' reasoning?

(A) If a drug found in drinking water is not a significant public health hazard, then its presence in the water will not have any discernible health effects.

(B) There is no need to remove low levels of pharmaceutical drugs from public drinking water unless they present a significant public health hazard.

(C) Even if a substance in drinking water is a public health hazard, scientists may not have discerned which adverse health effects, if any, it has caused.

(D) Researchers using older, less sensitive technology detected the same drugs several decades ago in the public drinking water of a neighboring town but could find no discernible health effects.

(E) Samples of City X's drinking water taken decades ago were tested with today's most recent technology, and none of the pharmaceutical drugs were found.

Argument Evaluation

This question asks us to find the answer choice that would most strengthen this argument.

Researchers in City X reason that because the levels of certain pharmaceutical drugs that have been found in the city's drinking water are so low—detectable only by use of the most recent technology—these drugs may well have been in the drinking water for decades. Furthermore, the researchers point out that there have been no discernible health effects from the use of the drugs. They conclude that the drugs are probably not a significant concern.

As it stands, the argument is quite weak. The researchers conclude only that the drugs *may have . . . been present for decades.* This leaves open the possibility that they were not present for that long. If they were not, then obviously the current lack of discernible health effects does not imply that there will be no such effects in the future.

We can strengthen the argument if we find solid information indicating that these drugs can be present in a city's drinking water at the levels found in City X's drinking water, or higher, for a long time without presenting any ill health effects.

A   This choice does not strengthen the argument. Note that there have not been any discernible health effects from drinking the water; this fact is compatible with this statement as well as with the drug being a significant public health hazard. Perhaps the reason there have been no discernible health effects is that the drugs have only recently entered the water supply.

B   This choice does not strengthen the argument's reasoning. Until we can establish that there is no significant health hazard—what the argument sets out to prove—we cannot know whether there is a need to remove these drugs from the drinking water.

C   This claim weakens the argument. It introduces the possibility that there may have been adverse health effects resulting from these drugs, yet the researchers have not been able to discern these effects, or have not been able to determine that they were effects of the drugs.

D   Correct. Researchers several decades ago, using less sensitive technology, were able to detect the same drugs in another town's public drinking water. This implies that the drug levels in that town were higher than those recently detected in City X's drinking water. Given that there have been no discernible health effects in this previous case, this lends support to the researchers' reasoning regarding City X.

E   This claim weakens the argument; it suggests that the drugs are a relatively new presence in the water. Therefore, the effects of these drugs might not have had time to arise.

The correct answer is D.

CR20521.01

211. Errors in the performance of repetitive or "boring" tasks—often attributed to a momentary lapse in concentration—can be serious in such activities as flying a passenger aircraft. Is there any method that would provide warning of such lapses—for example by monitoring brain activity? Researchers scanned the

brains of volunteers performing a repetitive task. When the tasks were being performed correctly, the volunteers' brains showed activity in cognitive-processing regions. However, these regions became less active several seconds before some errors were made, and another brain region, region X, became active. The researchers concluded that the monitoring of region X could provide warning of an impending error.

Which of the following, if true, most supports the researchers' conclusion?

(A) The cognitive effort required in performing a repetitive task diminishes significantly with increases in the number of repetitions of the task performance.

(B) Once a mistake was made and detected, brain activity in regions associated with cognitive effort sometimes increased.

(C) Other research found that whenever significant activity occurs in region X, it is generally with repetitive tasks, soon before an error occurs.

(D) The diminution of brain activity in cognitive processing regions and the increase of activity in region X began at least 5 seconds before the errors occurred.

(E) Reduced activity in brain regions associated with cognitive effort was accompanied by increased activity in regions that become active during sleep.

Argument Evaluation

This question requires us to find a statement that would provide additional support for the researchers' conclusion that monitoring region X can provide warning that an error is about to be made by someone engaged in a repetitive task.

Note that researchers had observed during brain scans that cognitive-processing regions of the brain remained active when a repetitive task was performed correctly. These regions became less active, and brain region X became active, several seconds before errors were made.

Certainly, further research showing such errors being preceded by the onset of activity in region X would strengthen the researchers' conclusion—this would help rule out that the researchers had simply noticed an unusual coincidence.

However, what would be even more helpful would be to indicate that *whenever* significant activity in someone's region X occurs, this person is definitively engaged in repetitive tasks and is about to make an error.

To see why this would be helpful, consider: if such activity in region X frequently happened, even when no errors were about to be made, monitoring such activity would not be helpful as a warning that an error was impending. Therefore, ruling this out would support the conclusion.

A   Note that this does not indicate that cognitive effort diminishes; it merely indicates that the amount of such effort required diminishes. Even more important, it tells us nothing about activity in region X.

B   This indicates what sometimes happens after errors are made. However, it gives us no information about what happens soon before an error. Information about that, of course, is what we need if we are trying to determine whether something can provide warning of an impending error.

C   **Correct.** As indicated above, the conclusion would be well supported by research suggesting that whenever region X has significant activity, this is usually during repetitive tasks and soon before an error occurs.

D   This does not provide additional support for the claim that monitoring region X will be useful as a warning of an impending error. After all, the statement that *activity in region X began at least 5 seconds before the errors occurred* rules out only that the increase in activity in region X occurred less than 5 seconds before the errors occurred. This statement does not rule out the possibility that the increase came, for example, many hours before the error occurred.

E   Such a discovery may help researchers discover why the errors occurred. However, it does not help support the claim that monitoring region X could provide a warning of impending error.

The correct answer is C.

CR46521.01

212. City resident: These new digital electronic billboards should be banned for light pollution since they are much too bright.

Outdoor advertising spokesperson: No, that's not true. Testing with a sophisticated light meter shows that at night they throw off less light than traditional billboards that are reflectively lit. Your mistaken perception that they are brighter comes from looking directly at the light source—the screen itself.

The underlying strategy of the spokesperson's response to the resident is most analogous to the underlying strategy of which of the following?

(A) A doctor dismisses a patient's claim to have had a heart attack, citing a cardiac enzyme blood test.

(B) A politician rejects an accusation of perjury by denying the credibility of witness testimony.

(C) An insurance agent rejects a claim, on the grounds that there is insufficient evidence to support the claimant's testimony.

(D) An investigator casts doubt on the results of a lie detector, citing the subject's report of illness during the test.

(E) A psychologist treats a mental illness by encouraging a patient to abandon inconsistent beliefs.

Argument Construction

This question requires us to identify the answer choice that that has an underlying reasoning strategy that is most analogous to the spokesperson's strategy.

The outdoor advertising spokesperson responds to the city resident by citing an objective test that shows the factual claims of the resident to be false.

A **Correct.** This choice is the most closely analogous to the spokesperson's strategy: the doctor uses an objective test to show the factual claims of the patient to be false.

B The politician does not use an objective test to reject the accusation of perjury. The politician merely denies the credibility of the witness; the basis for this denial is not stated.

C The insurance agent does not use an objective test as justification for rejecting a claim or for suggesting that there is sufficient evidence for the claimant's testimony.

D In this choice, the investigator rejects the results of what some might see as an objective test. However, the investigator does not use the results of an objective test to prove the factual claims of the subject to be incorrect.

E This choice does not involve rejecting a claim, nor does it involve any sort of objective test.

The correct answer is A.

CR02531.01

213. A fossil recently discovered in Marlandia, a chain of islands, proves that a present-day reptile indigenous to Marlandia is descended from an ancient reptile species that lived on the islands millions of years ago. The finding is surprising since the ancestral species was thought to have become extinct when Marlandia was submerged in a global sea-level rise twenty-five million years ago. Based on the new discovery, many scientists have concluded that the sea-level rise in question left at least part of Marlandia unsubmerged.

Which of the following would, if true, provide the most additional support for the scientists' conclusion?

(A) Reptiles in Marlandia have adapted to many environmental changes since the sea-level rise.

(B) Marlandia separated from a much larger landmass about eighty million years ago.

(C) No fossils that prove the relationship between the present-day species and the ancestral species have been found anywhere other than Marlandia.

(D) The present-day reptiles are able to thrive on very tiny Marlandia islands.

(E) The ancestral reptiles could not have survived long at sea.

Argument Construction

This question requires that we identify the answer choice that lends the most support for the scientists' conclusion. This conclusion states that the islands of Marlandia must not have been completely submerged during a global rise in sea level as had previously been thought.

Scientists arrived at this conclusion after being surprised to find that a present-day reptile indigenous to Marlandia is descended from an ancient reptile species that lived on the islands millions of years ago. They had believed that this prehistoric species had become extinct millions of years ago when Marlandia was submerged due to a global rise in sea level.

What are some ways that we can strengthen support for the conclusion? Information that rules out the possibility that the reptile could have survived even if the islands had been completely submerged would strengthen support. So would information that rules out the possibility that the reptile had migrated to somewhere other than Marlandia but traveled back to Marlandia after the islands were no longer submerged.

A   Even if it is true that reptiles on Marlandia have adapted to environmental changes since the sea-level increase, that does not support the belief that part of Marlandia never became submerged when the sea level rose. It does not rule out either of the two alternative explanations discussed immediately above, for instance.

B   The argument's conclusion is about whether some part of Marlandia never became submerged. Information indicating that Marlandia separated from a much larger landmass many millions of years before the global sea-level rise is not relevant to that conclusion.

C   It might seem that this choice supports the conclusion. If the ancestral species never lived anywhere other than Marlandia, then the present-day species could not have descended from this ancestral species elsewhere and only later, after the sea-level rise, migrated to Marlandia. That would help rule out an alternative explanation of how the present-day species survived the global sea-level rise. However, note that all we are told is that no fossils *have been found anywhere other than Marlandia*. Simply because no such fossils have yet been found does not indicate that these ancestral species

never existed elsewhere. Fossils are often deeply buried and hard to find. After all, the fossils on Marlandia that are discussed in the argument were only recently found; perhaps other such fossils will soon be found elsewhere. Thus, this answer choice does not support the conclusion.

D   This does not provide any particular support for the argument. Note that it is not the present-day reptile species that is presumed to have survived on Marlandia when sea levels rose. Rather, it is the ancestral species that is presumed to have survived.

E   **Correct.** This rules out that the ancestral species could have survived the sea-level rise simply by living at sea. It also reduces the possibility that the ancestral species had also lived elsewhere than Marlandia and had only later—after the sea-level rise—migrated to Marlandia.

The correct answer is E.

CR21041.01

214. Advertisement: Our competitors' computer salespeople are paid according to the value of the products they sell, so they have a financial incentive to convince you to buy the most expensive units—whether you need them or not. But here at Comput-o-Mart, our salespeople are paid a salary that is not dependent on the value of their sales, so they won't try to tell you what to buy. That means when you buy a computer at Comput-o-Mart, you can be sure you're not paying for computing capabilities you don't need.

Which of the following would, if true, most weaken the advertisement's reasoning?

(A)   Some less-expensive computers actually have greater computing power than more expensive ones.

(B)   Salespeople who have a financial incentive to make sales generally provide more attentive service than do other salespeople.

(C)   Extended warranties purchased for less-expensive computers can cost nearly as much as the purchase price of the computer.

(D)   Comput-o-Mart is open only limited hours, which makes it more difficult for many shoppers to buy computers there than at other retail stores.

(E)   Comput-o-Mart does not sell any computers that support only basic computing.

Argument Evaluation

This question asks us to weaken the argument's reasoning. The advertisement makes the following argument: because the salespeople at Comput-o-Mart are on salary rather than paid a commission for products they sell, the store's customers will not pay for computers that are more powerful than those that the customers need.

To weaken this reasoning, we need to drive a wedge between the given premises and the conclusion: we need to show that it is not necessarily true that, simply because salespeople do not have an incentive to sell more powerful computers, customers will not buy computers that exceed their own needs.

For example, consider a case where customers' computing needs are basic, but Comput-o-Mart sells only advanced computers. In this scenario, customers purchasing from Comput-o-Mart would almost certainly be paying for computing capabilities that they do not need.

A   The argument hinges on the fact that a customer may pay for computing power that he or she does not need. This statement simply notes that high computing power may in at least some cases not cost more than low computing power. In this case, if anything, it might be more likely that a customer would buy a computer more powerful than he or she needs. Even so, the statement is a general statement about computers rather than a statement specifically about those sold at Comput-o-Mart. We are not told whether Comput-o-Mart even sells any of these computers. If not, then this statement is irrelevant to the argument.

B   This statement suggests that the salespeople at Comput-o-Mart may be less attentive to customers than salespeople at Comput-o-Mart's competitors. That clearly does not give us a reason to think that a customer at Comput-o-Mart may end up paying for computing power that he or she does not need.

C   The argument discusses whether customers at Comput-o-Mart pay for computing power that they do not need. The costs of extended warranties are irrelevant to this discussion.

D   Again, this is irrelevant to the argument: Comput-o-Mart's hours, however limited, do not affect whether its customers pay for computing power that they do not need.

E   **Correct.** If Comput-o-Mart's customers require only basic computing and Comput-o-Mart sells only advanced computers, then it follows that Comput-o-Mart's customers are likely to pay for computing power that they do not need. That is, regardless of Comput-o-Mart's salespeople's payment structure (salary versus commission), if Comput-o-Mart sells only more advanced, more expensive models, then any customer at Comput-o-Mart who requires only basic computing would in fact be paying for unnecessary computing power.

The correct answer is E.

CR36441.01

215.   Consumer advocate: In our nation, food packages must list the number of calories per food serving. But most of the serving sizes used are misleadingly small and should be updated. The serving sizes were set decades ago, when our nation's people typically ate smaller portions than they do today, and, as a result, people eating typical portions today consume more calories than the package labeling appears to indicate that they will. It is time package labeling reflected these changes.

Which of the following is the main point of the consumer advocate's argument?

(A)   The number of calories per serving listed on most food packages in the consumer advocate's nation is misleadingly small.

(B)   Most serving sizes used on food packages in the consumer advocate's nation should be increased to reflect today's typical portion sizes.

(C)   People eating typical portions today often consume far more calories than the number of calories per serving listed on food packages in the consumer advocate's nation.

(D) The serving sizes used on food packages in the consumer advocate's nation were set when people ate smaller portions on average than they do today.

(E) The use of misleadingly small serving sizes on food packages in the consumer advocate's nation probably leads many people to consume more calories than they otherwise would.

Argument Construction

Of the answer choices given, which one most accurately states the consumer advocate's main point, that is, the advocate's main conclusion?

We are told that nutritional information on food packages currently is outdated and misleading. That is, the serving sizes that these packages show tend to understate the calories people will consume because people now typically consume greater amounts than people did when the serving sizes were set *decades ago*.

The consumer advocate's main conclusion is to recommend that serving sizes be updated to reflect the changes in food-consumption trends.

A The fact that serving sizes are misleadingly small is a premise of the argument rather than its conclusion.

B Correct. This accurately expresses the consumer advocate's main conclusion.

C The fact that people consume more calories per serving than the amount indicated on the packaging is a premise of the argument rather than its conclusion.

D The fact that serving sizes were set during a time when people consumed smaller portions is a premise of the argument rather than its conclusion.

E The fact that people consume more calories than they believe they consume because of misleading packaging is a premise of the argument rather than its conclusion.

The correct answer is B.

CR05941.01

216. Columnist: Metro City has a lower percentage of residents with humanities degrees than any other city of comparable size in our nation. Nationwide, university graduates generally earn more than people who are not university graduates, but those with humanities degrees typically earn less than do graduates with degrees in other disciplines. So the main reason Metro City has higher income per capita than any other city of comparable size in our nation must be its low percentage of residents with humanities degrees.

Which of the following, if true, would most strengthen the columnist's argument?

(A) Metro City residents with humanities degrees have higher income per capita than do people with humanities degrees in any other city of comparable size in the nation.

(B) The percentage of residents with university degrees is lower in Metro City than in any other city of comparable size in the nation.

(C) Nationwide, university graduates without humanities degrees typically earn more than do individuals without university degrees.

(D) Metro City residents with degrees outside the humanities have per capita income no higher than the per capita income of such residents of other cities of comparable size in the nation.

(E) In Metro City, a lower proportion of university graduates have humanities degrees than in any other city of comparable size in the nation.

Argument Evaluation

Which one of the five answer options provides the information that most strengthens the columnist's argument?

The columnist's reasoning seeks to explain why Metro City has higher per capita earnings than any city of comparable size. It attributes this to the fact that Metro City has a lower percentage of residents with humanities degrees than do these other comparable cities.

Suppose the residents with university degrees outside the humanities had a higher per capita income than such residents in the comparable cities nationwide. If that were the case, then that would indicate that the higher per capita income of such residents is sufficient to explain Metro City's divergence in per capita income from the comparable cities.

That is, if we have information to indicate that is NOT the case, the case for the explanation offered—a lower percentage of residents with humanities degrees—is strengthened.

A   This weakens the columnist's explanation by offering a potential alternative explanation: the higher per capita incomes of those with humanities degrees in Metro City might explain the higher per capita income of Metro City residents.

B   This does not lend additional support to the columnist's explanation. It suggests other possible explanations: first, the holders of degrees outside of humanities may have extraordinarily high incomes even for such graduates nationwide; second, Metro City may be unusual in having workers without university degrees who have an unusually high per capita income; third, both of these groups may have unusually high per capita incomes.

C   This does not lend additional support to the columnist's explanation. However, it is well-supported by the information offered in support of the argument's conclusion: university graduates generally earn more than others, and among university graduates, humanities graduates earn less than others.

D   Correct. As explained above, this information, by eliminating an alternative explanation to that offered in the argument's conclusion, strengthens the argument.

E   This information is consistent with the information provided in support of the argument's conclusion. It does not, however, provide additional support for the argument's conclusion. This information is consistent with alternative explanations for the higher per capita income of Metro City's residents. That is, for example, that

the holders of non-humanities degrees, or those with no degrees at all, have particularly high per capita income.

The correct answer is D.

CR87051.01

217. Psychologist: In a survey, several hundred volunteers rated their own levels of self-control and their overall life satisfaction. The volunteers who rated themselves as having better self-control also reported greater satisfaction with their lives. This suggests that self-control is one factor that helps people avoid situations likely to produce dissatisfaction.

In order to assess the strength of the psychologist's argument, it would be most helpful to know whether

(A)   people typically rate themselves as having significantly better self-control than expert psychological assessments would rate them as having

(B)   people's perceptions of how satisfied they are with their lives could be affected by factors of which they are unaware

(C)   there is a high level of self-control that tends to reduce overall life satisfaction

(D)   people's ratings of their overall satisfaction with their lives tend to temporarily decrease in situations likely to produce dissatisfaction

(E)   feelings of dissatisfaction significantly interfere with people's ability to exercise self-control

Argument Evaluation

Which one of the further pieces of information given in the answer choices would most help us evaluate the psychologist's argument?

A psychologist tells us that people surveyed who reported high levels of self-control reported high levels of life satisfaction also. The psychologist infers from this that self-control is one factor that helps people avoid situations likely to produce dissatisfaction with their lives.

Note that only answer options C and E directly address a possible causal link between degree of life satisfaction and degree of self-control. Answer option C tells us that a high degree of self-control can actually reduce life satisfaction.

However, this information, if accurate, does little to weaken support for the conclusion that self-control helps people avoid situations likely to create dissatisfaction. Furthermore, it provides no support for that conclusion.

That leaves E as the most likely candidate for the correct response. Suppose E were correct; that is, feelings of dissatisfaction make effective self-control less likely. This is compatible with the correlation between self-control and feelings of satisfaction—but also strongly suggests that self-control is the effect rather than the cause of feelings of satisfaction. And this undermines the conclusion of the argument.

A   This suggests that the self-ascribed levels of self-control of the participants in the survey may have been exaggerated. This weakens the psychologists' conclusion without completely invalidating this evidence.

B   This implies that survey participants were not fully aware of all the factors that affected their perceptions of life satisfaction. However, the conclusion does not depend on the participants' degree of awareness of the factors affecting their perceptions of life satisfaction.

C   This may be true, but even if true in some cases, this information does not necessarily invalidate the psychologist's conclusion in general.

D   This implies that people's ratings of their life satisfaction can vary, and be temporarily lowered, by encountering a situation likely to produce dissatisfaction. But such possible sources of random error would be allowed for in the statistical analysis of the survey results and do not necessarily invalidate the study's results.

E   **Correct.** As explained, this information undermines the psychologist's conclusion by providing an alternative explanation for the survey results.

The correct answer is E.

CR03161.01

218. Mansour: We should both plan to change some of our investments from coal companies to less polluting energy companies. And here's why. Consumers are increasingly demanding nonpolluting energy, and energy companies are increasingly supplying it.

Therese: I'm not sure we should do what you suggest. As demand for nonpolluting energy increases relative to supply, its price will increase, and then the more polluting energy will cost relatively less. Demand for the cheaper, dirtier energy forms will then increase, as will the stock values of the companies that produce them.

Therese responds to Mansour's proposal by doing which of the following?

(A)   Advocating that consumers use less expensive forms of energy

(B)   Implying that not all uses of coal for energy are necessarily polluting

(C)   Disagreeing with Mansour's claim that consumers are increasingly demanding nonpolluting energy

(D)   Suggesting that leaving their existing energy investments unchanged could be the better course

(E)   Providing a reason to doubt Mansour's assumption that supply of nonpolluting energy will increase in line with demand

Argument Construction

Which one of the answer options best describes the response of Therese to Mansour?

Mansour advocates that Therese and he should replace their investments in coal companies with investments in companies producing less polluting energy. He suggests this because there is both an increasing demand for and increasing supply of such energy.

However, Therese responds that as demand for clean energy increases, its prices will increase. These higher prices will increase demand for cheaper, dirtier energy. This will boost the stock prices of companies producing such dirty energy, for example, coal. The point of Therese's response is that since the stock prices of coal companies and other companies producing dirty energy will likely increase, investments in these stocks will increase in value. This provides a financial reason not to do what Mansour advocates.

A   Therese does not advocate that consumers use polluting energy; she simply predicts that the stock values of producers of polluting energy are likely to increase as the prices of polluting energy decrease relative to the prices of non-polluting energy.

B   Therese does not imply that there exist non-polluting uses of coal; in fact, she appears to agree with Mansour that coal is a dirty form of energy.

C   There is nothing to indicate that Therese disagrees with Mansour regarding whether consumers are increasingly demanding non-polluting energy.

D   **Correct.** This accurately captures the main point of Therese's response to Mansour: she provides a particular reason that maintaining their current investments could be a better option.

E   Therese does not directly address the question of whether this assumption of Mansour's is correct. Even if she implies that Mansour's assumption is incorrect, this is not the main point of her response to Mansour.

The correct answer is D.

CR04161.01

219. Scientist: In an experiment, dogs had access to a handle they could pull to release food into a nearby enclosure that contained a familiar dog and nothing else, contained an unfamiliar dog and nothing else, or was empty. The dogs typically released more food to the familiar dog than to the unfamiliar dog. This suggests that dogs are more motivated to help other dogs they know than to help unfamiliar dogs.

The scientist's argument would be most strengthened if it were true that, in the experiment, the dogs with access to the handle tended to release more food when

(A)   the behavior was being encouraged by a familiar person than when it was being encouraged by an unfamiliar person

(B)   the enclosure was empty than when it contained an unfamiliar dog

(C)   an unfamiliar dog in the enclosure was displaying hostility toward them than when an unfamiliar dog in the enclosure appeared friendly

(D)   a dog in the enclosure appeared uninterested in food already released into the enclosure than when it appeared interested in that food

(E)   a familiar dog was in the enclosure than when a familiar dog was visible but the enclosure was empty

Argument Evaluation

Which one of the five experimental outcomes, if added to the information given, would most strengthen the evidence for the scientist's conclusion?

There were three enclosures, two of which contained a dog. Only one of these contained a familiar dog. The dogs released more food to familiar dogs than to unfamiliar dogs. The scientists thereby concluded that dogs are more motivated to help familiar dogs than they are to help unfamiliar dogs.

However, it is possible that releasing the food to the familiar dog could have been motivated by other reasons. For example, the dog could simply be trying to communicate with the familiar dog rather than necessarily trying specifically to help this dog.

If the dogs released more food to a familiar dog while it was contained in an enclosure than when it was not enclosed yet nearby and visible, this would strengthen the idea of trying to "help" the other dog.

A   This information would weaken the scientist's argument. It introduces information suggesting the presence of a confounding variable in the experimental setup. That is, if the behavior was encouraged by a familiar person, we would not be able to tell whether it was this person's presence or the presence of the other dog that increased the behavior.

B   This would suggest that the dog's activation of the lever was not contingent on providing food to another animal. In other words, if the dog provides food even when there is no animal to provide food for, then it follows that the presence of the other dog is irrelevant to this behavior.

C   The experimental setup described here introduces the factor of friendliness. Adding this extra factor could easily confound testing of the original hypothesis, which suggested that simple familiarity increased the behavior.

D   The experimental setup described here introduces a factor of food interest. Adding this extra factor could easily confound testing of the original hypothesis, which suggested that simple familiarity increased the behavior.

E   **Correct.** This information would strengthen the hypothesis that a desire to help a familiar dog was operative in the dog's behavior.

The correct answer is E.

CR09461.01

220. Most geologists believe oil results from chemical transformations of hydrocarbons derived from organisms buried under ancient seas. Suppose, instead, that oil actually results from bacterial action on other complex hydrocarbons that are trapped within the earth. As is well known, the volume of these hydrocarbons exceeds that of buried organisms. Therefore, our oil reserves would be greater than most geologists believe.

Which of the following, if true, gives the strongest support to the argument above about our oil reserves?

(A)   Most geologists think optimistically about the earth's reserves of oil.

(B)   Most geologists have performed accurate chemical analyses on previously discovered oil reserves.

(C)   Ancient seas are buried within the earth at many places where fossils are abundant.

(D)   The only bacteria yet found in oil reserves could have leaked down drill holes from surface contaminants.

(E)   Chemical transformations reduce the volume of buried hydrocarbons derived from organisms by roughly the same proportion as bacterial action reduces the volume of other complex hydrocarbons.

Argument Evaluation

What new information, if added to the argument, would strengthen it?

The argument sets forth a novel hypothesis about how oil reserves are created. That is, oil reserves are created through bacterial action on complex hydrocarbons within the earth rather than through chemical transformation of hydrocarbons derived from organisms buried under ancient seas.

The argument notes that the volume of the hydrocarbons that bacteria transform to yield oil is greater than the volume of hydrocarbons derived from the buried organisms and concludes that total oil reserves are greater than most geologists believe them to be.

A   This suggests that most geologists might, if anything, be inclined to overestimate oil reserves. However, this consideration has little bearing on the chemical origin of oil or how much oil may remain buried in the earth.

B   This does not tell us whether the *chemical analyses* can identify whether the oil originated from hydrocarbons derived from buried organisms.

C   The existence of buried ancient seas has little, if any, relevance to the argument. This choice fails to provide evidence that by itself would help decide whether the hypothesized bacterial origin of oil actually supports the inference that oil reserves are greater than is currently assumed.

D   This suggests that bacteria have been found in some oil reserves; the potential importance of this discovery is unclear.

E **Correct.** This strengthens the argument: if it is true, then the greater abundance of complex hydrocarbons from which it is hypothesized that oil can be derived through bacterial action would predict much larger oil reserves than exist under most geologists' current predictions.

The correct answer is E.

CR66561.01

221. Meteorologists say that if only they could design an accurate mathematical model of the atmosphere with all its complexities, they could forecast the weather with real precision. But this is an idle boast, immune to any evaluation, for any inadequate weather forecast would obviously be blamed on imperfections in the model.

Which of the following, if true, could best be used as a basis for arguing against the author's position that the meteorologists' claim cannot be evaluated?

(A) Certain unusual configurations of data can serve as the basis for precise weather forecasts, even though the exact causal mechanisms are not understood.

(B) Most significant gains in the accuracy of the relevant mathematical models are accompanied by clear gains in the precision of weather forecasts.

(C) Mathematical models of the meteorological aftermath of such catastrophic events as volcanic eruptions are beginning to be constructed.

(D) Modern weather forecasts for as much as a full day ahead are broadly correct about 80 percent of the time.

(E) Meteorologists readily concede that the accurate mathematical model they are talking about is not now in their power to construct.

Argument Evaluation

Which one of the following would provide the best basis for arguing against the author's reasoning?

Meteorologists claim that the design of a mathematical model that would accurately capture all the complexities of weather dynamics would enable great precision in weather forecasting. However, according to the skeptical reasoning given, the meteorologists' claim cannot be evaluated, because any inaccuracies in weather forecasting would be attributed to shortcomings in the model.

It is important to consider that with the incremental improvement of capabilities for collection and analysis of data, including new types of data, model construction would improve to more accurately reflect weather dynamics. However, it would remain true that random factors affecting weather may continue to reduce accuracy of forecasts.

A This suggests that weather forecasting accuracy can be attained under certain unusual conditions, even in the absence of understanding complex factors that affect weather. Nevertheless, what is at issue in the skeptical reasoning given is how, or whether, overall forecasting accuracy can be attained under all conditions. Furthermore, it is unclear whether the meteorologists' aspiration to great precision and accuracy in weather forecasting can even be evaluated.

B **Correct.** This tells us that significant but incremental improvements in the accuracy of mathematical models result in gradual improvements in the accuracy of weather forecasting—even if wholly accurate and precise forecasts are never attained. This would allow evaluation of any progress in modeling and forecasting weather.

C Volcanic eruptions can affect weather but they do not rank as major ongoing causes of weather phenomena. The reasoning given refers to forecasting of weather under all conditions, whether the meteorologists' ideal is attainable or can even be evaluated.

D This suggests that current weather forecasting falls significantly short of the forecasting accuracy that the meteorologists mentioned aspire to. This idea reinforces the skeptical reasoning that suggests the meteorologists' ideal is not amenable to evaluation and may not even be attainable.

E   This does not convey a reason for thinking the meteorologists' claim can reasonably be subjected to evaluation; furthermore, it seems to provide some support for the skeptical reasoning given.

The correct answer is B.

CR38561.01

222. The lobbyists argued that because there is no statistical evidence that breathing other people's tobacco smoke increases the incidence of heart disease or lung cancer in healthy nonsmokers, legislation banning smoking in workplaces cannot be justified on health grounds.

Of the following, which is the best criticism of the argument reported above?

(A)   It ignores causes of lung cancer other than smoking.

(B)   It neglects the damaging effects of smoke-filled air on nonsmokers who are not healthy.

(C)   It fails to mention the roles played by diet, exercise, and heredity in the development of heart disease.

(D)   It does not consider the possibility that nonsmokers who breathe smoke-filled air at work may become more concerned about their health.

(E)   It does not acknowledge that nonsmokers, even those who breathe smoke-filled air at work, are in general healthier than smokers.

Argument Evaluation

Among the answer choices given, which one describes the most significant flaw in the reasoning, given the information provided?

Note that not all nonsmokers are healthy in every respect. This raises the possibility that tobacco-smoke exposure of some nonsmokers—those who already have some medical condition—could either worsen existing illnesses or cause new ones such as lung cancer or heart disease.

The risks in such exposure could be significantly greater for those unhealthy nonsmokers than for the healthy nonsmokers.

A   This choice is outside the scope of the argument. The argument addresses the issue of illnesses that could be caused by exposure to other people's smoke in the workplace. In this context, cancer-causing factors other than smoking are irrelevant.

B   **Correct.** The information provided does not mention health risks to unhealthy nonsmokers that exposure to other people's tobacco smoke in the workplace might cause.

C   This choice is outside the scope of the argument. The argument addresses the issue of illnesses that could be caused by exposure to other people's smoke in the workplace. It does not address general risk factors that contribute to anybody's risk of getting heart disease.

D   The argument does not consider whether nonsmokers might become concerned about their health risks in workplaces where they breathe smoke. The argument is about health risks, not about workers' attitudes to health risks.

E   The argument suggests that healthy nonsmokers are not unduly affected by cigarette smoke in the workplace. While possibly true, this claim is not a valid criticism of the argument as stated. The argument has no explicit comparison of the health levels of smokers and nonsmokers.

The correct answer is B.

CR78561.01

223. Since 1978 when the copyright law was changed, books that are less than fifty years old must not be photocopied without the publisher's permission. Thus, any book that has been photocopied since 1978 without the publisher's permission must be at least fifty years old.

The reasoning above exhibits a flaw similar to one in which of the following?

(A)   Any member of the solar system must be either a planet or a moon, so if an asteroid is neither a planet nor a moon, it must not be a member of the solar system.

(B)   Anyone who rides a city bus must buy a bus pass, and since Demetrios has a bus pass, he must be riding on a city bus.

(C) A driver who turns right must signal, so any driver who did not signal must not have turned right.

(D) Anyone who legally crosses a national boundary must have a passport; thus anyone who does not have a passport cannot legally cross a national boundary.

(E) Any wage earner residing in the state must pay state taxes, so since Blodwen pays state taxes, she must be resident in the state.

Argument Evaluation

The flaw in which one of the five arguments presented is most similar to the flaw in the given argument?

The conclusion of the given argument is adequately supported by its premises only if supplemented by a highly implausible assumption: *Since the 1978 copyright law came into force, no book published since 1978 has been photocopied without the publisher's permission.*

However, this would be unreasonable to assume: we have no reason to assume that the existence of a rule implies compliance with that rule.

A This argument contains no flaw; its conclusion follows logically from its supporting information.

B This argument is flawed because it is possible that Demetrios is not riding on a city bus but yet still owns a bus pass. However, this is not an argument regarding compliance or non-compliance with a rule.

C **Correct.** This argument has the same structure as the given argument. For the argument to work, it must be supplemented with the following highly implausible assumption: *No driver who fails to signal turns right.* That assumption is implausible because the existence of a rule is not always followed by compliance with that rule.

D The conclusion drawn here follows logically from the premise on which it is based. Therefore, the argument is not flawed.

E This argument is flawed: it is possible that Blodwen pays state taxes yet is not a resident in the state. The condition "liable to pay state tax" applies to all residents of the state, but we do not know that this applies *only* to residents of the state. That is, the class of those "liable to pay state tax" may in fact be larger than the class of those "resident in the state." In any case, the structure of this argument is significantly different from the given argument.

The correct answer is C.

CR10661.01

224. In the United States, injuries to passengers involved in automobile accidents are typically more severe than in Europe, where laws require a different kind of safety belt. It is clear from this that the United States needs to adopt more stringent standards for safety belt design to protect automobile passengers better.

Each of the following, if true, weakens the argument above EXCEPT:

(A) Europeans are more likely to wear safety belts than are people in the United States.

(B) Unlike United States drivers, European drivers receive training in how best to react in the event of an accident to minimize injuries to themselves and to their passengers.

(C) Cars built for the European market tend to have more sturdy construction than do cars built for the United States market.

(D) Automobile passengers in the United States have a greater statistical chance of being involved in an accident than do passengers in Europe.

(E) States that have recently begun requiring the European safety belt have experienced no reduction in the average severity of injuries suffered by passengers in automobile accidents.

Argument Evaluation

The argument suggests that passengers involved in automobile accidents in the United States typically are more seriously injured than those in Europe. Furthermore, in Europe, a different safety belt design is used. The argument suggests that these

European-style safety belts are more protective against serious injury than those used in the United States. Furthermore, it suggests that the United States would therefore benefit by adopting more stringent design standards for safety belts.

To clarify, the rate of severe injuries would indicate, for example, the number of seriously injured passengers per 100,000 passengers involved in automobile accidents. Note that this rate does not depend on the total number of passengers involved in automobile accidents.

However, many other factors could provide an alternative explanation for these differences in rate of severe injury. The question stem asks us which answer choice does NOT weaken the argument; in other words, we must find a factor among the answer choices that does NOT account for this difference in the rate of severe injury. Effectively, we will be looking for the answer that has no bearing on the rate of severe injury.

Which one of the statements given does NOT weaken the argument?

A   This choice weakens the argument. It suggests the possibility that the difference in rates of severe injury is due to the number of *people who actually wear* safety belts in the U.S. versus in Europe. This rate is, of course, irrespective of the functionality of the belts themselves. In other words, the effectiveness of the belt design is irrelevant if the belt is not being worn in the first place.

B   This choice weakens the argument. Training to understand how to minimize injury, rather than a safety belt design difference, may be a primary factor accounting for the lower severe injury rate in Europe.

C   This choice weakens the argument. The fact that cars constructed in Europe are more sturdy may account for the lower severe injury rate in Europe rather than the difference in the types of safety belts used.

D   Correct. This choice does not weaken the argument. The higher likelihood that one is involved in an automobile accident in the U.S. actually has no bearing on the higher rate of severe injury among passengers

who are involved in automobile accidents. That is, the rate itself is a proportion of the total number of passengers involved in accidents rather than the number itself. This rate would remain the same whether 10 accidents or 10 million accidents occurred.

E   This answer choice suggests that even implementation within the United States of the European safety belt design does not seem to change serious injury rates. This implies, of course, that some other factor is likely responsible for the differences in rates of serious injury between the U.S. and Europe.

The correct answer is D.

CR60661.01

225.   A country's Aeronautics Board (AB) employs inspectors who make routine annual inspections of all aircraft. On inspecting Azura Airlines' airplanes in December, they reported considerably more violations of AB rules this year, compared to a year ago. This fact explains why Azura had more accidents this year, compared to last year.

Which of the following, if true, would cast most doubt on the conclusion in the passage?

(A)   Some aviation experts in other countries consider certain AB rules to be too lax and too easy to get around.

(B)   Azura's routes are no more dangerous than are those of most other airlines.

(C)   The AB increased the length and rigor of its inspections this year, compared to last year.

(D)   Prior to last year Azura had an excellent safety record with very few accidents.

(E)   In both years the AB report on Azura did not include violations on airplanes owned by Azura but leased by another airline.

Argument Evaluation

During the Aeronautic Board (AB)'s annual inspection, it found more violations among Azura Airlines' airplanes this year than last. The argument suggests that this increase in the number of violations provides an explanation for why Azura Airlines experienced more accidents this year than last. We must choose the statement that most weakens the conclusion.

A   This statement is outside the scope of the argument; aviation experts in foreign countries' opinion of AB has no bearing on the AB and its evaluation of Azura Airlines.

B   This statement is outside the scope of the argument; even if Azura's routes are more dangerous than its competitors', the relationship between Azura's routes and other airlines' routes has no bearing on the AB and its evaluation of Azura Airlines.

C   **Correct.** This statement provides an alternative reason that the number of violations for Azura Airlines would have increased. That is, if the AB conducted more extensive and more rigorous inspections this year, then it is very likely that the number of violations found by the AB would increase. In other words, if more points are tested or existing tests are made stricter, then the increase in rigor of the testing would presumably lead to an increase in violations.

D   This statement is outside the scope of the argument; the argument only concerns last year as compared to this year. Azura Airlines' record prior to last year is irrelevant to this.

E   This information does not apply to the argument at hand; the argument only concerns the planes that were in fact counted both years. If we could take this information to imply that even more Azura-owned airplanes violate safety standards than previously thought, this would actually strengthen the argument rather than weaken it.

The correct answer is C.

CR13661.01

226. The more frequently employees take time to exercise during working hours each week, the fewer sick days they take. Even employees who exercise only once a week during working hours take less sick time than those who do not exercise. Therefore, if companies started fitness programs, the absentee rate in those companies would decrease significantly.

Which of the following, if true, most seriously weakens the argument above?

(A) Employees who exercise during working hours occasionally fall asleep for short periods of time after they exercise.

(B) Employees who are frequently absent are the least likely to cooperate with or to join a corporate fitness program.

(C) Employees who exercise only once a week in their company's fitness program usually also exercise after work.

(D) Employees who exercise in their company's fitness program use their working time no more productively than those who do not exercise.

(E) Employees who exercise during working hours take slightly longer lunch breaks than employees who do not exercise.

Argument Evaluation

The argument suggests that the greater the amount of time employees take to exercise during working hours, the fewer sick days these employees take. This is true even of employees who exercise just once a week during work hours.

Based on this evidence, the argument concludes that companies that start fitness programs will see a significant decrease in the absentee rate.

The question asks us to identify a serious weakness in the argument. The argument as stated does not address the following fundamental problem: the same employees who are frequently absent may also fail to make use of such a fitness program. If that is true, therefore, the evidence provided would give us little reason to believe that those who are currently frequently absent would be absent less often if such a program were implemented.

A   This answer choice may call into question the advisability of starting such a fitness program. That, however, is not what the argument's conclusion is about. The argument's conclusion states that company-run fitness programs will reduce absentee rates, but this choice tells us nothing about what effect, if any, such fitness programs would have on absentee rates.

B   **Correct.** The argument assumes that exercising during office hours will lead employees to be absent from work less frequently. However, this choice indicates that those who are frequently absent are the least likely to make use of a company fitness program. That could mean that these employees will use such fitness programs rarely, if at all. If so, we would have far less reason to believe that there would be a significant decline in the absentee rate if such a program were implemented.

C   This answer choice is outside the scope of the argument: we are not given any information about how exercise outside of work affects absentee rates.

D   This answer choice is outside the scope of the argument: the argument's conclusion is about absentee rates; the argument does not concern productivity.

E   This answer choice is outside the scope of the argument: there is no information to suggest any correlation between the length of lunch breaks and the use of fitness programs or the length of lunch breaks and rates of absence.

The correct answer is B.

Answer Explanations Verbal Reasoning

Critical Reasoning

Construction/Plan

CR67370.01

227. Distressed by his own personal tragedies, the Roman philosopher Cicero once asked himself whether a wise person should try to achieve the Stoic ideal of complete emotionlessness. Cicero reasoned that, however desirable the goal may be, a wise person could never attain it, since emotions are not simply irrational urges. They are, rather, a product of one's estimate of the goodness and badness of the events, people, and actions one witnesses.

Which of the following is an assumption required by Cicero's reasoning?

(A) Wise people inevitably evaluate at least some of the things they observe.

(B) Irrationality makes evaluation of what one observes impossible.

(C) Wisdom precludes attempting to attain what one cannot.

(D) If evaluations are based only on reason, then they are inaccurate.

(E) A wise person will not evaluate what cannot be directly observed.

Argument Construction

The question asks us to identify an assumption required by Cicero's reasoning.

Cicero reasoned that a wise person could never attain the goal of complete emotionlessness, because emotions are not merely irrational urges but *a product of one's estimate of the goodness and badness of events, people, and actions one witnesses.*

Why would Cicero have thought that this is a good reason to believe that a wise person could never be completely emotionless? He must have thought that wise people cannot completely avoid making evaluations of the goodness and badness of at least some of the events, people, and actions they witness. If he thought they could completely avoid making such evaluations, the reason he gave for his conclusion would not have supported it.

A **Correct.** As indicated above, Cicero's argument requires that wise people evaluate at least some of the things that they observe.

B Cicero's argument does not require this assumption. It makes sense to think that wise people would not be irrational. However, this assumption suggests that it is possible to avoid evaluations of what one observes, which is not helpful to Cicero's reasoning.

C If Cicero's conclusion is true, then this assumption helps support the claim that wise people should not attempt to attain the goal of complete emotionlessness. But the question does not ask you to identify an assumption that would allow you to infer that wise people should not attempt to attain that goal. Instead, the question asks you to identify an assumption that is required to infer that wise people cannot attain that goal. Whether you should try to do something is a different issue from whether you can do something.

D Cicero's argument is not about the accuracy of one's evaluations; rather, it assumes that wise people will inevitably make such evaluations.

E Cicero's argument is based on a premise about evaluations of the observed, not about evaluations of what is impossible to observe.

The correct answer is A.

CR49770.01

228. First discovered several years ago in North American lakes and rivers, the northern snakehead is a nonnative fish with no local predators. To keep the northern snakehead's population from growing, for the past three years wildlife officials have been paying recreational fishers for each northern snakehead they catch. In this way, the officials hope to stop the northern snakeheads from eliminating rare native fish species.

To evaluate the likelihood that the wildlife officials' plan will succeed, it would be most useful to determine which of the following?

(A) Whether the northern snakehead's population in local lakes and rivers could be reduced by introducing predators from its native habitat

(B) How local population numbers of rare native fish species have been changing since the wildlife officials started paying recreational fishers to catch northern snakeheads

(C) Whether the fish species on which the northern snakehead preys in regions to which it is native and in which it is abundant have become significantly depleted in recent decades

(D) What total number of northern snakehead have been caught by recreational fishers since the wildlife officials began paying for them

(E) Whether rare native fish species in the region face any threats to their survival other than the proliferation of northern snakehead

Evaluation of a Plan

In hopes of preventing the nonnative species northern snakehead from eliminating rare native fish species, wildlife officials have for the last three years been paying recreational fishers for each snakehead they catch. The northern snakehead has no predators in the area.

This question requires us to identify information that would be useful for determining whether the officials' plan will succeed.

Note that the plan has already been in effect. Nevertheless, we are given no information as to how well the plan has succeeded so far. To determine whether it is responsible to keep paying these fishers to catch northern snakehead, it is vital to understand whether the fishers' work up to this point has had any observable effect.

That is, it would be helpful to anyone who wants to determine whether the officials' plan is likely to succeed to have information about how the numbers of rare native fish species have been changing during that time.

A   This information would be useful for determining whether there may be alternative ways of reducing the northern snakehead population. However, it is not useful for determining whether the plan in question is likely to be successful.

B   **Correct.** As noted above, this information would be helpful in assessing whether the officials' plan is likely to succeed. If the numbers of rare native fish species have stayed constant or even declined throughout the period that the plan has been in place, it seems unlikely that the plan will ultimately be successful.

C   This information may provide a small amount of information as to how great a threat the northern snakehead might pose, but not much. For one thing, in its native region, the snakehead likely preys on different species from those in the region in question. More importantly, however, is the fact that this information is simply not useful to determining whether the officials' plan is likely to work in the region in question.

D   This might be useful for determining whether fishers have been motivated by the plan. This could potentially be useful for determining whether the plan will work; after all, the plan will not likely work if very few northern snakeheads are actually removed. Nevertheless, it is not as useful as noting the changes in the native fish population since the plan first went into effect.

E   Determining whether there are other threats to the rare native fish species would tell us whether the plan, if successful, is sufficient to save the rare fish species. Still, it is not useful in determining whether that plan is likely to be successful.

The correct answer is B.

CR51080.01

229. Scientist: A greenhouse gas, for example, carbon dioxide, forms a transparent layer that traps solar heat beneath it in the earth's atmosphere. Atmospheric levels of carbon dioxide are currently increasing, causing the climate to warm—an effect that is predicted by at least one computer model of the greenhouse effect. But the warming that has occurred is a great deal less than what would be expected based on the model. Therefore, _____.

Which of the following most logically completes the scientist's argument?

(A)   better measurements of atmospheric levels of carbon dioxide are needed

(B)   the definition of "greenhouse gas" should probably be reconsidered

(C)   there are factors besides the increase in greenhouse-gas emissions contributing to the warming of the climate

(D)   the computer model of the greenhouse effect must be incorrect in some respect

(E)   the likely consequences of any warming of the climate are unlikely to be much less damaging than predicted

Argument Construction

This question requires us to choose the option that most logically completes the scientist's argument.

The scientist's argument points out that at least one computer model has predicted that the amount of warming the atmosphere would by now have experienced as a result of the greenhouse effect would be significantly greater than what has actually occurred.

Because what precedes the blank is the word *therefore*, we must choose the statement that is most strongly supported by the information given.

A   It is reasonable to infer from the given information that some aspect of the computer model is incorrect in some way. One way that it might be incorrect is that the measurements of atmospheric levels of carbon dioxide used are inaccurate. Nevertheless, there is not sufficient information to infer that this is the specific flaw in the model.

B   The given information provides no reason for us to reconsider the definition of "greenhouse gas." Perhaps there would be a reason to do so if no warming had occurred whatsoever. However, the information tells us that warming has in fact happened, just not as much as predicted.

C   If there are factors in addition to greenhouse-gas emissions that lead to atmospheric warming, then presumably temperatures would have risen more than predicted, not less.

D   **Correct.** If the model were correct, its predictions would be confirmed by the data regarding warming. However, this has not occurred. It is therefore reasonable to infer that, in some way, the computer model is incorrect.

E   This does not follow from the argument: given the findings, it seems more reasonable to think that the likely consequences of any atmospheric warming would in fact be less damaging than predicted.

The correct answer is D.

CR09090.01

230. Beets and carrots are higher in sugar than many other vegetables. They are also high on the glycemic index, a scale that measures the rate at which a food increases blood sugar levels. But while nutritionists usually advise people to avoid high-sugar and high-glycemic-index foods, despite any nutritional benefits they may confer, they are not very concerned about the consumption of beets and carrots.

Which of the following, if true, would best explain the nutritionists' lack of concern?

(A)   Foods with added sugar are much higher in sugar, and have a larger effect on blood sugar levels, than do beets and carrots.

(B)   Most consumption of beets and carrots occurs in combination with higher-protein foods, which reduce blood sugar fluctuations.

(C)   Beets and carrots contain many nutrients, such as folate, beta-carotene, and vitamin C, of which many people fail to consume optimal quantities.

(D)   The glycemic index measures the extent to which a food increases blood sugar levels as compared to white bread, a food that is much less healthy than beets and carrots.

(E)   Nutritionists have only recently come to understand that a food's effect on blood sugar levels is an important determinant of that food's impact on a person's health.

Argument Construction

This question requires us to identify an explanation for nutritionists' lack of concern regarding consumption of beets and carrots, despite the fact that they have higher sugar levels than many other vegetables and rate high on the glycemic index.

Normally, nutritionists would advise people against consuming foods that rate high on the glycemic index, whatever their other nutritional benefits.

To explain why nutritionists might hold such apparently conflicting positions, consider whether there might be something notable about the consumption of beets and carrots that makes their consumption an exception to the rule.

A   The fact that some foods may be even more problematic than beets and carrots does not explain nutritionists' lack of concern about beets and carrots.

B   **Correct.** This provides a reason that consumption of beets and carrots may be, at least within the suggested context, exempt from nutritionists' concern about consumption of high-sugar, high-glycemic-index foods. Remember, nutritionists' general concern arises from the effects such foods have on those who consume them. If we suggest that beets and carrots are usually consumed with high-protein foods that counteract these unwanted effects, we have good reason not to be concerned about their consumption, at least in regard to their sugar level and glycemic index.

C   The nutritionists advise people to avoid foods high in sugar and high on the glycemic index *despite any nutritional benefits they may confer*. Therefore, the fact that beets and carrots have such nutritional benefits does not explain why nutritionists would not be concerned about consuming beets and carrots, given that they both high in sugar and rate high on the glycemic index.

D   Whatever measure the glycemic index is based on, we know that beets and carrots are high on that index. Furthermore, we

know that *nutritionists usually advise people to avoid high-sugar and high-glycemic-index foods, despite any nutritional benefits they may confer*. Therefore, the fact that beets and carrots are more nutritious than white bread does not in any way explain the nutritionists' lack of concern.

E   The fact that nutritionists have only recently become concerned about high-sugar and high-glycemic-level foods does not explain their particular lack of concern regarding beets and carrots.

The correct answer is B.

CR36601.01

231. Ozone in the stratosphere blocks deadly ultraviolet rays from the sun, but chlorofluorocarbons (CFCs) in aerosols and other products have thinned this protective layer. Evidence of this is the ozone hole that forms over the South Pole every Antarctic spring as temperatures drop below −78°C, the temperature at which ozone depletion occurs. Measurements of the ozone hole taken at various times this spring show that, compared with the same times the previous year, its area diminished by four million square kilometers. Nevertheless, scientists have not concluded that the ozone layer is recovering.

Which of the following would, if true, provide the strongest reason for the scientists' reaction to the measurements?

(A)   The ozone hole has steadily grown in size every year for the past decade except this year.

(B)   The length of time that the ozone hole persists fluctuates from year to year.

(C)   As a result of international treaties, CFCs have been completely banned for several years.

(D)   Weather patterns allowed unusual amounts of warm air to mix into the polar regions this year.

(E)   Human-made CFCs retain their ability to destroy ozone molecules for seventy-five to one hundred years.

Argument Construction

This question requires us to identify which of the answer choices would provide the strongest reason to support the scientists' skepticism about whether the ozone layer is recovering.

This skepticism exists despite the fact that measurements of the ozone hole taken at various times during the Antarctic spring have shown that the hole has diminished significantly from its size at the same times the previous year.

One major reason to be skeptical would be if there were some factor other than a recovery of the ozone layer that could reasonably account for the diminished size of the hole.

A   This does not give much reason to be skeptical that the ozone layer is recovering. Certainly one would not want to be too hasty in declaring a recovery after noting a trend of growth in the ozone hole's size. Nevertheless, something must account for this year's divergence from the trend. It seems reasonable to conclude, barring the discovery of some other factor that would explain the change, that a recovery in the ozone layer could be a factor in this year's divergence.

B   Each of the measurements was smaller than at the same time in the previous year. This fact would seem to indicate that fluctuations in the length of time the ozone hole persists do not justify the scientists' skepticism.

C   The fact that CFCs—which led to the thinning of the ozone layer—have been banned counts against the scientists' skepticism rather than supports it.

D   **Correct.** The hole forms when the temperature drops below −78°C during the Antarctic spring. If much of the area where the hole appears was significantly warmer than the previous year—perhaps above −78°C—there exists a reason other than a recovery in the ozone layer that explains the smaller size of this year's hole in the ozone. This would support the scientists' skepticism.

E   Even if CFCs retain their ability to destroy ozone molecules for many decades, something must account for the decrease in the size of the hole. Nothing in the passage indicates whether the amount of CFCs in the atmosphere has been increasing or

decreasing. If it has been decreasing for a long time, then this fact is compatible with a belief that the ozone layer is recovering.

The correct answer is D.

CR29111.01

232. The recycling of municipal solid waste is widely seen as an environmentally preferable alternative to the prevailing practices of incineration and of dumping in landfills. Recycling is profitable, as the recycling programs already in operation demonstrate. A state legislator proposes that communities should therefore be required to adopt recycling and to reach the target of recycling 50 percent of all solid waste within 5 years.

Which of the following, if true, most seriously calls into question the advisability of implementing the proposal?

(A)   Existing recycling programs have been voluntary, with citizen participation ranging from 30 percent in some communities to 80 percent in others.

(B)   Existing recycling programs have been restricted to that 20 percent of solid waste that, when reprocessed, can match processed raw materials in quality and price.

(C)   Existing recycling programs have had recurrent difficulties finding purchasers for their materials, usually because of quantities too small to permit cost-effective pickup and transportation.

(D)   Some of the materials that can be recycled are the very materials that, when incinerated, produce the least pollution.

(E)   Many of the materials that cannot be recycled are also difficult to incinerate.

Evaluation of a Plan

To answer this question, consider what information would call the advisability of implementing this proposal into question.

A state legislator proposes that communities be required to target recycling 50 percent of all solid waste within five years. This legislator argues for the plan in part on the basis that recycling programs already in operation are profitable.

To weaken this argument, consider whether there might be a reason that significantly changing the amount or types of solid waste currently disposed of would make currently profitable recycling programs unprofitable.

A   This does not cast much doubt on the advisability of implementing the plan. If some communities manage to get as many as 80 percent of their citizens to participate, the goal of recycling 50 percent of all solid waste within certain communities seems attainable.

B   Correct. This suggests that increasing the percentage of solid waste that is recycled to 50 percent may result in a significant amount of recycled, reprocessed material of inferior quality. If this material cannot match processed materials in quality and price, this may make recycling programs no longer profitable.

C   If the problem is a result of the small quantities, increasing the quantities of materials could alleviate the problem. Therefore, this does not cast doubt on the advisability of implementing the plan.

D   Even if some of these materials produce little pollution, they nevertheless may produce some pollution. It may still be beneficial to reduce or eliminate this pollution.

E   This indicates that these materials will most likely need to go into landfills. That does not call into question the advisability of recycling those materials that can be recycled.

The correct answer is B.

CR30721.01

233.   Biologist: Species with broad geographic ranges probably tend to endure longer than species with narrow ranges. The broader a species' range, the more likely that species is to survive the extinction of populations in a few areas. Therefore, it is likely that the proportion of species with broad ranges tends to gradually increase with time.

The biologist's conclusion follows logically from the above if which of the following is assumed?

(A)   There are now more species with broad geographic ranges than with narrow geographic ranges.

(B)   Most species can survive extinctions of populations in a few areas as long as the species' geographic range is not very narrow.

(C)   If a population of a species in a particular area dies out, that species generally does not repopulate that area.

(D)   If a characteristic tends to help species endure longer, then the proportion of species with that characteristic tends to gradually increase with time.

(E)   Any characteristic that makes a species tend to endure longer will make it easier for that species to survive the extinction of populations in a few areas.

Argument Construction

This question asks us to find an assumption that allows the biologist's conclusion to be logically drawn if made in conjunction with the premises of the biologist's argument.

The biologist claims that species with broader ranges are more likely to survive the extinction of populations in certain areas than are species with narrow ranges. The biologist concludes that over time the proportion of species with broader ranges will probably increase.

Note that the argument as it stands is not logically valid: it is possible that if species that now have broad ranges survive the extinction of populations with narrow ranges, the proportion of species with broad ranges could still decline. That is, decimation of populations in certain areas may in fact cause the ranges of species that now have broad ranges to shrink in size, thereby becoming narrow ranges.

Were this to happen at a faster pace than the extinction of species that currently have narrow ranges, the proportion of species with broad ranges would decline rather than increase. The correct answer to this question must rule out this possibility.

A   This choice does not rule out the possibility that the proportion of species that have broad ranges would decline.

B   This choice does not rule out the possibility that the proportion of species that have broad ranges would decline.

C   This choice does not rule out the possibility that the proportion of species that have broad ranges would decline. In fact, this assumption helps to support the claim that as certain populations of a species that once had a broad range die out, that species' range could narrow.

D   Correct. This assumption rules out the possibility described above; furthermore, it rules out any other possibility that allows the biologist's conclusion to be false even if the premises were true.

E   This choice does not rule out the possibility that the proportion of species that have broad ranges would decline.

The correct answer is D.

CR79731.01

234. Letter to the editor: If the water level in the Searle River Delta continues to drop, the rising sea level will make the water saltier and less suitable for drinking. Currently, 40 percent of the water from upstream tributaries is diverted to neighboring areas. To keep the delta's water level from dropping any further, we should end all current diversions from the upstream tributaries. Neighboring water utilities are likely to see higher costs and diminished water supplies, but these costs are necessary to preserve the delta.

Which of the following would, if true, indicate a serious potential weakness of the suggested plan of action?

(A)   Desalination equipment would allow water from the delta to be used for drinking even it if became saltier.

(B)   Water level is only one factor that affects salinity in the delta.

(C)   The upstream tributaries' water levels are controlled by systems of dams and reservoirs.

(D)   Neighboring areas have grown in population since the water was first diverted from upstream tributaries.

(E)   Much of the recent drop in the delta's water level can be attributed to a prolonged drought that has recently ended.

Argument Evaluation

This question requires us to find a potential weakness of the plan suggested. That is, the question requires us to find a reason that ending all current diversions from the Searle River's upstream tributaries might not be a good idea.

Note that the plan is designed to keep the delta's water level from dropping further. While there are costs to executing this plan, the letter claims that these costs are necessary to preserve the delta.

The letter begins with a discussion of how the dropping water levels in the delta will lead to saltier and less potable water, but it is unclear what role this plays in the letter's argument. That is, we do not know whether this is the primary reason for the concern about the delta's water levels. Given the information provided, it could be just one of many concerns. Given the letter says that the *costs are necessary to preserve the delta*, it appears to be just one among multiple concerns.

A   If the sole reason for wanting to keep the delta's water level from dropping further is to ensure that the river can provide drinking water, then this answer choice might suggest a weakness in the plan. That is, the plan itself would be unnecessary. Note, however, that the main reason given for the plan is *to preserve the delta*, not to ensure drinkability of the water. Bearing this in mind, there may still be reasons to carry out the plan even if the claim made in this answer choice is true.

B   The plan does not necessarily need to be able to solve the problem of increased salinity on its own. Even if it cannot, the plan may be an important part of solving the problem. Furthermore, there may be other reasons besides salinity for implementing the plan. This choice, therefore, does not give us a good reason to believe that the plan is not necessary.

C   This choice gives us a potential explanation of how the upstream water has been diverted. It does not, however, present a weakness in the proposed plan.

D   This choice suggests a reason that there may be costs to implementing the proposed plan; most clearly, the growing population will need water that it could get from the river. Nevertheless, the letter indicates that these costs are necessary to preserve the delta.

E   **Correct.** This gives us reason to think that the water levels may actually fix themselves. That is, the level will not continue to decline even if the plan is not carried out. The letter indicates that the specific reason to carry out the plan is to prevent the water level from dropping any further. So if the plan turned out to be unnecessary for preventing such a drop in water level, then the costs of the plan would have made the plan itself undesirable.

The correct answer is E.

CR47931.01

235. Researchers conditioned a group of flies to associate a particular odor with a weak electric shock. Twenty-four and forty-eight hours later the researchers conducted tests on the flies, both individually and in groups, to determine whether the flies retained the conditioning. When tested individually, the flies were significantly less likely to avoid areas marked with the odor. The researchers hypothesized that in the presence of the odor, a fly that retains the conditioned association gives off an alarm signal that arouses the attention of any surrounding flies, retriggering the association in them and thereby causing them to avoid the odor.

The researchers' hypothesis requires which of the following assumptions?

(A)   The flies do not give off odors as alarm signals.

(B)   Flies that did not avoid the odor when tested individually were not merely following other flies' movements when tested in a group.

(C)   Flies that did not avoid the odor when tested individually were less likely than the other flies to avoid the odor when tested in a group.

(D)   Prior to their conditioning, the flies would likely have found the odor used in the experiment to be pleasant.

(E)   An electric shock was used during the flies' conditioning and during the later tests.

Argument Construction

This question asks us for an assumption required by the hypothesis.

The researchers noted that the flies that had been conditioned to associate a particular odor with an electric shock were much less likely to avoid the odor when they were tested individually than when they were tested as a part of a group.

Based on this fact, the researchers hypothesized that the flies that had retained the conditioning would give off an alarm when they detected the odor. This alarm would then retrigger the association among the other flies, leading them to avoid the odor.

We must consider whether there is some other fact that could explain why the flies were more likely to respond to the odor in a group than when they are alone. If there were, that alternative explanation would severely call into question the researchers' hypothesis. The hypothesis therefore requires that any such alternative explanation be false.

A   It is possible that the flies do in fact give off odors as an alarm signal. Because the nature of the flies' alarm signal is not specified by the hypothesis, this is entirely consistent with the hypothesis and would not undermine it. Therefore, the hypothesis does not require that flies do not give off odors as alarm signals.

B   **Correct.** Suppose that the flies that did not avoid the odor when tested individually were more likely to avoid the odor when in groups. This may be simply because these flies were following the movements of the flies that were triggered. That is, the signal did not cause the other flies' reactions. Instead, the movements of the triggered flies did. It follows that this possibility must be ruled out in order for the hypothesis to be plausible, and this answer choice does precisely that.

C   The hypothesis would actually be more plausible if this statement were false. That is, the hypothesis would be more plausible if the flies that did not avoid the odor when tested individually were just as likely, when they were tested in a group, to avoid the odor as the other flies in the group.

D   The hypothesis is perfectly compatible with the assumption that, prior to their conditioning, the flies were entirely indifferent to the odor.

E   The principle of association—that the shock is associated with the odor even when the shock itself is not present—actually requires that this statement be false.

The correct answer is B.

CR02741.01

236. Kayla: Many people are reluctant to shop in our neighborhood because street parking is scarce. The city plans to address this by adding parking meters with time limits that ensure that parking spaces are generally available. But this plan will surely backfire— shoppers dislike paying at parking meters, so most will probably drive to other neighborhoods to shop at malls with free parking.

Which of the following, if true, would be the most logically effective rebuttal a proponent of the city's plan could make to Kayla's objection?

(A)   Most shoppers dislike hunting for scarce street parking spaces much more than they dislike paying for metered parking spaces.

(B)   The city could post signs with street parking time limits to ensure that parking spaces become available without forcing shoppers to pay at meters.

(C)   Currently, most shoppers in the neighborhood drive only occasionally to shop at malls in other neighborhoods.

(D)   The neighborhood already contains a parking lot where shoppers must pay to park.

(E)   The nearby malls with free parking have no parking time limits to help ensure that parking spaces in their lots become available.

Evaluation of a Plan

Which one of the answer responses provides the best rebuttal to Kayla's objection?

Kayla tells us that a city plans to install parking meters on streets where shoppers in a shopping neighborhood try to park. The meters would have time limits designed to ensure increased availability of parking.

Nevertheless, Kayla believes the plan will have the opposite effect since people dislike paying for parking and are likely to shop instead at a mall where parking is free.

It is important to determine whether shoppers are likely to be deterred from shopping at this mall because they dislike paying to park at time-limited meters.

A   **Correct.** Shoppers currently try to park on the streets where meters will be installed. These shoppers find searching for a parking space increasingly difficult. It is possible that shoppers actually dislike searching for parking spaces more than they dislike paying for parking spaces. If this is the case, there is no reason to believe that these customers will leave the neighborhood to shop elsewhere.

B   This answer choice suggests a potential alternative to installing parking meters. This does not provide a rebuttal to Kayla's objection.

C   While many shoppers do not often drive to other neighborhoods to shop, this could change once the meters were installed.

D   We are given no information concerning the cost or availability of parking in the parking lot, or its proximity to the shopping portion of the neighborhood.

E   We are given no precise information about the relative availability of parking spaces at the nearby malls. However, given Kayla's concern, it can reasonably be inferred that there is no significant shortage of free parking spaces at these malls.

The correct answer is A.

CR78551.01

237. A new handheld device purports to determine the severity of concussions by reading the brain's electrical signals and comparing them to a database

of 15,000 scans compiled at a brain research lab. The device is intended to help doctors decide whether an athlete who has received a blow to the head during a competition should be sent back into the game.

Which of the following would it be most useful to establish in order to evaluate the effectiveness of the device for its intended purpose?

(A) Whether the database of brain scans will regularly be updated with new scans

(B) Whether by use of this device doctors will be able to make a sound decision about whether to allow an athlete back into the competition before it ends

(C) Whether the device will be endorsed by a large number of medical professionals

(D) Whether the database includes scans of non-injured athletes in the same game as the injured athlete

(E) Whether team doctors have until now been mistaken in their assessments of whether an athlete can safely continue to play

Argument Evaluation

Which one of the answer choices would most help in determining whether the device is effective for its intended purpose?

A handheld scanning device has been developed to read brain signals and determine the severity of a concussion. The intended purpose of this device is to help doctors decide whether an athlete who has received a blow to the head during competition can be allowed back into the game.

A   If the database is regularly updated, it might increase the effectiveness of the device in the future. This is not relevant to answering whether the device will help doctors make medical decisions during games.

B   **Correct.** If the answer is yes, then the device is effective for its intended purpose. If the answer is no, then the device is not effective for its intended purpose: to help doctors make sound decisions about whether athletes who have suffered a head blow can safely resume play during a game.

C   Endorsement by medical professionals might help marketing of the device, but it is not directly relevant to deciding whether the device is technically suitable for its intended purpose. Simply being a medical professional does not necessarily make one an expert on such issues; that is, medical professionals in general are not involved in deciding whether athletes who have received a head blow in a game can safely resume play in the game.

D   In order to be technically useful, the database would have to be representative of functioning brains in a variety of activities. This includes both normally functioning brains and abnormally functioning brains. Note that even if this condition is met, it would not be sufficient to decide on whether the device is adequate for its intended purpose.

E   Previous mistakes by team doctors implies a genuine need for the device. However, this issue is separate from the issue of whether the device itself can help doctors make sound decisions. That is, while such a device may be needed, it is possible that this particular device still does not effectively help doctors make the decision to send athletes back into the game.

The correct answer is B.

CR30461.01

238. Mashika: We already know from polling data that some segments of the electorate provide significant support to Ms. Puerta. If those segments also provide significant support to Mr. Quintana, then no segment of the electorate that provides significant support to Mr. Quintana provides significant support to Mr. Ramirez.

Salim: But actually, as the latest polling data conclusively shows, at least one segment of the electorate does provide significant support to both Mr. Quintana and Mr. Ramirez.

Among the following statements, which is it most reasonable to infer from the assertions by Mashika and Salim?

(A) At least one segment of the electorate provides significant support neither to Mr. Quintana nor to Mr. Ramirez.

(B)   At least one segment of the electorate provides significant support to Ms. Puerta but not to Mr. Quintana.

(C)   Each segment of the electorate provides significant support to Ms. Puerta.

(D)   Each segment of the electorate provides significant support to Mr. Quintana.

(E)   Each segment of the electorate provides significant support to Mr. Ramirez.

Argument Construction

Which one of the five answer choices is most reasonable to infer from the information given by Mashika and Salim?

The information given allows us to make various deductive inferences. First, if each segment that significantly supports Ms. Puerta also significantly supports Mr. Quintana, then it follows, based on Mashika's statement, that no segment of the electorate that significantly supports Mr. Quintana also supports Mr. Ramirez. In other words, to support Ms. Puerta implies not supporting Mr. Ramirez; therefore, if the segments supporting Mr. Quintana include all the segments supporting Ms. Puerta, there can be no segments that support both Mr. Ramirez and Mr. Quintana.

However, Salim tells us that there is such a voter segment: at least one segment significantly supports both Mr. Quintana and Mr. Ramirez. From this, it follows that the hypothesis *if those segments also provide support to Mr. Quintana* must be untrue; in other words, there exists at least one segment of the electorate that significantly supports Ms. Puerta but not Mr. Quintana.

A   We are told that there is a segment that significantly supports both Mr. Quintana and Mr. Ramirez, but this provides no basis for concluding that there is also a segment that significantly supports neither of the two.

B   **Correct.** The previous explanation indicates that at least one segment supports Ms. Puerta but not Mr. Quintana.

C   If support for Ms. Puerta and support for Mr. Ramirez are mutually exclusive, then this must be false given that we know that at least one segment supports Mr. Ramirez.

D   The information provided indicates that this is false: there is at least one segment that significantly supports Ms. Puerta but not Mr. Quintana.

E   If support for Ms. Puerta and support for Mr. Ramirez are mutually exclusive, then this must be false given that we know that at least some segments support Ms. Puerta.

The correct answer is B.

CR98461.01

239. The proportion of manufacturing companies in Alameda that use microelectronics in their manufacturing processes increased from 6 percent in 1979 to 66 percent in 1990. Many labor leaders say that the introduction of microelectronics is the principal cause of the great increase in unemployment during that period in Alameda. In actual fact, however, most of the job losses were due to organizational changes. Moreover, according to new figures released by the labor department, there were many more people employed in Alameda in the manufacturing industry in 1990 than in 1979.

Which of the following, if true, best reconciles the discrepancy between the increase in unemployment and the increase in jobs in the manufacturing industry of Alameda?

(A)   Many products that contain microelectronic components are now assembled completely by machine.

(B)   Workers involved in the various aspects of the manufacturing processes that use microelectronic technology need extensive training.

(C)   It is difficult to evaluate numerically what impact on job security the introduction of microelectronics in the workplace had before 1979.

(D)   In 1990 over 90 percent of the jobs in Alameda's manufacturing companies were filled by workers who moved to Alameda because they had skills for which there was no demand in Alameda prior to the introduction of microelectronics there.

(E)   Many workers who have retired from the manufacturing industry in Alameda since 1979 have not been replaced by younger workers.

Argument Construction

Which one of the five answer choices given best reconciles the increase in unemployment with the increase in manufacturing employment?

In Alameda, the use of microelectronics in manufacturing increased elevenfold within 11 years. Unemployment in Alameda increased during that period but—contrary to what labor leaders argue—most of the job losses were due to organizational changes. According to the latest official statistics, many more people were employed in manufacturing in Alameda at the end of that period.

One idea to consider is whether manufacturing that involves use of microelectronics in equipment requires employees with a different mix of skills from those traditionally used by employees carrying out manual tasks associated with manufacturing.

A   This choice provides an example of automated manufacturing, but the given information does not specifically mention manufactured products that contain microelectronic components.

B   The given information tells us that the increased unemployment was due to *organizational changes.* But the additional information here is not a sufficient basis for attributing the increase in unemployment to gaps in training.

C   This simply suggests that there may be some inaccurate data underlying claims about employment trends in manufacturing in Alameda prior to 1979. But the question concerns trends from 1979 to 1990.

D   **Correct.** This suggests that an influx of new workers to Alameda with the new skills needed in manufacturing may in fact have displaced other employees. These people may still live in Alameda yet be jobless.

E   This information is not sufficient to reconcile the increase in unemployment among those previously employed in manufacturing with the increase in total manufacturing jobs. Retirement of employees from certain types of occupations

does not increase unemployment in those occupations.

The correct answer is D.

CR00561.01

240. The retinas of premature babies are not fully developed at birth. Because their retinas are so delicate, premature babies sometimes lose their sight. Methods for preventing this syndrome, which is called retinopathy of prematurity, have improved, but the proportion of premature babies who lose their sight because of this syndrome has increased.

Which of the following, if true, best reconciles the apparent discrepancy described above?

(A)   When premature babies are born, their retinas are developmentally unprepared to deal with light and air in the environment outside the womb.

(B)   The oxygen that must be administered to premature babies at birth can sometimes have a damaging effect on the babies' retinas, but the oxygen is now administered in less damaging concentrations than it used to be.

(C)   The effects of retinopathy of prematurity can be reduced by controlling the exposure of premature babies to light and oxygen, but this method cannot completely prevent the syndrome.

(D)   The improvement of methods to prevent retinopathy of prematurity has been a gradual process, and there is still a need for further knowledge.

(E)   Improved medical technology is saving the lives of premature babies who would previously have died, but these babies have even more delicate retinas than do other premature babies and are more apt to lose their sight.

Argument Construction

What could reconcile the fact that, even though technology has improved the likelihood of saving premature babies' sight, a greater percentage of premature babies are losing their sight than in the past?

Retinopathy of prematurity (ROP) can lead to blindness in babies born prematurely. However, methods for preventing ROP have improved. Given that, it is puzzling that the proportion of premature babies who go blind due to ROP has increased.

It is important to carefully distinguish among three different groups: the proportion of premature babies who survive; the proportion who have ROP; and the proportion of those who have ROP who become blind as a result.

A change in the proportion of premature babies that have ROP does not necessarily imply a similar change in the proportion of ROP cases that lead to blindness. Thus, even with an increased survival rate of premature babies and improved prevention of ROP, a greater proportion of babies with ROP can go blind.

For example, suppose the severity of ROP at birth among surviving premature babies is greater. Then we could expect that a greater proportion of ROP cases would lead to blindness, absent a measure to prevent this occurring.

A This choice does not explain why a greater proportion of ROP cases lead to blindness; it simply suggests some of the conditions in prematurity that can cause retinopathy.

B This choice does not resolve the apparent contradiction described; it merely suggests one factor that can damage premature babies' retinas.

C This choice does not resolve the apparent contradiction; it merely indicates how some severe consequences of ROP may be moderated.

D This choice does not resolve the apparent contradiction; it merely indicates that there is more for medical science to discover about how to prevent or treat ROP.

E **Correct.** Among the ROP cases that currently occur, a significant number of them are more severe than in the past. This is an indirect result of the increased survival rate of premature babies, which is also due to technological advances. The greater severity of the ROP among those babies who have it could easily explain the greater proportion of ROP cases that lead to blindness.

The correct answer is E.

CR60561.01

241. Although elementary school children have traditionally received considerable instruction in creating visual art, there has been no such instruction in music. Consequently, in contrast to the situation for visual art, most people as adults do not recognize the artistic intentions of composers. To remedy this situation, a few educators now recommend teaching elementary school students to compose music.

Which of the following, if true, is the strongest basis for arguing that implementation of the recommendation will not lead to the desired result?

(A) Few elementary school students are likely to create superior compositions.

(B) Traditional education facilitates the appreciation of visual art, but not the recognition of the artistic intentions of artists.

(C) More people report that they enjoy music than report that they enjoy visual art.

(D) Some composers have had little formal instruction in composition.

(E) The recommendation is based on the results of a controlled longitudinal study conducted in three schools within a single city.

Evaluation of a Plan

Which answer choice most suggests that implementing the recommendation will not lead to the desired result?

Most elementary school children receive education in creating visual art but no education in composing music. Although most adults recognize the artist's intentions in a work of visual art, the same is not true for most adults' ability to recognize the composer's intentions in a piece of music. Based on these facts, it is advocated that elementary school children be taught to compose music.

It is important to note that we are not told that most adults are able to recognize an artist's intentions specifically because of elementary-level instruction in creating visual art.

A   The goal of the recommendation is not for elementary school students to create superior compositions in music.

B   **Correct.** This indicates that traditional education in visual art—including, presumably, such education for elementary school students—does not generally result in ability to recognize the artistic intentions of artists. By analogy, the recommended education in music composition would be unlikely to lead to a recognition of the artistic intentions of composers.

C   Ability to enjoy music or visual art does not necessarily imply the ability to recognize the artistic intentions of visual artists or composers.

D   Composers' formal instruction is entirely irrelevant to the recommendation as well as to whether the recommendation achieves its intended purpose.

E   This suggests that the recommendation is based on scientifically collected data. That does not suggest that the recommendation would fail to achieve its intended purpose.

The correct answer is B.

CR47561.01

242. Pharmaceutical companies spend more than ever on research and development; yet the number of new drugs patented each year has dropped since 1963. At the same time, profits—at constant 1963 dollars—for the industry as a whole have been steadily increasing.

Which of the following, if true, is the single factor most likely to explain, at least in part, the three trends mentioned above for money spent, drugs patented, and profits made?

(A)   Government regulations concerning testing requirements for novel drugs have become steadily more stringent.

(B)   Research competition among pharmaceutical companies has steadily intensified as a result of a general narrowing of research targets to drugs for which there is a large market.

(C)   Many pharmaceutical companies have entered into collaborative projects with leading universities, while others have hired faculty

members away from universities by offering very generous salaries.

(D)   The number of cases in which one company's researchers duplicated work done by another company's researchers has steadily grown.

(E)   The advertising budgets of the major pharmaceutical companies have grown at a higher rate than their profits have.

Argument Construction

Of the five factors indicated in the answer choices, which one most helps to explain all three of the trends?

The information provided about the pharmaceutical industry indicates three long-term trends since 1963: increased research spending, increased profits, and reduction in the number of patents granted.

Note that in a case where the pharmaceutical industry produced fewer—yet more lucrative—new drugs as a result of its increased research investment, its profits might increase even if fewer new patents were granted.

A   Although the stringency of government regulations could help explain increased research spending and the granting of fewer patents, it fails to explain why profits would increase in the long term.

B   **Correct.** This helps explain all three factors. It suggests that each company has had to boost its research spending, but with a narrowing of focus to produce mass-market drugs with enormous potential for profit. This narrowing of focus could explain why fewer drugs are being patented.

C   Collaboration between pharmaceutical companies and leading universities would not help explain all three trends. It could indicate that the pharmaceutical companies have reduced their investment in their in-house research infrastructure. That is, perhaps these companies find it less expensive to farm out research to universities where a powerful research infrastructure already exists. Even if this could help explain increased research spending, nothing indicates that it would help explain the trends in profits or patents.

D   Companies doing similar or duplicative research could indicate certain inefficiencies in research spending, which could help explain the research-spending trend and the trend regarding patents. Nevertheless, it still fails to explain the trend of increasing profits.

E   This does not explain the trend regarding research spending or the trend regarding patents.

The correct answer is B.

CR97561.01

243. Under the agricultural policies of Country R, farmers can sell any grain not sold on the open market to a grain board at guaranteed prices. It seems inevitable that, in order to curb the resultant escalating overproduction, the grain board will in just a few years have to impose quotas on grain production, limiting farmers to a certain flat percentage of the grain acreage they cultivated previously.

Suppose an individual farmer in Country R wishes to minimize the impact on profits of the grain quota whose eventual imposition is being predicted. If the farmer could do any of the following and wants to select the most effective course of action, which should the farmer do now?

(A)   Select in advance currently less profitable grain fields and retire them if the quota takes effect.

(B)   Seek long-term contracts to sell grain at a fixed price.

(C)   Replace obsolete tractors with more efficient new ones.

(D)   Put marginal land under cultivation and grow grain on it.

(E)   Agree with other farmers on voluntary cutbacks in grain production.

Plan Evaluation

Of the plans described in the five answer choices and equally available to the farmer, which one would be the most effective to pursue?

It is expected that the grain board of Country R, which purchases surplus grain production from farmers at guaranteed prices, will, within a few years, impose quotas on each farmer's grain production in order to limit overproduction.

This plan will limit each farmer to a flat percentage of the grain acreage previously cultivated. The quota will be calculated based on pre-existing grain acreage (presumably averaged over a few years). Therefore, it would make the most sense for the farmer to boost grain acreage for the next few years, even if some of the acreage increase involves using land not optimal for grain production.

A   Selecting less profitable land now would make sense if no other course of action did. However, it would still entail some immediate reduction in profits: the land in question is currently *less profitable*, not unprofitable.

B   Long-term fixed-price contracts would presumably ensure the farmer's profitability from grain cultivation. But that might not occur if the total cost of agricultural inputs for grain cultivation were to significantly increase without the contracts safeguarding against such a case. Perhaps the most important factor, however, is that such long-term contracts could significantly limit the farmer's ability to profit from future upward trends in market demand for grain.

C   We are given no information to help us gauge how machinery obsolescence and major investment in new machinery might affect the profits from grain cultivation.

D   **Correct.** Since any quotas issued in a few years will be calculated as a percentage of the farmer's pre-existing grain-production acreage, the farmer would benefit from increasing his or her grain-production acreage even if some of the new acreage is suboptimal for grain cultivation.

E   To agree with other farmers on voluntary cutbacks might help forestall or at least delay the introduction of grain quotas by the grain board. However, it could have much the same effect as quotas even if it is sufficient to pre-empt mandatory quotas.

Furthermore, it would carry the risk that some farmers would defect from any agreement if they perceived an advantage in doing so.

The correct answer is D.

CR69561.01

244. Exports of United States wood pulp will rise considerably during this year. The reason for the rise is that the falling value of the dollar will make it cheaper for paper manufacturers in Japan and Western Europe to buy American wood pulp than to get it from any other source.

Which of the following is an assumption made in drawing the conclusion above?

(A) Factory output of paper products in Japan and Western Europe will increase sharply during this year.

(B) The quality of the wood pulp produced in the United States would be adequate for the purposes of Japanese and Western European paper manufacturers.

(C) Paper manufacturers in Japan and Western Europe would prefer to use wood pulp produced in the United States if cost were not a factor.

(D) Demand for paper products made in Japan and Western Europe will not increase sharply during this year.

(E) Production of wood pulp by United States companies will not increase sharply during this year.

Argument Construction

Which one of the statements gives an assumption on which the argument depends?

The argument claims that exports of U.S. wood pulp will increase this year. Support for this claim is provided by the suggestion that as a result of the falling value of the dollar, paper manufacturers in Japan and Western Europe will be able to purchase wood pulp (the raw material for paper) more cheaply from the United States than from any other source.

This would be true because, if the dollar prices of U.S. wood pulp did not increase, firms in Europe and Japan would pay a smaller dollar-equivalent of their own currencies.

Note that this argument can easily fail: if U.S. wood pulp does not meet the minimum quality requirements of any paper manufacturers in Japan or Western Europe, then those manufacturers will purchase elsewhere. It follows that the reasoning depends on assuming that U.S. wood pulp does in fact meet those quality standards.

A   Even if factory output of paper products did not increase this year, manufacturers in Japan and Europe might import more U.S. wood pulp this year as raw materials for next year's production.

B   Correct. The predicted increase would likely not occur unless U.S. wood pulp met the manufacturers' minimum-quality standards.

C   The reasoning does not have to assume that cost is the sole factor. However, it clearly assumes that cost is an important factor. Nevertheless, it does not make any assumption regarding what the relative importance of cost and other factors might be. For this reason, it neither assumes nor implies what might happen in the case that cost is not a significant factor.

D   The reasoning does not need to assume that no such sharp increase will occur this year. In fact, if such an increase were to occur, it would be even more likely that exports of U.S. wood pulp would increase this year if U.S. wood pulp became internationally more competitive on price this year.

E   Given the prediction that U.S. wood-pulp exports will increase, there is no reason to assume *no sharp increase* in U.S. wood pulp production *during this year*. Such an increase might even be likely if exports were to *rise considerably*. Therefore, option E is not assumed by the argument.

The correct answer is B.

CR79561.01

245. A company's personnel director surveyed employees about their satisfaction with the company's system for awarding employee performance ratings. The survey data indicated that employees who received high ratings were very satisfied with the system. The personnel director concluded from these data that the company's best-performing employees liked the system.

The personnel director's conclusion assumes which of the following?

(A) No other performance rating system is as good as the current system.

(B) The company's best-performing employees received high ratings.

(C) Employees who received low ratings were dissatisfied with the system.

(D) Employees who receive high ratings from a performance-rating system will like that system.

(E) The company's best-performing employees were motivated to perform well by the knowledge that they would receive performance ratings.

Argument Construction

Which one of the following states an assumption on which the personnel director's conclusion depends?

The assumption we seek must provide a needed logical connection between the given information and the conclusion drawn. From the information given, it seems reasonable to think that the employees *very satisfied with the system* also *liked the system*. Furthermore, we are told that the employees who received high ratings were very satisfied with the system.

It follows that if the company's best-performing employees also received high ratings, then these same people—the best-performing employees—were very satisfied with the system. This would make it reasonable to conclude that the best-performing employees liked the system.

A The argument does not address the issue of whether the existing performance-rating system is the best available. Rather, it draws a conclusion about the existing performance-rating system based on specific data generated by the system.

B Correct. Assuming that the company's best-performing employees received high ratings enables the personnel director's conclusion to be logically drawn.

C This choice describes an association between ratings and satisfaction, rather than an association between performance and ratings, or between performance and satisfaction. The information given in the argument is compatible with the claim that all employees were at least somewhat satisfied with the system.

D This choice assumes that employees who are rated highly by a system will like that system, but that assumption is more general than anything assumed in the argument. This choice addresses employees' attitudes to a performance-rating system based on the ratings they receive under that system. However, it does not address any association between ratings, performance, and attitudes to the system.

E Employees' satisfaction with a performance-rating system might well play a role in motivating employees. However, the issue of motivation figures neither explicitly nor implicitly in the reasoning of the personnel director.

The correct answer is B.

CR00661.01

246. There are fundamentally two possible changes in an economy that will each cause inflation unless other compensating changes also occur. These changes are either reductions in the supply of goods and services or increases in demand. In a pre-banking economy the quantity of money available, and hence the level of demand, is equivalent to the quantity of gold available.

If the statements above are true, then it is also true that in a pre-banking economy

(A) any inflation is the result of reductions in the supply of goods and services

(B) if other factors in the economy are unchanged, increasing the quantity of gold available will lead to inflation

(C)   if there is a reduction in the quantity of gold available, then, other things being equal, inflation must result

(D)   the quantity of goods and services purchasable by a given amount of gold is constant

(E)   whatever changes in demand occur, there will be compensating changes in the supply of goods and services

Argument Construction

This question asks us which of the statements is most strongly supported by the information in the argument. Given no other relevant changes, two factors can cause inflation: a reduction in market supply of goods and services or an increase in market demand. The argument also indicates that the total quantity of money available—or, in a pre-banking economy, the quantity of gold available—determines market demand. Therefore, in a pre-banking economy, an increase in the quantity of gold available will increase demand. In a situation where supply remains constant, this increases demand for this fixed supply, thereby raising prices. In other words, increasing the quantity of gold in a pre-banking economy will cause inflation.

A   While this may be true in certain cases, it is not the argument made in the passage. The passage indicates that certain instances of inflation are caused by increased demand stimulated by an increase in available money (or gold).

B   **Correct.** According to the information in the passage, if the quantity of available gold in a pre-banking economy increases while supply of goods and services remains unchanged, demand for goods and services will increase relative to supply. This imbalance raises prices for the supply; that is, it causes inflation.

C   This answer suggests the opposite of the information in the passage. While the information in the passage indicates that an increase in the quantity of available gold may cause inflation, this choice suggests that a reduction in the available amount of gold will cause inflation.

D   This suggestion is contrary to the information in the passage: the passage suggests that in a pre-banking economy, the total available amount of gold determines the amount that a good or service will cost. This answer choice suggests that the total available amount of gold is irrelevant to the cost of given goods or services.

E   The passage nowhere indicates that economies will compensate for changes in demand by changing available supply. This suggestion may or may not be true in real-world terms, but there is no information in the passage to support it.

The correct answer is B.

CR20661.01

247. Clearbell Telephone provides slow-dialing (SD) service to customers for a low fee, and fast-dialing (FD) service to other customers who pay a somewhat higher fee. FD technology, however, is so efficient that it costs Clearbell substantially less per average call to provide than does SD. Nonetheless, accountants have calculated that Clearbell's profits would drop if it provided FD to all its customers at the current low-fee rate.

Assume that installation costs for FD are insignificant if the customer already has SD service. Which of the following, if true about Clearbell, best explains the results of the accountants' calculation?

(A)   The extra revenue collected from customers who pay the high fee is higher than the extra cost of providing SD to customers who pay the low fee.

(B)   The low fee was increased by 6 percent last year, whereas the higher fee was not increased last year.

(C)   Although 96 percent of customers regard FD service as reliable and more convenient than SD, fewer than 10 percent of them choose to pay the higher fee for FD service.

(D)   The company's competitors generally provide business customers with FD service at low-fee rates.

(E)   Profits rose slightly each month for the first three months after FD was first offered to customers, then fell slightly each month for the succeeding three months.

Argument Construction

The argument suggests that fast-dialing (FD) service costs Clearbell Telephone less to deliver per call than does slow-dialing (SD) service, which Clearbell delivers at a lower fee. There are no significant extra costs such as installation to switch to FD if a customer is already a user of SD. Nevertheless, accountants expect Clearbell's profits to decrease if the company were to provide the high-priced FD service at the lower SD rate. *Our goal here will be to find a reason for this apparent contradiction.*

A **Correct.** This answer provides a plausible reason for the contradiction. Ultimately, we do not know the amount of extra fee that FD customers pay relative to SD customers. If the higher FD fees make up a substantial portion of the company's revenues, then it is very possible that the proposed change would reduce revenues significantly enough to lower profits. Remember, the SD service actually costs *more* for Clearbell Telephone. Therefore, the balance to find is whether the current higher FD fees generate more revenue than the money saved by eliminating SD service and instead providing FD services at the low fee.

B This statement provides information about how Clearbell's current prices were set. However, it provides no information as to how the proposed changes might affect profits.

C This statement does not explain the results of the accountants' calculations. First, customers' preference is irrelevant to the accountants' results. Second, if we were to assume that 10 percent is a small figure, it is still possible that FD fees are great enough to offset the extra costs Clearbell incurs by providing SD service. Third, since the cost to Clearbell is less per call using FD service, Clearbell's profits may in fact increase if all customers were to be given FD service.

D This statement is outside the scope of the argument. First, practices of Clearbell's competitors have no bearing on the accountants' calculations. Second, we have no way to determine what the change in Clearbell's profits and its competitive position might be if Clearbell were to provide FD service at the low-fee rate to its business customers. Third, given the facts provided in the argument, it is entirely possible that Clearbell already gives preferential rates for FD service to its business customers.

E This information does not help explain the results of the accountants' calculations. Simply because the changes in profit and the introduction of FD service happened at roughly the same time, we cannot assume that one caused the other. That is, it is possible that these fluctuations in profit are due to normal, perhaps seasonal, fluctuations in profits. Therefore, these fluctuations would not necessarily negatively impact Clearbell's overall level of profitability.

The correct answer is A.

CR23661.01

248. Manufacturers sometimes discount the price of a product to retailers for a promotion period when the product is advertised to consumers. Such promotions often result in a dramatic increase in amount of product sold by the manufacturers to retailers. Nevertheless, the manufacturers could often make more profit by not holding the promotions.

Which of the following, if true, most strongly supports the claim above about the manufacturers' profit?

(A) The amount of discount generally offered by manufacturers to retailers is carefully calculated to represent the minimum needed to draw consumers' attention to the product.

(B) For many consumer products the period of advertising discounted prices to consumers is about a week, not sufficiently long for consumers to become used to the sale price.

(C) For products that are not newly introduced, the purpose of such promotions is to keep the products in the minds of consumers and to attract consumers who are currently using competing products.

(D) During such a promotion retailers tend to accumulate in their warehouses inventory bought at discount; they then sell much of it later at their regular price.

(E) If a manufacturer fails to offer such promotions but its competitor offers them, that competitor will tend to attract consumers away from the manufacturer's product.

Argument Evaluation

Which of the answer choices provides the strongest evidence for the claim that the manufacturers could indeed make more profit by not holding promotions?

To promote a product during a period when it is advertised to consumers, manufacturers sometimes sell the product to retailers at a discounted price. This often results in a large boost in manufacturers' sales to retailers. However, we are told that manufacturers could make more profit by not offering the promotions.

The manufacturers' total profits on the product increase during the period of reduced-price sales to retailers; note that the price reduction results in a *dramatic increase* in the volume of sales to retailers.

Nevertheless, it is possible that this temporary increase in sales volume would reduce future sales volume to retailers at non-discounted prices. In such a case, it would be more likely that the manufacturers' overall profits on the product would be reduced.

A   It is reasonable for manufacturers to calculate the minimum needed to draw attention to a product if they wished to minimize the costs of the product promotion. However, this information gives little if any support for the claim that manufacturers could make more profit by not discounting prices to retailers.

B   The argument does not provide any information to suggest that the length of the promotion affects manufacturers' profits. According to the passage, many promotions last a short time, so consumers do not come to routinely expect a lower price on a product and thereby avoid purchasing it at the higher post-promotion price. However, this new information gives little if any support for the claim that manufacturers could make more profit by not discounting prices to retailers.

C   This choice implies that the manufacturer would risk making less overall profit, not more, if these promotions were not held.

D   **Correct.** The retailer profits by purchasing large volumes of the product at a manufacturer's discounted price and selling it to consumers at the higher post-promotion price. It follows that the increase in sales at the discount might in fact detract from non-discount sales. As noted above, this gives the strongest support for the claim about the manufacturers' profits.

E   This suggests that sales promotions are essential for manufacturers to compete in relevant markets. However, it gives little if any support for the claim made about manufacturers' profits.

The correct answer is D.

CR33661.01

249. Advertisement: Today's customers expect high quality. Every advance in the quality of manufactured products raises customer expectations. The company that is satisfied with the current quality of its products will soon find that its customers are not. At MegaCorp, meeting or exceeding customer expectations is our goal.

Which of the following must be true on the basis of the statements in the advertisement above?

(A) MegaCorp's competitors will succeed in attracting customers only if those competitors adopt MegaCorp's goal as their own.

(B) A company that does not correctly anticipate the expectations of its customers is certain to fail in advancing the quality of its products.

(C) MegaCorp's goal is possible to meet only if continuing advances in product quality are possible.

(D) If a company becomes satisfied with the quality of its products, then the quality of its products is sure to decline.

(E) MegaCorp's customers are currently satisfied with the quality of its products.

Argument Construction

This question requires us to identify a statement that can be inferred on the basis of the statements made in the advertisement.

The advertisement states that every improvement in the quality of manufactured products leads to increased expectations among customers, yet that MegaCorp has a goal of meeting or exceeding its customers' expectations.

It follows that MegaCorp will continually be able to meet this goal only if it is possible for it to continue improving the quality of its products.

A   The information in the advertisement provides support for the idea that customers are more likely to buy products that are of the highest available quality. However, there is nothing in the advertisement to indicate that the only way for any of MegaCorp's competitors to produce the highest quality product would be to adopt MegaCorp's goal.

B   There is nothing in the advertisement to support this claim. A company could, for instance, improve the quality of a product in ways that are different from what customers expect.

C   **Correct.** To meet or exceed ever-increasing demands for improved quality requires that continuing advances in product quality are in fact possible.

D   The advertisement suggests that a company that is satisfied with the quality of its products can, at the very least, maintain the current quality of its products. There is nothing to suggest that the quality of these products will actually decline.

E   The passage provides no evidence that MegaCorp has been successful at reaching its goal of meeting or exceeding customer expectations.

The correct answer is C.

Answer Explanations Verbal Reasoning

Sentence Correction

Communication

SC21011.01

250. The prime lending rate is a key rate in the economy: <u>not only are the interest rates on most loans to small and medium-sized businesses tied to the prime, but also on</u> a growing number of consumer loans, including home equity loans.

(A) not only are the interest rates on most loans to small and medium-sized businesses tied to the prime, but also on

(B) tied to the prime are the interest rates not only on most loans to small and medium-sized businesses, but also on

(C) the interest rates not only on most loans to small and medium-sized businesses are tied to the prime, but also

(D) not only the interest rates on most loans to small and medium-sized businesses are tied to the prime, but also on

(E) the interest rates are tied to the prime, not only on most loans to small and medium-sized businesses, but also

Logical predication; Parallelism

The sentence tells us that the interest rates on two classes of loans are affected by the prime lending rate. The structure *not only . . . but also . . .* , consisting of two adverbial modifiers, conveys this.

The position of the two modifiers is crucial in order to know what each modifies. Furthermore, it is essential that the two things modified be parallel.

A In this choice, *not only are the interest rates . . . but also on* is not parallel.

B **Correct.** This choice uses a correctly parallel form *not only on . . . but also on . . .*

C In this choice, *the interest rates not only on . . . but also* is not parallel.

D In this choice, *not only the interest rates on . . . are . . .* is idiomatically incorrect: when *not*

only begins an independent statement, the order of subject and verb in the *not only* part must be inverted as in *not only are . . .*

E In this choice, *the interest rates not only on . . . but also* is not parallel.

The correct answer is B.

SC83811.01

251. Lacking information about energy use, people tend to overestimate the amount of energy used by <u>equipment, such as lights, that are visible and must be turned on and off and underestimate that</u> used by unobtrusive equipment, such as water heaters.

(A) equipment, such as lights, that are visible and must be turned on and off and underestimate that

(B) equipment, such as lights, that are visible and must be turned on and off and underestimate it when

(C) equipment, such as lights, that is visible and must be turned on and off and underestimate it when

(D) visible equipment, such as lights, that must be turned on and off and underestimate that

(E) visible equipment, such as lights, that must be turned on and off and underestimate it when

Rhetorical construction; Agreement

This sentence, as worded, has a subject-verb agreement problem: the noun *equipment*, not *lights*, serves as the subject of the verb *are*; because *equipment* is singular, *is* should be used. Furthermore, the sentence would read more clearly if *visible equipment* were used rather than *equipment . . . that [is] visible*. This would create a less wordy sentence that has a more parallel structure, in which *visible equipment* is contrasted with *unobtrusive equipment*.

A This version is flawed for the reasons given above.

B   This version has the same subject-verb agreement problem as in A. Furthermore, it is unclear what the referent of the pronoun *it* is here. Finally, this version, like A, is wordy, and its structure is not parallel.

C   This version correctly uses the singular verb *is*. However, as in choice B, the pronoun *it* has no clear referent. Finally, this version, like A and B, is wordy, and its structure is not parallel.

D   **Correct.** This version is free of subject-verb agreement errors and its structure is parallel.

E   Although this version is free of subject-verb agreement errors and appropriately uses a parallel structure, it retains the problem from choices B and C: the pronoun *it* has no clear referent.

The correct answer is D.

SC37561.01

252. Evidence of some shifts in the character of violence on television is emerging from a new study of 500 television <u>programs by the Center for Media and Public Affairs, a nonprofit research center in Washington, D.C., a study that is underwritten by a number of educational institutions</u>.

(A)   programs by the Center for Media and Public Affairs, a nonprofit research center in Washington, D.C., a study that is underwritten by a number of educational institutions

(B)   programs by the Center for Media and Public Affairs, a nonprofit research center in Washington, D.C., and it is underwritten by a number of educational institutions

(C)   programs underwritten by a number of educational institutions and conducted by the Center for Media and Public Affairs, a nonprofit research center based in Washington, D.C.

(D)   programs, a study underwritten by a number of educational institutions and conducted by the Center for Media and Public Affairs, a nonprofit research center in Washington, D.C.

(E)   programs, a study conducted by the Center for Media and Public Affairs, a nonprofit research center based in Washington, D.C., and it is underwritten by a number of educational institutions

Logical predication; Rhetorical construction

The sentence gives three pieces of information: that a new study suggests the nature of violence on television is changing; that it was funded by educational institutions; and that it was conducted by the Center for Media and Public Affairs, a nonprofit research center.

Our task is to order this information logically and grammatically. The most obvious defect in the given sentence is that the long phrase *a study . . . institutions* describing how the study was funded is placed too far from the first mention of the study (*a new study*), with too much distracting information in between.

A   This choice is incorrect for the reasons stated above.

B   In this choice, *it* is ambiguous: it could, for example, refer to the evidence or the new study.

C   In this choice, the modifying phrases *underwritten by . . .* and *conducted by . . .* appear to modify *programs*.

D   **Correct.** This choice clearly organizes the information in the sentence, with no ambiguity.

E   The pronoun *it* is ambiguous: it could refer to the new study or the evidence.

The correct answer is D.

SC48461.01

253. Judge Lois Forer's study asks why <u>do some litigants have a preferred status over others in the use of a public resource, the courts, which in theory are available to all but in fact are unequally distributed among</u> rich and poor.

(A)   do some litigants have a preferred status over others in the use of a public resource, the courts, which in theory are available to all but in fact are unequally distributed among

(B)   some litigants have a preferred status over others in the use of a public resource, the courts, which in theory are available to all but in fact are unequally distributed between

(C) do some litigants have a preferred status over another in the use of a public resource, the courts, in theory available to all but in fact are unequally distributed among

(D) some litigants have a preferred status to another in the use of a public resource, the courts, in theory available to all but in fact not equally distributed between

(E) does one litigant have a preferred status over the other in the use of a public resource, the courts, in theory available to all but in fact they are not equally distributed among

Diction; Parallelism

The word *do* between *why* and *some* is unnecessary here. It would be used if we were to present the question in quotation marks, for example: "Why do some litigants . . . ?" However, when simply reporting that a person has asked the question, we simply say *X asks why some litigants.*

Additionally, the sentence appears to be attempting to say that the rich have better access to courts than the poor. Given that there are only two groups, the appropriate preposition is *between* (used for two and only two things) rather than *among* (used for three or more things). That is, the sentence would more appropriately read *unequally distributed between rich and poor.*

A This choice is flawed for the reasons indicated above.

B **Correct.** This version of the sentence uses the appropriate preposition *between* and clearly conveys the intended idea.

C This choice has the same flaws as choice A. Additionally, remember that the sentence attempts to communicate that some litigants have preferred status over some others rather than simply over one specific person. For this reason, *over another* is incorrect; the correct wording would be *over others.* Finally, the wording of the final clause is unacceptable; *which in theory are available to all but in fact are unequally distributed* is preferable.

D The correct preposition to use after *preferred status* is *over*, not *to*. Additionally, as in

choice C, *others* rather than *another* would be correct. Finally, the sentence would be more clearly worded if *unequally* rather than *not equally* had been used.

E As in choice A, the use of *does* is unnecessary. Note also that the question regarding the preferred status in the use of a public resource is not about two particular litigants, but about litigants in general. Therefore, *one litigant . . . over the other* does not clearly convey the intended meaning. Furthermore, the use of *does* is unnecessary, and the final clause would be better worded *which in theory are available to all but in fact are unequally distributed between* than what is found here.

The correct answer is B.

SC30561.01
254. During an ice age, the buildup of ice at the poles and the drop in water levels near the equator speed up the earth's rotation, like a spinning figure skater whose speed increases when her arms are drawn in.

(A) like a spinning figure skater whose speed increases when her arms are drawn in

(B) like the increased speed of a figure skater when her arms are drawn in

(C) like a figure skater who increases speed while spinning with her arms drawn in

(D) just as a spinning figure skater who increases speed by drawing in her arms

(E) just as a spinning figure skater increases speed by drawing in her arms

Logical predication; Parallelism

Each of the incorrect answer choices makes a faulty comparison.

A Grammatically, the comparison here is between *the buildup of ice . . . and the drop in water levels . . .* on one hand and *a spinning figure skater* on the other. However, the appropriate comparison would be either between the figure skater and earth, or between the skater's rotation and the earth's rotation.

B   Grammatically, the comparison here is between *the buildup of ice . . . and the drop in water levels . . .* on one hand and *the increased speed of a figure skater* on the other. However, the appropriate comparison would be between the increased speed of earth's rotation and the increased speed of a figure skater. Furthermore, note that this answer choice nowhere suggests that the skater is spinning.

C   Grammatically, as in choice A, the comparison here is between *the buildup of ice . . . and the drop in water levels . . .* on one hand and *a spinning figure skater* on the other. However, the appropriate comparison would be either between the figure skater and earth, or between the skater's rotation and earth's rotation.

D   When *just as* is used to mean *in the same way as*, it must link two independent clauses. The clause beginning *who increases speed . . .* is a dependent clause.

E   **Correct.** In this version *just as* is appropriately used to create a comparison between the way the buildup of ice at the poles, along with the drop in water levels at the equator, increases the speed of earth's rotation and the way a figure skater increases the speed of her spin by drawing in her arms

The correct answer is E.

SC01561.01

255. <u>Added to the increase in hourly wages requested last July, the railroad employees are now seeking an expanded program of retirement benefits.</u>

(A)   Added to the increase in hourly wages requested last July, the railroad employees are now seeking an expanded program of retirement benefits.

(B)   Added to the increase in hourly wages which had been requested last July, the employees of the railroad are now seeking an expanded program of retirement benefits.

(C)   The railroad employees are now seeking an expanded program of retirement benefits added to the increase in hourly wages that were requested last July.

(D)   In addition to the increase in hourly wages that were requested last July, the railroad employees are now seeking an expanded program of retirement benefits.

(E)   In addition to the increase in hourly wages requested last July, the employees of the railroad are now seeking an expanded program of retirement benefits.

Logical predication; Agreement

The phrase *Added to the increase in hourly wages . . .* modifies what immediately follows the comma, *the railroad employees*. This would mean that the railroad employees themselves are being added to the increase in hourly wages, which is absurd.

The idea the sentence is intended to convey is that the railroad employees are now seeking to have an expanded program of retirement benefits added to the increase in hourly earnings requested last July.

The correct answer will be the choice that most clearly, idiomatically, and grammatically expresses this idea.

A   As indicated above, the phrase *added to the increase in hourly wages requested last July . . .* incorrectly modifies *the railroad employees*.

B   The phrase *Added to the increase in hourly wages which had been requested last July* modifies *the railroad employees*, which is not what is intended.

C   Unlike the prior two choices, this choice does not make any modification errors. However, *seeking an expanded program . . . added* is not correct; *seeking to have an expanded program . . . added* would be acceptable. In the other answer choices, *seeking* most nearly means *trying to acquire*. In this choice, however, because it is used in conjunction with another verb (*added*), *seeking* most nearly means *trying*. When used in this sense, *seeking* should be followed by an infinitive.

D   Like C, but unlike A and B, this choice does not have any modification errors. However, it has an agreement flaw: the noun *the increase in hourly wages* is singular, so the verb must be *was requested* rather than *were requested*.

E   **Correct.** This version clearly and correctly conveys the intended idea.

The correct answer is E.

SC21561.01

256. The use of gravity waves, which do not interact with matter <u>in the way electromagnetic waves do, hopefully will enable</u> astronomers to study the actual formation of black holes and neutron stars.

(A) in the way electromagnetic waves do, hopefully will enable

(B) in the way electromagnetic waves do, will, it is hoped, enable

(C) like electromagnetic waves, hopefully will enable

(D) like electromagnetic waves, would enable, hopefully

(E) such as electromagnetic waves do, will, it is hoped, enable

Rhetorical Construction; Diction

While the use of *hopefully*, as used in the sentence as written, to mean *I hope that* or *let's hope that*, is well established, this use is considered to be informal. For this reason, it is generally avoided in writing.

When it is used in this way in writing, however, it must be used at the beginning of a sentence or at the beginning of an independent clause, and be set off by the use of commas. In any case, the use of *hopefully* in this sentence is incorrect: in a technical sense, it implies that the enabling of the astronomers will be hopeful.

A   The use of *hopefully* here is incorrect, for the reasons given above.

B   **Correct.** The use of *it is hoped* (as opposed to *hopefully*) here properly conveys the intended meaning of the sentence. Furthermore, the use of *in the way* appropriately conveys, unlike the answer choices using *like* or *such as*, that what is being compared is the interaction, or lack thereof, of gravity waves, on one hand, and electromagnetic waves, on the other, with matter.

C   The use of *like* incorrectly implies that electromagnetic waves are a type of

matter. Furthermore, the use of *hopefully* is incorrect, for the reasons given above.

D   The use of *like* incorrectly implies that electromagnetic waves are a type of matter. Furthermore, the use of *hopefully* is incorrect, for the reasons given above.

E   The use of *such as* is inappropriate here: first, *such as* must be followed by a noun, or list of nouns, rather than a noun followed by a verb, as in *electromagnetic waves do*; second, the use of *like* incorrectly implies that electromagnetic waves are a type of matter.

The correct answer is B.

SC61561.01

257. <u>Many of them chiseled from solid rock centuries ago, the mountainous regions of northern Ethiopia are dotted with hundreds of monasteries.</u>

(A) Many of them chiseled from solid rock centuries ago, the mountainous regions of northern Ethiopia are dotted with hundreds of monasteries.

(B) Chiseled from solid rock centuries ago, the mountainous regions of northern Ethiopia are dotted with many hundreds of monasteries.

(C) Hundreds of monasteries, many of them chiseled from solid rock centuries ago, are dotting the mountainous regions of northern Ethiopia.

(D) The mountainous regions of northern Ethiopia are dotted with hundreds of monasteries, many of which are chiseled from solid rock centuries ago.

(E) The mountainous regions of northern Ethiopia are dotted with hundreds of monasteries, many of them chiseled from solid rock centuries ago.

Logical predication; Verb form

This sentence should indicate that *hundreds of monasteries* were *chiseled from solid rock*. As written, however, the phrase at the beginning of the sentence modifies the noun that immediately follows the comma: therefore, as worded, the sentence states that *the mountainous regions of northern Ethiopia* were what was *chiseled from solid rock*.

A   This choice is incorrect for the reasons described above.

287

B   This choice, like A, has an incorrect placement of its modifying phrase. As a result, it too says that *the mountainous regions* are what were *chiseled from solid rock*. The regions themselves were not chiseled; it was the monasteries.

C   The present continuous *are dotting* suggests that the *dotting* is something that is actively occurring at this moment. It would be more idiomatically appropriate to use the present tense *dot*.

D   The chiseling took place centuries ago. This requires the past *were chiseled* rather than the present tense *are chiseled*.

E   **Correct.** This version of the sentence clearly states the intended meaning: many of the monasteries that dot the mountainous regions of northern Ethiopia were chiseled from solid rock centuries ago.

The correct answer is E.

SC81561.01

258. Plausible though it sounds, the weakness of the hypothesis is that it does not incorporate all relevant evidence.

(A) Plausible though it sounds, the weakness of the hypothesis

(B) Even though it sounds plausible, the weakness of the hypothesis

(C) Though plausible, the hypothesis' weakness

(D) Though the hypothesis sounds plausible, its weakness

(E) The weakness of the hypothesis which sounds plausible

Logical predication; Rhetorical construction

The phrase *plausible though it sounds* modifies the noun that comes immediately after the comma, namely, *the weakness of the hypothesis*. As a result, the sentence says that the weakness itself is plausible. It is reasonably clear, however, that the sentence is intended to indicate that the hypothesis sounds plausible, not that the weakness does. Additionally, the referent of the pronoun *it* is ambiguous. The referent could be either *weakness* or *hypothesis*.

A   This choice suffers from the above errors.

B   This choice also inappropriately says that the *weakness* is what is *plausible*.

C   This choice also inappropriately says that the *weakness* is what is *plausible*

D   **Correct.** This version appropriately describes the *hypothesis* itself as *plausible*.

E   The phrase *which sounds plausible* should be set off with commas, or else *which* should be replaced with *that*. Furthermore, this choice fails rhetorically in that it does not covey, as it should, how surprising it is that the plausible-sounding hypothesis has this weakness.

The correct answer is D.

SC32561.01

259. In despite of the steady population flow out from rural areas into urban clusters, nearly 5 million farm households are still in Japan out of a total population of some 116 million people.

(A) In despite of the steady population flow out from rural areas into urban clusters, nearly 5 million farm households are still in Japan

(B) In spite of the steady population flow out from rural areas into urban clusters, nearly 5 million farm households are still in Japan

(C) Despite the steady population flow from rural areas into urban clusters, Japan's farm households are still nearly 5 million

(D) Despite the steady population flow from rural areas to urban clusters, there are still nearly 5 million farm households in Japan

(E) In Japan, despite the steady population flow out from rural areas into urban clusters, still there are nearly 5 million farm households

Rhetorical construction; Diction

In despite of is idiomatically incorrect; either *in spite of* or *despite* is acceptable. Also, *nearly 5 million farm households are still in Japan* is stated confusingly; the idea is not that the farm households are leaving Japan itself, but rather that people are leaving rural areas. The sentence would be more appropriately phrased if it said *there are still 5 million farm households in Japan*.

A   This choice is flawed for the reasons given above.

B   *In spite of* is correct, but, as in A, *nearly 5 million . . . are still in* fails to convey the intended meaning clearly.

C   *Japan's farm households are still nearly 5 million* is confusingly phrased. As worded, it seems to indicate that there are 5 million people on farms in Japan rather than that the number of farm households in Japan is 5 million. The intended meaning would be better conveyed if it said *there are still nearly 5 million farm households in Japan.*

D   **Correct.** This choice conveys the intended idea clearly and is grammatically correct.

E   The time indicator *still* should be placed after the verb *are.* That is, the appropriate sentence should read *there are still nearly . . .* As worded here, *still* could be read in a way that does not indicate time, but rather means something like *nevertheless,* which would be redundant, given the earlier occurrence of *despite.*

The correct answer is D.

SC52561.01

260. Financial uncertainties <u>from the accident at Three Mile Island may prove even more deterring to the nuclear industry than political opposition is.</u>

(A)   from the accident at Three Mile Island may prove even more deterring to the nuclear industry than political opposition is

(B)   from the accident at Three Mile Island may prove to be even more serious a deterrent to the nuclear industry than political opposition

(C)   from the accident at Three Mile Island may prove to be an even more serious deterrent to the nuclear industry than political opposition

(D)   resulting from the accident at Three Mile Island may prove to be an even more serious deterrent to the nuclear industry than is political opposition

(E)   resulting from the accident at Three Mile Island may prove even more deterring to the nuclear industry than political opposition

Grammatical construction; Parallelism

First, *deterring to the nuclear industry* is not correct, as *deter* is a transitive verb and requires a direct object. Furthermore, while *prove* does not have to be followed by *to be*, here *to be* is required for parallelism with *political opposition is.* Finally, even though *financial uncertainties from* is not strictly incorrect, *financial uncertainties resulting from* would be clearer.

A   This choice is flawed for the reasons above.

B   As worded, this choice can be read as comparing the degree to which the financial uncertainties are a deterrent with the degree to which the financial uncertainties are political opposition. To fix this, we must insert the verb *is* either before or after *political opposition.* Furthermore, the sentence would be clearer if it said *resulting from.* Finally, *even more serious a deterrent* would more appropriately read *an even more serious deterrent.*

C   The comparison is again faulty as in choice B. Also, the sentence would be clearer if it said *resulting from.*

D   **Correct.** This choice clearly conveys the intended meaning. While it is possible to argue that *is* would be better placed after *political opposition*, it is technically correct in either place. Realistically, this issue is minor compared to those in each of the other choices.

E   *Deterring to the nuclear industry* is not correct, as *deter* is a transitive verb and requires a direct object.

The correct answer is D.

SC72561.01

261. <u>Remembered almost as an epic among America's 12,000 Bosnian Muslims is the digging of Chicago's subway tunnels in the early 1900s, one of the proudest of family</u> legends.

(A)   Remembered almost as an epic among America's 12,000 Bosnian Muslims is the digging of Chicago's subway tunnels in the early 1900s, one of the proudest of family legends.

(B) Almost an epic among America's 12,000 Bosnian Muslims is the digging in the early 1900s of Chicago's subway tunnels, one of the proudest of family legends.

(C) Digging Chicago's subway tunnels in the early 1900s, America's 12,000 Bosnian Muslims remember it almost as an epic and it is the one of the proudest of family legends.

(D) America's 12,000 Bosnian Muslims remember almost as an epic the digging of Chicago's subway tunnels in the early 1900s, one of the proudest of family legends.

(E) One of the proudest of family legends, remembered almost as an epic among America's 12,000 Bosnian Muslims, is the digging of Chicago's subway tunnels in the early 1900s.

Logical predication; Rhetorical construction

An epic is a work of art or legend conveying heroic deeds. Therefore, presumably what is meant to be remembered *almost as an epic* is the family legend relating to the digging of Chicago's subway tunnels in the early 1900s. However, as it is worded, the sentence states that the digging itself is remembered *almost as an epic*.

Furthermore, it is not immediately clear what *one of the proudest of family legends* modifies. Whenever possible, it is best to place a phrase close to what it modifies.

A This choice is incorrect for the reasons described above.

B This choice does not describe the family legend as *almost an epic*. Instead, it describes the digging of the subways that way. Additionally, as worded, the sentence seems to say that Chicago's subway tunnels themselves are *one of the proudest of family legends*.

C In this choice, the phrase *digging Chicago's subway tunnels in the early 1900s* modifies *America's 12,000 Bosnian Muslims*. However, it was an earlier generation who dug the tunnels, not the 12,000 Bosnian Muslims currently living in America. Additionally, as in previous choices, this version of the sentence also describes the digging rather

than the legend as being remembered *almost as an epic*.

D This choice also incorrectly describes the digging of the subway tunnels, not the family legend, as being *almost as an epic*.

E **Correct.** This version clearly states that it is the family legend that is *remembered almost as an epic*.

The correct answer is E.

SC92561.01

262. Like the one reputed to live in Loch Ness, also an inland lake connected to the ocean by a river, inhabitants of the area around Lake Champlain claim sightings of a long and narrow "sea monster."

(A) Like the one reputed to live in Loch Ness, also an inland lake connected to the ocean by a river, inhabitants of the area around Lake Champlain claim sightings of a long and narrow "sea monster."

(B) Inhabitants of the area around Lake Champlain claim sightings of a long and narrow "sea monster" similar to the one reputed to live in Loch Ness, which, like Lake Champlain is an inland lake connected to the ocean by a river.

(C) Inhabitants of the area around Lake Champlain claim sightings of a long and narrow "sea monster" similar to Loch Ness's, which, like Lake Champlain, is an inland lake connected to the ocean by a river.

(D) Like Loch Ness's reputed monster, inhabitants of the area around Lake Champlain, also an inland lake connected to the ocean by a river, claim sightings of a long and narrow "sea monster."

(E) Similar to that reputed to live in Loch Ness, inhabitants of the area around Lake Champlain, also an inland lake connected to the ocean by a river, claim sightings of a long and narrow "sea monster."

Logical predication; Rhetorical construction

As written, the phrase *Like the one reputed to live in Loch Ness . . .* compares *the one* to what comes immediately after the comma directly after the *river*, namely *inhabitants of the area around Lake Champlain*. That is surely not the intended comparison.

The intended meaning of the sentence, of course, is that the "sea monster" reputedly sighted at Loch Ness is like the "sea monster" reputedly sighted at Lake Champlain.

An additional problem with this sentence is that the separation between *one* and *"sea monster"* is too great; as a result, it is not clear what the word *one* refers to.

A   This choice suffers from the problems indicated above.

B   Correct. This choice clearly and efficiently conveys its intended meaning.

C   This version of the sentence appears to assert that the Loch Ness "sea monster" actually exists. Furthermore, it inappropriately uses the phrase *is an inland lake* to modify *Loch Ness's [sea monster]*, not *Loch Ness*.

D   As in choice A, this version of the sentence inappropriately compares *Loch Ness's reputed monster* to *inhabitants of the area around Lake Champlain*.

E   This version of the sentence inappropriately uses the phrase *Similar to that reputed to live in Loch Ness* to modify *inhabitants of the area around Lake Champlain*.

The correct answer is B.

SC43561.01

263. A star will compress itself into a white dwarf, a neutron star, or a black hole after it passes through a red giant stage, depending on mass.

(A)   A star will compress itself into a white dwarf, a neutron star, or a black hole after it passes through a red giant stage, depending on mass.

(B)   After passing through a red giant stage, depending on its mass, a star will compress itself into a white dwarf, a neutron star, or a black hole.

(C)   After passing through a red giant stage, a star's mass will determine if it compresses itself into a white dwarf, a neutron star, or a black hole.

(D)   Mass determines whether a star, after passing through the red giant stage, will compress itself into a white dwarf, a neutron star, or a black hole.

(E)   The mass of a star, after passing through the red giant stage, will determine whether it compresses itself into a white dwarf, a neutron star, or a black hole.

Logical predication; Rhetorical construction

The sentence attempts to convey the idea that a star will compress itself into one of three forms after it passes through the red giant stage: a white dwarf, a neutron star, or a black hole. The sentence also indicates that which one of these three forms the star will compress itself into is determined by the star's mass. As worded, these ideas are not clearly and unambiguously conveyed. For example, it is not clear what the modifying phrase *depending on mass* is supposed to modify. Because of its placement, it appears to modify *red giant stage*; it should, however, modify *star*. Given this problem, the sentence fails to convey its intended meaning clearly.

A   As indicated above, this version fails to convey its intended meaning clearly.

B   The referent of the pronoun *its* is unclear. Given that *red giant stage* is the only noun before *its*, the sentence would seem to indicate that *red giant stage* is the referent, but the meaning would be correct only if *its* refers to *star*. Furthermore, the modifying statement *depending on its mass* appears to modify *red giant stage* rather than *star*.

C   The modifying phrase *After passing through a red giant stage* modifies *a star's mass* but it should describe the star itself. Given that the mass is not what passes through the red giant stage, this is incorrect.

D   Correct. In this version, it is clear that the sentence is saying that the star itself passes through the *red giant stage* and that the star will ultimately compress itself into one of the three listed options: *white dwarf, neutron star, or black hole*.

E   The pronoun *it* refers to *the mass of a star*, rather than *a star*, as intended. Likewise, the star itself passes through the red giant stage, not its mass.

The correct answer is D.

SC53561.01

264. Although many art patrons can readily differentiate a good debenture from an undesirable one, they are <u>much less expert in distinguishing good paintings and poor ones, authentic art and</u> fakes.

(A) much less expert in distinguishing good paintings and poor ones, authentic art and

(B) far less expert in distinguishing good paintings from poor ones, authentic art from

(C) much less expert when it comes to distinguishing good paintings and poor ones, authentic art from

(D) far less expert in distinguishing good paintings and poor ones, authentic art and

(E) far less the expert when it comes to distinguishing between good painting, poor ones, authentic art, and

Idiom; Parallelism

The preferred idiomatic form is *distinguishing X from Y*, rather than *distinguishing X and Y*.

A This version uses the incorrect idiomatic form *distinguishing X and Y*.

B Correct. This version uses the preferred idiomatic form *distinguishing X from Y*.

C This version uses the incorrect idiomatic form *distinguishing X and Y*. Furthermore, *expert when it comes to* is excessively wordy in comparison to *expert in* as seen in choices A, B, and D.

D This version uses the incorrect idiomatic form *distinguishing X and Y*.

E Although the form *distinguishing between X and Y* is an acceptable alternative to *distinguishing X from Y*, this version fails to capture that what art patrons have difficulty distinguishing between are good paintings and poor ones on the one hand, and authentic art and fakes on the other.

The correct answer is B.

SC83561.01

265. <u>A site once used as an observatory by the Anasazi, ancient pueblo dwellers of New Mexico, has been recently discovered where patterns of light and shadow were employed to establish the precise limits of the positions of the Sun and Moon over a nineteen-year cycle.</u>

(A) A site once used as an observatory by the Anasazi, ancient pueblo dwellers of New Mexico, has been recently discovered where patterns of light and shadow were employed to establish the precise limits of the positions of the Sun and Moon over a nineteen-year cycle.

(B) A recently discovered site was once used as an observatory by the Anasazi, ancient pueblo dwellers of New Mexico, where patterns of light and shadow were employed to establish the precise limits of the positions of the Sun and Moon over a nineteen-year cycle.

(C) At a recently discovered site once used as an observatory by the Anasazi, ancient pueblo dwellers of New Mexico, patterns of light and shadow were employed to establish the precise limits of the positions of the Sun and Moon over a nineteen-year cycle.

(D) Patterns of light and shadow were employed to establish the precise limits of the positions of the Sun and Moon over a nineteen-year cycle at a site that was recently discovered and was once used by the Anasazi, ancient pueblo dwellers of New Mexico.

(E) Patterns of light and shadow were employed to establish the precise limits of the positions of the Sun and Moon over a nineteen-year cycle at a recently discovered place that the Anasazi, ancient pueblo dwellers of New Mexico, once used the site as an observatory.

Logical predication; Rhetorical construction

The most reasonable interpretation of this sentence is that there is a recently discovered site that was used as an observatory by the Anasazi, who were ancient pueblo dwellers of New Mexico. At this observatory, patterns of light and shadow were employed to establish the precise limits of the Sun and Moon over a nineteen-year cycle.

The correct answer choice will clearly convey this idea. However, the sentence as worded does not do so. There is no clear indication of when the patterns of light and shadow were employed for the indicated purpose.

A This choice is incorrect for the reason indicated above.

B   This choice suggests that the entire clause *where patterns of light and shadow were employed to establish the precise limits of the positions . . .* actually modifies *New Mexico* rather than *observatory*.

C   **Correct.** This choice eliminates the above flaws; it clearly and cleanly conveys the intended idea.

D   This choice does not clearly convey the idea that the Anasazi used the site as an observatory, nor that they employed patterns of light and shadow for the purpose indicated.

E   This choice does not clearly convey the idea that the Anasazi employed patterns of light and shadow for the purpose indicated. Furthermore, *at a recently discovered place that the Anasazi . . . once used the site as an observatory* unnecessarily inserts *the site*, which is redundant (with *place*) and renders the sentence grammatically incorrect.

The correct answer is C.

SC93561.01

266. The cathedrals of the Middle Ages were <u>community centers just as much as they were purely religious edifices; and they were structures that represented a city's commitment to a public realm, the opposite of being a private one</u>.

(A)   community centers just as much as they were purely religious edifices; and they were structures that represented a city's commitment to a public realm, the opposite of being a private one

(B)   community centers as much as purely religious edifices; they were structures representing a city's commitment to a public realm, as opposed to private

(C)   community centers as well as purely religious edifices; they were structures that represented a city's commitment to a public realm, not private ones

(D)   as much community centers as purely religious edifices, structures that represented a city's commitment to a public realm, as opposed to a private one

(E)   as much community centers as they were purely religious edifices, structures representing a city's commitment to a public realm, opposite of a private one

Rhetorical construction; Diction

The given sentence conveys the idea that the medieval cathedrals were community centers as well as religious edifices. Therefore, these cathedrals represented cities' commitment to a public realm.

A   In the sentence as written, the referent of the pronoun *they* is unclear. Furthermore, the sentence is unnecessarily wordy: *just as much as* would be better written *as much as*, and the word *being* is unnecessary.

B   In this choice, the referent of the pronoun *they* is unclear. Furthermore, the phrase *as opposed to private* is misplaced; it would be correct if placed immediately before *realm*.

C   In this choice, the plural phrase *not private ones* refers to the singular *a public realm*.

D   **Correct.** This choice avoids using a pronoun with no clear referent and correctly expresses the comparison between *a public realm, as opposed to a private one*, where both noun phrases are singular.

E   This choice uses *opposite of a private one* to refer to *a public realm*, unreasonably suggesting that a public realm cannot coexist with a private realm.

The correct answer is D.

SC14561.01

267. The newspaper story accurately recounted the history of the colonial <u>mansion, that it contained thirteen rooms, and that it had a reputation for being a haunted house</u>.

(A)   mansion, that it contained thirteen rooms, and that it had a reputation for being a haunted house

(B)   mansion, that it contained thirteen rooms, and that it had a reputation of being haunted

(C)   mansion, that the mansion contained thirteen rooms, and said that it had a reputation for being haunted

(D)   mansion, said that it contained thirteen rooms and had a reputation for being a haunted house

(E) mansion and said that the mansion contained thirteen rooms and had the reputation of being haunted

Logical predication; Grammatical construction

The given sentence consists of three disjointed pieces; the second and third each begin with *that*. The verb *recounted* appropriately takes *history* as its object. Note that the two *that*-clauses that also appear, inappropriately, to be objects of the verb *recount*. Furthermore, the noun *history* and these *that*-clauses are not parallel.

Note that these *that*-clauses work better as objects of the verb *said* rather than the verb *recount*. The correct answer option will need to better integrate the two *that*-clauses into the sentence as a whole. A common way in which different thoughts are made into one sentence is by use of *and*. Choice E succeeds in creating an integrated sentence using *and* to combine three different thoughts.

A   In this choice, the two *that*-clauses inappropriately appear to be objects of the verb *recount*.

B   In this choice, the two *that*-clauses inappropriately appear to be objects of the verb *recount*.

C   In this choice, the first *that*-clause inappropriately appears to be the object of the verb *recount*.

D   In this choice, the referent of the pronoun *it* is unclear. Furthermore, *had a reputation for being a haunted house* is wordy and would be better phrased *had the reputation of being haunted* as in choice E.

E   **Correct.** This choice correctly uses the *that*-clause as the object of the verb *said* and uses the appropriate, less-wordy predicate *had the reputation of being haunted*.

The correct answer is E.

SC24561.01

268. An archaeological excavation at <u>what might have been a workshop where statues were reproduced yielded 1,532 fragments of human figures, including</u> 7 intact statues.

(A) what might have been a workshop where statues were reproduced yielded 1,532 fragments of human figures, including

(B) what might have been a workshop where statues were reproduced yielded 1,532 fragments of human figures and

(C) the site of a possible workshop where statues were reproduced yielded 1,532 fragments of human figures and

(D) the site of a possible workshop where statues were reproduced yielded 1,532 fragments of human figures, including

(E) the site of a possible workshop where statues might have been reproduced yielded 1,532 fragments of human figures, including

Logical predication; Grammatical construction

The sentence tells us that an excavation yielded fragments of human figures as well as 7 intact statues. However, as written, the sentence implies that these 7 intact statues were actually fragments. This contradiction is presumably not intended.

A   This choice is incorrect because it incorrectly implies that the 7 *intact statues* are fragments.

B   **Correct.** The use of the word *might* makes clear that the suggestion that the structure was a workshop and that statues were reproduced there is just a hypothesis.

C   This choice is incorrect because it suggests, nonsensically, that the statues were reproduced in a *possible workshop*.

D   This choice is incorrect because it suggests, nonsensically, that the statues were reproduced in a *possible workshop*. Furthermore, it incorrectly implies that the 7 *intact statues* are fragments.

E   This choice is incorrect because it suggests, nonsensically, that the statues were reproduced in a *possible workshop*. Furthermore, it incorrectly implies that the 7 *intact statues* are fragments.

The correct answer is B.

SC34561.01

269. Sophisticated laser-guided land graders can now flatten uneven farmland almost perfectly <u>so as not to waste rainwater</u> in runoff down sloping fields.

(A) so as not to waste rainwater

(B) so that rainwater is not wasted

(C) so that there is no wasted rainwater

(D) and thereby not waste rainwater

(E) and there is no rainwater wasted

Logical predication; Rhetorical construction

The sentence is meant to indicate that the purpose of flattening uneven farmland is to prevent the waste of rainwater in runoff.

Note that purpose can be expressed in various ways, including by the use of a clause beginning with *so that.*

A   In this choice, the implicit subject of the verb *waste* is the *graders.* That is, it suggests that these machines would themselves waste water unless they flattened land.

B   Correct. This choice avoids errors found in the other choices and contains no other errors.

C   This choice is incorrect because it unnecessarily uses the wordy *there is . . .* form; it would be more concise to use the passive-voice verb form *no rainwater is wasted,* as in choice B.

D   As in choice A, this choice suggests that the graders themselves might waste rainwater.

E   This choice omits the element of purpose conveyed by *so that* in choice B: *and* fails to convey purpose. As in choice C, the wordy form *there is . . .* is used.

The correct answer is B.

SC54561.01

270. <u>Because there is not a linguistic census in France, as there is for Britain, there is difficulty in estimating</u> the number of speakers of Breton, a Celtic language.

(A) Because there is not a linguistic census in France, as there is for Britain, there is difficulty in estimating

(B) Because there is no linguistic census in France, unlike Britain, it is difficult to estimate

(C) Unlike Britain, there is no linguistic census in France, and that fact makes for difficulty in estimating

(D) There is not a linguistic census in France, as there is for Britain, a fact making for difficulty in the estimation of

(E) There is no linguistic census in France, as there is in Britain, a fact that makes it difficult to estimate

Logical predication; Rhetorical construction; Parallelism

The sentence suggests that because France, unlike Britain, has no linguistic census, it is difficult to estimate how many people in France speak Breton.

A   This choice is incorrect because *in France* is not parallel with *for Britain.* Furthermore, this choice uses the wordy construction *not a linguistic census* as opposed to the clearer *no linguistic census* as in choice E.

B   This choice is incorrect because *in France* is not parallel with *unlike Britain.*

C   This choice is incorrect because *in France* is not parallel with *unlike Britain.*

D   This choice is incorrect because *in France* is not parallel with *for Britain.* Furthermore, this choice uses the wordy construction *not a linguistic census* as opposed to the clearer *no linguistic census* as in choice E. Furthermore, the construction *making for difficulty in the estimation of* unnecessarily turns the adjective *difficult* and the verb *estimate* into nouns.

E   Correct. This choice uses the parallel *in France* and *in Britain* and correctly uses the comparison structure *there is no X as there is Y.*

The correct answer is E.

SC65561.01

271. When adjusted for body weight, <u>children of various age groups in the United States have a caffeine intake that ranges from 36 to 58 percent of the average amount consumed by adults</u>.

(A) children of various age groups in the United States have a caffeine intake that ranges from 36 to 58 percent of the average amount consumed by adults

(B) the caffeine intake of children of various age groups in the United States ranges from 36 to 58 percent of the average amount consumed by adults

(C) various age groups of children in the United States range in caffeine intake from 36 to 58 percent of that consumed by the average adult

(D) in the United States, children of various age groups have a caffeine intake that ranges from 36 to 58 percent of the average adult's consumption

(E) in the United States, the caffeine intake of children in various age groups ranges from 36 to 58 percent of that consumed by the average adult

Logical predication; Rhetorical construction

In a study quantifying caffeine intake averages among children in the United States, an adjustment in the children's caffeine-intake averages was made for body weight, which varies with age group.

A   In this choice, the modifying phrase *adjusted for body weight* is incorrectly applied to *children*.

B   **Correct.** The modifying phrase *adjusted for body weight* correctly applies to *the caffeine intake of children of various age groups*. Furthermore, the *caffeine intake of children* is correctly compared with the *average amount consumed by adults*.

C   In this choice, the modifying phrase *adjusted for body weight* is incorrectly applied to *various age groups of children*.

D   In this choice, the modifying phrase *adjusted for body weight* is incorrectly applied to *children of various age groups*.

E   The word *that* in the phrase *of that consumed by the average adult* actually refers to caffeine intake. This creates a nonsensical redundancy suggesting that the *caffeine intake* itself is what is *consumed*.

The correct answer is B.

SC06561.01

272. When bitter managerial <u>conflicts plague a small company, conflicts that in the past might have led to dissolution of the business, executives are likely to</u> turn to outside professional counselors to help resolve disagreement.

(A) conflicts plague a small company, conflicts that in the past might have led to dissolution of the business, executives are likely to

(B) conflicts plague a small company, conflicts that might have in the past led to its dissolution, executives likely will

(C) conflicts plague a small company, which in the past it might have led to the business's dissolution, executives are liable to

(D) conflicts, which in the past might have led to dissolution of the business, plague a small company, executives are liable to

(E) conflicts, which in the past might have led to its dissolution, plague a small company, executives tend to

Logical predication; Rhetorical construction

The sentence is in order as it stands; the best answer choice is option A. The other four answer choices have significant errors.

A   **Correct.** This choice is the best answer. It contains neither the errors in the other choices nor any other errors.

B   The placement of the adverbial phrase *in the past* creates redundancy because *have* already indicates a past tense. Placing the phrase *in the past* preceding *might*, as in choice A, indicates that the adverbial phrase correctly modifies the entire verb *might have led*. But *likely will . . .* is common in speech and somewhat informal; in a formal writing context, *are likely to*, as in choice A, is better.

C   This construction appears to make *it* the subject and *which* the object of the verb *led*, but the pronoun *it* has no logically plausible referent. *Liable* is sometimes used informally as a synonym of *likely*, but in formal written English, it is typically used only where the potential outcome is undesirable. In this sentence, *likely* is rhetorically a better choice.

D   The phrase *the business* is inappropriate given that no business has, by this point, been mentioned. The verb *plague* is too far removed from its subject *conflicts*, making the sentence awkward and difficult to read.

E   The possessive adjective *its* is meant to refer to *a small company* and could only do so if a company had already been mentioned. The verb *plague* is too far removed from its subject *conflicts*, making the sentence awkward and difficult to read.

The correct answer is A.

SC17561.01

273. A natural response of communities devastated by earthquake or flood is to rebuild on the same site, <u>overlooking the possibility that the forces that caused it could be repeated</u>.

(A)   overlooking the possibility that the forces that caused it could be repeated

(B)   overlooking the possibility that the forces causing it could be repeated

(C)   overlooking that the forces that caused the disaster could also cause another one

(D)   without considering that the forces causing the disaster could be repeated

(E)   without considering that the forces that caused the disaster could also cause another such disaster

Rhetorical construction; Logical predication

Communities hit by an earthquake or a flood naturally desire to rebuild in the same place, yet sometimes fail to consider that the forces that caused the disaster could cause another, similar disaster.

A   In this choice, *possibility* is redundant with *could*. Furthermore, this statement incorrectly suggests that the *forces . . . could be repeated* rather than that the disaster itself could be repeated. Note also that the pronoun *it* has no clear referent.

B   This statement incorrectly suggests that the *forces . . . could be repeated* rather than that the disaster itself could be repeated.

C   This choice uses the idiomatically incorrect form *overlooking that*. This choice is confusing also because *overlooking* has a physical meaning that can apply, for example, to a *site* but does not fit with *overlooking that*.

D   This statement incorrectly suggests that the *forces . . . could be repeated* rather than that the disaster itself could be repeated.

E   **Correct.** This choice clearly conveys the meaning of the sentence and has none of the flaws mentioned above.

The correct answer is E.

SC67561.01

274. <u>Avalanches at Rogers Pass in Glacier National Park killed more than 200 people between 1885 and 1910, but they</u> are now controlled if not prevented; cannons are fired at the slopes to make snow masses fall before they become dangerous.

(A)   Avalanches at Rogers Pass in Glacier National Park killed more than 200 people between 1885 to 1910, but they

(B)   More than 200 people have been killed by avalanches between 1885 and 1910 at Rogers Pass in Glacier National Park, but they

(C)   Between 1885 and 1910, more than 200 people were killed by avalanches at Rogers Pass in Glacier National Park, but they

(D)   More than 200 people have been killed by avalanches at Rogers Pass in Glacier National Park between 1885 and 1910, but such avalanches

(E)   Avalanches at Rogers Pass in Glacier National Park killed more than 200 people between 1885 and 1910, but such avalanches

Logical predication; Verb form

In the sentence as written, the referent of the pronoun *they* is unclear. It may look, at first, as if the referent is the noun phrase *Avalanches . . . 1910*. However, this does not work as intended: obviously, avalanches that occurred at the turn of the nineteenth century cannot now be *controlled*. It is therefore clear that *they* does not refer correctly.

A   In this choice, the pronoun *they* does not refer correctly.

B   In this choice, the pronoun *they* does not refer correctly. Furthermore, it unnecessarily uses the passive form *people . . . killed by avalanches*.

C   In this choice, the pronoun *they* does not refer correctly. Furthermore, it unnecessarily uses the passive form *people . . . killed by avalanches*.

D   In this choice, the verb form *have been killed* suggests a recent event that perhaps continues to the present. It would be inappropriate to use this to refer to events that happened near the turn of the nineteenth century. Furthermore, it unnecessarily uses the passive form *people . . . killed by avalanches*.

E   **Correct.** This choice avoids the unclear pronoun and uses the active form *glaciers . . . killed*, which produces a simple and rhetorically effective sentence. Furthermore, the phrase *such avalanches* refers, as intended, to actual or possible avalanches in more recent times than those mentioned in the sentence.

The correct answer is E.

SC77561.01

275. Because 70 percent of the people of India use wood as their sole fuel, ten million acres of forest have been lost there since 1960, <u>resulting in wood now costing eight times as much to collect and distribute than</u> in 1960.

(A)   resulting in wood now costing eight times as much to collect and distribute than

(B)   resulting in wood now costing eight times as much to collect and distribute as

(C)   resulting in wood now costing eight times as much to collect and distribute than it did

(D)   and as a result wood now costs eight times as much to collect and distribute as it did

(E)   and wood now costs eight times as much as a result to collect and distribute than

Idiom; Grammatical construction

Logically, the sentence attempts to say that the loss of forest has increased the price of wood. In the sentence as written, as well as choices B and C, the participle *resulting* modifies *ten million acres of forest* rather than the loss.

Note that any of the choices containing the comparison error *as much . . . than* are incorrect. This disqualifies A, C, and E. That leaves only B and D for consideration.

A   This choice is incorrect for the reasons stated above. Furthermore, it is unclear what role *costing* plays: it could be either an adjective form of the verb *to cost* or a noun form of *to cost*.

B   This choice is incorrect because the participle *resulting* modifies *ten million acres of forest* rather than the loss. Furthermore, it is unclear what role *costing* plays: it could be either an adjective form of the verb *to cost* or a noun form of *to cost*.

C   This choice is incorrect because the participle *resulting* modifies *ten million acres of forest* rather than the loss. Furthermore, it is unclear what role *costing* plays: it could be either an adjective form of the verb *to cost* or a noun form of *to cost*.

D   **Correct.** This clearly expresses the consequence that the loss of forest has increased prices of wood and uses the correct comparison *as much . . . as*.

E   This choice is incorrect because it uses the incorrect comparison *as much . . . than*.

The correct answer is D.

SC09561.01

276. In a crowded, acquisitive world, the disappearance of lifestyles such as those once followed by southern Africa's Bushmen and Australia's Aboriginal people, <u>requiring vast wild spaces and permitting little accumulation of goods, seem inevitably doomed</u>.

(A) requiring vast wild spaces and permitting little accumulation of goods, seem inevitably doomed

(B) requiring vast wild spaces and permitting little accumulation of goods, seems to be inevitably doomed

(C) which require vast wild spaces and permit little accumulation of goods, seem to be inevitably doomed

(D) lifestyles that require vast wild spaces and permit little accumulation of goods, seem inevitable

(E) lifestyles requiring vast wild spaces and permitting little accumulation of goods, seems inevitable

Logical predication; Agreement

In the sentence as written, the singular subject *the disappearance of . . .* and the plural verb *seem* do not agree in number. It does not make sense to say that *the disappearance* is *inevitably doomed;* presumably the sentence intends to suggest that the *lifestyles* themselves are inevitably doomed or perhaps that *the disappearance of . . .* these lifestyles is inevitable.

A   For the reasons explained previously, the sentence as written is incorrect.

B   This choice fixes the verb error: *the disappearance of . . .* and *seems* agree in number. However, it retains the problem that *the disappearance* is what is described as *inevitably doomed.*

C   In this sentence, the subject *the disappearance of . . .* and the verb *seem* do not agree in number. Furthermore, the pronoun *which* incorrectly refers to *Aboriginal people* rather than to *lifestyles.*

D   In this sentence, the subject *the disappearance of . . .* and the verb *seem* do not agree in number.

E   **Correct.** This sentence is well formed. The singular subject *the disappearance* agrees in number with the singular verb *seems.* Furthermore, it is clearly *the disappearance* that *seems inevitable.*

The correct answer is E.

SC42561.01

277. Before Colette, the female writers of France had been aristocrats, from Mme de Lafayette to Anne de Noailles; there <u>were no Jane Austens or</u> Brontë sisters, perhaps because there were almost no clergymen's daughters.

(A) were no Jane Austens or

(B) were not Jane Austens or

(C) was not Jane Austen nor the

(D) was not a Jane Austen or the

(E) was no Jane Austen or no

Idiom; Diction

The sentence attempts to convey that, before Collette, female writers in France were members of the aristocracy. Furthermore, the sentence suggests that the explanation of why there were no non-aristocratic writers—as there had been in England—may be because there were almost no clergymen's daughters.

The sentence exemplifies the non-aristocratic writers of England by reference to Jane Austen and the Brontë sisters. However, the sentence uses these authors to indicate a particular type of author. That is, the point is not to say, for example, that Jane Austen herself did not write in France at the time, but rather to say that no author like Jane Austen wrote in France at the time.

This is conveyed idiomatically by saying *there were no Jane Austens or Brontë sisters,* which the sentence correctly uses to indicate "there were no authors of the Jane Austen or Brontë sister type." Several of the answer choices do not present this idiom correctly.

A   **Correct.** As indicated above, the sentence is clear and idiomatically correct.

B   *Were not Jane Austens or Brontë sisters* is not idiomatically correct.

C   *Was not Jane Austen nor the Brontë sisters* is not idiomatically correct.

D   *Was not a Jane Austen or the Brontë sisters* is not idiomatically correct.

E   *Was no Jane Austen or no Brontë sisters* is not idiomatically correct.

The correct answer is A.

SC73561.01

278. Chinese public buildings erected under a construction code of the Sung dynasty have withstood earthquakes well because the white cedar <u>used has four times the tensile strength of steel and the timber frame, incorporating</u> many joints and few nails, is flexible.

(A)   used has four times the tensile strength of steel and the timber frame, incorporating

(B)   used in them has four times the tensile strength of steel has and the timber frame, incorporating

(C)   that was used in them has four times the tensile strength steel has, and the timber frame, incorporating

(D)   that was used has four times as much tensile strength as steel, and the timber frame incorporates

(E)   that was used has four times the tensile strength steel does, and the timber frame incorporates

Logical predication; Grammatical construction

The sentence presents two reasons the Chinese buildings built under the code described have withstood earthquakes: the white cedar used in them has four times the tensile strength of steel, and the timber frame, which incorporates many joints and few nails, is flexible. The sentence is correct as worded because it clearly specifies these reasons.

A   **Correct.** As stated above, this version clearly conveys the intended meaning.

B   The construction *has four times the tensile strength of steel has* is idiomatically incorrect.

The correct construction is *has four times the tensile strength of steel*.

C   The comma after *has* breaks up the sentence in such a way that only the great tensile strength of white cedar is offered as an explanation of the buildings' ability to withstand earthquakes, rather than both white cedar's tensile strength and the timber frame's flexibility. The statement regarding the timber frame's flexibility is mentioned simply as a separate fact not falling under the scope of *because*.

D   This choice presents a similar problem to the one in choice C: the comma after *steel* breaks up the sentence in such a way that only the great tensile strength of white cedar is offered as an explanation of the buildings' ability to withstand earthquakes, rather than both white cedar's tensile strength and the timber frame's flexibility. Furthermore, *the timber frame incorporates many joints and few nails, is flexible* is ungrammatical.

E   The construction *has four times the tensile strength steel does* is incorrect. The correct construction is *has four times the tensile strength of steel*. Furthermore, the comma after *does* creates the same problem that the initial commas in choices C and D cause, suggesting that the only factor allowing the buildings to withstand the earthquakes is the white cedar's tensile strength. Finally, the sentence ends with the same ungrammatical construction as in choice D: *the timber frame incorporates many joints and few nails, is flexible*.

The correct answer is A.

SC28561.01

279. Some historians of science have argued that science moves forward not so much <u>because of the insights of great thinkers but because of</u> more mundane developments, such as improved tools and technologies.

(A)   because of the insights of great thinkers but because of

(B)   because of the insights of great thinkers as the results of

(C)   because of the insights of great thinkers as because of

(D)   through the insights of great thinkers but through

(E)   through the insights of great thinkers but results from

Idiom; Parallelism

The sentence contains a comparison introduced by *not so much*. However, the comparison is executed with correct idiomatic usage only in one of the answer options.

As written, the comparison *not so much . . . but . . .* is incorrect. This is also true in choices D and E.

A   This is incorrect for the reason stated above.

B   In this choice, *because of* is not parallel with *the results of.*

C   **Correct.** This uses the comparison *not so much . . . as . . .* correctly and correctly makes *because of* parallel with *because of.*

D   In this choice, *because of* is not parallel with *through the insights of.*

E   In this choice, *because of* is not parallel with *through the insights of.*

The correct answer is C.

Answer Explanations Verbal Reasoning

Sentence Correction

Grammar

SC27561.01
280. Indoor air pollution can threaten the health of closely confined farm animals and the workers who tend them and <u>perhaps as well impairs the quality of such farm products like</u> eggs, poultry, and pork.

(A)   perhaps as well impairs the quality of such farm products like

(B)   perhaps as well impairs the quality of such farm products as

(C)   perhaps also impairs the quality of such farm products like

(D)   may also impair the quality of such farm products like

(E)   may also impair the quality of such farm products as

Agreement; Diction

In the sentence as written, the phrase *as well* is used incorrectly as a substitute for *also*. Furthermore, the incorrect construction *such . . . like* is used rather than *such . . . as*.

A   This choice is incorrect for the reasons mentioned above.

B   This choice incorrectly uses *as well* as a substitute for *also*.

C   This choice correctly uses also, but it uses the incorrect construction *such . . . like*.

D   This choice correctly uses also, but it uses the incorrect construction *such . . . like*.

E   **Correct.** This choice correctly uses the construction *such . . . as* and correctly uses *also* instead of *as well*.

The correct answer is E.

SC12811.01
281. Carbon-14 dating reveals that the megalithic monuments in Brittany are nearly 2,000 years <u>as old as any of their supposed</u> Mediterranean predecessors.

(A)   as old as any of their supposed

(B)   older than any of their supposed

(C)   as old as their supposed

(D)   older than any of their supposedly

(E)   as old as their supposedly

Diction; Grammatical construction

The sentence suggests that, based on carbon-14 dating evidence, the megalithic monuments in Brittany are 2,000 years older than certain other monuments previously believed to predate them.

The construction *2,000 years as old as . . .* fails to convey this age difference; the sentences using this construction are nonsensical and can be firmly eliminated as possibilities.

A   This choice uses the nonsensical construction *2,000 years as old as*.

B   **Correct.** This choice uses the correct construction *older than* and correctly uses the adjective *supposed* to modify the noun *predecessors*.

C   This choice uses the nonsensical construction *2,000 years as old as*.

D   This choice uses the correct construction *older than*. However, it incorrectly uses the adverb *supposedly* to modify the adjective *Mediterranean* rather than using *supposed* as an adjective modifying *predecessors*.

E   This choice uses the nonsensical construction *2,000 years as old as*. Furthermore, it incorrectly uses the adverb *supposedly* to modify the adjective *Mediterranean* rather than using *supposed* as an adjective modifying *predecessors*.

The correct answer is B.

SC68461.01
282. Some biographers <u>have not only disputed the common notion that Edgar Allan Poe drank to excess but also questioned whether he drank</u> at all.

(A)   have not only disputed the common notion that Edgar Allan Poe drank to excess but also questioned whether he drank

(B)   not only have disputed the common notion that Edgar Allan Poe drank to excess but also over whether he drank

(C)   have disputed not only the common notion that Edgar Allan Poe drank to excess but also whether he may not have drunk

(D)   not only have disputed the common notion that Edgar Allan Poe drank to excess but also questioned whether or not he had drunk

(E)   have disputed the common notion not only that Edgar Allan Poe drank to excess but also questioned whether he may not have drunk

Parallelism; Idiom

All the possible answer choices here use the construction *not only . . . but also . . .* We can easily eliminate the choices that use the construction inappropriately. The construction is used appropriately only if what immediately follows *not only* and *but also* are grammatically parallel. For example, if what immediately follows *not only* is an adjectival phrase, then what immediately follows *but also* must also be an adjectival phrase. If what immediately follows *not only* is a verb phrase, then what immediately follows *but also* must also be a verb phrase. And so on. The sentence here correctly uses the *not only . . . but also . . .* construction: what immediately follows *not only* is a verb phrase (*disputed the common notion . . .*), and what immediately follows *but also* (*questioned whether he drank at all*) is a verb phrase as well.

A   **Correct.** This choice uses *not only . . . but also . . .* appropriately, employing appropriately parallel structures.

B   This choice does not use *not only . . . but also . . .* appropriately, because what immediately follows *not only* is not grammatically parallel with what immediately follows *but only.*

C   This choice does not use *not only . . . but also . . .* appropriately, because what immediately follows *not only* is not grammatically parallel with what immediately follows *but only.*

D   This choice does not use *not only . . . but also . . .* appropriately, because what immediately follows *not only* is not grammatically parallel with what immediately follows *but only.*

E   This choice does not use *not only . . . but also . . .* appropriately, because what immediately follows *not only* is not grammatically parallel with what immediately follows *but only.*

The correct answer is A.

SC90561.01

283. The large populations and impressive cultural achievements of the Aztecs, the Mayas, and the Incas could not have come about without corn, which was not only nutritious but also was able to be dried, transported, and stored for long periods.

(A)   which was not only nutritious but also was able to be

(B)   which not only was nutritious but also could be

(C)   which was not only nutritious but also it could be

(D)   not only nutritious but it could also be

(E)   not only nutritious but also able to be

Parallelism; Grammatical construction

To answer this question, we need to understand the correct use of the construction *not only . . . but also . . . .* We can easily eliminate the choices that use the construction inappropriately. Note that whatever immediately follows *not only* and *but also* must be grammatically parallel.

In this sentence, what immediately follows *not only* is an adjective (*nutritious*), but what immediately follows *but also* is a verb phrase (*was able to be dried, . . .*). Therefore, this sentence does not use *not only . . . but also . . .* correctly, because what follows *not only* is not grammatically parallel with what follows *but only.*

Furthermore, *could be dried* is more idiomatically correct than *was able to be dried*, as is used here.

A   This choice is incorrect for the reasons discussed above.

B   **Correct.** This choice uses *not only . . . but also . . .* correctly. What immediately follows *not only* is a verb phrase (*was nutritious*), as is what immediately follows *but also* (*could be dried, . . .*). Therefore, this choice has an appropriate, grammatically parallel structure.

C   This choice does not use *not only . . . but also . . .* correctly, because what follows *not only* is not grammatically parallel with what follows *but only*. What immediately follows *not only* is an adjective (*nutritious*), whereas what immediately follows *but also* is an independent clause (*it could be dried, . . .*).

D   This choice uses a slight variation on the *not only . . . but also* construction. It is idiomatically acceptable to separate the *but* and *also*; for instance, rather than writing *but also could be*, you could correctly write *but could also be*. This variation, however should function in essentially the same way as *not only . . . but also* does. Grammatically parallel structures must be associated with both *not only* and *but . . . also . . .* But that is not the case in this choice: what is associated with *not only* is an adjective (*nutritious*), but what is associated with *but . . . also . . .* is an independent clause (*it could also be dried, . . .*). Therefore, this choice is not correct.

E   This choice does not use *not only . . . but also . . .* correctly, because what follows *not only* is not grammatically parallel with what follows *but also*. What immediately follows *not only* is an adjective, whereas what follows *but also* is a verb phrase. Furthermore, *could be dried* is more idiomatically correct than *able to be dried*, as is used here.

The correct answer is B.

SC91561.01

284. The Rorschach test is gaining new respect as a diagnostic tool because it takes only one hour to expose behavior and thought processes <u>that may be unlikely to emerge in other procedures or weeks of ordinary interviewing</u>.

(A)   that may be unlikely to emerge in other procedures or weeks of ordinary interviewing

(B)   whose emergence is unlikely in other procedures or weeks of ordinary interviews

(C)   that might not emerge in other procedures or in weeks of ordinary interviews

(D)   that may not emerge under other procedures or weeks of ordinary interviews

(E)   likely not to emerge during weeks of ordinary interviewing or in other procedures

Parallelism; Rhetorical construction

As worded, it is unclear whether *other* modifies both *procedures* and *weeks* or *procedures* only. To clarify that *other* does not modify both *procedures* and *weeks*, the correct phrasing here would be *in weeks*. Also, the construction *that may be unlikely to emerge* is needlessly wordy; *that might not emerge* is preferable.

A   This choice is flawed for the reasons given above.

B   This choice is also unclear as to what *other* is intended to modify. Also, *whose* is generally restricted to use with people (or, more rarely, animals) rather than with abstractions such as *behavior and thought processes*.

C   **Correct.** This choice clearly expresses the intended idea.

D   Although *may* and *might* are often interchangeable, this is not true of *may not* and *might not*. This is because *may not* can be interpreted to mean *are not permitted to*. This is of course not the intended meaning here; *might not* cannot be interpreted in this way, and so would be preferable.

E   In this choice, the meaning is unclear. The word *other* can be interpreted as being contrasted to ordinary interviewing rather than to the Rorschach test; however, it is clear that the sentence intends for these other procedures to be contrasted with the Rorschach test. Furthermore, this version expresses unlikeliness more strongly than the other versions do: something that is *likely not to happen* is something that has a very low probability of occurring, while something that is *unlikely to happen* has a relatively higher chance of occurring.

The correct answer is C.

SC82561.01

285. The overall slackening of growth in productivity is influenced less by government regulation, although that is significant for specific industries like mining, than <u>the coming to an end of</u> a period of rapid growth in agricultural productivity.

(A)   the coming to an end of

(B)   the ending of

(C)   by the coming to an end of

(D)   by ending

(E)   by the end of

Parallelism; Diction

As worded, the sentence is not parallel: *less by* must be made parallel by using *than by*. Thus, the sentence needs to read *is influenced less by . . . than by*. For this reason, the first two answer choices can be ruled out.

To choose among the remaining three options, consider which of *the coming to an end of*, *ending*, and *the end of* best conveys the most likely intended meaning: that *the overall slackening of growth in productivity* is largely influenced by the fact that *a period of rapid growth in agricultural productivity* is coming to an end.

A   As noted above, this version is not parallel; it lacks the *less by . . . than by* construction.

B   This version is also not parallel; it lacks the appropriate *less by . . . than by* construction.

C   **Correct.** This version correctly uses the *less by . . . than by* construction. It clearly expresses the most likely intended meaning, discussed above.

D   This version sounds as if it is saying that the period of rapid growth of agricultural productivity is intentionally being ended. This deviates from the intended meaning of the sentence.

E   We can understand this choice to say that the *slackening of growth in productivity* is largely influenced by the final part of the *period of rapid growth in agricultural productivity*. This also deviates from the intended meaning.

The correct answer is C.

SC13561.01

286. It may someday be worthwhile to try to recover uranium from seawater, but at present this process is prohibitively expensive.

(A)   It may someday be worthwhile to try to recover uranium from seawater

(B)   Someday, it may be worthwhile to try and recover uranium from seawater

(C)   Trying to recover uranium out of seawater may someday be worthwhile

(D)   To try for the recovery of uranium out of seawater may someday be worthwhile

(E)   Recovering uranium from seawater may be worthwhile to try to do someday

Verb form; Rhetorical construction

This sentence is well-formed. It appropriately uses the construction *to try to* rather than the common yet idiomatically inappropriate *to try and*. It also uses the idiomatically correct construction *recover . . . from*.

A   **Correct.** This choice is correct for the reasons discussed above.

B   This choice uses the idiomatically incorrect construction *to try and*.

C   This choice suggests that what is prohibitively expensive is *trying to recover uranium . . .* rather than the process of recovering uranium itself.

D   *To try for* is idiomatically incorrect, as is *the recovery . . . out of*.

E   *To try to do*—as opposed to *to attempt*, for example—is awkward and unnecessarily wordy.

The correct answer is A.

SC23561.01

287. The spraying of pesticides can be carefully planned, but accidents, weather conditions that could not be foreseen, and pilot errors often cause much larger deposits of spray than they had anticipated.

(A)   weather conditions that could not be foreseen, and pilot errors often cause much larger deposits of spray than they had

(B)   weather conditions that cannot be foreseen, and pilot errors often cause much larger deposits of spray than

(C)   unforeseeable weather conditions, and pilot errors are the cause of much larger deposits of spray than they had

(D)   weather conditions that are not foreseeable, and pilot errors often cause much larger deposits of spray than

(E) unforeseeable weather conditions, and pilot errors often cause much larger deposits of spray than they had

Parallelism; Rhetorical construction

The only plural nouns that could potentially be the referent of *they* in this sentence are *weather conditions* and *pilot errors*. However, neither of these makes logical sense within the context of the sentence.

For the purposes of this sentence, it is clearer to use the impersonal *than anticipated* rather than *than they had anticipated*. This is because it is not important who is anticipating the conditions under which the pesticides are sprayed. In other words, the statement is universal; the point is that these are unknowable conditions, rather than that some particular group failed to anticipate correctly the size of spray deposits.

A   As indicated above, there is no reasonable referent for the pronoun *they*.

B   **Correct.** The idea is conveyed clearly and cleanly.

C   *They* has no reasonable referent.

D   *Weather conditions that are not foreseeable* is an awkward construction. Either *unforeseeable weather conditions* or *weather conditions that cannot be foreseen* would be preferable.

E   *They* has no reasonable referent.

The correct answer is B.

SC33561.01

288. <u>To read of</u> Abigail Adams' lengthy separation from her family, her difficult travels, and her constant battles with illness is to feel intensely how harsh life was even for the so-called aristocracy of Revolutionary times.

(A)   To read of

(B)   Reading about

(C)   Having read about

(D)   Once one reads of

(E)   To have read of

Parallelism; Verb form

A common device used to associate two verbs is structured by using the following parallel form: [infinitive phrase] is [infinitive phrase]. A well-known example of this "To know her is to love her." This sentence correctly follows this parallel form.

A   **Correct.** This choice is well expressed, correctly following the device discussed above.

B   This choice does not correctly follow the device discussed above.

C   This choice does not correctly follow the device discussed above.

D   This choice does not correctly follow the device discussed above.

E   This choice uses an infinitive phrase, but it is not parallel. The simple infinitive *to feel* is mirrored by *to have read*, which is not parallel. This fails to convey properly the association between the two verbs.

The correct answer is A.

SC74561.01

289. In the traditional Japanese household, most clothing could be packed <u>flatly, and so it was not necessary to have elaborate closet facilities</u>.

(A)   flatly, and so it was not necessary to have elaborate closet facilities

(B)   flat, and so elaborate closet facilities were unnecessary

(C)   flatly, and so there was no necessity for elaborate closet facilities

(D)   flat, there being no necessity for elaborate closet facilities

(E)   flatly, as no elaborate closet facilities were necessary

Diction; Rhetorical construction

Although the word *flat* is a standard adjectival form, it functions in this context as the more appropriate adverb, indicating the manner of packing clothing. That is, stated correctly, the clothing would be *packed flat*.

Note, however, that the adverb *flatly* is correctly used in different contexts, such as *he flatly denied it*.

A   This choice incorrectly uses the adverb *flatly*. Furthermore, the phrase *it was not necessary* is unnecessarily wordy.

B   Correct. This choice correctly uses the adverb *flat* and implies that the flat-packing of clothing led to the absence of closet facilities.

C   This choice incorrectly uses the adverb *flatly*. Furthermore, *there was no necessity for* is unnecessarily wordy; it would be better stated *were unnecessary*, as in choice B.

D   This choice incorrectly implies that clothing could be packed flat because closet facilities were unnecessary. Rather, the correct answer must imply that the flat-packing of clothing made closet facilities unnecessary.

E   This choice incorrectly uses the adverb *flatly*. It also incorrectly implies that clothing could be packed flat because closet facilities were unnecessary.

The correct answer is B.

SC75561.01

290. Many states, in search of industries that are <u>clean, fast-growing, and pay</u> good wages to skilled workers, are trying to attract high-technology industries.

(A)   clean, fast-growing, and pay

(B)   clean, grow fast, and that pay

(C)   clean and fast-growing and that pay

(D)   clean and grow fast, paying

(E)   clean, fast-growing, and paying

Parallelism; Verb form

The sentence lists three characteristics of the industries that many states most desire to attract. The answer choices each provide ways to conjoin these characteristics within the sentence.

Normally, a series of three nouns or adjectives would have a comma following each one, with *and* preceding the third. Note that this method requires adequate parallelism among the three items.

As written, the third of these characteristics is conveyed by a verb form, either *pay* or *paying*. However, the first of the three items is the adjective *clean*, which is of course not parallel with the verb *pay*.

A   This choice is incorrect for the reasons stated above.

B   The adjective *clean* is not parallel with *pay*.

C   **Correct.** Both *clean* and *fast-growing* are adjectives and are therefore parallel; they can correctly be conjoined by *and*. This choice creates a sentence with the relative clause *that pay . . . workers*. Notice that the sentence has another relative clause *that are clean and fast-growing*. This relative clause parallels the other one. Using *and* to conjoin these two clauses, each modifying *industries*, is logical and correct.

D   The adjective *clean* is not parallel with the verb *grow*.

E   The adjective *clean* is not parallel with the verb form *paying*.

The correct answer is C.

SC95561.01

291. Much of the hope for continued improvement of the economy lies in the <u>projection of increasing consumer spending</u> this year.

(A)   projection of increasing consumer spending

(B)   projection of consumers increasing spending for

(C)   projected consumer spending increase

(D)   consumer spending that is projected to increase

(E)   increase in consumer spending that is projected for

Agreement; Rhetorical construction

Consumer spending helps fuel the economy; when consumer spending increases, the economy tends to improve. The given sentence suggests that there is hope for continued improvement in the economy resulting from a projected increase in consumer spending this year.

Which one of the five answer options best conveys this idea?

A This choice focuses on *projection* rather than *increase*. Furthermore, the role of *increasing* is ambiguous: it can either be read as an adjective modifying spending or as a noun with spending as its object.

B In this choice, the preposition *of* incorrectly governs the phrase *consumers increasing spending*.

C This choice correctly focuses on the *increase* in consumer spending as a whole. However, it strings together too many adjectives; to make the sentence clearer and more readable, it would be preferable to state *increase* first as in choice E.

D This choice incorrectly focuses on what may be simply one portion of consumer spending: that which is expected to increase.

E **Correct.** With this choice, it is clear that the underlined portion of the sentence focuses on *increase*. Use of the preposition *for* also clarifies that the projected increase is attributed to *this year*.

The correct answer is E.

SC46561.01

292. <u>Rejecting its argument that the Masters Dog Training Club's primary aim was to teach people to train dogs, the court ruled the club ineligible for tax exemption as an educational group.</u>

(A) Rejecting its argument that the Masters Dog Training Club's primary aim was to teach people to train dogs, the court ruled the club ineligible for tax exemption as an educational group.

(B) In rejecting the Masters Dog Training Club's argument that their primary aim was to teach people to train dogs, the court ruled the club ineligible to be exempted of taxes as an educational group.

(C) Rejecting the argument that the primary aim of the Masters Dog Training Club was to teach people to train dogs, the court ruled that the club was ineligible for exemption from taxes as an educational group.

(D) The club was not to be exempted of taxes as an educational group, ruled the court by rejecting its argument that the primary aim of the Masters Dog Training Club was teaching people to train dogs.

(E) The court ruled the Masters Dog Training Club not eligible to be exempted from taxes as an educational group, rejecting the argument that the primary aim was to teach people to train dogs.

Rhetorical construction; Diction

As written, the possessive adjective *its* fails to make clear whether it is to the court or to the club that the argument mentioned is being attributed.

Note that choices B and D are immediately disqualified by their use of the incorrect preposition *of* immediately following *exempted*. The correct usages are: *exemption from, exempt from,* and *exempted from*.

A This choice is incorrect for the reasons mentioned above.

B This choice uses the idiomatically incorrect form *exempted of*.

C **Correct.** This choice uses the idiomatically correct form *exemption from* and conveys the meaning of the sentence in a clear, concise way.

D This choice uses the idiomatically incorrect form *exempted of*.

E This choice uses the idiomatically incorrect form *ruled the . . . club* rather than the idiomatically correct *ruled that . . .* Furthermore, the phrase *not eligible to be exempted* is wordy and would be more clearly stated *ineligible for exemption* as in choice C.

The correct answer is C.

SC56561.01

293. Sartre, an inadvertent guru, had an opinion on everything, painfully considered, elaborately reasoned, <u>often changed</u>.

(A) often changed
(B) and it was usually changed
(C) that was often changed
(D) changing often
(E) one he often changed

Parallelism; Diction; Logical predication

The sentence is intended to predicate frequent change of Sartre's opinions. We need to find the answer choice that most effectively does so.

Note that this modifier in option A, consisting of the adverbial modifier *often* and the verbal adjective *changed,* is most closely parallel to the two preceding predicates.

A   **Correct.** This choice is correct for the reasons stated above.

B   In this choice the pronoun *it* could refer either to *opinion* or to *everything,* and the force of *usually* is unclear. Furthermore, this choice is not parallel in structure to the preceding modifiers *painfully considered* and *elaborately reasoned.*

C   In this choice, the relative pronoun *that* normally has the closest preceding noun, pronoun, or noun phrase as its referent. However, in this context, *everything* is clearly not the intended referent. Furthermore, this choice is not parallel in structure to the preceding modifiers *painfully considered* and *elaborately reasoned.*

D   This choice is not parallel in structure to the preceding modifiers *painfully considered* and *elaborately reasoned.* This option also unnecessarily inverts the adjective and adverb, creating a different order from the order in the previous two modifiers.

E   This choice is not parallel in structure to the preceding modifiers *painfully considered* and *elaborately reasoned.*

The correct answer is A.

SC96561.01

294. One analyst of the liquor industry estimated that this year a few liquor stores have experienced <u>declining sales of up to fifty percent but predicted that the industry as a whole will maintain a volume of sales fairly close to last year.</u>

(A)   declining sales of up to fifty percent but predicted that the industry as a whole will maintain a volume of sales fairly close to last year

(B)   declines in sales of up to fifty percent but predicted that the industry as a whole would have maintained a volume of sales fairly close to last year

(C)   up to fifty percent in declining sales but predicted that the industry as a whole would maintain a volume of sales fairly close to last year's

(D)   sales declines of up to fifty percent but predicted that the industry as a whole would maintain a volume of sales fairly close to last year's

(E)   declines up to fifty percent of sales but predicted that the industry as a whole will have maintained a volume of sales fairly close to last year's

Verb form; Rhetorical construction

The sentence reports one analyst's views about the liquor industry's sales performance this year: there will be large declines in sales in a few liquor stores, and this year's sales volume will be close to last year's sales volume.

A   This choice is incorrect because it refers to sales themselves rather than to declines in sales. Furthermore, it compares a *volume of sales* with a *year.*

B   This choice incorrectly uses *would have maintained* after the simple past *predicted.*

C   The phraseology *have experienced up to fifty percent* is incorrect, since a percent cannot be *experienced.* The phraseology *up to fifty percent in declining sales* fails to indicate clearly that sales declined by *fifty* percent from the previous year.

D   **Correct.** This choice correctly refers to *declines,* uses the correct *would maintain,* and correctly compares this year's sales volume with last year's sales volume.

E   This choice incorrectly uses *will have maintained* after the simple past *predicted.*

The correct answer is D.

SC08561.01

295. <u>Television programs developed in conjunction with the marketing of toys, which was once prohibited by federal regulations, are</u> thriving in the free market conditions permitted by the current Federal Communications Commission.

(A)   Television programs developed in conjunction with the marketing of toys, which was once prohibited by federal regulations, are

(B)   Television programs developed in conjunction with the marketing of toys, a practice that federal regulations once prohibited, is

(C)   Developing television programs in conjunction with the marketing of toys, as once prohibited by federal regulations, is

(D)   Federal regulations once prohibited developing television programs in conjunction with the marketing of toys, but they are

(E)   Federal regulations once prohibited developing television programs in conjunction with the marketing of toys, but such programs are

Logical Predication; Agreement

The sentence is meant to indicate that federal programs once prohibited the development of television programs in conjunction with the marketing of toys, but such programs are now thriving in the free market conditions permitted by the Federal Communications Commission.

As worded, however, *which was once prohibited* . . . modifies *the marketing of toys*. This is clear for two reasons: first, the phrase immediately follows *the marketing of toys*; second, the verb *was* is singular and the noun *Television programs* is plural and must therefore be associated with the singular noun *marketing of toys*.

This indicates that the marketing of toys was once prohibited by federal regulations, but surely that is not what the sentence is supposed to mean. Rather, the sentence should assert that the development of television programs in conjunction with the marketing of toys was prohibited.

A   This choice is incorrect for the reason discussed above.

B   The singular verb *is* is incorrect. It is the *Television programs* that are thriving, so the plural verb *are* is needed.

C   This option has at least two problems. First, surely the sentence is intended to indicate that the television programs themselves are thriving rather than that the process of

developing such programs is. Second, it is unclear what the awkwardly worded *as once prohibited by federal regulations* is intended to modify. It could mean either that the development of television programs in conjunction with the marketing of toys was prohibited or that the marketing of toys itself was prohibited.

D   The intended referent of the pronoun *they* is unclear: it could be either *Federal regulations* or *Television programs*.

E   **Correct.** This choice best conveys the intended meaning.

The correct answer is E.

SC98561.01

296. Statisticians studying the health effects of uranium mining on Navajo communities have found others besides miners and millworkers to be affected; birth defects, children's cancer, and altered birth ratios of males and females are much higher in mining than in non-mining communities.

(A)   children's cancer, and altered birth ratios of males and females are much higher

(B)   cancer among children, and altered male and female ratios at birth are much higher

(C)   cancer among children, and altered birth ratios of males and females occur much more frequently

(D)   altered birth ratios of males and females, and children's cancer are much higher

(E)   altered male and female ratios at birth, and cancer among children occur much more

Diction; Logical predication

Statisticians have been studying the frequencies of various health outcomes in uranium mining areas in Navajo communities. They have found that certain kinds of bad outcomes occur much more frequently in mining communities than in non-mining communities.

We need to pick the answer choice that best expresses this finding. The use of the predicate *higher* is appropriate when applied to rates of illness. However, it is not appropriate when applied to medical conditions (except as an informal shorthand), e.g., a claim that *birth defects . . . are much higher.* That is, it is unclear what a *higher birth defect* might specify.

The meaning of *altered male and female ratios* is unclear, as opposed to *altered birth ratios of males and females.*

A   In this choice, the statement *altered birth ratios . . . are much higher* is unclear.

B   In this choice, the statement *altered . . . ratios at birth are much higher* is unclear.

C   **Correct.** The idea of the sentence is expressed clearly and the phrase *occur much more frequently* clearly specifies *altered birth ratios.*

D   In this choice, it is unclear what is higher: it could be *birth ratios of males and females, children's cancer,* or both.

E   In this choice, the modifier *at birth* implies, nonsensically, that the ratios were altered at the time of birth. Furthermore, *male and female ratios* implies that the ratios themselves are of male or female gender.

The correct answer is C.

SC19561.01

297. <u>The effect of the earthquake that caused most of Port Royal to sink into the Caribbean was</u> like the eruption that buried ancient Pompeii: in each case a slice of civilization was instantly frozen in time.

(A)   The effect of the earthquake that caused most of Port Royal to sink into the Caribbean was

(B)   As the result of an earthquake, most of Port Royal sank into the Caribbean; the effect was

(C)   In its effects, the sinking of most of Port Royal into the Caribbean was the result of an earthquake

(D)   The earthquake that caused most of Port Royal to sink into the Caribbean was, in its effects,

(E)   Most of Port Royal sank into the Caribbean because of an earthquake, the effect of which was

Logical predication; Parallelism

The sentence is meant to indicate that an earthquake caused most of Port Royal to sink into the Caribbean. However, the sentence as stated has two major flaws:

First, as the sentence is worded, the phrase *that caused most of Port Royal to sink into the Caribbean* modifies *The effect of the earthquake.* This implies that *the effect* is what caused *most of Port Royal to sink,* whereas it was the earthquake itself that caused most of Port Royal to sink.

Second, the comparison is faulty: *the effect* is compared to *the eruption.* Presumably, the earthquake itself is what is meant to be compared to the eruption.

A   This choice suffers from the two major flaws discussed above.

B   This choice attaches the modifier *as the result of an earthquake* to *most of Port Royal.* This implies, confusingly, that *most of Port Royal* was *the result of an earthquake.* Furthermore, the sentence improperly compares *the effect* to *the eruption,* whereas the earthquake itself is what should be compared to the eruption.

C   This choice places the modifying phrase *in its effects* immediately before *the sinking,* suggesting that we are discussing the effects of the sinking rather than the effects of the earthquake.

D   **Correct.** This choice properly compares the earthquake to the eruption that buried Pompeii.

E   This choice improperly compares an effect of the earthquake to the eruption that buried Pompeii.

The correct answer is D.

SC58461.01

298. Since the 1930s aircraft manufacturers have tried to build airplanes with frictionless <u>wings, shaped so smoothly and perfectly</u> that the air passing over them would not become turbulent.

(A)   wings, shaped so smoothly and perfectly

(B)   wings, wings so smooth and so perfectly shaped

(C)   wings that are shaped so smooth and perfect

(D)   wings, shaped in such a smooth and perfect manner

(E)   wings, wings having been shaped smoothly and perfectly so

Diction; Logical predication

The sentence as written is not stated clearly. For example, it is unclear what is *shaped so smoothly and perfectly*; it could be either the *airplanes* or the *wings*. Upon considering the likely intended meaning, along with a review of the other answer choices, it seems most likely that the phrase is intended to modify *frictionless wings*.

Next, we need to consider whether it makes more sense to say that the wings are *smooth* or *shaped smoothly*. This issue can be determined only by considering the most plausible intended meaning rather than by considering just the grammar of the sentence. The idea of being *smoothly shaped* would seem already to be part of the idea of being *shaped perfectly*, and therefore it is redundant. On the other hand, having a surface that is very *smooth* would be crucial in a quest to make an airplane wing frictionless; for this reason, it makes sense to point out that the *wings* themselves are *smooth*.

A   This choice is incorrect for the reasons stated above.

B   **Correct.** Given the repetition of the word *wings*, it is clear that what follows modifies wings and not airplanes. Describing the wings as *smooth* and *perfectly shaped* clearly conveys what is most likely intended.

C   In this version, note that shaped is modified. For this reason, proper grammar requires that the adverbs *smoothly* and *perfectly* are needed rather than the adjectives *smooth* and *perfect*. However, as discussed previously, the intended meaning of the sentence would be better conveyed if we used the adjective *smooth* to modify *wings* rather than the adverb *smoothly* to modify *shaped*.

D   It is initially unclear what is being described as having been *shaped in such a smooth and perfect manner*; it could be either the airplane or its wings. Even if that were clarified, however, the sentence would be flawed: the sentence is intended to describe the *wings* themselves, not the *manner* in which the wings were shaped. That is, this wording could be interpreted as referring to the nature of the wings themselves or to

the process through which they were made. This ambiguity makes the meaning of the sentence unclear.

E   This version is very awkwardly worded, mainly because of *having been*. Furthermore, this version describes the act of shaping the wings. Because the sentence is instead meant to describe the wings themselves, this choice is incorrect.

The correct answer is B.

SC29561.01

299. A study of children of divorced parents found that ten years after the parents' divorce, children who had been under six years of age at the time of the settlement were <u>not preoccupied, nor even very curious, about the reasons that led to their parents' divorces</u>.

(A)   not preoccupied, nor even very curious, about the reasons that led to their parents' divorces

(B)   not preoccupied with, or even very curious about, the reasons for their parents' divorce

(C)   neither preoccupied, nor even very curious, with the reasons that led to their parents divorce

(D)   neither preoccupied with the reasons that led to their parents' divorces or even very curious about them

(E)   neither preoccupied with the reasons that their parents divorced nor even very curious about it

Diction; Parallelism

The correct idioms are *preoccupied with* and *curious about*. In the sentence as it is written, because of the placement of the commas immediately after *preoccupied* and *curious*, the preposition *about* is associated not only with *curious*, which is idiomatically correct, but also with *preoccupied*, which is not correct.

Furthermore, *not . . . nor* is idiomatically incorrect. The correct forms are *neither . . . nor* and *not . . . or*.

A   As discussed above, this choice is flawed in its use of both *preoccupied about* and *not . . . nor*.

B   **Correct.** This choice is correct. Both *preoccupied with* and *not . . . or* are idiomatically correct.

C   This choice uses the incorrect construction *curious with*, rather than the correct *curious about*. On the other hand, its uses of *neither . . . nor* and *preoccupied with* are correct.

D   This choice uses the incorrect idiomatic form *neither . . . or.*

E   This choice incorrectly uses the singular pronoun *it* to refer to the plural *reasons*. On the other hand, its use of *preoccupied with, curious about*, and *neither . . . nor* are all correct.

The correct answer is B.

SC49561.01

300. When Medicare was enacted in 1965, it was aimed <u>at the prevention of a catastrophic illness from financially destroying elderly patients.</u>

(A)   at the prevention of a catastrophic illness from financially destroying elderly patients

(B)   at being a preventive against catastrophic illness financially destroying elderly patients

(C)   at preventing a catastrophic illness from financially destroying the elderly patient

(D)   to prevent a catastrophic illness financially destroying an elderly patient

(E)   to prevent elderly patients being financially destroyed by a catastrophic illness

Verb Form; Diction

Two issues can be identified here: first, we must determine what form follows the phrase *it*

was aimed, used to describe a goal or intended purpose; second, we must determine what preposition (if any) connects *prevent* or its cognates with the thing that is actually prevented.

A   This choice uses the idiomatically correct *was aimed at.* However, the word *prevention* incorrectly takes both the preposition *of* and the preposition *from;* this makes the sentence awkward and ambiguous. Furthermore, using the noun *prevention* makes the sentence wordier than choices using some form of the verb *to prevent.*

B   This choice uses the idiomatically correct *was aimed at.* However, using the noun *a preventative* makes the sentence wordier than cases using some form of the verb *to prevent.*

C   **Correct.** The phrase *at preventing* is correct in context: it describes Medicare's intended purpose. Furthermore, the preposition *from* correctly indicates a consequence that has been prevented.

D   This choice uses the idiomatically incorrect *was aimed to.* Furthermore, it fails to use the idiomatically correct *prevent from.*

E   This choice uses the idiomatically incorrect *was aimed to.* Furthermore, it fails to use the idiomatically correct *prevent from.*

The correct answer is C.

Appendix Answer Sheet

Quantitative Reasoning

Problem Solving
Counting/Sets/Series

1.
2.
3.
4.
5.
6.
7.
8.
9.
10.
11.
12.

**Equalities/Inequalities/
Algebra**

13.
14.
15.
16.
17.
18.
19.
20.
21.
22.
23.
24.
25.
26.
27.
28.
29.
30.
31.
32.

Geometry

33.
34.
35.
36.
37.
38.
39.
40.
41.
42.

Rates/Ratios/Percent

43.
44.
45.
46.
47.
48.
49.

Value/Order/Factors

50.
51.
52.
53.
54.
55.
56.
57.
58.
59.
60.
61.
62.

63.
64.
65.
66.
67.

Data Sufficiency
Counting/Sets/Series

68.
69.
70.
71.
72.
73.
74.
75.
76.

**Equalities/Inequalities/
Algebra**

77.
78.
79.
80.
81.
82.
83.
84.
85.
86.
87.
88.
89.
90.
91.
92.

93.
94.
95.
96.
97.
98.
99.
100.
101.
102.
103.
104.
105.

Geometry

106.
107.
108.
109.
110.
111.
112.
113.
114.
115.
116.
117.
118.
119.
120.
121.
122.
123.
124.

Rates/Ratios/Percent

125.

126.

127.

128.

Value/Order/Factors

129.

130.

131.

132.

133.

134.

135.

136.

137.

138.

139.

140.

141.

142.

143.

144.

145.

146.

147.

148.

149.

150.

Verbal Reasoning

Reading Comprehension

151.	184.	214.	245.	275.
152.	185.	215.	246.	276.
153.	186.	216.	247.	277.
154.	187.	217.	248.	278.
155.	188.	218.	249.	279.
156.	189.	219.		
157.	190.	220.	**Sentence Correction**	**Grammar**
158.	191.	221.	**Communication**	280.
159.	192.	222.	250.	281.
160.	193.	223.	251.	282.
161.	194.	224.	252.	283.
162.	195.	225.	253.	284.
163.	196.	226.	254.	285.
164.	197.		255.	286.
165.	198.	**Construction/Plan**	256.	287.
166.	199.	227.	257.	288.
167.	200.	228.	258.	289.
168.		229.	259.	290.
169.	**Critical Reasoning**	230.	260.	291.
170.	**Analysis/Critique**	231.	261.	292.
171.	201.	232.	262.	293.
172.	202.	233.	263.	294.
173.	203.	234.	264.	295.
174.	204.	235.	265.	296.
175.	205.	236.	266.	297.
176.	206.	237.	267.	298.
177.	207.	238.	268.	299.
178.	208.	239.	269.	300.
179.	209.	240.	270.	
180.	210.	241.	271.	
181.	211.	242.	272.	
182.	212.	243.	273.	
183.	213.	244.	274.	

GMAT™ Official Advanced Questions Online Index

GMAT™ Official Advanced Questions Online Index

ARE YOU USING BOTH THE BOOK AND THE ONLINE QUESTION BANK TO STUDY? If so, use the following index to locate a question from the online question bank in the book.

To locate a question from the online question bank in the book: Every question in the online question bank has a unique ID, called the Practice Question Identifier or PQID, which appears above the question number. Look up the PQID in the table to find its problem number and page number in the book.

PQID	Question #	Page
CR00561.01	240	179
CR00661.01	246	182
CR02531.01	213	166
CR02741.01	236	177
CR03001.01	209	164
CR03161.01	218	168
CR04161.01	219	169
CR05941.01	216	167
CR09090.01	230	174
CR09461.01	220	169
CR10661.01	224	171
CR13661.01	226	172
CR15380.01	207	163
CR20521.01	211	165
CR20661.01	247	182
CR21041.01	214	166
CR23661.01	248	183
CR29111.01	232	175
CR30370.01	204	161
CR30461.01	238	178
CR30721.01	233	176
CR31410.01	201	160
CR33661.01	249	183
CR36441.01	215	167
CR36601.01	231	175
CR38561.01	222	170
CR45650.01	203	161
CR46521.01	212	165
CR47561.01	242	180
CR47931.01	235	177
CR49770.01	228	173
CR51080.01	229	174

PQID	Question #	Page
CR53140.01	202	160
CR53870.01	206	162
CR60561.01	241	180
CR60661.01	225	172
CR61021.01	210	164
CR66561.01	221	170
CR66590.01	208	163
CR67370.01	227	173
CR69561.01	244	181
CR70870.01	205	162
CR78551.01	237	178
CR78561.01	223	171
CR79561.01	245	182
CR79731.01	234	176
CR87051.01	217	168
CR97561.01	243	181
CR98461.01	239	179
DS00502.01	142	38
DS01451.01	80	23
DS01951.01	82	23
DS02871.01	86	24
DS05502.01	122	33
DS05541.01	132	36
DS06110.01	77	22
DS06351.01	69	20
DS06402.01	141	38
DS07402.01	121	33
DS08402.01	94	26
DS08602.01	147	39
DS12402.01	118	32
DS16291.01	113	30
DS16402.01	75	21

PQID	Question #	Page	PQID	Question #	Page
DS17602.01	144	39	DS65291.01	134	36
DS18041.01	110	30	DS67410.01	125	34
DS18602.01	105	28	DS67602.01	104	28
DS19350.01	68	20	DS69402.01	96	26
DS21891.01	135	37	DS70061.01	83	23
DS24931.01	78	22	DS73402.01	149	40
DS26402.01	93	26	DS76602.01	100	27
DS27602.01	76	22	DS76851.01	81	23
DS28402.01	95	26	DS77302.01	115	31
DS29831.01	108	29	DS81502.01	98	27
DS29931.01	127	35	DS84302.01	89	25
DS32402.01	138	37	DS85100.01	129	35
DS33551.01	133	36	DS85502.01	143	38
DS34010.01	126	34	DS86602.01	101	28
DS34402.01	120	32	DS87602.01	123	33
DS35210.01	106	29	DS88111.01	107	29
DS36141.01	131	36	DS89302.01	91	25
DS37571.01	111	30	DS92931.01	109	29
DS37602.01	145	39	DS94502.01	99	27
DS38302.01	136	37	DS95491.01	71	20
DS38602.01	148	40	DS95850.01	130	35
DS41402.01	72	21	DS97602.01	146	39
DS44402.01	140	38	DS99302.01	137	37
DS45771.01	112	30	PS01661.01	53	18
DS46402.01	150	40	PS03502.01	22	11
DS47602.01	102	28	PS03551.01	13	9
DS47661.01	84	24	PS04502.01	25	12
DS48302.01	90	25	PS04851.01	51	17
DS48391.01	88	25	PS06502.01	28	12
DS48602.01	124	34	PS07602.01	12	9
DS49302.01	117	31	PS12502.01	49	17
DS50502.01	97	27	PS15302.01	36	14
DS50571.01	85	24	PS15402.01	11	9
DS51402.01	73	21	PS17302.01	43	16
DS52402.01	139	38	PS17402.01	62	19
DS53402.01	119	32	PS18302.01	38	15
DS53541.01	128	35	PS18871.01	15	10
DS53841.01	79	22	PS20502.01	20	11
DS54402.01	74	21	PS22502.01	41	15
DS56971.01	87	24	PS23502.01	23	11
DS57602.01	103	28	PS24831.01	2	7
DS58302.01	116	31	PS24851.01	52	17
DS59851.01	70	20	PS25302.01	58	18
DS61791.01	114	31	PS28602.01	66	19
DS64402.01	92	26	PS30402.01	60	19

PQID	Question #	Page
RC69461.01-40	189	157
RC69461.01-50	190	157
RC69461.01-60	191	157
RC69461.01-70	192	157
RC69461.01-80	193	157
RC79461.01	Passage	158
RC79461.01-10	194	158
RC79461.01-20	195	158
RC79461.01-30	196	158
RC79461.01-40	197	159
RC79461.01-50	198	159
RC79461.01-60	199	159
RC79461.01-70	200	159
SC01561.01	255	185
SC06561.01	272	190
SC08561.01	295	195
SC09561.01	276	191
SC12811.01	281	192
SC13561.01	286	193
SC14561.01	267	189
SC17561.01	273	190
SC19561.01	297	195
SC21011.01	250	184
SC21561.01	256	185
SC23561.01	287	193
SC24561.01	268	189
SC27561.01	280	192
SC28561.01	279	192
SC29561.01	299	196
SC30561.01	254	185
SC32561.01	259	186
SC33561.01	288	194

PQID	Question #	Page
SC34561.01	269	189
SC37561.01	252	184
SC42561.01	277	191
SC43561.01	263	188
SC46561.01	292	194
SC48461.01	253	185
SC49561.01	300	196
SC52561.01	260	186
SC53561.01	264	188
SC54561.01	270	190
SC56561.01	293	194
SC58461.01	298	196
SC61561.01	257	186
SC65561.01	271	190
SC67561.01	274	191
SC68461.01	282	192
SC72561.01	261	187
SC73561.01	278	192
SC74561.01	289	194
SC75561.01	290	194
SC77561.01	275	191
SC81561.01	258	186
SC82561.01	285	193
SC83561.01	265	188
SC83811.01	251	184
SC90561.01	283	193
SC91561.01	284	193
SC92561.01	262	187
SC93561.01	266	189
SC95561.01	291	194
SC96561.01	294	195
SC98561.01	296	195

Notes

CAUTION!

The penalties for cheating on the GMAT™ exam are severe.

The following is considered cheating:

- Hiring someone to take the test
- Taking the test for someone else
- Memorizing test questions
- Sharing answers with others

The penalties for cheating are:

- Cancellation of your scores
- Ban on future testing
- School notification
- Possible legal prosecution

Has someone been trying to get you to act illegally?

File a report by email: **pvtestsecurity@pearson.com** or **testsecurity@gmac.com**